The Au Pair and Nanny's Guide

TO WORKING ABROAD

Susan Griffith · Sharon Legg

Distributed in the USA by
The Globe Pequot Press, Guilford, Connecticut

Published by Vacation Work, 9 Park End Street, Oxford
www.vacationwork.co.uk

THE AU PAIR & NANNY'S GUIDE
TO WORKING ABROAD
by Susan Griffith & Sharon Legg

First published 1989
Subsequent editions 1993, 1997 and 2002
Fifth edition 2006

Copyright © Vacation-Work 2006

ISBN 10: 1-85458-347-6
ISBN 13: 978-1-85458-347-5

No part of this publication may be reproduced or transmitted
in any form or by any means without the prior
written permission of the publisher

Illustrations by John Taylor & Lorraine White

Publicity by Charles Cutting

Cover design by mccdesign ltd

Typeset by Guy Hobbs

Printed and bound in Italy by Legoprint SpA, Trento

Contents

PART I INTRODUCTION

INTRODUCTION...8
Au Pairs, Nannies and Mother's Helps..8
Origins of the Au Pair System..9
Who is Eligible? – Male Au Pairs – What Families are looking for...........10
Motives for Working with Children..13
Deciding to Go – Where should you go?...14
Red Tape – Regulations..17
Training and Experience – NVQs – Certificates and Diplomas – Other
Qualifications..19
Duties, Rewards & Risks..21

FINDING A JOB...25
The Internet...25
Agencies – Pros and Cons – Choosing an Agency – Accreditation Bodies
– Agency Procedures – North American Applicants – Working for Tour
Operators..27
Advertisements – *The Lady* – Other Publications..............................36
Word of Mouth...38
Job-hunting Abroad..38
Interviews – Preparing for the Interview – Conducting Yourself at Interview.........39

PREPARATION..42
Contracts – Nannies – Au Pairs..42
Health and Insurance – National Contributions.................................43
Learning a Language..45
Travel...45
What to Take – Money – Packing..46
While You're Waiting – Keeping in Touch – Last Minute Panics............48

PROBLEMS AND HOW TO COPE...50
Initial Traumas – Breaking the Ice – Your First Day – Coping with the Previous
Nanny – Winning the Children Over – Culture Shock – Homesickness....................50
Problems with Children – Resentment in Children – Crying – Disobedience
– Discipline – Tantrums – Eating Problems – Food Allergies – Sleeping and
Dreaming – Toilet Training – Bedwetting...56
Problems with Parents – Pay and Time Off – Requesting a Pay Rise
– Interference with your Social Life – Unrealistic Expectations – Maternal
Resentment and Jealousy – Employee Resentment – Conflict over Discipline
– Flirtatious Fathers – Marital Problems...64
Coping with a New Arrival – Telling the Children – Explaining the Facts of
Life – Coping with the Mother – Jealousy – Feeding – Nappy Rash – Colic
– Stimulating the Newborn..72

LEISURE TIME AND DEPARTURE...76
Creating a Social Life – Meeting Other Au Pairs/Nannies – Meeting Expatriates

– Meeting the Locals..76
Learning a Language – Language Courses Abroad..79
Time Off – Your First Day Off – Excursions and Activities – Use of a Car.............80
Departure – Giving Notice – Preparing the Children – Meeting the New Nanny
– Farewell..82

PART II COUNTRY BY COUNTRY GUIDE

Australasia 85	**Italy**...131
Austria..90	**Netherlands**....................................137
Belgium & Luxembourg................95	**Scandinavia**....................................142
Canada..100	**Spain & Portugal**...........................148
France...106	**Switzerland**....................................155
Germany.......................................116	**Turkey**..159
Greece...121	**United Kingdom**............................161
Ireland 125	**USA**..169
Israel...128	**Rest of the World**..........................180

PART III DIRECTORY OF AGENCIES.................183

PART IV APPENDICES

APPENDIX 1 – SAFETY IN THE HOME 295
Suffocation – Poisoning – Burns – Other Dangers 295
First Aid – Asthma – Bites – Burns and Scalds – Choking – Concussion – Cuts
and Bruises – Dislocation – Drowning – Emergency Procedures/ Resuscitation – Fits
– Foreign Bodies – Fractures – Hysteria – Insect Stings – Nose Bleeds –
Poisoning – Splinters – Sprains – Suffocation 296

APPENDIX 2 – CHILDHOOD AILMENTS...301
General Ailments – Chicken Pox – Colds – Constipation – Coughs and Sore
Throats – Croup – Diarrhoea –Earache – Eczema – Head-lice – Stomach Pains
– Teething or Toothache – Vomiting 301
General Care During Sickness 303

APPENDIX 3 – COOKING FOR CHILDREN 305

APPENDIX 4 – FUN AND GAMES.. 314

APPENDIX 5 – EMBASSIES IN LONDON & WASHINGTON........... 319

Preface

While the demand from modern working parents for young people to look after their children in their homes has been increasing exponentially, the supply of au pairs from certain countries has undeniably decreased. Fewer British school-leavers consider au pairing as an option than was the case a decade or so ago. Partly this is because so many exciting gap year schemes compete for their attention. Living with a family and looking after children is sometimes seen as less glamorous than conserving turtles in Costa Rica or working in a Nepali village school. This is a shame, as fluency in a European language and experience of dealing with children and family can be more rewarding and useful in future life than picking up elephant poo in Africa.

Young people who seek to become au pairs or nannies will soon discover that it is one of the most affordable ways to live and work abroad, whether on the continent or further afield in the United States and Australia. While gap year travellers are struggling to raise at least £3,000 for their adventure, the canny au pair is fixing up a family placement – at a cost of no more than £40 through an agency and often free - and saving up a little more for a no-frills flight to Barcelona, Berlin or Bergen. Even if they choose Boston, a free flight will be part of the deal when they are accepted onto an au pair exchange programme.

Family placements provide a safe and stable environment in which to practice a language and experience a culture. That is why so many au pairs from Central Europe have been flocking to the UK, etc., particularly the new EU member countries. Whatever part of Europe you come from, placements are relatively easy to arrange. Furthermore, candidates from outside Europe can often benefit from legislation that exempts them from work permit requirements.

Yet risks abound. Au pairing is a little like the children's rhyme about the little girl who had a little curl, which could be paraphrased: 'when it is good it is very very good, but when it is bad it is horrid.' While in some cases, the au pair forms a life-long bond with the family after a happy and fulfilling year abroad, in others there is exploitation and resentment. Often problems arise because the au pair embarks on the adventure ill-prepared. Part of the purpose of this book is to help readers avoid disappointment and conflict, and to set off cured of their naïveté.

The au pair placement industry is changing rapidly. This new edition of the guide takes account of the amazing changes that the internet has brought about, with a proliferation of online agencies aiming to bring job-seeking au pairs and nannies together with families looking for live-in childcare. Some argue that the unregulated matching of young girls with foreign families where there is an absence of screening and no back-up in the event of problems is highly dangerous. Yet in some ways, answering an advert seen on a website is not significantly different from answering an advertisement in a specialist magazine (like *The Lady*) which was the old-fashioned way of finding a live-in job. Horror stories abound of online matches going wrong, and these issues are explored in this book, alongside the advantages and otherwise of using an agency.

The Au Pair & Nanny's Guide will help you not only to decide whether the demanding experience of an au pair or nanny is for you, but it includes masses of concrete information about how to fix up a successful placement from Scandinavia to the Mediterranean, New York to New South Wales. Drawing upon the experiences of many others, it will help you make the most of your stay abroad.

Susan Griffith
Cambridge
January 2006

Acknowledgments

This completely revised fifth edition of *The Au Pair & Nanny's Guide to Working Abroad* would not have been possible without the assistance of the many women – and a handful of men – who shared their experiences as live-in child-carers. The authors wish to express their gratitude to all those whose names appear throughout these pages, who enlivened our task with their vivid descriptions of the children they cared for, whether beastly or angelic, and of their employers from Islington to Istanbul. **For this edition, special thanks are due to Jacqueline Edwards, Riitta Koivula, Aracelli Miranda Pereira and Esther Terpstra.**

Also, Sharon Legg would like to thank the families for whom she enjoyed working: the Wolf family, the O'Hallorans and *la famille* Decoster. Finally, our thanks are due to Dr. Philippa Swan for checking the medical accuracy of the text.

The Eurozone comprises Austria, Belgium, Finland, France, Germany, Greece, Netherlands, Ireland, Italy, Luxembourg Portugal and Spain. At the time of writing the Euro was worth 68 pence or US$1.18.
   Current exchange rates are available at the online Universal Currency Converter www.xe.net/ucc or on www.oanda.com.

While every effort has been made to ensure that the information contained in this book was correct at the time of going to press, details are bound to change, especially those pertaining to visa requirements for au pairs and nannies, exchange rates and the services offered by the agencies listed in Part III. Readers are invited to write to the authors c/o Vacation Work, 9 Park End Street, Oxford OX1 1HJ or email Susan Griffith on susan@vacationwork.co.uk with any new stories of their experiences; those whose contributions are used will be sent a free copy of the next edition or any Vacation-Work title of their choice.

PART I

Au Pairs, Nannies & Mothers' Helps

Working with Children
Deciding to Go
Finding a Job
Preparation
Problems and How to Cope
Leisure Times & Departure

Introduction

AU PAIRS, NANNIES AND MOTHER'S HELPS

The terms au pair, mother's help and nanny are often applied rather loosely, so it is worth spending some time clarifying the varying roles. All are primarily live-in jobs, concerned with tending to the needs of children, contributing to their emotional and mental development and imposing discipline when necessary.

Nannies are usually thought of as having some formal training, such as the Diploma in Childcare and Education (formerly the NNEB) or a Level 3 National Vocational Qualification. There are however 'nanny' positions open to women who have no paper qualifications but who have substantial experience of working with children. Nannies have sole charge of the children and are responsible for chores directly relating to them. They usually live in and command a full-time salary, since they will be on duty around the clock except on one or two days off per week. Daily nannying (i.e. live-out) is also a possibility after you have gained considerable experience. Salaries vary enormously at this senior level but are seldom less than £200 per week (or the equivalent abroad), and occasionally stretch up to £400; the average is £250 in London.

A more progressive term for Mother's help is 'Parent's help' which has gained limited currency over the past couple of years. But most agencies still refer to a live-in helper who will sometimes have sole charge but more usually will work alongside the parents as a 'mother's help'. They will assist wherever necessary and be expected to perform a variety of tasks related not only to the children but also to the household generally, including housework and/or cooking. They may be paid on a par with a trained nanny, but usually get less; £90 is the standard starting wage in the UK although many earn £150 net or more. The hours are normally eight hours a day, five and a half or six days a week plus several evenings of babysitting.

Au pairs are in a different category, though many of their duties overlap with those of a mother's help. The official purpose of the arrangement is to provide single women and men aged 18-27 with the chance to study a foreign language and culture while living as part of a family. Technically that means it is not possible to be an au pair in your own country or in one whose language you share, though there are exceptions, as in the case of the Au Pair in America scheme which is open to native English-speakers as well as to English-learners of all nationalities. Au pairs are meant to work for no more than 25 hours a week over five days, plus two evenings of babysitting, and get pocket money of not less than £55 a week in the UK or a considerably less generous €60 a week on the continent. Unlike nannies and mother's helps, au pairs do not sign a contract since the arrangement is an informal one. Au pairs should be treated more like family members than employees. An au pair has much less responsibility for the welfare of the children than does a nanny, and is not normally expected to take sole charge of a young child.

Holiday au pairs usually work from July to September and accompany the family on their holidays. Since the children are out of school, there may be less free time than during the academic year and often no chance to attend language classes. Otherwise the same rules should apply as for ordinary au pairing.

These are in broad outline the kinds of live-in childcare positions with which this book is concerned. The kinds of arrangement into which families and live-in helpers settle are in fact infinite, and many of the guidelines and definitions set out in the pages which follow are open to interpretation and subject to all kinds of permutations. Two variations are the au pair plus and the demi pair. The demi pair works a maximum of three hours a day, plus some babysitting, in exchange for £25 a week. This arrangement seems to have fallen out of favour somewhat and is offered by far fewer agencies and families than formerly. The au pair plus merges with the mother's help since she is often required by households with two working parents who are away from home the whole day but she usually gets paid less than a mother's help because she may not have had much childcare experience. The average weekly pay in the UK is currently £70 a week for working 30 hours and £80 for 35 hours. In the view of some at the elite end of the industry, au pairs plus and mother's helps are often euphemisms for domestic workers so anyone contemplating this role should find out in detail what will be expected of them.

All of these definitions can very easily become blurred, for example a number of jobs advertised as nannying positions are really mother's help jobs in disguise, i.e. there is more housekeeping than would normally be involved in a nannying job. A muddling of the two levels of responsibility had tragic consequences in the Louise Woodward case in 1997. In the press coverage of the death of a nine-month old baby in Boston in the care of the British au pair Louise Woodward, the term nanny was frequently used, whereas the accused 18 year old was a participant of one of the au pair programmes to the USA. She was unqualified and inexperienced and arguably should not have been permitted to take sole charge of a baby. The rules have been changed subsequently as described in the chapter on the USA.

To simplify matters, the term 'au pair' is used most often throughout, since this book is aimed primarily at those who want to go abroad to work. But much of what is said about au pairing is equally relevant to nannying either in the UK or abroad.

ORIGINS OF THE AU PAIR SYSTEM

The first recorded use of the word 'au pair', which means literally 'on equal terms' in French, is in 1897 in the *Girl's Own Paper*. It refers to English girls teaching their language in France in exchange for lessons in French. But soon the emphasis altered, and caring for children became the central duty of au pairs rather than teaching. Since then a great deal of grandiloquent prose and high-flown sentiments have been spouted on the subject of au pairing, describing it as the ideal way to experience a foreign culture from the inside, learn a language, etc. You would almost think that the only motive which families have in taking on an au pair is to help her appreciate their culture and learn their language. In fact it is usually a case of a harassed mother looking for a cheap home help. Between these two contradictory viewpoints, however, there is plenty of scope for successful and satisfying employer/employee relationships from which both parties benefit in the ways that are intended by the system.

The high moral line on au pairing, which views it as a road to self-improvement, is not a recent import. On the continent the system has its origins in Switzerland at the end of the last century when, for the first time, large numbers of single young women were moving away from home to take up jobs in the cities. The church and other groups who saw themselves as moral guardians anticipated that a decline in morals would accompany this independence, so they encouraged young women to live and work in families, not only for the sake of their morals, but so that they could acquire useful household skills. The language learning element came a little later, since German-speaking Swiss girls would be placed in French-speaking households, where they could learn Switzerland's second language.

The UK began au pair exchanges with Switzerland in the early 1920s, then with Austria in 1930. After World War II the number of participating countries and au pairs rose dramatically, so that today there are hundreds of thousands of au pairs in Europe. It is estimated that there are over 20,000 in Greater London alone. Although it began as a peculiarly European notion, it has been taken up in the USA as well and, more recently, in Australia. It is a concept which, although old-fashioned in many ways, is capable of shifting and adapting to modern times and of reflecting the attitudes of contemporary society.

WHO IS ELIGIBLE?

The greatest attraction of looking after children for many is that it is one of the easiest ways to fix up work abroad, since the demand is so great. It has been estimated that about half of all women with children in industrialised nations work full or part time. Often the qualifications for being hired by these working mothers are minimal and it is not unusual for young women aged barely 18 who have never worked and who have no experience with children beyond occasional babysitting to be successfully placed in a foreign household. Although agencies and families almost always state that they *prefer* au pair candidates to have had some practical experience of looking after children, most are prepared to consider anyone with a genuine liking for children, a positive attitude towards domesticity and a reasonably mature character. Most will require at least one reference which simply testifies to your reliability and common sense.

The second great advantage of au pairing over other jobs abroad, is that often it is easier to make your status legal. Work permits are notoriously difficult to get for 'proper jobs' in most countries of the world, but often exceptions are made for live-in help (see the section on *Red Tape* below). Au pairing is primarily for Europeans, though a handful of agencies in Canada and the US can arrange au pair placements for North Americans (see section in *Finding a Job.*

The minimum age can be a stumbling block for some school leavers who are not yet 18. The majority of agencies prefer not to accept applications from candidates younger than 18.

> **Australian Camilla Preeston (then resident in Hong Kong) discovered this for herself:**
> *I had decided even before I had finished school that I would take a year off between school and university, and au pairing seemed like the perfect way to do this. Being seventeen and a half made things much more difficult in the beginning though. I sent off endless letters to agencies in Britain and overseas but most flatly replied that I was too young, though a couple said that they would try anyway. I eventually had*

> *success with a Canadian agency who were happy to help me find a job in France. The reason they didn't turn me away may have been because the fee they levy is paid upfront before a family is found (though they claim to have placed all applicants to date). By the time they had found me a family in Calais, four months of my year off had already gone by and I was almost ready to give up. I immediately accepted the offer, perhaps a little hastily. However, had I refused it, I might not have found another family willing to accept me due to my age, and it was the first family offer I had received in the four months I had been trying.*

Obviously Camilla's youth did not prevent her from coping with what turned out to be a difficult situation, where she was expected to accept a lot of responsibility for the children (including a newborn baby) and the running of the household, while the mother was away for five days and two nights a week.

It is a universal requirement for au pairs to be single and certainly childless for obvious reasons. But it is not impossible for someone with a child to find a job looking after someone else's child abroad as well as her own, as a single mother of a two-year old son from Cheshire explains:

Although a lot of families would not accept someone with a child, some do, so it is always worth asking. I was able to find a job as a live-in au pair when I was staying in a village in southern Spain. In the end things didn't work out for us because our children didn't get on with each other. Also it was quite different for me at 30 living in someone else's house than it was at 20. So I found that I was able to afford to rent an apartment in the village (since it was so cheap) and continue working for the family on a daily basis.

MALE AU PAIRS

One very important category of applicant will not find the job hunt at all easy. Despite the progress made over the past couple of decades in trying to dismantle sexist stereotypes, it is still very difficult for men to arrange family placements. For once, the employment situation is reversed; normally it is women who must prove that they are better than men when competing for the same kind of job. But just to gain equal footing in childcare, men must have excellent references and plenty of experience. Many agencies refuse pointblank to register men simply because they are so rarely asked by families to supply a male au pair or nanny that it is not worth their while to process applications from males. According to an article in the British press, one experienced male nanny was turned down by 59 agencies before he was taken on and placed by a Surrey agency. In conservative societies in southern Europe, the situation can be even worse.

As recently as 1993, males were prohibited by law from becoming au pairs in the UK, even though this contravened EU Equal Treatment Directives. Due to heavy lobbying by youth exchange organisations, equal rights campaigners and Euro-MPs, the legislation was changed so that the definition of au pair in Britain no longer specifies gender, only age and nationality. A high percentage of au pair applications from Central Europe (mainly Hungary, Czech Republic and Slovakia) is now from males, and some agencies specialising in placing East European au pairs with British families aim to place about 10% males.

But no legislation can dismantle prejudice overnight. Men who reply to au pair/nanny adverts are often met with bemusement and, in some cases, hostility. Even broad-minded parents, who buy the sort of children's books which show fathers ironing and cooking, are often unreceptive to the idea of a male au pair. High profile cases of paedophiles working in children's homes have frightened many potential employers. Male applicants must be prepared to be asked outright by agencies and at interviews with parents whether they are gay or child molesters. Such assumptions are very discouraging in these supposedly

Hello! I'm the new au pair

enlightened times.

So rare and exotic a breed are male nannies that they are likely to become featured in newspaper articles. An article in the *Sunday Times* entitled 'Male nannies taking over in the nursery' turned out to be about the same individual as one on the same subject which appeared in the *Daily Telegraph* two and a half years later. Simon Willis, an Australian, encountered incredulity when he tried to get a job looking after children in London. He was asked by the woman who had placed the advertisement on a notice board at London University whether he was replying on behalf of his girlfriend. He had to employ all his male wiles and powers of persuasion just to arrange an interview. But he did get the job and the little girl instantly adored him.

But the situation is very slowly improving. Colleges offering childcare courses report a small increase in the number of enquiries from men whereas a few years ago they received none at all. Even the exclusive Norland College in Berkshire admitted its first male student a few years ago, a 22 year old from Japan whose parents run a private nursery.

> **Male au pairs are not so uncommon in some countries, including France where Ian Croker au paired for a year**
>
> *As a male au pair, I accept that I may be a rarity, though the picture is not quite as gloomy as many men think. Certainly in France, there are quite a few male au pairs (four in my village near Fontainebleau alone). In my experience the boys tend to get placed in families with a lot of energetic children or families that have had problems with a high turnover of au pairs. My agency claims that the boys they have placed have had fewer problems with homesickness and therefore more staying power. Parents are increasingly aware of the benefits of having a boy, and many feel that their children are safer when out with a guy, especially in the city. Two friends of mine (both guys) are also au pairs and none of us has ever experienced any ribbing from our family or friends. There certainly are narrow-minded people around, and I was rejected by several families purely on grounds of gender. But then*

applicants are turned down all the time because of their colour, religion or just on the grounds of their passport photo.

The best chance which young men have of fixing up a live-in position is to emphasise their willingness to teach the children English. Persistent sexism means that any men who do manage to find a family willing to take them on will probably find that they are not expected to do those domestic chores which their female counterparts would unthinkingly be given. Instead they will be sent to the local park with the kids and a football. Steve Ducker had a marvellous time in Rome. His duties extended no further than coaching the 12-year-old boy in English after school and amusing him by taking him on little expeditions. In exchange for this he had a luxurious flat to himself and had plenty of free time in which to explore Rome and environs.

WHAT FAMILIES ARE LOOKING FOR

An experienced au pair-cum-nanny claimed that to do the job well you need a 'sense of humour, the patience of a saint, a liking for children and the ability to leap over toy buildings in a single bound'. A love of children is an obvious prerequisite, and will cover up a multitude of sins. But other qualities which parents are looking for include a mature attitude to assuming responsibility. All parents want to feel confident about leaving their children in the care of another person, so they are looking for someone who is sensible, trustworthy, able to assume control, and who will report major mishaps as appropriate.

Families want somebody reliable who will drive carefully, remember to lock up and who will not invite guests indiscriminately into the home. They also expect to be able to trust you, not only with their valuables but with money for shopping, children's treats, etc. Any accidental damage in the home should immediately be admitted and an offer to replace it tendered. Most agencies will have encouraged families to take out liability insurance on their au pair or nanny's behalf which should cover major problems.

A cheerful disposition is greatly valued in family situations. All parents want a warm, healthy atmosphere in their homes, and are disconcerted by girls who are moody or volatile. A calm approach to life in general and little disasters in particular is what is called for. Live-in helpers who are reduced to hysteria by the sight of a spider or the squeak of a mouse won't do their charges any good.

Personal hygiene is just as important as making sure the children are kept clean and tidy. Parents resent it if you don't clean up after yourself, even if it is in your own room or on your day off, though none is likely to go as far as the wife of the former Israeli Prime Minister Benjamin Netanyahu who was reputed to make her nanny wash her hands up to 300 times a day.

A large number of agencies and families absolutely prohibit smoking among their staff. If you are a smoker but serious about nannying, you might want to consider giving up. It is no good pretending that you never touch cigarettes when you obviously do. Even if you manage to bluff your way into a job, you will be climbing the walls once you start and are not able to smoke freely. If you try to do so secretly, there'll be all sorts of tell-tale signs. Non-smokers have very sensitive noses.

All children have a tendency to be early risers so it helps if you are too. If you are a night hawk by nature, you will have to exercise self-discipline and resign yourself to reorganising your habits and your social life.

MOTIVES FOR WORKING WITH CHILDREN

For many, a childcare job is simply an easy transition to the world of work and a way of acquiring a higher standard of living than is normally possible in one's early working years. In addition to your own room, you may have your own TV, the use of a car, and the chance to accompany the family on exotic holidays. There will be no need to worry about organising or paying for transport to work, finding accommodation and all the other

If something goes wrong report it at once

headaches normally associated with starting a job in a new place.

In addition to the worthy goals of learning a language and experiencing a foreign culture, many people simply want to see the world and can't afford a straight holiday. Jane Newel was a trained nanny with two years residential experience in Britain when she noticed an advertisement in a national newspaper for an experienced nanny to care for a three-year-old girl:

> *It was January when I saw the job advertised and I was immediately interested because it involved a lot of travel. The winter blues were getting to me since I was extremely fed up with the British climate and longed for some sunshine.*

Others are less concerned about the climate and are trying to escape from a difficult or boring situation at home. Pam Bain was a nurse who, at the age of 22, decided to become a mother's help in Paris.

> *I was engaged to be married at the time the job was offered, but I jumped at the chance because I felt uncertain about marriage and needed some time alone to think.*

It can also be a very good way for young women to assert their independence from over-protective parents. Some au pairs learn to appreciate their own families more after intimate acquaintance with another family.

DECIDING TO GO

Living with a family abroad for an academic year is probably one of the best ways there is to learn a language and experience a culture. Yet the numbers leaving the UK to take part in this system have been declining. Some serious language students take part in structured exchanges like Erasmus, which count towards a degree course. Since the introduction of student fees, many students who at one time would have had no hesitation in flitting off to the continent for a summer's au pairing and travelling now feel obliged to earn money closer to home. Perhaps the change that has had the most impact on au pairing is the way the gap year industry has boomed in the past decade. A young woman who would once have arranged to au pair in Seville now invests several thousand pounds (often of daddy's money) in a gap year conservation scheme in Costa Rica. There is now an amazing array of jobs on offer via the internet, so the idea of au pairing with the restrictions it entails holds less appeal. First Britons and now Western Europeans are drifting away from the idea of au pairing, only to be replaced by armies of eager young women and men from the new EU countries (Poland, Czech Republic, Slovakia, Slovenia, etc.) with their good work ethic.

But the idea of becoming an au pair should not be dismissed lightly. For one thing, it is far more economical than expensive gap year schemes. It immerses you in a language and culture more successfully than some alternatives where much of the time is spent with your peers. For anyone who has a rapport with children, it is still an obvious choice.

A liking for children is certainly a pre-requisite. If you have had very little exposure to young children, try to arrange some since you may discover that you lack the appropriate quantities of patience to take charge of them for an extended period. If you do have experience of children you might give some thought to what age group you most enjoy. Nannies often have a favourite age, though every stage brings its own pleasures and problems. For example, babies can be carted around on private errands and you may find that they adapt to you more quickly than older children. But you might also find their dependence restricting and miss not being able to hold a conversation. A job as an au pair with school age children (except in the summer holidays) allows much of the day free. The more flexible you can be the better; you don't want to limit your choices too much, for this will make it harder to find a suitable job.

How much are you prepared to put up with? Could you cope with a major loss of privacy? Au pairs are occasionally made to share a bedroom with the children on holiday, which can be a shock to anyone who is not used to sharing. How much do you value your free time? In theory au pairs work no more than five hours a day, whereas a mother's help position is more like a full-time job.

What kind of lifestyle are you seeking? If you have visions of working for a celebrity family, living in the lap of luxury in some sunny part of the world, you are almost certainly going to be disappointed. And even if such a situation did materialise the reality might not match the anticipation. Rich and celebrated families can be very demanding, and you may have to work extremely hard for your material perks, with little free time to enjoy them. Furthermore you are more likely to be treated like a servant than a daughter. It all depends on the situation and on your own individual goals and aspirations.

WHERE SHOULD YOU GO?

After you have sorted out the general issues, you can then concentrate on particulars, such as which country to work in. Assuming you have no predilection for a certain country or language, it might be helpful to read through the country chapters in order to decide on a destination. In these chapters, we indulge in gross generalisations such as German standards of cleanliness are exceedingly high, American children are spoiled or British families tend to protect their privacy to the point of excluding their au pairs. Of course there are slovenly Germans, model American children and gregarious Brits. But we have made an attempt to provide something of the flavour of working in families around the world.

If you know someone who has visited or (preferably) lived in the country which interests you, try to find out from them what it is like, encouraging them to be as candid as possible in order to balance the inevitably rosy view conveyed in the tourist office literature (though of course this should be consulted too). Best of all of course is to meet someone who has worked in a family situation in that country. Experiences differ radically. Some say that Mediterranean people tend to be more demanding of their home helps, whereas others think that conditions are less favourable in northern Europe where you are more likely to be given heavy housework and not encouraged to engage in the relatively enjoyable task of speaking English to the children.

You will next have to establish whether or not it is feasible to work in your chosen country. The free exchange of labour within the European Union has made this much easier in the majority of cases but, as you will see from the country-by-country section of this book, certain countries require visas or work permits which may be difficult or time-consuming to obtain. Make enquiries of the agencies and of the appropriate embassy before you proceed.

Are you confident enough to commit yourself to go to a country far away or would you prefer to retain the possibility of getting home quickly if necessary?

What length of contract are you seeking? Except in the case of summer placements, most families expect you to stay at least six months, and contracts for the academic year (normally September to June) are also very common.

Do you satisfy the age requirements? Many agencies and families will not accept anyone less than eighteen (sometimes nineteen). A few countries like Belgium allow seventeen year old au pairs, though they will often have to provide parental authorisation. Some countries are reluctant to supply temporary work permits to people over a certain age, for example au pair visas for non-European au pairs in Germany are given only to young people under the age of 24.

How good is your knowledge of the relevant language? How much interest or aptitude do you have for learning it? Could you cope in a situation where you were reduced largely to sign language?

Can you afford the travel expenses? Bear in mind that in all but a handful of cases, the au pair is responsible for paying for her own travel. In exceptional cases, this outlay will be reimbursed on completion of a year with one family (for example this tends to happen in Iceland), but you still have to find the money upfront.

Assuming you won't have much say in where exactly you are placed, are you willing to adapt to a lifestyle which may be completely unfamiliar to you, for example if you are from a big city how would you fare in a remote rural setting and vice versa?

How many children are you prepared to care for? You will not be paid five times as much for looking after five children instead of one, so you have to ask yourself whether or not you would be happy living with a large family. Very large families are a rarity these days, of course, and it is unusual to have more than two or three charges. You should also consider whether or not you are prepared to work for a pregnant mother. The new arrival could bring a drastic change in the workload, especially if the mother plans to return to work shortly afterwards. Also your relationship with the other children may become more vexed, if they become jealous of their new sibling.

Not all families who require nannies are harmoniously united. In fact, there is an increasing demand for home helps as more and more marriages disintegrate. Would you be prepared to work for a one-parent family? This might involve greater responsibility for you, but you might be compensated for this by higher wages and more autonomy.

Are you prepared to work alongside the mother? If you enjoy taking on full responsibility and prefer to work alone, then obviously a sole-charge position is the best for you. It can be very trying to work with a mother, especially if you have very different views on how children should be raised.

Pam Bain realised too late how spoiled she had been by having been independent in her previous job

As a nurse, I had been used to my own routine and being left to get on with the job, so I found it difficult working so closely with the mother. It was hard to know when she wanted me around and when she didn't. She also seemed quite jealous of my relationship with the baby and that made things pretty strained between us at times.

On the other hand there is a certain advantage in being able to share the running of the home and to know that you are not completely alone if a crisis develops.

RED TAPE

The majority of countries in which au pairs wish to work are members of the European Union, which now consists of the UK, Ireland, France, Germany, Netherlands, Belgium, Luxembourg, Austria, Denmark, Italy, Greece, Spain, Portugal, Finland and Sweden, plus the ten new accession countries which joined the Union in May 2004: Cyprus, Czech Republic, Estonia, Hungary, Latvia, Lithuania, Malta, Poland, Slovakia and Slovenia. Regulations affecting the free movement of labour in and out of these new member countries differ but in most cases reciprocal transitional controls have been implemented for two years in the first instance and up to a maximum of seven years before full mobility of labour will be allowed. The au pair traffic is overwhelmingly away from these new member states into the 'old Europe'. The free reciprocity extends to countries of the European Economic Area (EEA), which includes Iceland, Liechtenstein and Norway. Switzerland is a special case but has also been shedding restrictions (see chapter).

Within the EU the red tape is minimal for nationals of the original 15 member states who wish to work, whether as au pairs, nannies, or in any capacity. A ten-year UK passport costs £42 for 32 pages and £54.50 for 48 pages, and should be processed by the Passport Agency within ten days, though it is safer to allow more time. The one-week fast track application costs £70 and an existing passport can be renewed in person at a passport office, but only if you have made a prior appointment by ringing the Passport Agency on 0870 521 0410 and are willing to pay £89 (£95.50 for 48 pages). Passport office addresses are listed on passport application forms available from main post offices. All relevant information can be found on the website www.passports.gov.uk.

Regulations differ among European countries regarding residence permits. Several countries like France and Spain have recently abolished the rule that EU nationals have to apply for a permit. The norm now is that Europeans simply register their address at the local town hall. Individual requirements are provided in the country chapters.

Outside Europe, legislation varies from country to country. Turkey, Canada, the United States, Australia, the Middle East and so on offer possibilities for au pairs, mother's helps and nannies. Although the red tape in North America is considerable, thousands of people do cross the Atlantic to work with families. The restrictions and procedures for obtaining the appropriate documentation are provided in each of the country chapters. Similarly there are schemes for Americans and Canadians to become au pairs in Europe (see later section in *Finding a Job*).

Whereas au pairs can benefit from sympathetic legislation in many countries which exempt them from work permit requirements and taxation, nannies and mother's helps will find that they encounter more difficulties over the formalities. Full-time nannying is considered a 'proper job' which means that the normal immigration rules for foreign workers are invoked. For example, in Britain mother's helps should technically be paid the national minimum hourly wage of £5.05, make contributions and pay tax. The usual practice is for the employer to apply to his or her local employment authority for permission to hire an 'alien' (anyone from outside the European Union if in an EU country). The family may have to prove that no national is available or qualified to undertake the job and that an earnest attempt has been made to fill the job with a local. Then the nanny must apply to the relevant embassy in her home country. It is most unusual to be allowed to apply for a work permit after arrival, though this rule does differ and the embassy literature should always be consulted.

Increased concerns about child protection mean that some agencies are now asking candidates to provide a police clearance form. In the UK, a CRB (Criminal Records Bureau) disclosure takes about six weeks to come through (see section below on 'Agency Procedures').

Au pairs are not always exempt from tax. An anomaly came to light in 2005 in Finland where au pairs are subject to tax, even though their earnings fall short of the threshold for social security cover. Tax deductions are also made in Norway (see chapter on Scandinavia).

REGULATIONS

The Council of Europe based in Strasbourg drafted a European Agreement on Au Pair Placements in 1969 (European Treaty Series Number 68). It sets out the rules which in an ideal world would govern all au pair placements, though many EU countries think that it is inadequate for the purpose and it is generally considered outdated. Twelve countries have signed the agreement (Belgium, Bulgaria, Finland, Germany, Greece, Moldova, Switzerland, Denmark, France, Italy, Norway and Spain) though only the last five in that list have ratified it, which is to say passed legislation which can enforce it. Britain is one of the countries which has refused to sign it, giving as its reason the following:

The United Kingdom has not signed that agreement because of concern that it would require a binding contract between the au pair and the receiving family which would conflict with the traditional informal arrangements and shift the emphasis from an opportunity to learn English and something on the way of life here as a member of a family to actual employment. There would also be the question of policing the arrangements and the considerable resources this would involve.

The terms of the Agreement are as follows:
(1) An au pair placement consists of a temporary family stay during which young foreigners can perfect their knowledge of the language and culture of the host country.
(2) Au pair placements can be extended for up to a maximum of two years.
(3) The au pair should be between the ages of 17 and 30 (though individual countries are permitted to specify different minimum and maximum ages).
(4) The au pair must have a medical certificate signed by a doctor within the past three months, stating that the candidate is in good health.
(5) The rights and duties of the au pair and of the host family should be set out in a contract or any written agreement before the au pair leaves the country of residence.
(6) The agreement should indicate to what extent the au pair will participate in the life of the host family and guarantee a certain level of independence and privacy.
(7) The au pair should receive all meals and a private room.
(8) Enough free time should be allowed for the au pair to attend a language course, to benefit from the cultural opportunities of the country and to attend religious services if she so wishes. She must have at least one day off per week, of which at least one per month should be a Sunday.
(9) The au pair should be expected to work no more than five hours per day, excluding meal times.
(10) In countries in which there is no official mechanism for providing social security the host family is responsible for obtaining private health and accident insurance for the au pair.
(11) The au pair arrangement should be terminated with no less than two weeks' notice on either side.
These are no more than guidelines but, viewed as guidelines, they are useful. There are of course numerous cases of abuse, for example families neglect to arrange insurance or they ask their au pair to look after the children all day, instead of just for five hours. But at least the official criteria provide a basis for discussion between families and helpers.

One important step forward in the late 1990s was the establishment of a regulatory association for au pair agencies, the International Au Pair Association (IAPA) has as one of its goals to lobby governments to better regulate au pair agencies, for example by introducing a licensing scheme. The Association has established a voluntary Code of Conduct among its members to promote professionalism in a field which is sometimes associated with abuses and exploitation. Discussions continue in the European Parliament about how to create an accreditation scheme for agencies involved in placing domestic workers which would be extended only to those agencies that commit themselves to minimum standards (such as charging reasonable fees, ensuring au pairs enter into a legally binding contract with their employers which clearly states rights, responsibilities and duties, and providing emergency help in cases of difficulty). Agencies could also be committed to doing background checks on both the prospective au pair and the prospective host family, which is not a requirement at present.

TRAINING AND EXPERIENCE

Women and men who are considering childcare as a career should investigate enrolling in a suitable training course. Although a paper qualification is not a prerequisite for employment as a nanny, increasingly it helps candidates in the job hunt (as well as in doing the job).

The range of training and vocational courses in childcare is vast. Many are awarded by CACHE, the Council for Awards in Children's Care and Education (Beaufort House, Grosvenor Road, St. Albans, Herts. AL1 3AW; 01727 818616; www.cache.org.uk). The Council grew out of the post-war National Nursery Examination Board (NNEB) and in 2001 merged with the National Association of Maternal and Child Welfare (NAMCW). The main courses that CACHE awards are National Vocational Qualifications (NVQs) at Levels 2, 3 and 4, and the Certificate and Diploma in Childcare and Education. A list of all its courses may be requested from CACHE or found on its website. CACHE can also send a list of CACHE-approved centres on request or their website has a searchable database. Most regional colleges throughout the UK offer courses in childcare. Some courses are over-subscribed, so early application is advised. The long list of qualifications acceptable to the government's Surestart Childcare Approval Scheme (see chapter on UK) may be read at www.childcareapprovalscheme.co.uk/carer/qualifications.asp.

NVQS

Trainees can pursue a National Vocational Qualification (NVQ) in Early Years Care and Education through colleges and independent training organisations or in the workplace. Government funding is available for many young people aged 18-24 who undertake NVQs. As the CACHE literature explains, 'NVQs are a system of awards that were introduced for people involved in vocational work – be it full-time or part-time, waged or unwaged. There is a series of NVQs specifically designed for those working in Early Years Care and Education i.e. work with children under eight years'.

Many courses are provided locally to trainees through colleges of further education and will require attendance in day or block release format. The experience gained in the workplace (including private employers) is supported by portfolios produced by trainees in their spare time. These courses require on-site assessment visits by an approved assessor to verify the trainee's competence. Level 2 in Childcare is the most basic course which can normally be completed in a year or 18 months. Level 3 is one of the key qualifications which nanny agencies look for. The NVQ3 is generally a two-year course during which a candidate is assessed in 11 compulsory skill areas in the workplace and through a portfolio. Examples of the unit topics are 'management of behaviour' and 'establishing and maintaining relationships with parents'. The candidate must demonstrate both practical competency and theoretical understanding.

CERTIFICATES AND DIPLOMAS

The Qualifications & Curriculum Authority (83 Piccadilly, London W1J 8QA; www.qca. org.uk/nq/subjects/childcare-accred.asp), in co-operation with CACHE, has established a framework of nationally accredited qualifications in early years education, childcare and playwork which should serve to standardise the requirements for qualifications in the field. As with NVQs, Level 2 is a basic certificate level; Level 3 is a higher diploma level. The Level 2 CACHE Certificate in Childcare and Education (CCE) can be awarded after one year of full-time study which must include 390 hours of practical training. It qualifies you to work as a mother's help or nursery assistant.

The more advanced qualification which nanny agencies are looking for is the Level 3 CACHE Diploma in Child Care and Education (DCE), formerly known as the NNEB (Diploma in Nursery Nursing), a term which is still widely used by agencies and which has long been considered the Rolls Royce of qualifications. This is a two-year full-time vocational course including 750 hours and 12 modules of practical training which prepares candidates for employment in any childcare capacity. The Certificate and Diploma courses are offered at study centres throughout the United Kingdom with a couple in Ireland and New Zealand. Note that the Diploma is recognised nationally for university entrance and will allow progression to teacher training, nursing and related careers.

Two private fee-paying nanny colleges offer the Diploma course in England and their graduates enjoy an elevated reputation among the ruling classes (including royalty). Both charge very high fees (e.g. upwards of £10,000 a year); write for their prospectuses if interested:

Norland College, York Place, London Road, Bath BA1 6AE (01225 466202; mail@norland. co.uk; www.norland.co.uk). From £3,070 a term for six terms excluding accommodation. Subsidies and assistance with fees are available for the foundation course.

Chiltern Nursery Training College, 16 Peppard Road, Caversham, Berks. RG4 8JZ (0118-947 1847; www.chilterncollege.com). About £2,900 a term (£4,200 residential).

Another provider of well respected childcare and early education courses is the Montessori Centre International, 18 Balderton St, London W1K 6TG (020-7493 0165; www.montessori. ac.uk). Some courses are available by distance learning, though when learning to care for children, practical experience is of paramount importance.

OTHER QUALIFICATIONS

Anyone considering enrolling in a childcare course should make sure that the qualification for which they intend to study will be respected by potential employers and agencies. Other diplomas such as those granted by BTEC and City & Guilds are demanding courses, though they may not be as widely recognised as the CACHE qualifications. BTEC courses are awarded by Edexcel (0870 240 9800; www.edexcel.org.uk). The BTEC Higher National Certificate in Early Years is generally thought to emphasise academic achievement more than practical training. City & Guilds offer a range of relevant NVQs and other courses, including Certificate in Work with Children and Caring for Children aged 0-7; details from C&G, 1 Giltspur St, London EC1A 9DD (020-7294 2800; www.cityandguilds.com).

A sample of the standard list of the main acceptable qualifications is taken here from the literature from Au Pair in America's 'Au Pair Extraordinaire' programme for qualified child carers:

- O   CACHE Diploma in Early Childhood Care and Education
- O   Edexcel BTEC National Diploma in Early Years
- O   NVQ3
- O   HNC in Childcare and Education (Scotland)
- O   Diploma in Nursing (Children's Nursing)
- O   BSC Degree in Midwifery (+ 1 year's full-time experience)
- O   CACHE Certificate in Early Childhood Care and Education + 1 year's

experience
- Montessori Diploma (3-6 year olds)
- BA (Hons) Care & Education: Early Years and Disability Studies

A selection of childcare training centres in the UK includes the following:

Aston Training College, 109 Uxbridge Road, Ealing, London W5 5TL (020-8579 3955; www.happychild.co.uk/astontraining.htm).

Carshalton College, Nightingale Road, Carshalton, Surrey SM5 2EJ (020-544 4444; www.carshalton.ac.uk).

Godalming College, Tuesley Rd, Godalming, Surrey GU7 1RS (01483 423292; www.godalming.ac.uk).

London College of Early Years Care and Education (LCEYCE), 370-376 Uxbridge Road, London W12 7LL (020-8740 9538; www.lceyce.co.uk). Private training agency accredited by the British Accreditation Council for Independent Further and Higher Education as well as CACHE and City & Guilds.

MNT (Maternity & Nanny Training) Courses, Hawkwood, The Street, Old Basing, Hants. RG24 7BY (0870 220 2657; info@mynannynetwork.co.uk; www.mynannynetwork.co.uk). Full range of training courses for nannies, and maternity nurses, including induction course for UK government's Childcare Approval scheme.

New College Nottingham, c/o Basford Hall College, Stockhill Lane, Basford, Nottingham NG6 0NB (0115-916 2001; www.ncn.ac.uk).

Riverside Training Company, 29 Milligan St, London E14 8AT (020-7536 9566; riversidechild@btconnect.com). Childcare courses including 2-day Nanny Induction Course, aimed specifically at childcarers without qualifications. It can be used to register as an Approved Childcarer under the new government scheme. The course has also been accredited by CACHE.

West Kent College, Brook St, Tonbridge, Kent TN9 2PW (01732 358101; www.wkc.ac.uk).

The boom in nanny schools in Australia continues. One of the best known is The *Charlton Brown* centre in Brisbane (see entry in Directory) which runs various training courses. Their 'signature' course is a specialised 12-week intensive Nanny Award course that mixes theory with practical skills, designed to equip people for work as a nanny either in Australia or abroad. The centre also offers a Certificate and Diploma course in Children's Services. At one time the Pam Arnold Centre in Adelaide also offered full-time and part-time nanny training courses, but recently its courses have been available by distance learning based on their *Child Care Manual* (sold via www.childcareknowhow.com for A$49.95 plus A$10 postage). A post-course job placement service is promised.

In South Africa, the place to turn is the Mary Poppins Professional Au pair College in Cape Town (in South Africa au pair tends to be synonymous with nanny). This small private institute (+27 21-674 6689; poppins@telkomsa.net) established in 1998 provides a professional training for au pairs/nannies and full-time or part-time Early Childhood Development courses. It also acts as a placement service for Cape Town, UK and Europe (see Directory entry). Course participants who have a driver's license and their own vehicle qualify for the 'Earn while you Learn' option in which trainees get practical experience while earning the going wage.

Many successful nannies have landed high-paying jobs, including jobs with royalty, without the benefit of formal qualifications. Several agencies place inexperienced girls in homes in Britain as 'trainee nannies' at a fairly low wage, so that they can build up the necessary experience and references to move to more senior positions.

DUTIES

Au pairing and nannying can incorporate any number of duties beyond caring for children. It is worth emphasising that the job is often very demanding. Try not to have unrealistic expectations and never be seduced into thinking that you are on holiday. You will no doubt have opportunities that might not have come your way had you stayed at home, but first and foremost you are abroad to work.

Your primary duties will revolve around the children. Try to find out ahead of time what ages they are and, if you are inexperienced, read a childcare manual such as one by Miriam Stoppard or Penelope Leach.

Most families will expect you not only to keep their children's rooms tidy, but also to do some light housework. 'Light housework' is notoriously open to interpretation, however, so do be careful that you are not exploited. It is usual to be asked to dust, vacuum, wash dishes and keep the children's rooms clean.

It would be surprising not to be responsible for the children's clothes, though you should not be expected to do any hand washing. The vast majority of families who hire live-in helpers own a washing machine and usually a dryer, which should cut down the time taken to do this chore and on any ironing you may be expected to do.

Normally you will be expected to prepare the children's meals. You might even be required to cook for the adult members of the household sometimes, so be honest about how good you are at cooking and how much (or little) you enjoy it.

The amount of shopping you will be required to do varies considerably from family to family. Some will expect you merely to pick up a few items at the local grocery store while others will make you responsible for the entire food budget. Usually, the parents will go on a major shopping expedition once a week and leave you to purchase any extras that may be needed.

Candidates with driving licences are at a distinct advantage when applying for jobs since many parents will want you to ferry their children to school, to the doctor/dentist/dance class, etc. Not all parents are willing to lend their au pair or nanny a car, but if they do require you to drive, they will usually allow you to use the car to take the children out for day trips, or even allow you to borrow the car for your own private use during your free time. Always be scrupulous about paying for your own petrol, unless you have come to some arrangement. (The arrangement was not very satisfactory in Annie Stevens' case in Brussels where she was allowed to borrow the family's Mini but was charged a mileage rate which she calculated was exactly twice the cost of petrol.)

Some families in Europe prefer foreign nannies or au pairs so that they can assist the children with another language. Your task will be made a lot easier if the children share their parents' ideas about the benefits of language learning, not to mention have a certain aptitude. It may be a case of giving a scheduled lesson once a day or simply chatting to them in English or reading them stories.

Maree Lakey, an Australian au pair in Austria, found this language-teaching aspect of her job more problematic than she had expected:
I am basically there to help the four children aged 11-17 with their English learning, although this is not necessarily always easy. On the whole they have little desire to learn and see their lessons with me as more of a chore than anything else, but I guess that's not so unusual. I've found out how hard it is to try to speak correct English with them and to explain grammar rules which I have forgotten. It's also a bit difficult sometimes as my Australian English often differs from what the children have to learn. The children are of course not sympathetic to my difficulties, insisting that I should be infallible, being a native speaker.

REWARDS

If the arrangement works, it can be absolutely great. Emma Colgan says that her year off between school and university as an au pair in Hamburg was possibly the best thing that she ever did and she would recommend it to anyone and everyone:

I was very lucky in that I lived with a lovely family who really treated me as a member of the family (in fact they spoilt me rotten on occasion). I was included in family celebrations, outings and dinner parties, and was taken on holiday with them. If I was not going out in the evenings I was always welcome to sit with them, talking for hours or watching a good film over a bottle of wine. They were incredibly generous and kind, giving me extra money for school books, socialising, etc. They said to me over and over again, 'Our house is your house'. They trusted me implicitly and because they treated me so well, I naturally wanted to work hard for them.

Emma is probably right when she goes on to say that her situation was exceptional. Few au pairs have the good fortune to work for such ideal employers. In fact Emma didn't think of them as employers, but rather as her 'German parents'. She now considers them friends and keeps in touch with them regularly.

Even if your host family isn't quite as generous and as easy-going as Emma's you will almost certainly improve your knowledge of a foreign language. This is valuable not only for modern language students. Helen McMillan had planned to study for a degree in languages but was anxious to spend some time travelling before she settled down to university life, so she accepted a six-month contract as an au pair in Italy, which she greatly enjoyed:

All that sunshine and good life went to my head, and I found I couldn't face three more years of poverty as a student. My Italian was so good by then that I decided to skip further study and went to work for an Italian firm instead. I now travel all over Europe on business trips (and incidentally keep in touch with the family I worked for). When I think about it, that au pair position changed the entire course of my life.

Whereas some use their new-found facility with a foreign language to decide their future course or career, others take up a professional rather than a casual interest in childcare. There is a host of related careers, from teaching to running your own au pair agency which might develop from a successful stint as an au pair.

Almost all au pairs claim that the principal benefit of their experience (whether or not their relationship with their families was successful) is that they gain confidence in themselves. Susie Walton is one of the many who says that she came back from her year abroad (in her case the American Midwest) a changed person, much more assertive and confident about doing things on her own. It also helped her to get on better with people. Often a year of au pairing or nannying abroad teaches you to make friends quickly, which is surely a life-enhancing skill.

RISKS

The relationship of au pair to family is not like the usual employer/employee relationship; in fact the terminology sometimes used is 'hosts', 'hospitality' and 'guests', which is to view the arrangement in somewhat more idealistic terms than the reality will support. To be treated as a member of the family is splendid in theory, however it means that the success of the arrangement depends more than usual on whether or not individuals hit it off, so there is always an element of risk when living in a family of strangers. Some girls are decidedly opposed to the idea of being treated as a member of the family, since it means that they may not have fixed hours and duties. The families that throw up their hands in horror at the mention of a contract or the notion of being business-like about the arrangement are often the ones who expect you to be on call around the clock.

Few au pair experiences are an unmitigated success, and there is almost always an admixture of misery to a greater or lesser degree. Some randomly selected articles published in newspapers and magazines over the past few years are variously entitled 'Au Pairs - Look Before You Leave', 'Perils and the Au Pair Girl' and 'Sun, Seas and Servitude'. For practical tips on how to cope with specific difficulties when they arise, see the chapter in this book 'Problems and How to Cope'.

Homesickness is the most common problem and is probably unavoidable at the beginning of your sojourn abroad. You will feel yourself to be a million miles away from friends, family and a comfortable routine. But even after you settle into the life of your host family, loneliness can persist if you don't take positive steps to create a social life (see the section on *Leisure Time* below).

> **Much depends on your own attitude, as Pam Bain admits, after recounting how unhappy she was in Paris:**
> *I look back now and think that perhaps if I'd been in a more optimistic frame of mind, I might have tried harder to enjoy myself. I didn't feel much like socialising so I didn't make friends and, personally, I was glad to get back home.*

The relationship between parents (especially the mother) and au pair or nanny can be a fraught one. In many situations you are neither employee (with fixed hours and duties) nor friend (with the trust and affection which friends bestow on one another). If the relationship does not work out, it can lead to downright disaster. Few situations contain more potential for misery. Plenty of employed people are unhappy with their jobs and seek the consolation of family, friends and a social life. Others are stressed or unhappy at home but enjoy the atmosphere of their workplace. In a family placement, the two categories merge and an unhappy situation can be very difficult to escape from. Frances Thirlway, who was made miserable by the thoughtlessness of her employers in Munich, recalls how she used to retreat to the local library just to be out of summoning distance. She thinks that she read through the whole of German literature that year. And when the family took a holiday in the south of France, Frances would wander off into the hills with a book, which was a form of hiding from the family. It is possible to spend your free time less solitarily than Frances did. Annie Stevens, who disliked her employers in Belgium, signed up for French classes where she found a Chilean boyfriend, and Nicola Wenban spent all her free time in Vienna at a much more congenial home where an English friend was au pairing.

Even if you are treated well by your family, another common cause of complaint is the loss of independence noted above. Janet Renard, an American student who au paired in Sicily, thinks that the younger you are (preferably between 18 and 21) the easier it is to adapt to a family situation in which a great deal must be shared, including your time. Once you have tasted the independence of having your own flat, it is difficult to give up that freedom. But if you are fresh from school, you may appreciate the security and familiar pattern of family life.

There is another risk mentioned by a few veteran nannies, that their experiences have put them completely off the idea of having their own children. Others of course came away with an opposite attitude, since they are eager to put into practice what they have learned and to avoid the parental mistakes to which they have been exposed.

Of course some young au pairs are guilty of abandoning the safe haven of a family placement and embracing risk. Agents tell dreadful tales of young women aged 18 or 19 leaving their placements after meeting a stranger who offers them what they assume will be a more appealing situation. For example a 19 year old Slovenian girl who arrived at the home of one of the *Jolaine Agency's* client families in late 2005, left abruptly after meeting a stranger on Oxford Street who persuaded her that it would be advantageous for her to rent a room from him and take a paid job that he would find for her. Meanwhile her parents in Slovenia could not contact her and were anxiously calling the English family where she should have been. When her host mother warned her that her decision to trust this stranger was potentially risky, she replied that having done her military service in Slovenia, she was able to look after herself.

Finding a job

The prospects for finding a childcare job abroad, even for the unqualified, are very good. As an increasing number of mothers in the developed world pursue their careers and the divorce rate rises, the demand for all kinds of live-in helpers escalates. The four main ways of finding a childcare position abroad are: through traditional specialist agencies, via the internet (including online agencies), through print advertisements (largely replaced by the internet) and finally word of mouth.

THE INTERNET

Cyberspace buzzes with an exchange of information about live-in childcare. Everywhere you look on the internet potentially useful links can be found. Virtually all conventional agencies have a web presence and introduce their services via their websites. But this is not the same as an online agency which simply provides a database of families on the one hand and people looking for live-in jobs on the other so that they can match themselves up.

Internet databases like these enable families and applicants to engage in DIY arrangements. Prospective au pairs register their details, including age, nationality, relevant experience and in many cases a photo, to be uploaded onto a website which then becomes accessible to registered families. The families then make contact with suitable au pairs after paying an introduction fee to the web-based agency. Registration is usually free or reasonably priced for the job-seeker. Be very wary of sites that require any significant payment. Online agencies (for example the *Au Pair Company, Almondbury Agency, 4nannies.com Inc, Au Pair Connect,* etc. with entries in the 'Directory of Agencies') operate like any online employment recruitment service. Terms and conditions vary widely. In many cases it is free to upload your details but a fee will be charged to search the database, for instance US$50 for three months. Another possibility is that it is free to search but you must pay a fee when you make a match. Whatever the system, the site-cum-agency has to make money somehow.

A great many sites for online au pair matching have sprung up, in addition to the ones included in the Directory, including www.greataupair.com, www.au-pair-box.com, www. eaupair.com, www.aupairsearch.com (based in South Africa), www.aupairs.co.uk, www. aupair-world.net (German-based), www.findaupair.com (affiliated to the Chester Agency in the UK), www.perfectaupair.com (based in Bristol, England), www.learn4good.com/jobs (Search 'Au Pairs' or 'Childcare/Nannies' for interesting agency postings in date order), www.aupair-plus.com, www.aupairz.com, www.au-pair.net and Au Pair on the Net (www. aupaironnet.com).

The internet can also assist job-seeking nannies; try for instance www.nannyjob.co.uk which allows you to search its database for au pair, mother's help or nanny vacancies in various regions of the UK, Europe and beyond. At the time of writing it claimed to have more than 2,300 live job vacancies and a database of 2,100+ CVs for job-seekers. Another possibility is www.globalappointments.com.

Before a prospective au pair decides to look for a family on the internet, it is worth considering the relative advantages and disadvantages of using the web as opposed to a conventional agency as described below. Making the arrangement directly with a family sight unseen and with no agency back-up carries potential risks. No doubt many of the matches result in successful outcomes. Typically a family contacts a promising looking candidate or a job-seeker contacts a promising sounding family; they make contact via email and then telephone and decide whether they are compatible. Assuming each party is upfront and keeps to their part of the bargain, all should be well.

> **Without any mediating agency, however, there will always be lingering anxiety and nagging doubts, as expressed by Pearl Chan from the US**
> *I am a junior at a prominent university in the United States and I was looking to au pair abroad for the summer. I have corresponded with a family in the South of France and both parties are ready to seal the deal, after finding each other's profiles through an online agency, eaupair.com. I am almost positive no services are provided after a match. Therefore, in the case that anything were to happen, who should I contact in the country? While the family sounds like a wonderful one, I must be cautious because I will be abroad and have no contacts once there.*

This is a standard dilemma and the only reply is to go on your instincts and have a contingency plan in place (i.e. enough money) if things go wrong.

If it happens that either side is not committed to the arrangement to which they have signed up, the other side can be badly let down and have no recourse. For example an employer might change his or her mind between inviting a young girl to come and the start date. It is not unknown for families to issue several invitations and choose the one they like the look of better after arrival. In this case, an au pair could be turned away on the doorstep, without fluent English or much money. Similarly, families that are expecting an au pair to arrive on a certain date can find themselves disappointed.

Far worse problems can be imagined. There is nothing to prevent a predatory male registering as a family and tricking an unsuspecting young woman into arriving at his private address. Come to that, a family might unwittingly invite an axe murderer into their homes. These worst case scenarios verge on the absurd but make the same point that conventional agencies make, that without the support of an agency, it is very difficult to carry out any effective screening of either party. Some of the websites do publish black lists naming and shaming employers who have misled young foreigners, but these are far from comprehensive. Websites also have to protect their paying client families and so publish the names of au pairs/nannies about whom they have received complaints, as one did:

Warning to All families, Agencies, Au pairs - Thursday, August 18, 2005:
Dear clients, Please be aware that the agency perfectaupair has found that one of their candidate has breached the au pair programme. This was evidenced when the family's

mother has caught the candidate sleeping with the father. As we are regulated to ensure that all candidates have certain moralities. We are also under the family's trust to provide awareness of such situation. The candidate name is Miss Stephanie... residing in Lille, Country France. If you require additional information or details, please do not hesitate in contacting me.

If relying on the internet it is essential that you ascertain exactly the nature of the situation and the expectations of your new employer. Work out in your mind what you will do in the event the arrangement does not work out. If the agency is simply a database-provider, they will be able to offer little or no back-up. (On the other hand, the same is true of answering a conventional print advertisement).

Via the internet, Jayde Cahir found an agency, was emailed several families' portfolios from which she was able to make direct contact, and eventually chose a family in Germany. In initial discussions with the host family, she was misled on several counts and found that she was expected to be more a paid companion for the neglected wife than an au pair. Even though she did develop a good relationship with the wife and boy, the husband took against her and unceremoniously dismissed her:

> *I left the house within two hours of receiving his note asking me to leave or he would 'throw me out'. So I was left in a foreign country, unable to speak the language with nowhere to live. In most cases, the agencies are there to support you; however mine never returned my phone calls. This ended up being a very expensive experience as am still owed unpaid wages.*

AGENCIES

The primary role of au pair, nanny and domestic agencies is to network with partner agencies abroad in order to introduce prospective au pairs/nannies to suitable families. Whilst the matching of families with au pairs is first done on paper, the normal practice is for partner agencies to arrange for families to conduct telephone interviews with any prospective au pairs, so that all parties are aware of the requirements of the position. Agents act as clearinghouses for various application forms and try to satisfy the requests of families with the applicants registered with them. If a Spanish family wants a Roman Catholic, English-speaking dog-loving, non-smoking au pair with a driving licence, then the local Spanish agent will pass on this request to a counterpart British agent (for example) who will try to find a suitable candidate. A professional agency will go to great lengths to match applicants

with the right family since it is in their business interest to satisfy their clients with an acceptable commodity, you. They go on to provide a back-up service to the candidate for the duration of his/her stay.

Au pair placement was something that was always done by telephone and correspondence between agencies rather than requiring a face-to-face interview, so it is an activity that now makes extensive use of electronic communication. However some agencies continue to pride themselves on their personal contact with their clients. Since candidates normally apply from their home country, au pair agencies normally depend on their partner agencies abroad for screening and checking. Over years of co-operation, agencies build up a good relationship with their partners and can be confident that the candidates who come via this route are the ones deserving to be placed in the best positions. A good agency also vets the families that register with it; some even make personal visits to the homes of client families. Nanny agencies are different since most applicants for nanny posts are personally interviewed by their agency and their references verified.

In recent years, established au pair agencies have lost a great deal of business to internet agencies and are adamant that the protection they provide is valuable to both parties.

Elizabeth Elder, who is currently the elected chair of the Childcare section of the Recruitment & Employment Confederation in the UK (see below), describes some of the problems that have arisen from internet matches:
One of the issues we are particularly concerned about currently is the danger both families and au pairs and nannies are exposing themselves to by finding families and childcarers through unregulated internet sites and independent of respectable agencies. Every day there are horror stories ranging from families who find their au pairs promoting themselves on pornographic sites, to the sad stories of au pairs arriving with no papers, references, medical notes or police checks only for the family to discover that the au pair cannot drive, or do any of the things promised beforehand. These young people are then unable to register with agencies such as ours to find new families because they do not have any of the necessary paperwork, and they then disappear into the illegal black market workplace, exposing themselves to unscrupulous gang leaders, etc. We are really concerned that this is a highly dangerous way of finding work and likewise highly dangerous for families who are trusting their most treasured possessions into the care of unchecked people.

It is illegal for agencies in the UK to charge job-seekers a fee, however it is normal for agencies in most countries to charge a fee for au pair placement abroad.

According to the Employment Agencies Act, which can be viewed on the Department of Trade & Industry website (www.dti.gov.uk/er/agency/regs-pl971.htm#agencies):
Employment agencies and employment businesses are prohibited from charging fees to workers for finding or seeking to find them jobs... This includes those that deal with au pairs and with freelance or self-employed workers as well as those that deal only with workers on a normal contract of employment... [There are a few exceptions] An agency which uses the services of an agent abroad in finding a post for an au pair outside the United Kingdom is allowed to charge a fee to the au pair for finding the position, but the fee must not exceed £40 and cannot be charged until the au pair has accepted the post offered - see the Employment Agencies Act 1973 (Charging Fees to Au Pairs) Regulations 1981 (SI 1981 No 1481).

Au pair agencies on the continent are not restricted by such legislation and many agencies in France, Italy, Spain, Switzerland, etc. typically charge prospective au pairs a substantial fee up to €250. Normally this fee is applicable only to local applicants who want to fix up a childcare job in another country, e.g. the UK or US, but it is wise to check before applying.

PROS AND CONS

Using an agency is certainly the most reliable way of finding work. Angie Copley is just one satisfied customer who was favourably impressed with the ease of fixing up a job abroad:

> *After passing a BTEC course in Social Caring, I decided I would go to Italy for a year and work as a nanny. I found the address of an agency in your book and wrote to them. Before I knew it, they had found me a family in Sardinia. I couldn't believe that it was so easy. All I had to do was pay for a flight out there and that was that.*

The primary advantage of using a conventional agency is that it works closely with a partner agent in the target country, who can provide a local back-up service if things go awry. If an initial placement does not work out for some reason, an agency should be prepared to find a replacement (au pair or family) quickly. Although the level of service varies among agencies, a good agency will go to a great deal of trouble to help the new arrival with the logistics, e.g. advise on travel and visas, facilitate contact with other au pairs in the vicinity, etc. For example members of BAPAA (British Au Pair Agencies Association) organise large-scale social events for au pairs placed by its member agencies, e.g. welcome information sessions, Christmas party, river trip in the spring and so on. None of this is available to the isolated au pair who has fixed up a family over the internet.

Judith Twycross's experience with the Sussex agency that arranged a placement in Seville for her was a textbook success:

> *The main advantage of going through an agency was that I was given a choice of five or six families over a three-week period whom I could ring up and speak to myself or ask the Spanish agent to check various details. This was very important to me as I had certain specifications from which I was not prepared to waver, such as I wanted to have at least two set evenings off a week and all day Sunday. I also did not want babies under the age of two and I wanted to guarantee that I would be able to attend language classes. The English-speaking agent in Madrid was very helpful when I was trying to choose a family. She rang twice to speak to me and the family during my first month to check everything was going well and to clear up any misunderstandings. She also arranged a meeting between me and another au pair working in Seville which made the task of settling in and developing a social life considerably easier.*

However, alongside the advantages of using an agency, the system is not guaranteed to be trouble-free. Once you have lodged an application the uncertainty can be irritating or even nerve-racking. There may be a long delay while the agency tries to find a suitable match, especially if you choose to apply direct to an agency abroad. Then suddenly the offer of a family may come through which you are obliged to accept or reject immediately, and quite often for an almost immediate starting date. It is a good idea not to assume too much, and to keep in close communication with the agency to check on the progress of your application.

Some au pairs have complained that if you go through an agency you are taking potluck. Reputable agencies should help you to avoid problems, however less scrupulous ones might promise more than they can deliver. For example, you should probably give a wide berth to any agency that suggests you lie or exaggerate on your application form (e.g. that you speak the language, have more childcare experience than you actually have). Sally Stanley was told by her agent in London that the Spanish family to whom she was being sent would be having a holiday in Majorca at some point, though this was never even mentioned after she arrived. Meanwhile the agent (either in England or in Spain) had told the family that Sally was planning to stay for a whole year, although she had made it quite clear on her application form that she had to resume her studies in October. The agency had given her an urgent starting date which she scrambled to meet, only to find that her charges would be away on holiday for a further week. This series of fiascos is not typical but it is best to seek out the most reputable agency you can (see information about accreditation bodies below).

Many misunderstandings can be avoided by direct communication between family and au pair. Most agencies do encourage an exchange of information once an au pair has accepted a placement, assuming there is time and a common language, but it is still difficult to form a complete and accurate picture. Always make a point of obtaining the family's email address and phone number from the agency and also the contact details of their agent abroad. A couple of long distance phone calls could clarify many things and set your mind at rest.

CHOOSING AN AGENCY

The list of agencies with entries in the Directory of Agencies in this book is by no means exhaustive. Thousands of agencies large and small exist to supply live-in childcarers to working families. Finding agency details is very easy with a few clicks of a mouse. Your first port of call should be the website of IAPA (described below) from which web links can take you to established agencies in many countries. For agencies working in the UK, the commercial site www.BestBear.co.uk aims to provide a definitive list of reputable UK childcare agencies. According to a *Which?* report, of the 1,000 agencies investigated by BestBear, only a quarter are recommended on its site.

With so much choice of agency, it is a good idea to contact several agencies initially, in order to compare their services. If you want to find a childcare agency in a specific city or area, it is possible simply to check the online Yellow Pages, e.g. www.yell.com for the UK, www.yellowpages.ca for Canada, etc. Any search engine will guide you to the *Paginas Amarillos* of Spain or the *Gelbe Seiten* of Germany. For France go to www.pagesjaunes.fr, for Italy www.paginegialle.it and for Norway www.gulesider.no.

After comparing agency terms, it is advisable to choose just one agency with whom to register. If you are unhappy with their service for any reason, you should contact them and tell them that you are going to apply to another one. Sharon Legg, one of the authors of this book, registered with several agencies at once and lived to regret it:

I learned my lesson the hard way. While I was looking for work in France, I used three different agencies simultaneously and it all became extremely confusing. I was receiving phone calls from families and, because their English was often poor and my French non-existent, I found it difficult to establish which agency they were connected with. It all became very awkward indeed and I upset a lot of people!

If you apply too widely, it can work to your disadvantage. One Italian agency refused to try to place one girl whose application she had received from six different agents.

In the first instance check the website, then email, phone or write, briefly describing any relevant experience you might have, what kind of position you are seeking and requesting an application form and general information about the agency. You should be able to conclude a certain amount from the tone and style of the agency literature. On the one hand you may receive a glossy and professionally packaged dossier with detailed country-by-country information, on the other a badly photocopied application form with little background information. Amateurish presentation isn't necessarily a bad sign, since it might indicate that the agency is a one-person operation possibly run from a private home. Sometimes this means that you will get more personal service though they are unlikely to have as great a choice of client families.

Another thing to watch out for is whether regular office hours are maintained and whether personal visits are encouraged. It is unusual for interviews to be compulsory (unless you are going for full-time nanny jobs) however an informal meeting with the agency staff is a good idea if geographically feasible. A few agencies seem to operate with a telephone answering machine, which is not ideal if you have any questions or last-minute panics.

For candidates who are looking for placements abroad, it is often possible to apply directly to an au pair agent in your target country, though not all continental agencies are prepared to consider privately lodged applications. Make sure that the fee they charge local girls for sending them abroad will not be levied on you. While some agencies in Austria and Switzerland charge at least the equivalent of a week's pocket money, for example, others charge nothing. Applying directly may work out satisfactorily, especially if applicant and agent rely mainly on e-mail, but it might also result in a higher degree of insecurity while you wait to be offered a job. Unless the agency has advanced on-line facilities, you are likely to incur some expense in postage, phoning and faxing.

The Roman Catholic organisation ACISJF (Association Catholique Internationale au Service de la Jeunesse Féminine) provides an au pair placement service in some of the countries in which it operates; the website www.acisjf-int.org has links to its branches worldwide. The YWCA in some cities runs an au pair referral service, though usually for people already in town.

If in any doubt about an agency, ask them to refer you to one or more au pairs on their books who may be willing to describe their experiences with the agency and (even more importantly in some cases) with their partner agency in your destination country. The services offered abroad differ drastically.

ACCREDITATION BODIES

Obviously you will want to choose a reputable agency. As mentioned earlier, employment agencies in the UK no longer have to be licensed by the Department of Employment. There is no regulation of agencies whatsoever and anyone can start up an au pair agency without having undergone any inspection or external monitoring. The potential dangers of exploitation and worse are a great cause of concern to many in the industry. Young women and men can find themselves in families where no checks have been made and with no one to turn to when things go wrong.

One way of checking quality control is to find out if the agency you are considering belongs to a trade association. Agencies that belong to the main regulatory bodies, e.g. the International Au Pair Association (IAPA) or the British Au Pair Agencies Association (BAPAA), have signed up to a code of conduct, which provides some safeguards for au pairs. Other countries have their own associations such as NAPO in the Netherlands (see country chapters).

Many leading au pair agencies and youth exchange organisations in Europe belong to IAPA, the International Au Pair Association, an international body trying to regulate the industry. The IAPA website www.iapa.org has clear links to its member agencies around the world and also prominently lists the reasons why registered agencies are the safest way to arrange an au pair placement; just click on 'Protect Yourself'. IAPA was formed 12 years ago to regulate the industry worldwide. Entries in the Directory of Agencies indicate membership in IAPA or any other association.

Agencies can become members only after demonstrating their credentials over at least two years of operation. The official address of the IAPA is c/o FIYTO (Federation of International Youth Tourism Organisations), Bredgade 25 H, 1260 Copenhagen K (tel 33 33 96 00/fax 33 93 96 76). IAPA agencies try to apply standard vetting procedures on prospective au pairs and families. They meet at an annual conference so that they have face-to-face contact with their partner agencies around the world.

The British Association of Au Pair Agencies (BAPAA) was founded in 2003 by the 23 UK members of IAPA. BAPAA's contact details are: Lower Ground Floor (L C & C), 10/11 Gray's Inn Square, London WC1R 5JD; www.bapaa.org.uk. As the UK is the only

EU country with no compulsory registration for au pairs/nannies or agents, it was felt that it would be appropriate to set up a regulatory body to promote high standards. BAPAA continues to lobby for government recognition.

The standards of service that can be expected from a BAPAA agency are

- ✪ Thorough screening procedures
- ✪ Courteous and efficient handling of customers
- ✪ On-going support for families and au pairs
- ✪ Guidance to families on how au pairs should be welcomed
- ✪ Guidance to au pairs on how to make the most of the au pair experience
- ✪ Financially sound business
- ✪ Nationwide ability to support au pair requirements through BAPAA network

---

A selection of au pair and nanny agencies belong to the *Recruitment and Employment Confederation* or *REC* (36-38 Mortimer St, London W1N 7RB; 020-7462 3260; www.rec.uk.com) which is the national trade association for the recruitment and staffing industry in the UK. The REC has 70 member agencies operating in the childcare sector, which are listed by region on the REC website. They seek to uphold rigorous standards of conduct within the industry and tend to be at the elite end of the market and mainly deal with positions in the UK. If you are dissatisfied with the services given by an REC agency, you may take advantage of the REC's disciplinary procedures. If it can be shown that an REC agency misled either a family or candidate in any way or was guilty of bad practice then they would be subjected to the disciplinary procedure which could result in an enquiry with the Department of Trade and Industry. Of course anyone who feels that they have become involved with a rogue agency or who encounters unprofessional practices is free to report that agency directly to the DTI for investigation.

A new voluntary association was set up in 2004 called the *Association of Nanny Agencies* which launched its own website in the summer of 2005: www.anauk.org. ANA grew out of the Professional Association of Nursery Nurses or PANN (2 St. James' Court, Friar Gate, Derby DE1 1BT; 01332 372337), an independent registered trade union for nannies. Representatives of the REC have expressed concern that the voluntary and informal nature of this new organisation means that it lacks the legal backing and expertise to be a voice for the industry. So far, the website does not provide a list of members, but anyone interested can enquire via admin@anauk.org.

Other agency groupings exist, though these are more like a trade association for joint marketing purposes such as the Universal Au Pair Association (UAPA; www.uapa.net) which has only a handful of members.

But there are still a great many privately run agencies which are not members of any regulatory body. Some are excellent, providing a service equal to that of the established agencies brandishing the logo of an international association. Others are not. One disincentive for a small independent agency to join an association is the annual subscription fee, though in the case of BAPAA this is only £100 a year and of IAPA €600. In short, the whole field is notoriously difficult to regulate and it will be a long time before au pairs and nannies will be protected by formal legislation in whatever country they choose to work.

AGENCY PROCEDURES

The time taken to make a placement depends on how flexible you are about dates and location, and the number and size of partner agencies. Email has transformed the matching process, and instantaneous placement is possible if you have an appropriate background and happen to apply at a time when suitable unfilled vacancies are available. Quick placement is seldom possible for summer assignments, for which most agencies insist on early application, and are rare for male applicants. The vast majority of au pair openings coincide with the academic year, lasting from September to June. The next most popular time for starting a job is January, since many jobs become vacant after Christmas.

The downloaded or posted application form should be filled out meticulously. In all

When sending photos take care to project the right image

likelihood it will be the principal information on which the matching with a family is based and making a good impression is of prime importance. There might also be a questionnaire which will help the agency to get to know your requirements in greater detail.

In addition, the application dossier which you are asked to submit usually includes one or more photos, at least two letters of reference (which in some cases is required by law), a declaration of good health signed by a doctor, a curriculum vitae and/or a handwritten letter addressed 'Dear Family' describing yourself and your reasons for wanting to work as an au pair.

Recently au pair agencies have been asking for a police check and indeed it is essential for nanny applicants. In the UK this document is provided by the Criminal Records Bureau and many entries in the directory mention a 'CRB check' as a requirement of application. Normally it is the responsibility of registered agencies or employers rather than individuals to apply to the CRB. The standard fee charged for a CRB standard disclosure is £29 and an enhanced disclosure is £34. Further details are available from www.crb.gov.uk or www. disclosure.gov.uk; the CRB Information Line is 0870 90 90 811. The CRB has recently advised that all overseas au pairs, nannies and mother's helps should obtain a certificate of good conduct from their Embassy, though this is not yet a widespread practice.

If applying from abroad or supplying a photo to an au pair matching website, it does not have to be a professional shot, but you should take care to project the right image. A head and shoulders photo, preferably with an engaging smile is best. Another good idea is to send a family shot, preferably with you with one of your previous charges or a young cousin. Resist the temptation to send a party photo, in which the cocktail or pint of bitter you are clutching will probably create a negative impression no matter how flattering the photo may be. If you are in doubt, send along a selection from which the agency can choose.

References are not as important as they are in many other jobs, though of course the more glowing the better. The normal procedure for au pairs is for you to collect them yourself rather than have them sent to the agency directly. References for nannies, by contrast, will be followed up and verified so you need only provide the name and contact details, normally telephone. It is advisable to send photocopies in case you need the originals again later. School or college-leavers will need to provide a reference from their head teacher (though a few agencies specify that they are not interested in academic references), plus one of a domestic nature. This might be from a mother whose children you regularly babysit, or perhaps from a holiday job which involved domestic chores.

The letter introducing yourself should mention where you were born and brought up, a description of your family and their interests, any travelling you have done either in an organised group or independently, what kind of schooling you have had and your attitude to it, any jobs, hobbies or ambitions and of course why and for how long you want to work abroad and why you think your personality is suitable.

The doctor's certificate can be a simple statement signed by a physician that you are 'mentally and physically fit for work abroad'. Most (but not all) GPs charge £10-£20 for this statement. Things get more complicated when the medical certificate is a requirement of the visa (see country chapters) and needs to be translated into the relevant language.

NORTH AMERICAN APPLICANTS

Many North Americans are eager to learn the language and absorb the culture of European countries, and indeed some do become au pairs, though the term is not universally recognised in the US and Canada. The red tape is more difficult for them, especially in certain countries like Italy and Spain, than for au pairs from European countries, however they are rarely prohibited from spending six months or a year working with families.

The following agencies, all but one in Canada, have au pair programmes in Europe for North Americans:

Au Pair Canada, 15 Goodacre Close, Red Deer, Alberta T4P 3A3, Canada (tel/fax 403-343-1418; aupaircanada@shaw.ca). Au pairs to France, Netherlands, Switzerland and Germany (see entry).

Club Aventure - Aventures Jeunesse, 757 Mont-Royal Est, Montreal, Quebec H2J 1W8, Canada (1-877-527-0999/ 514-527-0999; fax 514-527-3999; info@aventuresjeunesse. com; www.aventuresjeunesse.com). Au pairs (mainly from French-speaking Canada) to England, Scotland, France, Denmark, Iceland and Netherlands (see entry).

Globetrotters Education Consulting Inc, 1784 Rosebank Road, Pickering, Ontario, L1V 1P6, Canada (905-839-0090 or 416-839-4420; fax 905-839-0063; laura@ globetrotterseducation.ca; www.globetrotterseducation.ca). Jobs in Spain, Italy, France, UK, Australia and Germany.

InterExchange Inc., 13th Floor, 161 Sixth Avenue, New York, NY 10013 (212-924-0446; fax 212-924-0575; info@interexchange.org/ www.interexchange.org). Au pairs to Austria, Finland, Netherlands, Italy, Norway and Spain (see entry).

Le Monde Au Pair, 7 rue de la Commune Ouest, Bureau 204, Montréal, Québec H2Y 2C5, Canada (514-281-3045; fax 514-281-1525; www.generation.net/~aupair). Au pair placements in Denmark, France, Germany, Austria, Italy, Netherlands, Norway, Spain, Switzerland, UK, Australia, New Zealand and USA.

Scotia Personnel Ltd., 6045 Cherry St, Halifax, Nova Scotia B3H 2K4, Canada (902-422-1455; fax 902-423-6840; scotiap@ns.sympatico.ca/ www.scotia-personnel-ltd.com). Au pairs to USA, England, France, Holland, Germany, Australia, Spain, Switzerland, Iceland, Denmark, Ireland, Austria and Italy (see entry).

The British Home Office does not allow Americans to become au pairs in Britain on the principle that they share a common language. But live-in jobs are available to students participating in the 'Work in Britain' programme run by BUNAC USA (see chapter on the United Kingdom).

WORKING FOR TOUR OPERATORS

Qualified nannies will have no trouble finding a seasonal job with a British tour operator who have difficulty filling all their posts in this booming field. Partly because parents are having children later in life, after they have become more affluent, tour operators have tried to lure this new market by brushing up their child-friendly image. Over the past decade, many with names like 'Family Ski' have started offering kids' clubs and crèche facilities. All the major camping tour operators like Eurocamp (01606 787525) and Canvas Holidays (01383 629018) employ children's couriers to run activity programmes (mainly for children over four) and are often looking for experienced nannies to fill these positions.

Some UK nanny agencies have contracts with the biggest tour operators to supply nannies, for example *Nannies Abroad* based in Winchester and *Babysitters/Childminders* in London (see entries). The major tour operator Mark Warner (George House, 61-65 Kensington Church St, London W8 4BA; 0870 033 0760; www.markwarner-recruitment. co.uk) recruits a large number of childcare staff for the six-month summer season in Mediterranean resorts and for the winter in the Alps. Nannies must be qualified (NNEB, NVQ or equivalent). Winter vacancies occur in Austria and France and summer jobs are available at the company's Beachclub Hotels in Corsica, Sardinia, Greece, Turkey, Portugal, Egypt and Sri Lanka.

Many ski tour operators now employ nannies and children's reps. Specialist ski recruitment websites can be extremely helpful in tracking down this kind of job. The superb Natives.co.uk posts current vacancies on behalf of a selection of the major operators and also includes detailed resort descriptions. Try also Season Workers (www.seasonworkers. com), Free Radicals (www.freeradicals.co.uk) and www.voovs.com, all of which consider themselves to be one-stop shops for recruitment of winter staff for Europe and North America. Sun Search Recruitment (www.sunsearchrecruitment.com) recruits qualified nannies (NVQ level three or equivalent) to work in luxury chalets in the French Alps for the winter or in Spanish and Portuguese resorts in the summer. The company has telephone contact numbers in England and Spain.

Other companies that hire nannies for resorts in a number of countries include:

Club Med International Recruitment, 11-12 place Jules Ferry, 69458 Lyon Cedex 06, France (recruit.uk@clubmed.com; 08453 676767 in the UK; www.clubmed-jobs.com). Nannies who can communicate in French for upmarket holiday villages in Europe and North Africa. NNEB nannies to work in Baby Clubs (for babies and toddlers) and those with at least 2 years experience with older children (ages 5-17) and with first aid certificate. North American applicants can apply online at www.clubmedjobs.com.

Cosmos Holidays, Wren Court, 17 London Road, Bromley, Kent BR1 1DE (020-8695 4724; overseasdept@cosmos.co.uk; www.cosmos-holidays.com/jobs.php). 30 children's representatives and crèche staff for Balearics, Canaries, Portugal, Turkey and Greece. Nannies must have recognised childcare qualification. Seasonal contracts last for 6 months but high season contracts available for 3-4 months. £460 per calendar month, payable into UK bank account. Flights to and from resort and accommodation are provided.

Crystal Holidays, King's Place, Wood St, Kingston-upon-Thames KT1 1JY (020-7420 2081; www.shgjobs.co.uk). TUI SHG recruits nannies with at least an NNEB or NVQ Level 3 for Thomson as well as Crystal.

Esprit Holidays, 185 Fleet Road, Fleet, Hants. GU51 3BL (01252 618318; recruitment@ esprit-holidays.co.uk). Nannies should have NNEB, NVQ3, BTEC or RGN qualification.

First Choice/Skibound, Jetset House, Lowfield Heath, Crawley, W. Sussex RH11 0PQ (0870 750 1204; www.firstchoice4jobs.co.uk). 150 children's reps are hired for flexible periods between March and October for resorts in Spain (including Canaries and the Balearics) Portugal, Greece, Cyprus, Turkey and Bulgaria. Must have NNEB, BTEC or NVQ level 3 in Childcare, a Diploma in Nursery Nursing or an equivalent UK qualification.

In2action Ltd, 11 York Ave, East Cowes, Isle of Wight, PO32 6QY (01983 200 953; www. in2actionuk.com). 30+ childcare placements in partnership with First Choice Holidays in overseas holiday resorts in Costa Del Sol, Lanzarote, Mallorca and Turkey, among others. Must have NNEB/CACHE Level 3. Monthly salary of £578 with meals and accommodation provided.

MyTravel, Holiday House, Sandbrook Park, Sandbrook Way, Rochdale, Lancs. OL11 5SA (24-hour Recruitment hotline 0870 241 2642; www.mytravelcareers.co.uk). Nursery nurses and children's reps recruited for brands Airtours, Direct Holidays, Panorama and Manos Holidays in wide range of European resorts.

Neilson, Locksview, Brighton Marina, Brighton, BN2 5HA (0870 241 2901; skijobs@ neilson.com or for summer positions recruitment@neilson.com). Nannies for summer season in Greece, Croatia, Egypt and Turkey; and ski season in Andorra, Austria, France, Italy, Norway, etc.

Powder Byrne, 250 Upper Richmond Road, London SW15 6TG (020-8246 5342; www. powderbyrne.com). Upmarket company operating in Switzerland, France and Austria in winter and France, Cyprus, Italy, Portugal, Mallorca, Tunisia, Mauritius and Dubai in summer. Upmarket company employing nannies to manage resort crèches.

Sunsail Ltd, The Port House, Port Solent, Portsmouth, Hants. PO6 4TH (02392 222329; hr@sunsail.com; www.sunsail.com/hr/overseas_job.html). Qualified nannies needed for watersports hotels in Mediterranean resorts, especially Greece and Turkey.

And if resorts are not exotic enough for your tastes, consider trying to get a job as a nanny or children's rep on a cruise ship. Cast-a-way-UK recruits candidates with a recognised childcare qualification and/or a minimum of two years' experience to work onboard ships on six-month contracts, mainly out of Miami. The pay is approximately $1,000 a month for working up to 12 hours a day. Further details are available from Cast-a-way (PO Box 145, Birchwood, Warrington WA3 7WH (info@cast-a-way.co.uk; www.cast-a-way.co.uk).

ADVERTISEMENTS

The old-fashioned way of looking for live-in vacancies was by answering or placing advertisements in *The Lady* magazine Many of the most prestigious nanny agencies continue to advertise in its pages. However nowadays, the majority of vacancy advertisements appear elsewhere, particularly on-line on a thousand different websites rather than in print, some of which are listed above. English-language expat magazines and newspapers (whether online or in print) are often good sources of au pair/nanny vacancies and are mentioned throughout the country chapters.

Whatever the medium, when you answer an advertisement and deal directly with prospective employers, matters are more in your own control than if you rely on the offices of an agency. You are free to make all your own arrangements, which some independent-minded people prefer. The advantage for families of relying on adverts rather than on agencies, is that they are spared any agency fee. The disadvantage for both parties is that if something goes wrong, there is no one who can be asked to mediate.

THE LADY

The Lady is a weekly magazine founded in 1885, published every Tuesday and costing £1. On the front cover of every issue they proclaim 'Jobs for Nannies, Au Pairs, Mothers' Helps, Cooks, Chefs, Wardens, Matrons and other vacancies'; the inclusion of wardens and matrons perhaps gives a flavour of the magazine. Few magazines held such a monopoly on their field of specialisation as *The Lady* did. But its readership (judging from the advertisements for stairlifts and will writing services) is not really aimed at young au pairs and nannies. The gold-plated nanny and household staff agencies still advertise but very few private families. In a randomly chosen issue at the time of writing, there were just six listings under the heading 'Overseas Domestic Situations Vacant (Cooks, Housekeepers, Mother's Helps, Nannies)' and all of them for housekeepers or carers for the elderly, whereas a decade ago there would have been scores of adverts for nannies.

The pickings aren't quite so slim for domestic jobs in Britain though again the majority are for housekeepers and carers with just a few for nannies. The best time of year to check is the summer since many vacancies need to be filled for the beginning of the school year. It is a good idea to have copies of your cover-letter and CV already prepared as well as plenty of stamps, so that postal applications can be despatched without delay. The first few applications to arrive will probably receive the most detailed attention. Again, it is a good idea to send a stamped addressed envelope for the reply. Here is an example of a cover-letter:

> *Your Full Address*
> *Your Telephone Number*
> *Date*
> *Dear...*
>
> *I read your advertisement in* The Lady *[or other] magazine this morning with great interest, and now I am forwarding my curriculum vitae in the hope of being considered for the post. I hope you will find me a suitable applicant and I look forward to your reply.*
>
> *Yours sincerely (or faithfully)...*

If the name of the prospective employer is known, address him/her by name and sign the letter 'Yours sincerely'; if you are replying to a box number and the name of the family is not included in the advertisement, address the letter 'Dear Family' and use 'Yours faithfully'. (In most cases it will be the woman of the house with whom you will initially be dealing, but there is no need to assume that at this stage.)

You should write the letter in your own handwriting (unless you are afflicted with an illegible or unattractive scrawl) to lend a personal touch. It is of course preferable to write to a foreign family in their own language. Some people, who have little or no knowledge of the language, are tempted to enlist the help of a linguistically talented friend or relative; however this is risky since it is bound to set up false expectations should you get the job, and so it is probably better to write in English.

Your CV (known as resumé in North America) should be typewritten and include the following: name and address, telephone number, date of birth, nationality, details of education and work experience (including babysitting), additional skills (e.g. swimming or first-aid) and hobbies. Don't list too many extracurricular interests (especially if they include clubbing) or the family may wonder how on earth you ever fit work into your hectic schedule. If you drive, don't forget to mention it, and also let the family know if you are a non-smoker.

You can of course place your own advert, as Julie Richards did, again some years ago:

> *I had difficulty in getting a job when I was at home in the UK, as I didn't have any experience or qualifications as a nanny. In the end I put an advert in The Lady, and had about 30 offers of jobs.*

A sample advert might read: 'Au pair, age 20, seeks position with family abroad. One year's similar experience with good refs. Driver. Non-smoker. Enthusiastic and hard-working.' Unless you want to protect your privacy with a box number, you will get faster results and a better response by including a phone number.

Although the magazine is not widely distributed abroad, past advertisers have received replies from all over the world (including North America) to a single advert. *The Lady* can be contacted at 39-40 Bedford Street, London WC2E 9ER (020-7379 4717/fax 020-7836 3601; classified.ads@lady.co.uk). Any advert that private advertisers place must be sent in by post and prepaid; the first ten words cost £22, and each further five words or less £9.90, including VAT. The use of a box number will add £8 to the cost. The text and payment must be received by the Wednesday morning preceding the issue in question.

OTHER PUBLICATIONS

Professional nannies should look at the weekly magazine *Nursery World* (0870 444 8628) with articles, adverts and listings of interest to nannies and mother's helps. It is published on Thursdays, costs £1.30 and is available in W. H. Smith's. Their website lists vacancies for high level jobs abroad; check www.nurseryworldjobs.co.uk where the vacancy listings remain in place for a fortnight after publication. As a random example, one week's vacancies were in Zurich, Venice, Bahrain, Singapore, San Francisco, the south of France, among others.

You can try to check the classified ads in a newspaper from the country you plan to work in, preferably online. Similarly, you can place your own advertisement in foreign publications either directly or through their UK-based agents. This will be very expensive in print (estimated minimum £50) but might be worthwhile if you have your heart set on an unusual destination like Singapore or Helsinki or in countries to which access is difficult.

Another newspaper which might be worth checking is *LOOT* (24-32 Kilburn High Road, London NW6 5TF; 020-7328 1771) which bills itself as 'London's noticeboard'. Among its many categories of classified ads (which are free to private advertisers) are 'Au Pair Jobs Offered/Wanted'. It is just one of many free newspapers worldwide in the Free Ads Paper International Association, usually printed on coloured newsprint. It is possible to advertise free of charge in any of these papers (from San Diego to Sofia, Rio to Ravenna) which are listed in each issue of *LOOT* with instructions for placing ads.

WORD OF MOUTH

Sometimes au pairs who have worked abroad are asked by their employers to find a replacement upon their return home. If you happen to have a friend or acquaintance working for a family overseas, and you are considering doing likewise, you might end up being the replacement. It can be a great advantage knowing your predecessor who can give you first-hand information about the parents' strengths and weaknesses as employers and about the children. On the other hand, if the job doesn't work out and you decide to leave prematurely, it could embarrass your friend.

Hannah Start suggests contacting English language schools in your hometown to find a position. Professional people from abroad on short intensive language courses might well be looking for an au pair on whom to practise their English once they return home. Hannah fixed up a plum job in Paris this way.

JOB-HUNTING ABROAD

If you are already abroad, check the adverts in the local press, assuming you can read them or can find someone to translate them for you. It is worthwhile in many cases consulting any English language publications such as the *Athens News* which are mentioned whenever relevant in the country chapters. You can visit the offices of au pair agencies abroad who might be able to place applicants on the spot with little delay (see Directory for addresses).

Other ways of hearing about openings are to check notice boards at the local English-speaking churches or bookshops, in supermarkets (especially in resorts), and at the local university, to ask the headmistress of a junior school if she knows of any families looking for an au pair, to put up notices at play-groups, or visit a school at the end of the school day and chat with the mothers and au pairs who are there to collect their charges. Clinics, laundrettes, newsagents and second-hand children's clothes shops may also post relevant notices.

Sometimes foreign cultural organisations such as the Alliance Française, Goethe Institut or British Council can be helpful. If you sign up for a language course abroad or simply cultivate the company of the students, you'll probably get to know some au pairs and through them the names of families in need of home help.

The demand for live-in help and babysitters in ski resorts around the world is very strong.

In some cases, there are even notices up in the local tourist office of ski resorts from Crans-Montana in Switzerland to Thredbo Australia asking for domestic and childcare help.

INTERVIEWS

Unless you apply for an au pair position once you are already abroad, you probably won't have an interview with the family nor with the agency, except in special cases. This is not true however with nanny and mother's help jobs where, in almost all cases, the candidates will be interviewed by the family, the agency or someone appointed by the employers.

Some foreign parents arrange an interview to coincide with a trip to Britain. You might meet one parent while on a business trip or the whole family on holiday. Occasionally the interviewing is left to the present or most recent nanny. It is very rare to be transported to the family home abroad for a meeting. They will often come to London rather than elsewhere in Britain so it is an advantage if you are prepared to travel up to the city if necessary. Travel expenses are not usually reimbursed, so some money should be set aside for this purpose.

PREPARING FOR THE INTERVIEW

The first thing you should do is prepare any questions you might want to ask the parents. Try to commit these to memory and introduce them into the conversation at appropriate intervals, rather than laboriously read them from a long list. The more enjoyable and interesting you can make the meeting, the better impression you will make. Some experienced nannies feel that it is as much a case of the nanny interviewing the family as the other way round.

If you lack practical experience, it might be an idea to read a reference book on childcare such as those by Miriam Stoppard or Penelope Leach, favoured childcare gurus. It is also worth looking at *Bringing Up a Family 0-9 Years* by Mary Batchelor, *Healthy Eating for your Child* by H. Bampfylde and J. Dickerson and even *Dr. Spock's Baby* and *Childcare Book* by Benjamin Spock.

> **In Matt Tomlinson's view, this is especially important for males:**
> *If you've never seriously looked after kids before, do your homework. Get loads of ideas on things to do and read a couple of books. Mothers are quite useful, if only so you can avoid the mistakes they've made! My mother was quite supportive, giving me lots of good advice and also a copy of Penelope Leach's seminal guide to raising small children, which I recommend strongly for anyone hoping to work with under 5s.*

It is very important to look presentable at any interview and nannies and au pairs are no exception. Avoid wearing jeans and trainers even though this will probably be your 'uniform' once you start work. On the other hand, don't go to the interview dressed to kill. The parents will probably find it hard to envisage you cleaning up after the children and subconsciously dismiss you as unsuitable. Most families are looking for someone who projects herself as tidy and reliable. Try to present a balanced image of someone who is sensible but fun, polite but informal.

Sometimes you will meet the family at the office of the agency, but it is more common to meet them at a hotel or private house (but never agree to an interview in a hotel bedroom). If the venue is an unfamiliar place, allow plenty of time to find it. If long distances are involved and you have friends or relatives who live in the interview area, ask if you can stay with them the night before. It'll save you having to arrive at the interview looking creased and worn out from travelling.

CONDUCTING YOURSELF AT INTERVIEW

If the interview has been arranged for you by an agency, there will probably be other candidates present and you might not be seen straightaway. You can put this waiting period to good use, however, depending on the circumstances. The children might be there and if this is the case, you must try to familiarise yourself with them. It will give you an opportunity to determine whether or not you would enjoy being their nanny and, besides, you would be wise to show an interest in them. A candidate who ignores prospective charges will not be rated very highly. On the other hand do not gush all over them, since this is sure to alienate them. Do not underestimate the power which children wield. If they take a shine to you, the parents might hire you in spite of a lack of formal qualifications. Similarly, if you pay them little or no attention, they are unlikely to support you, and the parents will notice your lack of enthusiasm.

The same applies to the current nanny. If she is present, make a point of chatting to her for she is a wealth of information. Try to interpret her attitude towards the family, and take note of how they interact with her. Does she seem to enjoy working for them, and do the parents treat her in a friendly manner? The nanny might also be in a position to influence the parents' choice, so don't be lulled into a false sense of security. Keep the conversation fairly business-like and don't give anything away that could be interpreted as a negative trait later on.

If you are left in a room by yourself use the time to go over any points you plan to raise at the interview. You will probably start to feel particularly nervous at this time but try to relax by breathing deeply and reminding yourself that the parents are not professional interviewers and are probably dreading the ordeal as much as you are.

They will usually begin the interview by giving you more details of what the job involves. Try to leave with a clear idea of what will be expected of you. Ask what your day(s) off will be and how much you will be paid, remembering that wages vary considerably depending on the country and type of situation. Take note of any fringe benefits on offer (use of car, for example) since these might compensate for an otherwise low salary. Topics you might raise are what the children eat (i.e. how much cooking will be expected of you), their attitude to television and discipline generally. Don't forget to raise subjects such as pets. They can mean extra work for you, and if you have any animal allergies they could make your life a misery. If the children aren't present, ask to see photos of them. The parents will be pleased at your interest.

Remember to ask about the previous nannies, since the way the parents talk about their former employees could well be revealing. Barbara Henson, an American woman who decided to look for a nanny job after she arrived in London, found a job in Camberwell but realised too late that the family had had eight nannies in two years and her predecessor had attempted suicide. Also find out whether you will be living as part of the family or as a more formal employee. Try to discover whether they enforce strict rules (and will therefore back you if a punishment is meted out) or allow their children a free rein.

Once questions on both sides have been answered, don't try to prolong your time with them unless otherwise invited to do so. It is likely they will be waiting to see other applicants so just shake their hands, smile brightly and thank them for their time.

If you come away from the interview feeling that you are interested in the job, take some notes on what has taken place. It's amazing how quickly important details can be forgotten, especially if you are being interviewed by more than one family within a short time. It's also a good idea to write a brief note to the parents, thanking them for their hospitality (most families will have provided some sort of refreshment at the interview), telling them how much you enjoyed meeting them (assuming that is true) and that you are enthusiastic about the job. Writing such a note may seem a little crawling, but it's proof of good manners, which might give you the edge over the competition. If you obtained the interview through an agency, you should phone them when you get home to tell them how you think it went, and whether or not you are interested.

An hilarious dissection of the nanny interview can be found in the opening chapter of the fictional *Nanny Diaries*. Here is a brief extract:

We will dance around certain words, such as 'nanny' and 'childcare' because they would be distasteful and we will never ever actually acknowledge that we are talking about my working for her. This is the Holy Covenant of the Mother/Nanny relationship: this is a pleasure - not a job. We are merely 'getting to know each other'... The closest we get to the possibility that I might actually be doing this for money is the topic of my babysitting experience, which I describe as a passionate hobby, much like raising Seeing Eye dogs for the blind. As the conversation progresses I become a child development expert, convincing both of us of my desire to fulfill my very soul by raising a child and taking part in all stages of his/her development...I feel my eyes twinkle and imagine twirling my umbrella à la Mary Poppins. We both sit in silence for a moment picturing my studio apartment crowded with framed finger paintings and my doctorates from Stanford.

CHECK LIST
TICKETS   CAMERA
PASSPORT   CLOTHES
CONTRACT   SHOES
INSURANCE HAIR
TENNIS RACKET GRIPS
MARMITE   OTHER
CHEESE   GLASSES
ADDRESS BOOK
DIARRHOEA TABLETS.
TAPE PLAYER
MARS
ALARM CLOCK
PRESENTS FOR KIDS

Preparation

After you have secured a job, there may or may not be a waiting period during which you will have a chance to organise the practicalities of moving abroad and to prepare yourself in other ways. If you are going to a country that requires immigration procedures (e.g. Canada and Switzerland), you may find that you will have several months at your disposal. In addition to deciding what to take and which ticket to buy, you should think about health and travel insurance, necessary documents such as visas, and about having a contract drawn up.

The Professional Association of Nursery Nurses or PANN (2 St. James' Court, Friar Gate, Derby DE1 1BT; 01332 372337) sells a photocopied booklet 'All You Need to Know about Working as a Nanny' for £5 with basic information for professional nannies and a template of a contract. One of PANN's briefs is to lobby for legislation that would require nannies to be professionally qualified and registered. Whereas childminders must be registered with their local authority and submit to a police check, there is no legal requirements for nannies, although the voluntary Childcare Approval Scheme introduced in April 2005 is a step in the right direction. Potential problems are periodically highlighted by tragic incidents in which babies are abused or abducted by those caring for them, though there have been no high profile cases involving nannies since 2000.

CONTRACTS

Once you have received a job offer and have decided to accept, what happens next? If you are dealing with an agency, the offer will probably come from them. Au pair and nanny agencies are never more than referral services. If you have a contract, it will be with the family not the agency, though the agency may facilitate drawing up a contract. If a contract is sent to you direct from your future employer, you should inform the agency that an offer has been made and accepted, since they will want to collect their fee from the family. You should be totally honest with them at all times, as they have been instrumental in finding you a job and you may want to employ their services again.

NANNIES

This is the point at which a formal contract or alternatively an informal agreement should be drawn up, either with the guidance of the agency or independently. In the UK, all employers are obliged by law to provide written Particulars of Employment within the first eight weeks of employment. This should set out clearly the extent of your duties and free time, the length of stay, wages and the amount of notice which must be given on either side, whether the family will pay for health insurance and what will happen in the event of sickness. If the family has had a bad experience with a nanny, they might want to list acceptable reasons for disciplinary measures (i.e. verbal warning in the first instance, written warning and finally dismissal) such as unsatisfactory dress standards, unreliable timekeeping, after-hours behaviour which might harm the reputation of the employer, etc. The reasons for immediate dismissal are usually theft, drunkenness and philandering with the boss or his friends.

If the contract is provided by your agency or employers, study the agreement carefully before signing, making sure they have remembered to append their signatures. Sign the original and take a photocopy before returning the original to them, accompanied by a less formal note.

Although contracts are mainly intended to benefit the employee and to safeguard her against exploitation, it is a legally binding document and, in extreme cases, its violation could result in a lawsuit for breach of contract. This however is very rare: although it is not uncommon for nannies to leave their employers without due notice, resulting lawsuits are almost unheard of. Leaving prematurely is not to be recommended, however, since the family will also sign in good faith, and the contract should be maintained by both parties until it is mutually desirable to terminate it. You will soon learn that it is necessary to be a little flexible. One of the main disadvantages of this kind of work is that you can't always clock off when you are expecting to. Rather than viewing this as a breach of contract, try to recall the times when you receive unexpected bonuses, for example when the mother decides to take the children out by herself one afternoon, thus leaving you with more free time than you had anticipated.

AU PAIRS

Contracts are not very common in au pairing jobs. It is customary to receive only a letter of invitation from the family which may not specify hours, duties or pocket money. If there is time, you might wish to write to the family to ask them to provide a written agreement. It is always preferable to have something in writing in case of serious disagreement. If this is impossible, you should at least have a business-like discussion about these matters either on the telephone beforehand or in person once you arrive and make notes during or immediately afterwards (see the section on *Problems* below). Sometimes families are reluctant to put things in writing, since they want the arrangement to be entirely informal and flexible. You will have to use your judgment whether or not to insist on something in writing.

HEALTH AND INSURANCE

Some families pay for or contribute towards the cost of medical insurance and it is essential to find out well in advance whether your employers are prepared to do this. In some countries they are compelled by law to provide insurance, so check the country chapters in this book and with your agency. Even if you are allowed to participate in the national scheme of the country you are going to, you may find that there are important exclusion clauses such as for dental treatment, non-emergency treatment, prescription drugs and so on.

No matter what country you are heading for, but especially if it is an EU country, you should obtain the Department of Health leaflet T6 *Health Advice for Travellers* available from post offices, doctor's surgeries or by ringing the Health Literature Line 08701 555455 or read it online at www.dh.gov.uk, which also has country-by-country details.

If you are a national of a European Economic Area country and will be working in another EEA country, you will be covered by European Social Security regulations. The information leaflet SA29 *Your Social Security Insurance Benefits and Health Care Rights in the European Economic Area* was last updated October 2004 and can be read online at www.dwp.gov.uk/international/sa29 or obtained from the Centre for Non Residents, Room BP1301, Benton Park View, Newcastle-upon-Tyne NE98 1ZZ (0845 915 4811; www.inlandrevenue.gov.uk/nic).

In 2005 the new Europe-wide European Health Insurance Card (EHIC) was introduced to replace the old European health cover form E111 as well as the E128 for students and people working in other member states. In the first phase of introduction, the EHIC will cover health care for short stays and by 2008, the electronic card will cover longer stays as well.

At present this reciprocal cover is extended only to emergency treatment. Given the limitations of state-provided reciprocal cover, you should seriously consider taking out comprehensive private cover which will cover extras like loss of baggage and, more importantly, emergency repatriation. The cost of bringing a person back to the UK from any overseas country in the event of illness or death can run to thousands of pounds. In all other countries not listed above comprehensive private medical insurance is essential.

Most insurance companies offer a standard rate that covers medical emergencies and a premium rate that covers personal baggage, cancellation, etc. as well as health. Always read the fine print. Your nanny agency might be able to advise on matters of insurance. An American company which specialises in insuring au pairs is predictably enough called Au Pair Insurance (15 Cottage Avenue, Fifth Floor, Quincy, MA 02169; 617-328-1565; www.aupairinsurance.com) which is not exclusively for US au pairs. A British company which has a special policy for au pairs is Geoffrey Wallis Ltd. (111 World's End Lane, Green Street Green, Orpington, Kent BR6 6AW; 01689 860888). CareMed International Travel Insurance in Germany (Oscar-Romero-Allee 15, Bonn, 53113; +49 228-555 4900; www.caremed-travel.com) is a member of the International Au Pair Association and is accustomed to recommending policies to au pairs.

Some travel insurers to consider for long-stay insurance cover abroad include:

Club Direct Travel Insurance, Dominican House, St. John's St, Chichester, West Sussex, PO19 1YQ (0800 083 2455; www.clubdirect.com). One-year basic 'Backpacker' travel policy costs £176, comprehensive £220 with baggage cover.

Endsleigh Insurance, Endsleigh House, Cheltenham, Glos. GL50 3NR (www.endsleigh.co.uk). From £180 for 12 months cover in Europe, £245 basic worldwide and £370 comprehensive cover worldwide. Offices in most university towns.

Europ-Assistance Ltd, Sussex House, Perrymount Road, Haywards Heath, W Sussex RH16 1DN (01444 442365; www.europ-assistance.co.uk). World's largest assistance organisation with a worldwide network of doctors and agents.The Voyager Travel policy covering periods from 6 to 18 months costs £265 for 12 months in Europe and £545 worldwide. The policy is invalidated if you return home during the period insured. American readers can obtain details from Worldwide Assistance, 1825 K St NW, Suite 1000, Washington, DC 20006 (1-800-821-2828; www.worldwideassistance.com).

NATIONAL CONTRIBUTIONS

In countries where no Social Security agreement exists, the leaflet NI38 *Social Security Abroad* gives an outline of the arrangements and options open to you. If you fail to make National Insurance contributions while you are out of the UK, you will forfeit entitlement to benefits on your return. You can decide to pay voluntary contributions at regular intervals or in a lump sum in order to retain your rights to certain benefits. Unfortunately this entitles you only to a retirement/widow's pension, not to sickness benefit or unemployment benefit.

> **Sharon Legg regretted not having given more careful consideration to these matters:**
> *While working abroad as an au pair, I was foolish enough not to consider medical insurance because I was confident that nothing serious would ever happen to me. On my last day, I was taken suddenly and seriously ill and required urgent medical attention. One is not paid very much as an au pair but luckily I had managed to put most of my earnings aside. In less than 24 hours, I had blown all my money on medical fees. Then, when I returned to Britain, I was refused sickness benefit on account of insufficient National Insurance contributions, since I hadn't paid while I was out of the country. I learnt my lesson the hard way, so leave nothing to chance.*

As mentioned above, it may be the family's responsibility to make contributions on your behalf (as it is in the UK for employees earning more than £91 a week) however one cannot assume that the family will automatically abide by the regulations.

LEARNING A LANGUAGE

Having even a limited knowledge of the foreign language before you set off is invaluable, so it is always worth trying to improve your standard before leaving home. Evening language classes offered by local authorities usually follow the academic year. Intensive courses offered privately are much more expensive. If you are really dedicated, consider using a self-study programme with books and tapes (which start at £30), online course or broadcast language course. Even if you don't make much headway with the course at home, take it with you since you will have more incentive to learn once you are immersed in a language.

Although many people have been turning to the web to teach them a language, many conventional teach-yourself courses are still on the market for example from Berlitz (020-7518 8300), the BBC (08700 100222), Linguaphone (0800 282417; www.linguaphone. co.uk) and Audioforum (www.audioforum.com). All of them offer deluxe courses with refinements such as interactive videos and of course these cost more (from £150). Linguaphone recommends half an hour of study a day for three months to master the basics of a language.

No matter what your level of proficiency, a good dictionary and phrase book will prove an invaluable ally, so be sure to pack one. If you have started learning the language, keep a notebook with new words you have learned and keep adding to it. If you are worried about being stumped on the basics, you can purchase a travellers' picture dictionary and just point.

TRAVEL

Except in the case of highly prized professional nannies, you must pay for your own travel costs. Very occasionally a family will pay for your fare home if you have completed a one-year contract. There are exceptions, for example the programmes which place au pairs in the USA in which your flight is organised for you and paid for by the family. In a few cases, your placement agency may be able to offer advice on travel, but mostly you will have to sort out your own arrangements. Since the family may offer to meet you at the airport, last minute bargains are not ideal. It is always better to have an open return ticket, so that you will feel more in control of the situation. Also, certain countries require a return or onward ticket as a condition of entry. To cover the contingencies of wanting to cut short or to extend your term of employment, it is not advisable to book a return date which cannot be altered without incurring great expense. Check the travel section of the country chapters for ideas and a rough guide to ticket prices.

Discount travel agents advertise in London weeklies like *TNT* and *Time Out*, as well as in the travel pages of newspapers like the *Independent*. Phone a few outfits and pick the best price or compare web fares. A good starting point is www.cheapflights.co.uk which has links to other useful sources of travel information (but does not include no-frills airlines like Ryanair and easyjet). Alternatives are www.travelocity.com, www.opodo.com and www. lastminute.com. Users can log onto their destination and then see a list of prices offered by a variety of airlines and agents.

The principal agencies specialising in travel for student, youth and budget travel are:

STA Travel - 0870 160 6070; www.statravel.co.uk. Specialists in student and youth travel offering low cost flights, insurance, etc. 50 branches in the UK and 450 worldwide.

Trailfinders Ltd, 194 Kensington High St, London W8 7RG (020-7938 3939 longhaul; 0845 050 5940 Europe). Also more than a dozen branches in UK cities plus Dublin and five in Australia.

Marco Polo Travel, 24A Park St, Bristol BS1 5JA (0117-929 4123; www.marcopolotravel. co.uk). Discounted airfares worldwide.

Flight Centre 0870 499 0040; www.flightcentre.co.uk). Many branches in London and around the UK (1200 shops worldwide). Cheap student flights and extra services like working holiday packages.

North South Travel, Moulsham Mill Centre, Parkway, Chelmsford, Essex CM2 7PX (01245 608291). Discount travel agency that donates all its profits to projects in the developing world.

Quest Travel – 0870 444 5552; www.questtravel.com.

Bridge the World – 0870 444 1716; www.bridgetheworld.com.

On the whole the railways of Europe are expensive, even with under-26 discounts. Tickets and rail passes are available from Rail Europe offices in selected railway stations and travel agents; the central number for Rail Europe is 08705 848848 (www.raileurope.co.uk).

Eurolines is the name given to all the separate national coach services of Europe working together and selling various coach passes. To find out about a straightforward journey from England to the Continent, just book through National Express offices or website (www. nationalexpress.com). Prices start at £49 return for London-Amsterdam. Passengers under the age of 26 are eligible for a 10% discount.

If you suffer from travel sickness, try taking Stugeron tablets for sea and air travel. These seldom cause drowsiness so you should still be quite alert when you arrive. If seasickness is a particular problem, tuck a small book (a passport will do) into the waistband of your skirt or trousers. Having something solid near one's stomach seems to help.

WHAT TO TAKE

MONEY

If at all possible try to save a certain amount of money so that you won't be financially dependent on the family if things don't work out. Bear in mind that you might not be paid for the first fortnight or month, so you will need some money to tide you over, preferably in Euros or US dollars as appropriate. The rest should be in travellers' cheques, which can be purchased from any bank and most building societies. Be sure to keep the serial numbers of the cheques separate from the cheques in case they are stolen. A credit card can also be a handy asset when you are abroad, unless you are given to improvidence.

PACKING

As the day of departure draws closer, you will need to sort out your wardrobe and select clothes that will be compatible with the climate you are going to. For hot countries take at least one pair of comfortable leather sandals or rubber flip-flops which will allow your feet to breathe. Natural fibre clothes, especially cotton, are much better in hot climates than synthetics for the same reason. Some light-weight, long-sleeved clothes would not go amiss to protect you from sunburn and insect bites. Remember too that in some countries standards of modesty are different from what you may be used to, so you should be prepared to abide by the laws and customs of your host country.

For cold climates pack thermal underwear, two pairs of gloves or mittens which can be worn together and a woolly hat. A lined coat and non-slip boots are also a must. If you don't already own suitable clothing, it is probably better to wait until you arrive, so you can buy things as you need them and won't have to lug them around with you.

Try not to overload yourself, since by the end of your contract you will have accumulated as much again. It will probably be a while before you establish a social life, so concentrate mainly on your working necessities. You can always get things sent out later by post, if your family and friends are obliging. Some nannies are happy to live in jeans, shorts and T-shirts, but you will have to adapt this according to your preference and that of your employers. Whatever you decide, try to look neat and presentable at all times.

Leah Wilmoth, an American au pair in Montpellier France in 2005, passes on her packing suggestions and other tips on the website www.frenchamericancenter. com

- *Bring clothes that you can mix and match with a lot of things. Pack less than you usually would! You're going to want to buy gifts and souvenirs that you will have to bring back with you in your suitcase! So make room for them beforehand.*
- *Bring books and music in English: sometimes you will have cravings to see and hear your own language.*
- *Bring ONE nice dress and shoes that are comfortable to wear and look good with a lot of outfits*
- *Bring pictures of family and friends*
- *Ask a lot of questions even if that means making a few mistakes while speaking! try to speak to yourself in the language as much as you can before, during and after your stay.*
- *Pick up a Language Survival Guide for the country you're going to be working in*
- *Keep a well documented journal of feelings, excursions and names of places visited everyday.*
- *And take a lot of pictures! You'll be grateful for this after you return home!*

In addition to local maps and a dictionary, you might want to take a fat paperback to keep you company in your own language while you're finding your feet. Two suggestions would be *The Diary of an American Au Pair* by Marjorie Leet Ford (based on her memorable year au pairing in Britain many years ago) and *The Nanny Diaries* by two ex-nannies in New York, Nicola Kraus and Emma McLaughlin.

If cooking will be among your duties, a copy of a basic cookery book could be invaluable; Mig Urquhart claims to owe a sizeable debt to her old edition of *Delia Smith's Complete Cookery Course*. Avoid taking electrical appliances to countries whose systems differ from Britain's. Although most of Europe is on 220 volts alternating at 50 cycles per second as in Britain, the plugs are not compatible. The Standard North American voltage supply is 110, so Americans will have to buy a transformer as well as a plug adaptor if they decide to take a hair-dryer or some other appliance. These can be more easily found in Britain than in the US.

You might also want to pack a few small items of sentimental value which will help make your new room more familiar and homely. It is a good idea to buy each of the children a small gift to present to them upon arrival. These needn't be expensive; small souvenirs of your home town might suffice, and help to win them over initially. In due course they will also be interested in seeing photos of your family and friends.

WHILE YOU'RE WAITING

If there is a delay before you are due to set off, you can use the time to improve your knowledge of the language with teach-yourself tapes or even a short intensive language course. Check the facilities at your local library, since language tapes can be very expensive to buy. At the least invest in a good dictionary which will probably prove more useful than a phrase book.

You should also investigate the courses available near your new job, either by asking the family, the agency or some relevant organisation such as the Spanish or Italian Institute. Remember that most schools close down during the summer and, besides, many families will move to beach or mountain locations in the summer, far removed from any language institutes. Further information about language courses can be found in the chapter *Leisure Time* below.

Another way of putting your time to good use is to attend a first-aid course. British nanny agencies can often recommend a local course. For example in London Safe and Sound delivers Child Safety and First-Aid courses; ring 020-8449 8722 or check their website www.safe-and-sound.org.uk to find out dates and locations. An alternative is provided by R.E.D.I. Training (020-7610 0710; www.redi-training.co.uk) which puts on first-aid courses for carers and parents.

All kinds of medical emergencies can occur which can be alarming unless you are prepared. Also consult the appendices on *Safety in the Home* and *First-Aid*, though reading is no substitute for practical demonstrations and participation.

Once you know exactly where you'll be living, you should do as much preparatory reading about the country you're destined for as you can. One of the most useful pieces of research you can do is to locate your new address on a detailed city map. It is also useful to have some notion of where key places and public transport routes are in relation to where you'll be living. You will probably be able to print off a map from the internet or buy a good guide book with maps from a specialist travel bookshop like Edward Stanford Ltd. (12-14 Long Acre, Covent Garden, London WC2).

Sharon has an unusual further suggestion for preparing yourself for departure:

I always make a point of writing a letter to myself before the trip, and taking it with me to read in times of homesickness. It sounds very strange but it helps! In it I remind myself of all the reasons why I wanted to leave home (painting it as black as I possibly can!) and then I emphasise all the good things I hope to achieve by working abroad. A little reminder goes a long way to renewing enthusiasm.

KEEPING IN TOUCH

In the interval before taking a job, it is important to keep the lines of communication open by dropping the family a line from time to time. You could begin by sending the children some postcards of Britain. After all, there's no need to wait until you arrive before starting to develop a relationship with them. Do not hesitate to use the telephone unless there are serious linguistic problems. This will save both parties needless anxiety that the other side has had a change of mind or heart.

Be very careful to make a detailed plan for meeting your employers, and also a contingency plan in case there are unexpected delays. If you have never met the family, ask for a photograph and an identifying feature (e.g. hat, umbrella, etc.) One agency suggests using brightly coloured luggage labels and sending an identical set to the family to bring with them to the airport. Pam Robb worried for the whole ten-hour flight to Western Canada how she would recognise the family, which turned out to have been quite unnecessary since Edmonton Airport is so small that by the time she cleared customs, the only person left was her employer.

LAST MINUTE PANICS

Don't be surprised if you get cold feet as the time of departure approaches, especially during the last few days when your family and friends will make a fuss over you as they bid their farewells. Circumstances may have changed somewhat if there has been a considerable lapse of time between application and departure, but try not to change your mind, since a termination at this late stage is bound to cause a great deal of distress and aggravation. Your new family has put their trust in you and expect you to fulfil your part of the bargain. Unless you are sure you can cope, your nearest and dearest are best left at home once you have decided to leave the house. Tearful farewells from parents and friends (especially boyfriends) will just make you feel worse. Sometimes the lead-up to leaving is far harder than actually getting on the plane/boat/train. Once you're aboard, you will soon regain your initial excitement and enthusiasm for what lies ahead.

Problems and how to cope

This chapter may seem disproportionately and discouragingly long. In fact the whole book is peppered with stories which illustrate various kinds of problems and disasters great and small which can beset au pairs and nannies. After reading this you may be left with the impression that whoever thought up the idea of au pairing should have been locked away forever with a self-willed three-year-old given to tantrums. However we hope that by bringing out the full range of problems which can arise you may feel a little better prepared (whether psychologically or in practical terms) for the particular problems which you encounter.

INITIAL TRAUMAS

If you have already met the family at an interview, arriving should not be too traumatic since you will know roughly what to expect. However most au pairs and some mother's helps will be meeting the family for the first time at the airport or station in which case they should have detailed instructions about where to meet and how to recognise the family.

It is important to consider your appearance when you arrive. Nobody expects you to look like a model from *Vogue* but try to make an effort. Choose reasonably smart but comfortable clothes that won't look too crumpled after a journey. A subtle spray of perfume should make you feel fresher, especially if you have had to sleep in your clothes. Knowing you look as good as possible will promote a positive image and help boost your confidence.

BREAKING THE ICE

Don't assume that the task of breaking the ice is solely the family's responsibility. People's personalities and cultural traits vary enormously and your new family may feel even more awkward and shy than you do. To overcome your own shyness, focus your attention on the children, especially if you don't feel at home with the language. No one will expect you to be a great conversationalist, but some attempts at general small talk (e.g. questions about their country) will not go amiss. You may want to draw some comparisons with your own country, without of course implying criticism of theirs. If the children are withdrawn at first, do not shower them with unwanted attention. But don't treat them as though they don't exist either. When they begin to thaw, then you can pay them more attention to which they are bound to respond.

No matter how tired you are when you first arrive, spend a little time socialising with the family before going off to your room. You will probably be given a tour of the house and be offered some refreshment. It would be unusual if you were expected to do any work on your first day but show your willingness to help even if you are very jet-lagged and ready to fall into bed. Families nearly always expect you to eat your first meal with them so you can get to know each other better. You should always offer to help clear the dishes before you take your leave for the night.

Providing you're not too exhausted, it's a good idea to unpack as soon as possible. A bare and unfamiliar room can be depressing to wake up to, so try to get it organised before you go to bed.

YOUR FIRST DAY

Your main objective on the first day is to gain some idea of the family's routine and try to slot yourself into it as smoothly as possible. Don't attempt to reorganise anything at this point, even if you think it would be beneficial to the family. You need to find your feet before adopting such responsibilities.

Here is a list of tasks to which you might give priority in the first few days:

(1) Make sure your new family knows the name, address and telephone number of your next of kin.
(2) Make a list of all the emergency telephone numbers and keep it handy.
(3) Locate the first-aid box, fuse-box, etc.
(4) Learn how to operate household appliances.
(5) Ask for a set of keys to the house. Find out where spare ones are kept, in case you find yourself locked out.
(6) Take note of any house rules.
(7) Establish when you can expect to be paid and how much you will have to pay in deductions (if applicable).
(8) Sort out which chores are to be allocated to you. You might find it useful to draw up some sort of rota for house duties so you can organise them and fit them in each week.
(9) Ask when your first day off will be, so you can plan accordingly, and have something to look forward to.

COPING WITH THE PREVIOUS NANNY

Au pairs almost never overlap, however sometimes families will ask the nanny being replaced to stay on for a limited period to help make the transition a little smoother. This short period of overlap can either be a great help or an extra source of aggravation, depending on the circumstances and your point of view.

On the good side of the equation, the initial workload will be halved and you will be able to adjust gradually to the household responsibilities. The nanny will be able to give you lots of tips on the various quirks of each family member, and answer questions that you might not like to ask the parents at this stage. She will be able to introduce you to her friends and will have more time than the mother to show you around.

Unfortunately, the previous nanny can also be somewhat intimidating. She will seem much more capable and efficient than you, and your already fragile sense of confidence could totally disappear. The children will make it blatantly obvious that they would much rather have *her* than *you* and, understandably, this makes your task even more difficult. Try not to be overcome by your feelings of inadequacy and remember that it is only a matter of time before you become equally efficient and just as treasured by parents and children alike. Being new in any job is an uncomfortable feeling, and as a live-in helper, it is doubly hard because it is your home as well.

Wendy never used to do that

Even when your predecessor - either au pair or nanny - is no longer present, the family's fond memories of her can be enough to make you grind your teeth. They may, for example, refer to your room as 'Wendy's room' even though Wendy has been long gone. When you hear things like, 'Wendy did it this way' or 'Wendy never used to do that' it can be infuriating but it is something you just have to learn to live with. Try to be tolerant of this reaction in the children. We all feel suspicious of change and it is normal for them to miss someone who was such an important part of their world. The phase will pass as you learn how they prefer to have things done and the family becomes more used to your ways.

WINNING THE CHILDREN OVER

In the beginning, the children may well have difficulty adjusting to you, and you will have to work quite hard to earn their trust and co-operation. This can be especially difficult because you have so many other practical problems to deal with, as well as adjustment worries of your own. The first few weeks are vital, however, in building a relationship with your charges since this could set the tone for the duration of your stay. Therefore you want to make sure that things get off to a good start.

One of the best things you can do is to be flexible and adapt as well as you can to the established routine. It will help the children feel more secure if you are consistent and continue the daily patterns they are used to. Obviously no one should expect you to be a clone of the previous live-in helper or the mother, but try not to impress your personality too forcefully at first.

If the children are being generally difficult, try to avoid confrontations as much as possible by making it fun for them to co-operate instead. For example, if they are deliberately dawdling over getting dressed in the mornings, try starting a race to see who finishes first, and reward the winner with a treat after breakfast. You could also pretend to be dependent on them. Make them feel important by saying how much you need their help to show you where everything is. Ask them to take *you* to school because you're frightened of getting lost (which may, indeed, be no exaggeration).

Should they be particularly nervous of new-comers and create a fuss every time you go near them, remember that they are not being deliberately bad-tempered but are probably feeling insecure. Try to be tolerant and don't force the issue. Subtly involve them in play by doing anything that will attract their attention. Perhaps you could start by making something out of modelling clay or Lego and as they become increasingly interested they will probably want to try it themselves. Before you know it, they'll be joining in and you'll be on your way to building a friendship as well as a Lego castle. It might take a lot of patience, but you will probably be rewarded for it eventually.

Winning the Children Over

CULTURE SHOCK

One of the hardest things you'll have to cope with in your first few weeks is culture shock. This is bound to strike whenever anyone drastically changes his or her lifestyle and encounters unfamiliar attitudes, customs and even food. In some cases you may be faced with the truth of certain stereotypes, such as Spaniards are lax about punctuality or Germans obsessive about cleanliness. In other cases you may find the stereotypes upended (e.g. a punctilious Spaniard, a slapdash German, a stand-offish American) and this can be even more disconcerting. If you're lucky the family will make allowances for your culture shock, though ultimately it is you who must do the adapting. If you are having real difficulties adapting to one aspect of your new life, it is better to mention it (tactfully of course) than to let it fester. It is hard enough to pick up signals of distress in your own culture, let alone across cultural barriers, so you should not expect your new employers to be mind-readers. Besides they will probably respect you for being forthright, even if they cannot immediately alter whatever is worrying you.

You might even discover that some of their strange ways are actually better than what you are used to. Yvonne Standard tried to be as flexible as possible when she worked for a family in the States:

> *I was very unadventurous about food before I went but rather than make a scene by saying I didn't like something, I would try everything that was offered. I didn't know much about cooking before I went, but helped the wife in the kitchen a lot (she was a good cook) and I learned quite a bit.*

The more you know about the family ahead of time, the easier it will be to cope with the shock of your new situation (and vice versa). If you are a vegetarian, a compulsive jogger or a transcendental meditator, it might be best to inform the family before you arrive and discover their attitude. Emma Colgan, who is a vegetarian, was treated with the greatest respect by her German family who forbade her from washing up the meat pans, whereas another vegetarian au pair went to another carnivorous family in Austria, and she had to work in a kitchen dangling with sausages and to prepare and cook the meat while herself living on ice cream.

Small children may not understand your need for privacy

One of the most difficult things to adjust to is a loss of privacy. In the vast majority of cases you will be given your own room, though there may be some pressure on you not to retire to it very often nor to close the door. Small children cannot be expected to understand your need for privacy especially if in their culture there is a stronger emphasis on the extended family and communal living. A few ground rules will have to be laid down and enforced as gently as possible. In a few cases you may be asked to share a room with one of the children. This should probably be resisted if at all possible though sharing with small infants who sleep through the night is usually not too troublesome. However it is a point that should always be established before you accept a job.

If you are used to living in a city and end up with a family in a village (or vice versa) your culture shock will be exacerbated.

This was just one of the several factors that contributed to the unhappiness of Finnish au pair Riitta Koivula when she was placed with a family with three daughters in a village on the Greek island of Kos, though her story has a happy ending:
My journey to Greece began in September with the help of the Allianssi agency in Finland. First I was so excited about my new family and about the new place to live. I had never been in Greece before and loved the sun and the beach. I lived in a small village called Pily where almost no one spoke English. I got tired of the village quite soon because winter came, tourists left and it wasn't warm enough to spend time on the beach. I have always lived in a much bigger town in Finland. I got tired of the family – the girls did not speak English and I could not speak Greek, so communication was quite difficult – and the kids were quite lively. I also did not like the fact that the mother and father were arguing all the time and after one month I also noticed that the father was interested in me. He asked me once if I wanted to sleep with him – I was shocked about that. The working hours were also terrible. I worked from about 8am-12am and then in the evenings from 4pm to 10pm, every day except Sundays. I was very homesick because I was only 19 and still living with my parents in Finland.

So I left Kos in November and went to Athens. Thanks to Popy Raekou [now of the Nine Muses agency] there was a new family for me. I fell in love with Athens and its people right away. I met other au pairs and one Finnish au pair became my best friend. The new family was the best and we are still close. I didn't even remember my homesickness any more. I saw so many places in and outside Athens and learned so many things, even to read and write and speak Greek. We took lessons during the spring with Popy as our teacher. I also learned to be independent and brave. I learned to take care of myself and to stand up for my rights. I returned home in July having also learned to appreciate my own country more.

HOMESICKNESS

This can hit at any time throughout your trip, but it will probably be particularly acute during your settling-in period. You are bound to feel a little lost at first and think more fondly of your real home, so many miles away. British au pairs should be prepared to find themselves gasping for some fish and chips, English bacon, BBC Radio, a favourite TV programme and newspaper (though the latter can usually be bought a day or two late in major European cities). These feelings are natural and you must try to understand them as something that will pass, rather than an indication that moving abroad was a big mistake.

Keeping busy is always a good way to keep worries at bay, so concentrate on establishing yourself in your new situation. Usually the job will occupy your time, though in a few cases au pairs have minimal duties and might find themselves with a great deal of time on their hands in which to mope. Turn to the chapter on *Leisure Time* for advice on how to build a social life and keep amused.

If your job consists mainly of caring for a young child and you are not accustomed to the need for constant vigilance, you may find yourself getting bored and missing the fun of your previously unencumbered life at home, as Janet Renard did in Sicily:

The baby was fine, but it's true that the exotic surroundings couldn't make up for the fact that baby care is monotonous.

If you find yourself becoming unduly depressed or bored, it is probably a good idea to express your feelings to your employers who may give you more free time in which to take advantage of your new setting and to help overcome your longings for home.

It may not be much fun for a vegetarian au pair working for a carnivorous family

PROBLEMS WITH THE CHILDREN

RESENTMENT IN CHILDREN

It is quite common for a child left in the care of a full-time helper to feel resentful of his or her mother's absence. Unfortunately the child sometimes channels this resentment towards his au pair/nanny instead, and so reacts badly towards her or him. This is more common in the early stages when a new helper has taken over and a stable relationship with the child has not yet had a chance to develop. Children's sense of logic tells them that if they can drive the au pair away, then mummy will be restored to them. Of course, things aren't that simple, and it is very easy for a state of conflict to set in. Try not to take a child's reaction towards you as a personal affront. He or she would probably have reacted the same way to anyone in your shoes, and it is more your role in their life that they are rebelling against, rather than a person.

Camilla Preeston found her introduction to the children of the French couple with which she planned to spend six months discouraging:

> *When I arrived, I was made to feel very welcome, although I was exhausted from the 14-hour flight from my home in Hong Kong and the 6-hour time difference. Monsieur and Madame had prepared my room and Mme provided me with just about everything from a bathrobe to a toothbrush. She told me that she wanted me to be more of a big sister to the little girls (aged 2½ and 3½) than an au pair. However the next day, my*

first efforts with helping Mme were met with a slap on the face from the youngest girl. It was only natural of course for them to feel some resentment. Mme was preparing a thesis in medicine and couldn't afford to spend a great deal of time with her children, plus she was expecting a new baby. I found out that the girls had been looked after by other people almost since their birth, which might have explained their resentment.

When trying to cope with such resentment, encourage children to articulate their feelings by asking leading questions. Something like: 'I used to feel sad when my mummy went off to work/out for the day when I was a little girl.' Substitute whatever you think appropriate. Once you've confirmed the source of the resentment, you might try reasoning, assuming the child is old enough to understand. Justify the mother's absences. For example: Mummy goes to work to earn enough money so she can pay for the family's treats, such as holidays, etc. You could also mention that she went to great lengths to find someone like yourself to be her special assistant. Stress all the fun things you have planned and how you're looking forward to spending time with the children (even if they are being so unreasonable that you dread the very sight of them).

The next thing to do, is grit your teeth and summon up as much patience and tolerance as you can possibly muster. As the children learn to trust you, it won't be too long before your positive feelings towards them become genuine and mutual.

CRYING

Obviously, it is less disquieting when older children cry because they can articulate their feelings through speech. Once you know what's wrong, you can deal with the matter appropriately. With babies, however, it's more complicated because crying is just about the only way they can communicate. There is nothing more alarming than a screaming baby when you can't discover what's wrong.

As you become more familiar with a child, you will begin to distinguish his or her needs according to the type of cry. For example, a cry of hunger will sound different from a cry that indicates tiredness. If you're not sure, though, it's better to work your way through a basic check-list. Check nappies to see if they need changing; if they don't, give the child something to drink, and if that fails try a bottle of feed. A cry of distress could indicate colic or teething (discussed later) or some other less obvious source of pain. For example, something sharp like a safety pin may be sticking into the child.

On the other hand, he could be just plain bored or lonely, in which case a back rub and a few soothing words would help, or play some music and dance with him in your arms. If you're trying to finish some chores, put the baby in a carrier and carry him around with you if he's not too heavy and do both at the same time. Alternatively, take him out for a walk.

There may be times when children are so over-tired that nothing you can do will placate them. This situation should be avoided in the first place if at all possible, by sticking to a regular sleep schedule. Put them gently to bed with some soothing music playing in their room and leave them to cry themselves to sleep. Check on them every ten minutes or so, just to be on the safe side. Crying sometimes makes babies thirsty, so you might need to offer them another drink. If a child continues to cry but you're sure that there's nothing seriously wrong, accept that you've done all you can and remove yourself to a distant part of the house, for your own sanity.

DISOBEDIENCE

When you first begin your job, chances are the children will 'play up' a bit. This is quite normal because they are testing you to see how far they can go. It is very important that you impose firm but fair limitations on their behaviour and be consistent in what you will and will not accept from them.

Suppose they continue to be uncooperative; what do you do? Well, there are times when you may be tempted to think that a quick smack is in order, but this is always forbidden.

Even if parents are smackers themselves, they are most unlikely to tolerate someone else using corporal punishment. A new law in Britain has made smacking illegal if it is hard enough to leave a mark. In any case, a nanny or au pair should never raise a hand in anger against a child in their chair. Besides, violence begets violence. Counting to ten before you mete out any punishment sometimes helps to get things into perspective first. Disagreeable small children can be banished to a corner of the room without anything to amuse them, which usually works in a surprisingly short period of time. Remember that young children have a different concept of time, and ten minutes can seem like an eternity to them, so don't overdo it. Anyone who watched the strangely compelling Channel 4 series *Supernanny* in 2005 will be familiar with the 'naughty stair' or the 'naughty bench'. Whenever Supernanny Jo Frost was called in by desperate parents to help them cope with their badly behaved children, she invariably nominated a certain place of banishment for children who misbehaved, after it was clearly explained what the misdeamenour was that had resulted in punishment. The Channel 4 website includes a page of tips on 'Taming Your Tyrant' and Jo Frost has written a book *Supernanny* though many think that the book has less substance than *Nanny Wisdom: Our Secrets for Raising Healthy, Happy Children - From Newborns to Preschoolers* by Justine Walsh and Kim Nicholson.

With older children, threatening to cancel a planned event might be all you need to exert some control. Be prepared to carry out such threats, though, or the child will simply ignore what you say in future. Make sure the punishment is justified by the crime. You shouldn't be unfair about it or they will rebel against you constantly. For minor disobediences you could withhold part of their usual snack on that particular day, and for something more major you could cancel a trip to the swimming pool or a planned picnic. Don't make threats a habit, though, or they will become meaningless, and habitual shouting often goes unheeded. Ask yourself if what you're angry about is really worth all the aggravation, and save a stern tone of voice for when it's really needed.

Try to avoid using sweets as a way of manipulating your charges. No one respects bribery, and it can prove expensive as well as damaging to their teeth. Consider whether or not the children are getting enough positive attention from you. If being naughty is the only time you really communicate with them, the chances are they'll be continually unco-operative. To a child, negative attention is better than nothing. Use an award system instead. The more you praise a child for good behaviour, the more likely he is to reproduce it.

DISCIPLINE

This can be a very touchy subject, especially if your idea of discipline is vastly different from that of the parents. Discipline means teaching a child what is acceptable behaviour and what is not, but this is open to interpretation. What is naughty to you (such as failing to say 'please' and 'thank you') may be the norm in your new household. Occasionally you may find the reverse is true. If you are unclear about a discipline issue, you must discuss it with the parents since, once again, consistency is very important. Avoid disciplining the children when the mother is present and obviously in charge. Keep in the background and never interfere in an issue between parent and child.

Children feel much more secure when they are taught to live within certain boundaries. Try not to restrict the child unnecessarily, but do offer guidance and set an example. It is better to substitute requests for demands, but there will be times when a command is unavoidable, for example, to warn a child who is approaching danger. Save your 'Nos' for when it really matters and always explain your reasons why. 'Because I said so' is not good enough.

During your first week, it is perhaps better not to be too much of a disciplinarian. You don't want to alienate the children before you've even had a chance to settle in. Remember that your goal is to build a loving relationship, not terrify them. On the other hand, this doesn't mean that you should pander to them either. If you do, it will be much harder to establish your authority later on. Aim to strike a balance, exerting more influence as you

Children can play up a bit

settle in; this process usually takes place in the natural course of things in any case.

Children will be doubly receptive to discipline which is applied with sensible good humour and inventiveness so they do not perceive it as discipline at all. For example Sharon invented a game which she called 'Mr. Plaque' to encourage young children to clean their teeth. She would tell them that Mr. Plaque and his band of merry men were hiding between their teeth, hoping to damage them unless they were scrubbed away with a toothbrush. She would examine the inside of their mouths and say that she just saw Mr Plaque behind a tooth. They enjoyed chasing him with brushes so much that her problem was getting them to stop!

One difficult problem is whether or not to inflict corporal punishment for bad behaviour. Personal views and cultural traditions do vary but generally parents do not encourage their nannies and au pairs to smack their children. Some find the idea anathema. When Frances Thirlway dropped a casual remark, little more than a jest, to her employer about some children needing a good hiding, the mother reared back in horror, and went around for weeks muttering darkly about what a monster of violence Frances must be. If the parents are set against physical punishment (or indeed if you are) you will have to substitute other ways of disciplining them.

Even if you are granted a free hand, smacking should be used only for extremities of naughtiness and as a last resort. Try to avoid carrying out such punishments in front of others. There is no need to inflict the additional burden of public humiliation upon a child.

A discussion of the problems which arise when there is a major discrepancy between your ideas of discipline and that of the parents follows in the section *Problems with Parents*.

TANTRUMS

Many childhood tantrums could be avoided if those in charge of them learnt to read the warning signs before they got out of hand. Allowing a child to become so tired or cold or hungry or bored that he ends up distraught, is poor planning and unnecessary. Also, if the au pair or nanny is inconsistent, conflict may arise over misunderstandings. For example, if a toddler is allowed to walk most days, he may well resent it if you suddenly insist he has to ride in the push-chair. Explain to him the reasons for your change of routine.

Sometimes, though, whatever you do, a tantrum ensues. This is especially common in the two to three year old age group when children are striving to exert their independence. Remember that the more attention you give them, the more you are indirectly rewarding them for undesirable behaviour. Stand firm and tell the child that if he or she wants your attention, they will have to stop the tantrum first. Say it once and then totally ignore them until they stop. This is much easier if you're at home than in a public place, where an unpleasant scene can be highly embarrassing. Try to deal with the problem as soon as you sense it arising. Don't wait until a child is already screaming and kicking on the floor before you act. If it does get to this stage, try whispering in their ear. Sometimes kids will stop screaming as curiosity gets the better of them and they decide to quieten down so they can hear what you have to say. If the child is so angry that he holds in his breath, splash his face with cold water, since the shock will force him to take in air.

If you are in the home, removing the child to a separate room may be an immediate solution. It gives you a chance to calm down and deprives the child of an audience. Alternatively, try distracting him by doing something unusual. Mimic his actions and stage your own tantrum. With any luck, you could both end up laughing.

EATING PROBLEMS

You should encourage your charge to stick to a routine of meals. If the children are used to snacking at liberty, they might whine a bit once you start imposing a meal system, but you must stick it out or you'll be preparing food constantly, half of which will go to waste. Children soon learn, and it is just as much for their convenience as for yours since once they start school, they won't be able to eat at will.

Try not to over-react if you're landed with a fussy eater. The angrier you get at meal times, the more power the child exerts over you, so it's best to ignore picky eating.

Sharon Legg encountered a particularly worrying case:

I was once looking after a little boy of two who was a very fussy eater and I had a lot of trouble trying to persuade him to eat nutritious things. At one point, I was so worried that I took him to see a doctor who reassured me that it was just a phase and that the child would eventually start eating a more normal diet of his own accord. Sure enough, his eating gradually improved. Have you ever noticed how, for example, when you've been eating a lot of sweet food in any one day, you suddenly develop a craving for something savoury? Well, I think it's nature's way of redressing the balance, and even children will automatically crave something their body lacks. Also, once I had the doctor's reassurance that there was nothing seriously wrong, I became much more relaxed at meal times and I think this attitude was communicated to my charge.

Make sure a poor eater comes to the table hungry. Perhaps it's better to eliminate snacks. Give small portions of food so he isn't overwhelmed by the task in front of him. Don't make an issue out of finishing everything on his plate; children know when they've had enough and you should respect this. Warn him that there'll be nothing more to eat until the next meal break. If he complains of hunger a short time later, then that's just too bad; make him wait.

The same applies to picky eaters. If children are deliberately playing with their food, put a reasonable time limit on meal times and then clear away whether they have finished or not. Don't force them to eat something they hate. Children do go through fads so continue to give balanced meals and let them select what they like. They will start to eat properly long before they are in danger of starving to death!

FOOD ALLERGIES

Some foods, especially those with a lot of E-additives, have been shown to cause hyperactivity in some children. This can be a very disturbing condition whereby the child is very excitable, lacks concentration, appears to need very little sleep and can be very destructive. If you suspect that the child in your care is a sufferer, keep an eye on his diet which may give you a clue as to how to improve his behaviour. It has been found, for example, that some children respond badly to Tartrazine, an artificial dye used in certain orange drinks. If your charge behaves exceptionally badly after consuming a particular kind of food, there may be an allergy link. Try eliminating the suspect pabulum from their diet and observe any alteration in conduct. Obviously, if there is a dramatic improvement, the offending food should be avoided.

Research concerning a possible connection between diet and hyperactivity is far from conclusive, however, so it is best to seek medical advice when dealing with the problem. Indeed, what you consider to be hyperactive might actually be normal high spirits. If you have little or no previous experience of dealing with children, it can come as a shock to discover just how active and exhausting some of them can be. Giving them extra scope for letting off steam may be all that is required, so make sure your charges have plenty of opportunity for physical exercise.

SLEEPING AND DREAMING

If your charge usually has trouble getting off to sleep at nights, try taking him for a walk before bedtime. A relaxing bath usually helps. It's best to give the children some sort of notice that bedtime is approaching so that they don't suddenly have to disrupt their play. If they put up resistance, be firm with them and stick to a set routine. Give them their bath at the same time each evening and put them to bed straight afterwards. A bedtime story is an additional way of helping them to wind down. Avoid robust games or television programmes which will excite them, and choose a book that is calming rather than scary. Ask them if there is anything they need before they go to bed; it will save delaying tactics later on. They'll eventually adapt to, and respect, your rules. Allow older children to have a light on for a limited period of time, so they can read to themselves. Then be firm and consistent about switching the light off.

If you use an intercom make sure you have it the right way round

Babies sometimes confuse day with night. Try to prevent them from falling asleep before bedtime by stimulating them, otherwise you'll have problems getting them to sleep at the right time. The same applies to naps. If they are sleeping too long, gently wake them up. Give them their bottle in a dim light to help emphasise the closing in of the day and the approach of bedtime. Adding a little cereal to the final feed should abate hunger through the night.

If the parents are going out in the evening, it can be a little unsettling for the children if the departure coincides with their bedtime routine. Should this happen often, you would be justified in suggesting that they leave at a more convenient time whenever possible. After the children have already fallen asleep is ideal, but this isn't always practicable. Therefore, encourage the children to say goodbye to their parents so that they understand that you will be in charge for the evening. They'll probably make a fuss initially, but once the parents have gone, they usually settle down. Distracting them with something amusing should help.

A trick with toddlers is to spray a little perfume or put a dab of handcream on their hand and then tell them to sniff the scent until it's gone. The scent itself, combined with deep breaths should be enough to relax them so they fall asleep.

Fear of the dark is very common and you should be sympathetic. Leave the door open and the hall light on, and give the child a cuddly toy to hug. Try putting a radio in the room with the volume turned low. Nightmares can usually be dealt with by giving calm reassurances. Lying down with them until they go back to sleep is also very comforting, but time-consuming for you. If the bad dreams persist, and are particularly frightening for a child, they might warrant professional counselling. Sleepwalkers should be walked back to bed and precautions should be taken. For example, a gate across the top of the stairs and child-proof window catches, or bars on the windows. It is quite normal for children to sleepwalk occasionally because their minds are so active, but if you are concerned that there might be an underlying emotional problem, do seek professional advice.

Early risers can be deterred from disturbing the whole household by putting a collection of absorbing play-things beside the bed. Do this after the child is asleep, though, otherwise he'll be playing all night. Leaving out a covered bowl containing dry cereal or crackers will also stave off early morning hunger. Setting an alarm clock and telling older children not to disturb anyone before it rings will keep them in their rooms (you hope). Don't forget to show them how to switch it off.

Finally if you use an intercom which has a wire running from the child's room to the sitting room or kitchen so you can hear from a distance if they start crying, make sure you have the speaking and listening ends the right way round. One family we know were delighted at how soundly their child slept until they discovered that they had the device back to front so that the child could hear everything that was said downstairs but the parents could hear nothing from upstairs.

TOILET TRAINING

Many children respond well to toilet training between the ages of eighteen months and two years. However, every child is different, so if you seem to be having problems, try stopping the training for a few weeks and then pick up where you left off.

Children learn mainly by imitation, so if you don't feel too inhibited, allow the toddler in the loo with you sometimes or rope in a compliant older brother or sister instead. Incorporate whatever language the family uses to describe the body's processes so the child becomes familiar with the terms with which he needs to express himself. Once you have gained some idea of your charge's habits, put him or her on the pot around that time. Providing some books or music can help amuse children while you are training them to sit in the bathroom. Turning on the taps or whistling may also encourage them to urinate. If you don't get the desired result, try not to be impatient. The more tension involved, the worse it will become.

Never punish your charge for 'accidents', since it is harmful to make a child feel guilty about an action he hasn't yet learned to control. Involve them instead in the cleaning-up process, for this will teach them responsibility. Letting them wear plastic pants instead of nappies around the house also encourages them to exert more control in the absence of a safety-net.

Many children respond well to toilet training

Above all, reward children for any successes because they will then be more inclined to repeat them. Praise them when they tell you that they want to 'go' - even if the cry comes too late. Emphasise in a calm but firm tone that next time he should tell you before instead of after.

Sometimes a child who is already trained will revert to soiling his pants again. This could be a sign of tension in his life. Perhaps he has just started play-school or there's a new baby in the family. It may be necessary to repeat part of the toilet training but if you relieve the cause of the anxiety, the problem should resolve itself.

BEDWETTING

This is only to be expected if you are currently trying to toilet train a child, but sometimes older children can have difficulty as well. Again it may be a sign of tension: perhaps a change of schools has caused it, or even a change of au pair. Try to find the root cause and remedy it if you can. A little reassurance might be all that is needed. You should consult a doctor if bedwetting becomes a habit, because it can sometimes indicate an allergy to cow's milk or other problem.

If a child is prone to wet the bed, the first thing you should do is to protect the mattress by covering it with a plastic sheet; do it as unobtrusively as possible so as not to draw unnecessary attention to the problem, making the child feel guilty or ashamed. They might also become subconsciously aware that the bed is 'safe' and so exercise little control over their bladder muscles.

You could try restricting fluid intake shortly before bedtime, but if bedwetting is a real problem this will just reduce the amount of fluid passed. Besides, a child who is thirsty probably won't settle down to sleep. Taking him to the loo before you go to bed yourself might improve things. They will be half asleep, of course, but don't take over completely. By leading him through the motions they will learn the routine and begin to do it automatically. Pick them up out of bed and lead them by the hand to the toilet; don't carry them. You might have to do this regularly for a few nights before you meet with success. If a child's bed is still wet in the morning, get them to help you strip it and put the sheets in the washing machine. Teach them, in a kindly way, to take responsibility for their actions. Above all, reassure the child that he or she will grow out of it.

PROBLEMS WITH THE PARENTS

Even if you have sole charge or a liberal degree of autonomy, you are still answerable to the parents, and it is imperative that you maintain a good relationship with them. If the parents are agreeable but the children difficult, the work will be tolerable. It tends not to work the other way round, though. If you don't get on with the parents it can be utter misery and lead to your premature departure or dismissal. Sometimes there is a personality clash whereby it is no one person's fault but it just seems impossible to see eye to eye. If this situation cannot be resolved, it is better for all concerned if you look for another job. But before you consider such a drastic measure always discuss the problem with the parents. Many disagreements could be sorted out if only they were discussed long before they reached crisis proportions.

PAY AND TIME OFF

Since both au pairing and nannying are often such flexible and informal jobs in comparison to, say, a secretary in a large firm, things can be a bit untidy when it comes to regular pay cheques and time off. Sometimes there is a genuine reason for such lapses. It is quite conceivable that a busy mother could forget pay-day once or twice and pay you late, and parents working shifts can sometimes become muddled over free time. How should you proceed, though, if this becomes a habit?

First of all, have a mutually arranged date so you know when to expect your wages and free time; otherwise *you* may become confused. If discrepancies arise, some sort of routine will make it easier to sort out. Being paid on the first day of every month, for example, is much better than a vague 'every few weeks'. If the parents are slap-dash about this, be firm. You've earned your money and you have a right to regular wages. Keep a note of when you are paid and how much, if it isn't always a fixed sum, for example, if the parents pay you to work an extra day instead of compensating for the time later on. You should ask in advance of a public holiday whether you will be compensated for it. If your pay-cheque is overdue, don't let it run to more than a week before reminding them. You may hate the thought of haggling over money, but once in a while it may be necessary to assert yourself. Don't delay until it gets out of hand; the bigger the sum grows, the harder it will be to ask for it and you'll only become resentful.

If you're having a hard time extracting your pay, an agency can come in very handy. It is useful to have an intermediary in these matters, and the agency staff will probably be more experienced and professional in dealing with such problems. Never ask an agency to sort out your trouble for you until you've tried talking over the discrepancy with the family first. Agencies should only be brought in as a last resort. Au pair and nannying positions are usually fairly easy to come by, so if your situation is intolerable, don't be afraid to look for another job. Estrangement for financial reasons, however, is very rare. Most families who hire help make sure that they can afford the salary.

Discrepancies over free time are more common because there are no hard and fast rules. Your job description should give you some guide as to how much free time you can expect but this is often implemented rather loosely. For example, you may find you are required to babysit a few evenings more than was originally agreed, but it is up to the individual to decide how much extra time she is prepared to give. As long as your co-operation is

If you have a hard time extracting your pay

appreciated, it's worth being flexible over certain requests, e.g. staying in an extra evening or two in the week. Think of the opportunities you have to run personal errands when, in theory, you are supposed to be working for your employer. A formal company would never be that flexible.

By all means speak to the employers, if you feel your time is being taken advantage of. Just because the parents work shifts or go on business trips, there is no reason for you to miss out on entire days off. You will have to fit in with their schedule, of course, but you should still be compensated for any time owing to you.

Holiday time can be problematic, unless it has been discussed at the beginning. Sometimes families are reluctant to promise a holiday until they get to know and trust their live-in helper and want to reward her. In some countries (like Belgium and Switzerland) au pairs are entitled by law to paid holiday if they fulfil their six month or one year contract. In general, if you have worked for a family for a whole year, you should be given at least two weeks off with pay. Most parents give you the option of an independent vacation or one taken with the family. Consider the pros and cons carefully. Holidays with young children are seldom restful, and if it is a self-catering affair it will be even worse. There are advantages, however, since the holiday expenses will normally be paid for by your employers and the trip might be one you couldn't normally afford. Make sure you know in advance what your options are. Obviously, if the parents are paying for the holiday, it is only fair that you give them some assistance in return, but it would be very disappointing to work as normal, only to discover afterwards that it counted as your vacation.

If you feel strongly about having Christmas and Easter off, there's no harm in trying to arrange it with parents. Remember, though, that most families could do with your help on these occasions and you will probably have to compromise. If you get on well with the family, it can be a very enjoyable time to be with them, especially the children. Some families may prefer privacy at these times, in which case you should respect their wishes and find an alternative place to celebrate.

REQUESTING A PAY RISE

Only you can judge whether or not you are paid your worth, bearing in mind the fringe benefits you receive and the overall budget of the family concerned. However should a mother become pregnant while you are still in her employ (see below), you have the right to negotiate a pay rise if she expects you to be working for her after the baby is born. A new arrival can have a significant impact on your work load, especially if the mother plans to resume her career afterwards.

The best time to request a pay rise is when you can expect the least number of interruptions and the parents are at their most relaxed. If the request is denied, you must decide if you are willing to continue working there at the current rate. If a rise is agreed, establish exactly how much so you can decide if it is satisfactory.

It is worth mentioning here that few au pairs or nannies work in private families because of the money. There are some lucrative positions around, but generally girls offer their labour in exchange for experience and the pleasure involved in performing a worthwhile job with plenty of scope for enjoyment.

INTERFERENCE WITH YOUR SOCIAL LIFE

Decent families should understand that your life does not revolve exclusively around them. In other words, you are entitled to a social life. No one has the right to tell a fully grown woman what time she ought to come in at night, providing she isn't noisy when she returns and her job performance is not adversely affected by, for example, over-sleeping and/or a hangover. Nobody wants to leave their child in the care of someone who is only half-awake - or half-dead. If the parents complain about your late nights, ask yourself if they could be justified in doing so. This is one situation where it is frequently the au pair who is being inconsiderate.

Some families can be very awkward about allowing you to bring friends home. Sometimes this can be for security reasons; if their home harbours a lot of valuables, you can understand their concern about strangers entering their house. Use your discretion and always ask your employers for permission in advance of receiving guests. Throwing parties in the parents' absence is definitely out, unless they specifically invite you to do so. Having one or two friends over during your free time seems reasonable enough. After introducing them to your employers, it's best to entertain them in your own living quarters so that you don't impose on the family's privacy. Conducting a romance under these circumstances is more tricky, but if your family is reasonably hospitable, they may not mind. If you have permission to enjoy dinners *à deux* once the children are in bed, make a point of replacing the extra groceries which you have consumed. Your employers are responsible for feeding you only, not your circle of friends as well.

Even if your family is particularly liberal, most do not approve of their nanny's boyfriend spending the night in her room. Save your nocturnal activities for his apartment or somewhere other than your place of work. There should be no reason why you shouldn't sleep elsewhere on your nights off, providing this doesn't interfere with your work the next day.

UNREALISTIC EXPECTATIONS

Au pairs and (occasionally) nannies are sometimes expected to do an unreasonable amount of work. While au pairs are supposed to be learning about the German/French/Italian way of life, they may end up learning only Frau Rottbleit's/Mme. Travailleur's/Senora Mostruoso's way of life or at least of housekeeping, with all its irrationalities and eccentricities.

If the employers are reasonable, you should be able to discuss what you consider to be an excessive burden of work. Many mothers unthinkingly pile on more duties when they see that their au pair or nanny is coping adequately with the present ones. The best line of argument in this case is that you feel you will be neglecting the children if you attempt too much cleaning and laundering.

Other employers are just plain neurotic and you may achieve nothing by complaining. For example the wealthy Italian family for whom Susie Walton worked made her do all the laundry, except the sheets, by hand since they didn't approve of washing machines. Frances Thirlway worked for a pair of German psychiatrists who, when on holiday in

France, hoovered the garden patio daily and expected Frances to share their standards of cleanliness. Camilla Preeston's host mother in France expected her not only to do the washing and drying up but to disinfect the sink, brushes, sponges, tap and rubbish bin on every occasion. But this was only the beginning of the burdens placed on her just-turned-18 shoulders:

Mme decided she wasn't getting enough work done on her thesis (which she partly blamed on me, not the fact that instead of working she would do things such as wash the girls' dolls' clothes). So she decided to spend five days including two nights away from home. This change made a big difference to my working hours and I had sole charge of the three children for up to two days at a time. To help, Mme drew up a timetable for me, which started at 7am and ended at 8pm (which left no room for my French lessons). I had by this time taken almost full responsibility of the new baby, which to my surprise also meant on my days off on more than one occasion. Mme expected me to pick up the two girls from school by bus with the baby which wasn't too easy. Needless to say, I was very tired by the time I went to bed and even more so when the baby started teething and wouldn't sleep during the day.

Like most au pairs, Camilla found it very difficult to talk to her host about her hours and missed French lessons. Because she had only two months left to go, she decided that it wasn't worth the effort of arguing.

MATERNAL RESENTMENT AND JEALOUSY

When a mother works or has other obligations, she often doesn't spend as much time with her children as she would like. Hiring a home-help is one way of relieving the pressures on her, but for many women a degree of conflict remains. It is quite possible for a mother to resent your role in her child's life even though she has arranged things that way and is otherwise glad of your help. Problems such as these may be diminished by a little sensitivity on your part. When the mother arrives home and has had a chance to catch her breath, ask her whether or not she needs your help. This gives her the option of spending some time alone with her children. Natalia de Cuba adopted a technique which the mother greatly appreciated, of leaving detailed notes on the kids' behaviour, little successes, nightmares, etc.

You may find yourself beginning to occupy first place in the child's affections, which can create a very awkward situation. After working for a busy family in Rome for several months, Emily Hatchwell was appalled when the four-year-old girl rushed to her instead of to the mother when the two adults entered the room together. At that point she began purposely to distance herself from the little girl, and this strategy seemed to be effective.

Au pairs often have problems when they find themselves working alongside a mother who has quit a satisfying job to have children. Inevitably some of these mothers feel envious of their husbands who continue to enjoy the satisfaction of their careers, and they may channel their resentment towards the live-in helper. One of the first things that Carla Mitchell's employer in Paris did (a psychiatrist who was no longer practising) was to give her a book to read called *Mother's Day is Over*, a radical feminist argument that the impulses of motherhood are *not* universal to women. Carla found this quite disconcerting and rightly diagnosed deep unhappiness in her employer.

If you do end up working alongside the mother, it can be difficult to determine when your services are required and when they are not. Explain that you are going off to do some chores, but are available if she needs you to take over with the children. This way, you are not avoiding your duties, but at the same time you are leaving her in control.

EMPLOYEE RESENTMENT

One of the most galling problems that a few au pairs face is that they are treated not as a member of the family but as a servant, and this can lead to real bitterness. For example, the parents may fail to introduce their live-in helper to visiting friends and yet ask her to fetch or serve things. You have to get used to being invisible, which is hard on the ego. You have to be fairly lucky to find employers who will treat you as an equal but there is plenty of scope for decent treatment between these two,

> **The author of *The Diary of an American Au Pair* (who travelled from San Francisco to London and Scotland to work for an upper class English family) does not agree:**
> *As part member of the family and part servant, half of me has risen to a much higher class. This is the class I feel naturally cut out for. The other half of me has sunk. The people I've met have not seen me as a little bit of each class; each has put me in one slot or the other. It's the males who seem to see me as I see myself – as one of their own. The females almost uniformly see me as their inferior.*

A less predictable form of resentment can arise if you have grown extremely close to the children. Then, when the parents come home, the children abandon you and you suddenly feel superfluous. This is sometimes so blatant that it can become hurtful, and you resent the mother for taking over. Even though you recognise the rightness of the children preferring their parents, you may still find it difficult to remain detached.

There are occasions when you have had a particularly enjoyable day with your charge(s)

a pair of German psychiatrists liked the lawn hoovered every day

and everything goes fine until the mother comes home. All hell seems to break loose, and you end up wishing she hadn't bothered to return. Once again, this is quite common behaviour. Children sometimes store up all their bad feelings so they can give vent to them when the parents return. Don't blame the mother or father for this reaction or feel guilty that it's somehow your fault. It may be that the children are subconsciously punishing their parents for having left them.

By contrast, it can sometimes seem as though the mother or father gets to do all the fun things with the children while all the hard work is left to you. You can perhaps console yourself that at least you may be helping to strike a blow for equality within marriage, since if you weren't there to do the drudgery, it would probably be the mother who would have to do most of the scivvying, leaving the father to adopt the role of kindly godfather. In any case, you too can participate in the fun. If you organise your chores properly, there should always be time for you to do enjoyable things with the children. Try taking the initiative and organise some outings of your own to the zoo, to exhibitions, or whatever you like. All work and no play will make you a dull (and resentful) person.

An unexpected source of resentment can develop once you start making friends with other nannies. You get a privileged insight into how other families operate and sometimes end up feeling that you have a raw deal. Au pairing and nannying positions do vary enormously and, chances are, there will always be someone with an apparently better job than you. Try to establish whether or not your envy is justified and then take steps to resolve it, if you can. Either accept what you have and appreciate it, or look for another job. Seething resentment is not a good atmosphere in which to raise children.

Beverley Smith from South Africa deeply resented that she was put in an awkward position on the night of her arrival at the home of a single mother near Rotterdam:

From the very first night there were danger signs: the mother went to her boyfriend's house in the middle of the night without saying a word to me, and only returned at 8am the next morning. At 2 in the morning I was roused by hysterical crying, to discover my three-year old charge outside my bedroom door. After pacifying her (language barrier and all) and putting her back to bed, I spent the rest of the night awake. I was furious with the host mother for thrusting that kind of responsibility on me when I had just arrived and didn't even know the child well enough to communicate properly. I left that job a month later and returned home, sorry that I didn't get to experience Dutch culture to its fullest.

CONFLICT OVER DISCIPLINE

If you and your employers have vastly different views on how to raise children, a great deal of bad feeling can result. Usually it is a case of the parents being more lenient with their offspring than the helper thinks is appropriate, leaving the au pair or nanny to suffer the consequences of the parents' indulgence. Once again, communicating your feelings as tactfully as you can and then compromising is the best policy, and you may even learn something from an exchange of ideas. British parents tend to be stricter with their children than many other nationalities and you may come to appreciate the advantage of a more relaxed approach to child-rearing. It is important to remain open-minded about attitudes that are different from the experiences of your own upbringing.

This was a bitter lesson that Maree Lakey from Australia had to learn when she au paired for a wealthy family in Germany
I come from a very modest background and was shocked at the amount of toys, clothes and other possessions which the children had. I witnessed with disbelief how the children were 'disciplined' by the parents. If something didn't quite go their own way, they would fly into a screaming rage. The mother, who was also extremely

> *excitable, would yell back at the children at first. She would however never stick to her guns; instead she would eventually back down and the children would later receive some sort of present to 'make everything good again'. My attempts at discipline would most likely end in the children going to the mother or grandmother, who would promptly disregard what I had tried to enforce and give them what they wanted. I could never compete with this. It was an impossible situation. Once I was totally fed up and uncharacteristically voiced my disapproval. My outburst was met with shock and a quick assurance from the mother that of course the children must obey my decisions as much as those from the parents. These were empty words and so I just had to accept the situation.*

If you do think that some basic change in routine would benefit family relations or the behaviour of the children, you should consider trying to discuss the possibility with the family, employing all your skills of diplomacy. In some cases you will find the parents more than willing to take advice from their live-in helper, if they have come to respect her judgment and native good sense. For example a 20 year old Irish woman, who got on famously with her sophisticated New England employers, noticed that the little boy was becoming increasingly spoilt. She identified the source of the problem as the parents' tendency to lavish too much attention on him whenever they were together. Maeve advised the mother to ignore the boy for half an hour on her return from work and then play with him. Not only did the mother take the advice but the boy became much easier to handle and better behaved almost immediately. So it is possible to make some useful contributions.

Sometimes the parents are unwilling or unable to see your point of view in which case you are bound to accept their way of doing things. They are, after all, paying for a service, and in this respect it is you who must be more flexible. Au pairs have far less responsibility than nannies for the discipline of children, but in both cases there is a limit to what you can achieve or how much you can interfere. Some au pairs, like Jesse Lane, think that it is a waste of energy trying to inculcate any manners or habits which have not been taught by the parents:

> *The bringing up of a child is up to the parents and don't forget it. I am sure that had I let the children have their own way, I would have got on a lot better and had a much nicer time.*

This is of course much easier said than done, and the compulsion to correct bad manners or reprimand selfish and rude behaviour can be irresistible.

If you spend most of your time clenching your teeth and seething with silent fury it is best to look for another job. Unfortunately it is often not until you live with a family that such problems come to light.

FLIRTATIOUS FATHERS

The *idea* that fathers regularly make passes at their au pair or nanny is far more prevalent than the reality. Often the father is quite a remote figure and most are far too sensible or preoccupied to consider such an affair. It would be naïve to assume, however, that such events never occur, so how do you cope if it happens to you? It is simple common sense to distance yourself as soon as you sense danger. Different cultures can have conflicting views on such matters, and this can sometimes lead to misunderstandings. When in doubt, however, trust your instincts and leave the room. If he persists, communicate in no uncertain terms that you are not interested. If that doesn't do any good, threaten to tell his wife. If it becomes necessary to carry out your threat, be prepared for dismissal. If things have progressed to that stage, it's probably time to leave in any case. No job is so good that it's worth putting up with harassment. If the attraction is mutual, you should do your best to discourage the feelings. You are there to benefit the family, not to destroy it.

The idea that fathers regularly make passes at the au pair or nanny is more prevalent than the reality

One prospective au pair heading off to Paris was so worried about this problem that she chose a single parent family which seemed to offer ideal conditions. Not long after her arrival she discovered that the woman who was her employer (whose profession had been described as 'stylist' on the forms) was a pornographer. This combined with the fact that the boy was a complete brat brought her to such a low ebb that she burst into tears one evening, whereupon the employer began stroking her hair. She left the next day.

MARITAL PROBLEMS

With marital breakdown at an all-time high around the world, you may find yourself working in an atmosphere of tension and unhappiness. Any marriage problems are unlikely to be evident to you until you are actually in their midst. This of course puts pressures on the children who will sense the strain and fear the disintegration of their family.

The extent of such a problem depends on the personalities and actions of the people involved and is, therefore, largely out of your control. You are not a marriage guidance counsellor, so refuse to be drawn into any marital disputes. Remain as impartial as possible, even though your loyalties may lie more with one parent than the other, and concentrate on the children. They will need a great deal of affection, encouragement and distraction during such turbulent times. Matt Tomlinson enjoyed his stay with a young French family so much that he continued to visit them on return trips to France, so he was sorry to learn that they were divorcing. His advice is to try and keep the children out of it and be your usual self, since they will need something solid more than ever.

If you are working for a family in which the parents are already divorced, the situation is bound to have affected the children to some degree. The apparent loss of a mother or father causes them to feel bereft and insecure. Male au pairs or nannies can be of help in redressing the balance in cases where the father has left the family and it is a great shame that this option is so rarely available.

One young woman wrote to describe the problems she encountered as an au pair in Denver Colorado:

It was a disaster from the word go. I had been told by the host mother that she was a single parent, divorced a year earlier, with all problems resolved. But they hadn't even started. On arrival, I discovered that not only had she just started divorce proceedings, but she was utterly miserable and constantly depressed. You can imagine what it was like for the two young children aged 8 and 6. I was caught in the middle. The mother expected me to side with her against the father which included using the children to send nasty comments across town when they visited him. I was determined to remain impartial but that only depressed the mother more. The children progressively viewed me as their 'lost' father and vented all their anger and frustration on me which included terrible screams and swearing and beating me. When I broke down in tears and confronted the mother (which I should have done earlier) I was accused of lying and sacked. Thank goodness my second placement was happier.

COPING WITH A NEW ARRIVAL

The arrival of a new-born baby in the family will generate much joy and excitement, but it will also mean more work for you and bring its own unique set of problems.

One of the first things to consider when a mother informs you of her pregnancy is whether or not you will still be working for her by the time the baby is born. If your contract is due to expire shortly before or after the birth and you have no plans to extend it, remind your employer of your proposed leaving date. This should give her plenty of time to arrange for someone to replace you before the birth.

During the pregnancy, be prepared for mood swings, exhaustion and complaints from the mother. She may be feeling resentful that her body is no longer her own and she can't do everything she was used to doing. If the au pair is the only person around, she will bear the brunt of the moaning.

Naturally, a new infant adds considerably to the workload. Even if the mother looks after the baby, you will be left with other tasks which were previously shared. Prior to the baby's arrival you should establish if a maternity nurse will be hired, and what new duties will ensue. Consider, for example, the increase in laundry and your possible involvement in night feeds. Make sure you fully understand what will be expected of you.

TELLING THE CHILDREN

Usually it is the mother who will announce the imminent birth to her children, so do not broach the subject first without her consent. Nine months can seem like a very long time to little children so it is best not to relay the news too early in the pregnancy. When this time has come, be prepared to answer any questions they might ask you.

In the meantime there are some practical things you can do to help prepare them. Talk about the baby, emphasising how tiny and vulnerable he or she will be, and how you need the children to help you look after the new little one. Encourage them to mix with infants so they learn what to expect. Above all, reassure them that affection does not come in limited supplies and they will be loved just as much as their new brother or sister.

Generally speaking children are greatly interested in the prospect of a new arrival and thrive on the general air of expectation and excitement. When the baby is born they should be encouraged to handle him or her and play their part in the new regime so that some of the glamour of the event rubs off on them. Children's natural curiosity means they are likely to be very keen on all the details surrounding and following the birth.

EXPLAINING THE FACTS OF LIFE

You'll never have a more natural opportunity to explain the facts of life than when there is a pregnancy in the family. The mother might prefer to deal with this subject herself, however, so you should first establish how involved she wants you to be, if at all.

If the parents wish to handle the matter by themselves, and your charge is asking you awkward questions, reply in a casual tone of voice that you do not know the answer but suggest he asks his mum or dad. Nannies more than au pairs, usually find that their involvement in the child's sex education is expected. If you are given this responsibility, don't introduce the subject yourself but wait until your charge takes the initiative. Answer the questions only when he or she poses them and reply in language appropriate to the child's age. If a child is old enough to ask the question, he is old enough to receive a reply.

The most common question children will ask is, where do babies come from? Don't elaborate unnecessarily by bombarding them with too much information. A simple explanation that babies grow in their mummy's tummy should suffice for the time being. The mother will probably allow her children to feel the baby kicking inside her. Should your charges ask how the baby got there, just tell them that he grew from a tiny seed that was planted inside his mother.

Older children may require more advanced explanations depending upon the knowledge they have already acquired to date. Keep your answers direct and uncomplicated, and try not to be unnaturally solemn. This can add tension to what should be a relaxed discussion. A humorous picture book on the subject is Babette Cole's *Mummy Laid an Egg!* aimed at 6-8 year olds.

WHEN THE MOTHER IS IN HOSPITAL

Unless a relative comes to help out while the mother is in hospital, this could be an exceptionally busy time if you are not used to sole charge. You might have to curtail your evening social life for a while, leaving the father free to visit his wife. It would be nice if you offered to work your days off during the mother's absence, especially if the father is struggling to cope alone. Suggest taking some extra time off in a month or so instead, once the baby has arrived and a new routine has been established. Your thoughtfulness will be appreciated and you will have the opportunity to take a mini-holiday later on.

Providing the parents have no objections, take the children to visit their mother. This will reassure them that they have not been abandoned, and help to familiarise them with the new baby.

COPING WITH THE MOTHER

The first few weeks after giving birth and returning home can be a particularly difficult time for a mother, even if she has been through it all before. She may be prone to mood swings as a result of hormonal changes in her body, and suffer from fatigue. You should encourage her to rest as much as possible, offering to take over the care of the infant when necessary. Avoid interfering and dominating the proceedings, however. The mother will want some time alone to enjoy her new child, so concentrate more on the other children and on keeping the house running smoothly. For the first couple of weeks you may have to adopt chores, such as grocery shopping, that were not previously your responsibility.

Post-natal irritability or tearfulness can be difficult to understand, but try to be tolerant, sympathetic, and offer support and reassurance whenever needed. If you are used to sole charge, it will take time to adapt to your new supporting role.

JEALOUSY

Deirdre, an experienced nanny in Istanbul, started a new job just after her employer had given birth to a second child:
My main problem was that I came into a household with a new baby. There were many visitors and family friends, some of whom stayed days or weeks at a time. The little girl I was responsible for found it hard to adjust to the situation of a new baby brother, new nanny and lots of visitors, as she was only 18 months old. She was extremely jealous of the baby and therefore had many problems including a bad sleep pattern. However she has now settled down and attends a play school twice a

> *week. Every child and every family are different and it takes a good three months to build a relationship with a child, so don't give up.*

By encouraging older children to help with the baby, you may be able to defuse their feelings of displacement. You cannot entirely make up for this, but spending as much time as possible with the older children will further help to alleviate their insecurity. Try also to plan more activities than you normally would and grant new privileges, emphasising that it's because they are so grown up, now that they have a younger brother or sister. For example, if parents are in agreement, you could extend bedtime by fifteen minutes.

Listen to any outbursts from the older children and reassure them that you understand. Tell them a story about how you felt towards your own baby brother. Be watchful for acts of aggression towards the baby but make allowances for any mild acts of jealousy since drawing attention to them could make things worse.

FEEDING

Not all women are able to breast-feed and if the mother chooses to return to work shortly after the birth, you will have to take over feeding by bottle. Fresh milk should not be used for new-borns because of its high sodium and phosphate content. Commercial feeds are suitable and can be bought either in powder or liquid form. Make the formula up exactly as directed by the manufacturer. If you make it too concentrated, you will over-load the baby's kidneys.

It is essential that all bottle equipment is washed and sterilised before use. You can do this by soaking the bottles and teats, etc. in boiling water for five minutes and then leaving them to drain under a cover. This method will cause more wear and tear, however, and there is an easier way of doing things. It is possible to buy a special tank which you fill with a hypochlorite solution. All feeding equipment can be sterilised in that, until it is needed again. Do not prepare and keep feeds warm for any length of time because milk is a culture medium for bacteria. The bottles can be made up twenty-four hours in advance, however, and stored in the fridge. Throw away any left-over milk once it has been heated.

Warm up the bottle just before a feed by standing it in a jug of hot water. Microwaves can also be used though it is difficult to obtain a balanced temperature. It is very easy to overheat the formula and then you will be left with a hungry baby screaming for his dinner while you frantically try to cool the bottle under running water. Always test the feed on the back of your hand or your wrist before giving it to the child, to make sure it is tepid and not too hot. If the formula becomes cold during feeding, re-heat it. Babies seem to prefer heated liquid, probably because breast milk is warm.

The teat hole should be big enough to allow a regular flow of milk. Too little and the baby will become frustrated; too big and he will take too much, possibly causing him to choke. To make the teat bigger, pierce with a sterilised needle. Ideally, it should take about fifteen minutes to complete a feed. Bottle-fed babies tend to suffer more from wind, so you should stop half-way through to burp him. If the baby gulps his milk, give him one or two tablespoons of cooled boiled water, just before his feed. It will take the edge off his appetite and he will drink more slowly. Babies like a drink of warm unsweetened boiled water anyway, so give him a few sips from time to time as part of his routine.

Mealtimes should take place in a quiet, relaxing atmosphere if at all possible. Place a bib around the baby's neck, prop him up into a half-sitting position and hold him close against your breast while feeding him his bottle. It helps if you are free to concentrate on your new charge, giving him plenty of eye contact.

This can be difficult if you have other children to care for too, so get them fed and settled with some amusement first. If meal times clash, give the older child a small snack to stave off his hunger.

Most babies need feeding every three hours but some more frequently. Don't try to force a child to finish his bottle. Just note how much he has drunk and he will probably make up for it later in the day.

NAPPY RASH

This is caused by bacteria from the baby's stools which breaks down his urine into ammonia, and burns the skin. The bacteria thrives in alkaline conditions which is why bottle-fed babies tend to suffer from it more. (The stools of breast-fed babies are more acidic.)

To avoid nappy rash as much as possible, change the baby frequently. Disposable nappies are easier but more expensive. Cloth nappies should be soaked and washed thoroughly to remove the ammonia. Avoid using plastic pants as these keep the urine close to the skin and will aggravate the rash. Air the baby's bottom regularly. Let him lie face-down on an old blanket to protect the carpet.

If a baby does get nappy rash, stop washing the baby's bottom with soap and water which will dry the skin and exacerbate the rash. Use a liquid cream instead, such as baby lotion. Make sure he is dried well after a bath; this can be done most efficiently with a hair dryer on a warm (not hot) setting. Apply a thick barrier cream to his bottom, such as zinc oxide or petroleum jelly, before securing a clean nappy. Seek medical advice if the rash seem particularly inflamed and persistent.

COLIC

Young babies up to the age of three months are sometimes afflicted with colic, which causes acute spasms of pain in the intestines. The child doesn't just cry, he screams, becomes red in the face, clenches his fists and draws both his legs up towards his stomach. Gripe water is a traditional remedy for this, but its effectiveness is unproven and, besides, you may have trouble obtaining it abroad. Warm drinks of boiled water can be given instead and encourage the child to burp by patting his back vigorously. Applying a warm (not hot) covered hot water bottle to his abdomen may also offer relief.

STIMULATING THE NEW-BORN

Babies are far more intelligent than they are sometimes given credit for, and they should not be ignored once their basic needs have been tended. Give the baby plenty of cuddles and spend some time singing or talking to him. It won't be long before he or she responds to your facial expressions.

New-born babies cannot focus their eyes on objects further away than one foot, so when amusing him don't hold the playthings too far away. Make his room as colourful as possible. You could begin by decorating his nursery wall with the parents' congratulation cards, providing they have given you permission to do so. Put bright transfers on the inside of his crib and hang a musical mobile over the side. It's a good idea to hang a second one over his change table to amuse him while changing his nappy. Putting a mirror on the wall beside him will also provide some entertainment.

Take your young charge for walks in his pram so he gets plenty of air and comes into contact with stimuli outside his home. It is very useful to double up on baby supplies for outings. This enables you to have a permanently packed bag ready for impromptu excursions except for the addition of a few last-minute articles. The following check-list might prove helpful: nappies, plastic bags for used nappies, safety pins for cloth nappies, spare set of clothes, baby wipes/cotton wool/tissues/toilet paper, plastic sheet for changing (washable wallpaper works just as well), baby lotion, barrier cream, talc, bottle and teat, formula, bib, playthings. Remember to replace all the non-perishables when you return, in preparation for the next outing.

Leisure time and departure

CREATING A SOCIAL LIFE

Building a social life from scratch is hard enough at any time but becomes even more difficult in an alien tongue and culture. Unless you are exceptionally lucky and find yourself content to socialise with your host family, you will have to take positive steps to meet people and participate in activities outside the confines of your employers' home. This may require uncharacteristically extrovert behaviour for you, but overcoming initial inhibitions almost always pays worthwhile dividends. There is no substitute for a friend when you are feeling low. Even an acquaintance (preferably one who speaks your language fluently) can go a long way to relieve some of the loneliness and isolation. There are plenty of on-line au pair chatrooms, some hosted by the major agencies (such as www.englishaupair.co.uk) which may help to break down feelings of isolation. But cyberspace is so big that it will be difficult to make contact with someone in your immediate neighbourhood.

MEETING OTHER AU PAIRS/NANNIES

Working for a family can get very claustrophobic and it is most important to make friends of your own away from the home. When work, children or parents are getting you down, it is essential to have someone else you can have a good moan with and so keep a sense of proportion about the usual stresses and strains of family life.

Don't wait until your first day off to begin the search for companions. Ask your employers to introduce you to other households who hire live-in helpers. Most will be more than willing to oblige if they know any, since it is in their best interests for you to be happy and to settle. You may be surprised at the number of foreign young people in your vicinity doing just what you are doing: for instance in a small village 80km south-west of Paris, Jessie Lane encountered no less than 17 English or English-speaking au pairs. Other au pairs can provide an important support network since you will be faced with similar problems.

Look out for other au pairs or nannies at parks, recreation centres, playgroups, etc. and while collecting the children from school. Many Mothers and Toddlers Groups (especially in parts of London) would be more accurately called 'Nannies and Toddlers'.

One of the great advantages of using agencies for placements abroad is that they are usually able to provide a list of a few au pairs in your destination neighbourhood, though it will be up to you to make contact. Some corresponding agents abroad arrange coffee mornings especially for new arrivals, as well as follow-up social events, some of which may be open to anyone and publicised in the local English language press. The ratio of women to men is usually chronically unbalanced as Nicola Wenban found in Vienna where there was one male au pair and hundreds of women.

Some au pairs have shown initiative in making contact with other au pairs. Leeson Clifton, who came from Canada to be a mother's help in Britain, placed an advertisement in the local paper for an au pair get-together which was a great success. Natasha Fox kept a record of the adverts she had noticed in magazines for live-in jobs in Helsinki and contacted the addresses after arrival. Making the first move to contact strangers can be a bit nerve-racking, but you would have to be very unlucky to meet with a lukewarm response to such an overture.

MEETING EXPATRIATES

If there is a shortage of congenial au pairs or nannies in your vicinity or if you are tired of conversations about nappy rash and tight-fisted parents, you might well benefit from the company of your fellow countrymen/women to combat loneliness or homesickness. The local English language bookshop might prove a useful source of information about forthcoming events for English speakers, as will any newspapers or magazines published in English such as the *Bulletin* in Brussels or the *Athens News* in Greece. Seek out the overseas student club if there is a university nearby. Even the least devout of au pairs have found English-speaking churches to be useful for arranging social functions and offering advice. If there is a bar in town which models itself on a British or Irish pub, you will no doubt find a few die-hards drinking Guinness, who might be more than willing to befriend you.

The most obvious way to meet other foreigners is to enrol straightaway in a language course or perhaps classes in art and civilisation (see the section *Learning a Language* below). Even if you are not particularly serious about pursuing language studies, language classes are the ideal place to form vital social contacts with people from around the world. You can also join other clubs or classes aimed at residents abroad. During Emma Colgan's very successful year as an au pair in Germany, she joined the English amateur dramatics group called the Hamburg Players:

Admittedly this did not benefit my German at all, but I enjoyed myself and made very good friends, especially with a girl my age who still visits me in England.

MEETING THE LOCALS

Meeting the local residents may prove more difficult, though circumstances vary enormously according to whether you live in a small village or a big city, with a gregarious family or a socially isolated one, and so on. If you don't spend all your free time moping at home, you are bound to strike up conversations with the locals, whether in cafés, on buses or in shops. Admittedly these seldom go past a superficial acquaintance, but they still serve the purpose of making you feel a little more integrated in the community.

> **Annabel Roberts enjoyed her stay in Germany but reported**
> *I didn't meet any young Germans. Most of us au pairs found that they only held an interest in you as foreigners, and when the novelty wore off they lost interest. This seems harsh, but all the girls I spoke to agreed.*

Annabel goes on to recommend taking a supplementary job if possible, such as private tutoring in English, to meet the locals. Her 'pupil' often invited her out with a group of friends.

Again students will probably be more socially flexible than others and it is worth investigating the bars and cafés around the local university or polytechnic. If you have a particular hobby, sport or interest, find out if there is a local club where you will meet like-minded people; join local ramblers, clubbers, folk music buffs, Amnesty International, etc. You only have to become friendly with one local person to open up new social horizons if you are invited to meet their friends and family.

Australian Mary Scollen, working as a mother's help in England, asked a young London policeman directions to Carnaby Street, got chatting, exchanged telephone numbers and finished up going out on a date with him a few days later.

LEARNING A LANGUAGE

Until you feel reasonably comfortable in the language, you will not only find it difficult to meet the local people, but you will not enjoy simple tasks like shopping or answering the telephone. It is surprising how miserable you can feel when you can't communicate with anyone and, equally, how quickly you will acquire a certain facility if you are forced to survive in the language. Au pairs consistently report that when they have no choice but to speak daily in a foreign language, they learn more in a month than during years of study at school.

Au pairs are in fact less prone to complain that communication with their family is impossible than that their employers insist on speaking English, thereby preventing them from improving their own fluency in the local language. On the other hand, people who have no knowledge of foreign languages would be unwise to fix up a job with a non-English speaking family.

LANGUAGE COURSES ABROAD

In some countries such as Switzerland and Finland, the au pair visa is contingent on enrolling in formal lessons. In most countries, au pairs from outside Europe are obliged by the terms of the arrangement to enroll in language classes. Whatever the rules and whatever your standard, it is a very good idea to sign up for a course, if only for the social advantages. It should be easy to find out about local courses from your agency, your family, the tourist office or even just the Yellow Pages. Fees vary wildly, but state-funded courses are invariably cheaper than commercial ones. In some countries, it is customary for the family to pay part or all of the fees (as in Sweden), though this is usually at the discretion of the employers.

Jessie Lane was determined to learn French so tried not to spend all her spare time with her fellow au pairs and faithfully attended classes at a local college. The classes helped her come to terms with the grammar with which she had always struggled.

A big consideration before going abroad (assuming there will be other English speakers there) is to make up your mind whether you are going to have a good time or to learn the language.

Obviously it is possible to combine these by following a prescribed course where your knowledge of the language is sure to improve, as will your social life.

Lessons are not of course essential to learning a language, especially if you speak no English with the children you are looking after; but they always help. In some cases it can also provide an actual qualification. Emma Colgan found that it was helpful in her situation when returning to England (to pursue a university course in international business and German) clutching some sort of exam certificate as concrete proof to the folks back home that she hadn't spent the whole time changing nappies and sipping German lager.

PROBLEMS

Some au pair positions are as far from a form of study as it is possible to be. Improving your knowledge of the language may be difficult or impossible for any number of reasons: because you have too little free time or are worked so hard that you are too shattered to use your leisure time to study, because the language classes are inaccessible (financially or literally) or closed (as is usually the case during the summer vacation), because the family insists that you speak English to them and their children, and so on. If the latter is the case, discuss your dilemma with the parents and try to find a compromise whereby you speak English at certain times and their language at others. Speaking with children can be one of the best (and least embarrassing) ways to improve your vocabulary and pronunciation, since your little charges won't hesitate to correct you when you make a mistake while reading their favourite stories.

If your family isn't co-operative, you will either have to exert a lot of self-discipline (i.e. study from books and force yourself to speak to native speakers outside the home whenever you can), or find another family where it will be easier to make progress. If your primary aim is not being achieved, you will only become increasingly resentful and disappointed unless you take action.

TIME OFF

Au pairs and nannies find a thousand ways to spend their afternoons, days, or weekends off. The key is to get out of the house, and so avoid the possibility of being called upon. The value of using your spare time to attend language classes has already been stressed. But you will also want to explore your new environment either by yourself or with a new-found friend. Daytime excursions on your own (to parks, museums, galleries, shops, etc.) will probably be more enjoyable than venturing out alone in the evenings.

YOUR FIRST DAY OFF

On your days off you will want to explore further afield, but don't get too carried away with sightseeing plans at the beginning. There will be plenty of time for that later on, and many chores may require urgent attention first, for example, opening a bank account, visiting your agency, etc. Perhaps this will also be your only chance to investigate and then enrol in classes or get in touch with any contacts you have been urged to look up by the folks back home. It is also an idea to locate the British Consulate (if you are living in a city) and ask them what services they provide for British residents either on a day-to-day basis or in an emergency.

On your first night out, do not alarm your new employers by returning at an ungodly hour and try to be especially quiet. As they get to know and trust you, their anxiety should fade away on this score, though you should be aware that some families impose a curfew especially during the week, partly out of concern for their young au pair's safety.

EXCURSIONS AND ACTIVITIES

Your location will to a large extent dictate your range of amusements. Those who are lucky enough to be within easy reach of Rome or Paris will never exhaust the beautiful and interesting places. But people on a German army base or in a small industrial town in northern Spain may have more difficulty. If you know you are going to be some distance from a major centre, consider acquiring a vehicle of some kind, whether a bicycle, moped or even car. A lack of transport may not be the only impediment to organising excursions, if you find yourself working for an over-protective family who disapprove of too much independence (see *Problem Parents: Interference with your Social Life).*

Even if you find yourself a long way from a wide range of entertainments, it is possible to have an enjoyable time abroad. One outlet is sport. Lucy Sumner was lucky enough to fix up an au pairing job in the small alpine resort of Monêtier-les-Bains in France and used her free time in the obvious way. Not only did she take up skiing for its own sake, but she found it an excellent way to meet both residents and tourists. But this doesn't always work. Irene Platt thought that a good way to meet the locals in her small French town was to join the tennis club, but was dismayed to have her application turned down on the grounds that she would be there for too brief a time.

HOLIDAYS

Although you probably won't get paid enough to contemplate a holiday on the grand scale, make an effort to organise at least one complete break away from your place of temporary residence. Even a couple of days by the seaside or visiting a tourist attraction in the region can revitalise your interest in being abroad and provide a refreshing break from routine. If you stay in a youth hostel, you'll see new faces and hear new viewpoints on the culture in

Throwing parties in the parents' absence is definitely out

which you have been immersed. And if nothing else, it will give you a chance to mingle with your peers instead of children.

Holidays with the family can be a real perk, and some lucky au pairs find themselves spending weeks aboard the family yacht or at a mountain lodge. One of the highlights of Natalia de Cuba's experience of au pairing in France was the week which was spent at the family's country house in the south of France; part of the reason for the success was that 'the family was very relaxed when freed from schoolwork and business'.

But be careful to distinguish ahead of time between your holiday time and theirs, since you will probably end up working much harder than usual when the children are out of school and demanding more attention (see the section *Problem Parents: Pay and Time Off*).

In each of the country chapters which follow, an attempt has been made to suggest specific ideas for using your leisure time and to pass on tips from au pairs and nannies who have discovered all sorts of diversions.

USE OF A CAR

Many families, especially in country areas, will allow their au pair or nanny to use a car in the evenings or during their time off. This is a privilege and should be seen as such. You will already be using the car as part of your work, for shopping or taking the children out so you will have checked that the insurance covers you as an additional driver. If you are using a family car for your own purposes you should return it with the same amount of petrol in the tank as when you borrowed it and be particularly careful to drive sensibly and not drink. If something goes wrong report it at once.

DEPARTURE

GIVING NOTICE

Once your contract is drawing to an end and you know you will not be extending it, or if your circumstances have changed and you wish to leave earlier than expected, try to give the family as much notice as possible. This will give the parents time to find a suitable replacement, and the children time to adjust to the idea that you will no longer be living with them.

Avoid leaving impetuously during the heat of an argument. It would be a shame to undo all the good work you've invested in building up a decent relationship with your employers, and it isn't very fair to the children who will be affected by your sudden departure. If you want to terminate your contract, it shouldn't be done suddenly and on bad terms. Bid the children farewell in as friendly a manner as possible, even if it isn't from the heart. It can be awkward, working your notice if things are difficult between you, and in many cases the employers will insist that you leave straightaway. But if they don't, stick it out for the sake of the children. Any unexpected disruption in their home-life is bound to have an upsetting effect on them, and children's feelings should not be hurt unnecessarily. If you cannot avoid leaving under a cloud just pack your things quietly, say goodbye to the children and leave.

Similarly, moonlight flits are undesirable. At least have the courtesy to tell your employers that you wish to leave, face to face. The worst thing about slipping away without a word of warning (apart from being sneaky) is that you deny the children an opportunity to say goodbye to you. This is especially cruel if you have been with them long enough to develop a trusting relationship. If you don't bid them a formal farewell, they will probably go on expecting your imminent return.

PREPARING THE CHILDREN

If your contract has been a successful one, your charges will have grown to love you (although they may have strange ways of showing it sometimes!), depend on you and generally regard you as one of the family. Therefore, when the time comes for you to leave, it can be quite traumatic for them even if they've always been told that you won't be their nanny forever. Six months or longer may seem like a lifetime to children and they will have forgotten that your stay was always going to be temporary.

Bed-time is not a good time to break the news because they may lie awake worrying about your departure. Fears always seem much worse at night when one is tired and surrounded by darkness. On the other hand, don't be surprised if they greet your news with little concern or curiosity. Not all children express their feelings in obvious ways. They may become more clingy than normal, calling for you in the night or misbehave more than usual. Try to read the signs with tolerance and answer them with reassurance. Tell them stories about your family and describe your home in detail, if you haven't already done so. It helps if they have some idea of where you're going and that you can be contacted by phone or letter. This is especially important since you will probably be moving out of visiting range. If so, try to send postcards from your new abode to let them know that they aren't forgotten. Above all, reassure them at every opportunity that you will still love them, even though they will no longer be in your care.

Children have an uncanny knack for becoming particularly endearing during your last week; or perhaps it's because you interpret their behaviour more positively now that you know your time together is coming to an end. Either way, it is very flattering if your charges are averse to your being replaced and make it plain that they would prefer you to stay. Don't encourage any last-minute acts of devotion towards you, however, in preference to the new nanny. Of course the children will miss you, and you them, but it is your duty to help make the transition as smooth as possible. Tell the children all about her and display her in a good light, so they have a positive image of her. This will help them to adjust once she takes over.

MEETING THE NEW NANNY

It's quite common to be introduced to the new nanny and be asked to show her the ropes before you leave. This is better for the children because it gives both parties a chance to adapt to each other before the new girl's contract formally begins. Try to help her as much as possible because the more quickly she settles in, the better it will be for the family.

Tell her all about the children's routine and maybe make a few notes if you think it might help her. If you're very public-spirited, you can leave notes on evening entertainment, libraries, etc. and draw a few maps so the new au pair or nanny will have some idea of where the shops, children's school and local park are. Show her how to use the household equipment but try not to bombard her with too much detail. Avoid gossiping about your employers. Let the girl form her own impressions, just as you did. When you live with a family, they allow you a privileged insight into their intimate lives, and you should treat this with respect and confidentiality.

Encourage her to take the lead with the children, while you drop into the background as much as possible. If she considers it necessary to discipline them in your presence (or if she fails to discipline them when you think it is called for), it can be tempting to interfere if you think she's handling the situation badly. Bite your tongue. She's in charge now and you must allow her to get on with it. NEVER criticise her in front of the children, thereby undermining her authority, since this can lead to problems. If you want to give her the benefit of your experience, do so in private. Concentrate on the household chores, leaving her with the children as much as possible.

FAREWELL

Saying good-bye can be very sad and difficult, but it doesn't mean the end of the relationship. Many au pairs and nannies remain in close contact with the families they have worked for, receiving photos and keeping up-to-date with their news. You may be sent drawings at Christmas, gifts on your birthday, Valentine cards in February and through this correspondence, you can follow the children's development, albeit from a distance.

Part II

Country by Country Guide

Rules & Regulations
Advantages & Disadvantages
Specialist Agencies

AUSTRALIA	ISRAEL
AUSTRIA	ITALY
BELGIUM & LUXEMBOURG	NETHERLANDS
	SCANDINAVIA
CANADA	SPAIN & PORTUGAL
FRANCE	SWITZERLAND
GERMANY	TURKEY
GREAT BRITAIN	USA
GREECE	REST OF THE
IRELAND	WORLD

Each chapter contains a section on the advantages and disadvantages of working in that particular country, how to fix up a job either through an agency or independently, the regulations affecting visas and health insurance, general points about what to do in your leisure time and a list of the agencies which deal with that country. Agencies that are italicised in the text are included in the Directory of Agencies at the end of the book.

Australasia

AUSTRALIA

Australia and to a much lesser extent New Zealand are increasingly promising destinations for people interested in working with children, either professionally or as part of a working holiday. Many people under 30 are eligible for a working holiday visa for up to a year which can facilitate temporary nannying and au pairing (see section on Red Tape below).

The concept of au pairing is not foreign to Australians and several agencies include the word in their names, for example *Au Pair Australia* in Sydney's inner suburb of Glebe, *Australian Nanny & Au Pair Connection* in Melbourne, *Family Match Au Pairs & Nannies* and *JCR Au Pairs & Nannies*. These agencies are familiar with the working holiday programme and are prepared to try to place foreign au pairs in families for periods of less than three months (to satisfy the terms of the visa). Holiday positions for the summer (December-February) and for the ski season (July-August) are available.

Many agencies are able to offer a choice of posts at short notice. When Julia Stanton from Harrow left one job after a week of working, because of the long hours (very little time off between rising at 7am to walk the dog and 8.30pm when the children went to bed), Rosemary McCormack of the agency *Australian Nanny & Au Pair Connection* found her a more suitable job the same day.

> **The introductory letter from one of the agencies gives a flavour of working as an au pair in Australia:**
> *We have helped hundreds of girls to find work in Sydney, the Blue Mountains, the Gold Coast of Queensland, Brisbane and country areas. You do not need experience, only the love of children. It is certainly an excellent way of working and living here as well as gaining a better understanding of our culture. As an au pair you will be working an average of 25-40 hours per week. In most cases weekends are free to discover Sydney and meet with friends. You can become part of the family, sharing in outings and family life, or choose to have independent activities on your time off. Most families have the luxuries of swimming pools and/or tennis courts, and sometimes they allow use of the family car.*

FINDING A JOB

The demand for live-in and live-out childcare is enormous in Australia and a few agencies in Britain cater to the demand, such as *Childcare International*. A number of London nanny agencies have strong links with counterparts downunder, primarily to recruit Australian and New Zealand nannies for families in southern England but also to place some British childcarers in Antipodean homes. For example *Family First International* lists its several partner agencies in Australia and New Zealand on its website, while *Tinies* and *Occasional & Permanent* both have counterpart agencies downunder.

A number of au pair agencies place European and Asian women with working holiday visas in live-in positions. Most agencies will expect to interview applicants and check their references before placement. The policy of Placement Solutions (a division of *International Nannies Services*) is typical of professional nanny agencies: applicants have to be personally interviewed and have three childcare references, first aid, police clearance and a driving licence. As in the UK, some of the more prestigious agencies have been lobbying for more regulation in the industry especially in the wake of the cause of the Australian nanny, Louise

Sullivan, who in 1999 was charged with the murder of a baby in her care in London. The Australian Association of Nanny Agencies (AANA) did not survive long and now the main regulatory body is NICA (National In-home Childcare Association).

Not all au pair placements require childcare experience, though confidence and maturity are important. Nannies are usually rigorously checked; many Australian nannies have a qualification early childhood education. As in America, a driving licence is a valuable asset and sometimes essential.

Check the websites of the following agencies to find out if their services might be appropriate:

AAA Nannies, PO Box 157, Sanctuary Cove, Queensland 4212 (head office 7-5530 1123; www.nanny.net.au). Charges placement fee of $400 for international applicants.

ANZAA (Australia New Zealand Nanny Au-pair Agency) International, Head Office, PO Box 326, Nerang, Queensland 4211 (tel/fax 7-3319 6999; www.anznaa.com). Established in 2000 to provide young people from around the world an opportunity to travel the world, while caring for children; UK contact 020-7078 4130.

Care for Kids – www.careforkids.com.au – Sydney-based online childcare agency.

Care for Kidz, PO Box 871, Bulimba, Bristane, QLD 4171 (1800 763 288; brisbane@ careforkidz.com.au)

Charlton Brown Group, Level 16 300 Adelaide St, Brisbane, Qld, 4000; 1300 301 888; 7-3221 3855; fax 7-3221 6855; nannies@charltonbrowngroup.com.au; www. charltonbrowngroup.com.au. Has a nanny college.

Childcare Team, Ground Floor, 7 Parkes St Parramatta, NSW 2150 (2-9891-4377; fax 2-9891-4366; info@childcareteam.com.au; www.childcareteam.net. Formerly Affordable Au Pairs.

Help on the Way, Level 1, 139 Glen Eira Road, East St Kilda, VIC 3183 (3-9528 6688; wehelp@helpontheway.com.au; www.helpontheway.com.au)

Mary Poppins, Suite 3,18 Napier Cl, Deakin, Canberra, ACT 2600 (2-6282 8155; fax 2-6282 8633; info@marypoppins.com.au; www.marypoppins.com.au). Local and international nanny placements.

Perfect Solution Babysitters and Au Pairs, 56 Rolfe St, Manly, NSW 2095 2-9976 2214; www.perfectsolutions.com.au)

Susan Rogan Nannies, Level 2 156 Collins Street, Melbourne VIC 3000 (3-9654 6377; www.susanrogan.com.au)

Tinies Childcare - 1-300-308 875; www.tinieschildcare.com.au. Counterpart of Tinies agency in UK (see Directory entry).

The Wright Nanny, PO Box 562, Pyrmont, Sydney, NSW 2009 (2-9660-6621; fax 2-9660-7277; enquires@thewrightnanny.com.au; www.thewrightnanny.com.au)

The wonderfully named *Bub Hub* in Australia calls itself Australia's most comprehensive online directory of baby and toddler services. It keeps an updated list of nanny agencies at www.bubhub.com.au/servicesnanniesnsw.shtml. Other agencies can be found in the Yellow Pages for the major cities under the heading 'Nannies', 'Babysitters' or 'Domestic Services'.

The long-established *Dial-an-Angel* agency (www.dial-an-angel.com.au) covers all the types of childcare vacancies from au pairs to experienced housekeepers. The company has offices around Australia:

Canberra ACT: PO Box 663 Woden, ACT 2606 (2-6282 7733; canberra@dialanangel. com)

Lindfield NSW: PO Box 188, Lindfield, NSW 2070 (2-9416 7511; lindfield@dialanangel. com)

Penrith NSW: PO Box 7, Penrith, NSW 2751 (2-4722 3355; penrith@dialanangel.com)

Newcastle NSW: Suite 3, 71-73 King Street, Newcastle, NSW 2300 (2-4929 3065; newcastle@dialanangel.com)

Central Coast NSW: PO Box 181, Gosford, NSW 2250 (2-4323 6688; centralcoast@

dialanangel.com)
Woollongong NSW: 2-4227 2611; wollongong@dialanangel.com)
Brisbane QLD: PO Box 203, Indooroopilly QLD 4068 (7-3878 1077; brisbane@ dialanangel.com)
Gold Coast/Sunshine Coast QLD, PO Box 2072 Southport Business Centre, QLD 4215 (7-5591 8891; goldcoast@dialanangel.com)
Adelaide SA: 'Angel House', 78 Melbourne St, North Adelaide, SA 5006 (8-8267 3700; adelaide@dialanangel.com)
Melbourne VIC: PO Box 52, St Kilda, VIC 3182 (3-9593 9888; melbourne@dialanangel. com)
Ballarat/Bendigo VIC: Freecall: 1800 683 707
Perth WA: Suite 12a, 18 Kearns Crescent, Ardross, WA 6153 (8-9364 5488; perth@ dialanangel.com)
Rowena Caverly was very pleased with the help which *Dial-an-Angel* gave her in finding a nannying job:

> *As someone who finds crowded hostel life a bit wearing, nannying provided me with both a roof and a job. I first approached Dial-an-Angel in Melbourne. Since I was on a working holiday visa, I knew I would only be in Melbourne for a couple of months and that seemed acceptable. It is best to offer the agency an honest time limit. It took a few weeks to get a job offer; although their books were full, many families required a minimum of six months. I took on a live-in job with a part South African part Canadian family which was originally for six days but I stayed a month. I remained in touch with people I had met at the hostel and made a few of them green with my tales of regular meals, constant hot water and access to a car. A temporary joy for sure. Months and many miles later, I arrived in Brisbane with only a month of working time left to offer. I approached the local branch of Dial-an-Angel and was in luck. The Melbourne office sent a glowing reference (thank God) and there were some short-term and one-day jobs available.*

Some overseas nannies accept jobs as day-nannies and stay long-term in backpackers' accommodation, though it is usually preferable (and cheaper) to hang on for a live-in position.

As one might expect in the relatively classless society of Australia, the distinction between nanny and au pair is not as pronounced as it is in the UK and Europe. However as in Europe, agencies in Australia will expect to interview prospective nannies and check their references before placement, while agencies may accept advance applications from au pairs on working holidays and make a placement sight-unseen.

Another possibility is to register with an employment agency that supplies staff to day care centres as Catharine Carfoot from Essex did:

> *One surprisingly successful route to employment was through Select Education (109 Pitt St, Level 1, Sydney 2000). There is plenty of work at the moment. It depends on how you feel about being left in sole charge of (for example) 16 3-4 year olds or 6 babies. I should emphasise that I was never left as the only member of staff in the building even if it felt like that sometimes. Select provides childcare workers for kindergartens, pre-schools, day care or whatever.*

An on-the-spot job hunt is easy to conduct. Applicants are often interviewed a day or two after registering with an agency and start work immediately.

Geertje Korf's experience in Tasmania while she was on a working holiday illustrates the ease with which childcare work can be found

> *I decided to go to Tasmania for a cycling holiday. At the second place I stopped I got offered a job as a nanny to four children, just by mentioning I had been nannying in Sydney. The place had beautiful surroundings, restaurants, etc. so I decided to accept. It was a good job and I left quite a bit richer.*

Posts are also advertised in daily papers, particularly the *Sydney Morning Herald* and Melbourne *Age*. Check the Monday Job Market of the *Herald* under the 'Situations Vacant - Domestic and Rural' column. In fact almost all the jobs listed are in the city rather than the country.

WORKING IN AUSTRALIA: PROS AND CONS

The standard starting wage for a 30-hour-a-week au pair job is A$150-$180 a week, while mother's helps normally earn A$200-$250, live-in nannies A$250-$350 and live-out A$400-$450. As well as long term posts, holiday positions for the summer (December-February) and for the ski season (July-September) are available. According to one agency, the easiest time to find a placement is between April and August when some families will pay above the standard rate. The hourly rate for casual nannies is in the range $15-$25 depending on qualifications and duties.

Most agree that Australians are excellent employers and Australia a wonderful country in which to spend some time in a family, including Matt Tomlinson who became a nanny in Australia on the strength of the year he'd spent as an au pair in Paris. He found that there were a few Australians willing to go against tradition and entrust their children to a young man while on ski holidays:

Being a male nanny in Australia was an interesting experience. I got used to being asked if I was a child molester. I found the only solution was to stay very cool and not take it personally. On the upside, I was also offered a number of live-in jobs in Melbourne. And in case you're wondering, yes, I did get a lot of ribbing from the Aussie guys when I told them what job I was doing. One of the nicest things about nannying in Australia, you tend to get treated as an equal by the parents, whereas barmen, waiters and ski lift operators do not. I got references from a few of my most regular clients. If I hadn't had to go back for my final year at university I would probably be a very well paid nanny in Melbourne by now.

The chaffing he endured didn't prevent him from setting himself up as a freelance nanny in the ski resort of Mount Buller in Victoria:

The work was a bit irregular but when it was busy, the money was good ($500 a week) which gave me enough for my lift pass and snowboard gear. Being a nanny was a real laugh. It was being paid quite a lot of money to sledge, build snowmen, snowball, eat crisps and build dens. Sure, I had my fair share of monsters, but as I rarely had the same children for more than a few days there was always light at the end of the tunnel.

An interesting angle for those with childcare experience and basic skiing is the Ski Kindergarten. In Buller they take 3-6 year olds but most of the other resorts have a crèche too.

At least the cold conditions at Australian ski resorts remove one common anxiety. Anyone considering a childcare position in more tropical conditions might be interested in Rowena Caverly's experiences:

I looked after a 15-month old boy at a permaculture farm set in a rainforest. The job taught me new skills daily, such as how to persuade a baby that the Huntsman Spider on the wall really does not want to play. My task in summer was to teach him to toddle heavily to scare off snakes. Otherwise a nasty situation might have developed (and my money would not necessarily be on the baby as the victim).

Non English-speaking au pairs can be directed to local language schools according to their first language, since there is excellent provision for English teaching throughout the country. A few European agencies run programmes for students which combine language study and living in with a family, usually on a demi-pair basis (free accommodation in return for 15-20 hours a week). European agencies like *3 Esse* in Italy can assist; see Directory for others. If interested, ask any English language school in Australia or New Zealand for guidance. For example the Phoenix English Language Academy in Perth (8-9227 5538; www.phoenixela. com.au) offers demi-pair placements and the Capital Language Academy in Wellington (49-51 Courtney Place, PO Box 1100, Wellington; enquiries@cla.co.nz) is developing a demi-pair programme for students from Argentina, Canada, Chile, Denmark, France, Germany, Hong Kong, Ireland, Italy, Japan, Korea, Malaysia, Netherlands, Singapore, Sweden, Great Britain and Uruguay; email emma.k@cla.co.nz for details.

RED TAPE

The number of working holiday visas for Australia has risen steadily from 33,000 in 1995 to 88,750 now. Australia has reciprocal working holiday arrangements with Britain, Ireland, Canada, Netherlands, Germany, Japan, Korea, SAR of Hong Kong, Taiwan, Sweden, Denmark, Finland, Norway, Cyprus, Malta, France, Belgium, Italy and most recently Estonia. The working holiday visa is valid for 12 months. Americans aged 18-30 are eligible for a four-month working stay in Australia.

The visa is for applicants between 18 and 30 without dependent children intending to use any money they earn in Australia to supplement their holiday funds. Working full-time for more than three months for the same employer is not permitted. Those eligible for a working holiday in Australia, whether as mother's helps or anything else (fruit picker, typist, etc.), can now apply for the visa online (www.immi.gov.au/e_visa/visit.htm) or in the traditional way from a specialist agent like Visas Australia (01270 626626; www.visas-australia.com) or Consyl Publishing (3 Buckhurst Road, Bexhill-on-Sea, East Sussex TN40 1QF; 01424 223111). The non-refundable processing fee in the UK is currently A$170 (£70). You must have enough money for your return fare and savings of a minimum of A$5000/£2100. At present US nationals may apply for special programme visa 416 which allows them to work for up to four months, and then they can stay on purely to travel for a further three months.

WORKING IN NEW ZEALAND

New Zealand also has a Working Holiday visa for many nationalities, including an unlimited number for British nationals aged 18-30 who want to stay up to 23 months on a working holiday. The internet-based agency Au Pair The Kiwi Connection (PO Box 15866 New Lynn, Auckland; +64 9-826 0083; kiwiaupair@xtra.co.nz; www.kiwiaupair.com) includes information about visas for New Zealand on its site. There are also of course professional nanny agencies like Poppetts in Auckland (2A Fitzroy Street, Ponsonby; 9-376 7774; info@poppetts.com; www.nznanny.co.nz). Experienced nannies in New Zealand cities are paid NZ$11-$18+ per hour. Live-in nannies normally earn NZ$350-$550 a week.

Another agency which imports and exports nannies from New Zealand and the UK is KiwiOz Nannies started by two New Zealand women in 2002 and based in Auckland and London. The New Zealand agency can be contacted at PO Box 56, 168 Dominion Road, Auckland (+64 9-629 2941; contact@kiwioznannies.co.nz; www.kiwioznannies.co.nz) whereas the website of the London agency in Notting Hill is www.kiwioznannies.co.uk). Experienced childcarers in Auckland can also register as weekend babysitters; the hourly rate is NZ$12-$14 for a minimum of three hours.

Note that the Auckland agency *International Working Holidays (IWH)* in the Directory has only an outgoing programme for New Zealand nannies.

DIRECTORY REFERENCES

For agencies based in Australia, see: **Au Pair Australia** (Glebe, Sydney), **Australian Nanny & Au Pair Connection** (Kooyong, Melbourne), **Charlton Brown Group** (Brisbane), **Childcare Team** (Parramatta, NSW), **Dial-an-Angel** (Sydney, Brisbane and interstate), **Family Match Au Pairs & Nannies** (Kincumber, Sydney), **Global-Nannies** (online service based in Brisbane), **International Nannies Services** (Alphington, Melbourne), **JCR Au Pairs & Nannies** (Bentleigh, Melbourne), **Just for Kids** (Manly, Sydney) and **People for People** (Warringah, Sydney).

An agency based in New Zealand is **International Nannies** (Auckland).

For agencies in Britain which deal with Australia and occasionally New Zealand, see: Academy, Au Pair Search Ltd, Childcare International, Occasional & Permanent, Quick Au Pair & Nanny Agency, Sunflowers Childcare, Tinies Childcare andTop Notch Nannies.

Other agencies abroad that send au pairs to Australia/New Zealand include:

Canada: Globetrotters Education Consulting, Le Monde, Scotia Personnel

France: Butterfly et Papillon, Institut Euro' Provence, Inter-Séjours, NACEL, Nurse Au Pair Placement.

Germany: Aupair-Ark.de, Experiment E.V., GSAP

Italy: 3 Esse, International Study Vacation, Roma Au Pair, STI Travels

Netherlands: Activity International, House-o-Orange Au Pairs, S-AuPair Intermediate

Spain: Interclass

ASIA

HONG KONG

Since Hong Kong became a Special Administrative Region of the People's Republic of China in 1997, there has been far less scope for British people working there in any capacity. Chinese families normally employ Cantonese speakers as babysitters and nannies, and even if expat families want to employ a British nanny, the red tape has become more difficult.

Apart from Hong Kong, the Far East affords few opportunities. The traffic in mother's helps is in the opposite direction, with many Asian women, particularly in the Philippines, aspiring to work in Western households. Although there is plenty of wealth in Japan, virtually no Japanese families have foreign staff to care for their children since this is not part of Japanese culture. A smaller proportion of middle-class Japanese women go out to work in the west and the majority still stay at home to look after the children and the household themselves. Of course there are plenty of Western families posted to Japan and throughout Asia who may be looking for a nanny. Contact one of the nanny agencies that operates worldwide (listed at the end of the Country chapters).

Austria

Austria, together with Switzerland, was one of the first countries to host au pairs so there is a well-developed tradition. Well-established agencies between them place more than a thousand au pairs in Austria each year. Most of the families live in the cities of Vienna, Salzburg and Linz, where there are enough au pairs to reduce any feelings of isolation. The agencies will try to place friends who apply together near one another. This is usually possible for the standard stay of September to June, but much less easy for summer placements. Many Austrian families visit the Alps during the summer and this can provide a good opportunity to see some of the most scenic areas in Europe.

The cost of becoming an au pair is high in Austria: the agency fees are usually equivalent to one week's pocket money, while the recommended insurance costs from €170 for six months. The minimum pocket money of €60 per week is about standard in Europe; check the current minimum on the German-language website of the Arbeitsmarktservice website (www.ams.or.at/download/aupair-info.pdf). Au pairs plus normally earn €75-€85 a week. Furthermore Austrian cities have a high cost of living so it is essential to take some money with you for travel and emergencies.

Austrians are reputed to be exacting employers, though it is impossible to generalise. Writing from Austria, Maree Lakey cheerfully reported that she had enjoyed the first three months of her placement, despite the four teenage children's unwillingness to knuckle down to English conversation lessons with her (as agreed) and the substantial amount of housework. However her host mother treated her with respect which in Maree's view makes all the difference. Many Austrian families speak little English, so a grounding in German will make your stay much more tolerable and in any case is a requirement of most placements.

The agencies offer a back-up service and will try to find you another family if things don't work out. They even extend their advisory services to au pairs who have not arranged their families through the agency. Nicola Wenban's relations with her Viennese employers deteriorated over the first few months until she was barely on speaking terms with them and was pointedly excluded (Harry-Potter-like) from any family treats. She found the level of ingratitude for all her hard work and extra hours breathtaking and finally she gave her week's notice. She then went to her agency and poured out her tale of woe; they were very attentive and sympathetic and immediately offered to find her another family. But by then she was so fed up that she was longing to go home to England, and regretted that she had not gone to the agency much earlier. They asked her to fill out an assessment form, which she was delighted to do in the hope of preventing other girls from going through what she had.

FIXING UP A JOB

The long established Catholic agency Auslands-Sozialdienst in Vienna has discontinued its au pair exchanges and the Vienna-based agency *Au-Pair4You has* stepped into the breach. A number of private agents based in cities around Austria offer a service for incoming au pairs. Most are accustomed to dealing with direct applications from abroad, though almost all expect to communicate in German. In addition to the ones in the Directory, here are some to try:

Au-Pair Agentur Calimer, Stelzhamerstr.2/2/9, 4020 Linz (732-666233; fax 732/666244; office@calimero.co.at; www.calimero.co.at). Contact Katerina Unterluggauer.

Au Pair-Agentur Lederle Brigitte, Kaufmännen 40, 6850 Dornbirn (5572-36 809; fax 5572-36 809 – 11; brigitte.lederle@vol.at).

Au-Pair & Family, Blindengasse 52/1/3, 1080 Vienna (tel/fax 1-405 405 0; office@aupair-family.at; www.aupair-family.at). Second office at Ahornstrasse 8, 4481 Asten (676-41 40 150; fax 7224-68359). Contact Jana Varga-Steininger. IAPA member.

AuPair & Nanny for you, Freudenberg 2, 9064 Pischeldorf (4224-29 580; fax 4224-29 581; office@aupair4you.at; www.aupair4you.at). Contact Barbara Gruber-Leitner.

Au-pair Corner, Josef Buchinger Straße 3, 3100 St. Pölten (2742-25 85 36; fax 2742-21080; monika.essenhofer@essenhofer.at; www.au-pair-corner.at). Contact Monika Essenhofer.

Family Business, Hessstrasse 2.2, 3100 St. Pölten (2742-79 990; fax 2742-79 990 20; info@kinderbetreuung.at; www.kinderbetreuung.at).

Friends Au-Pair Vermittlungsagentur, Napoleongasse 7/18, 2301 Gross-Enzersdorf

(2249-4650; office@aupairvermittlung.at; www.aupairvermittlung.at). Contact Alexander Mutzek.
Au pairs in Austria must be aged 18-28. The agency requirements are not usually very strenuous when it comes to childcare, and many inexperienced 18-year-olds are placed, especially if they have done German at GCSE or A level.

> **The agencies can take a long time to reply to correspondence as Ann Derry found:**
> *I arranged an au pair position with a family near Salzburg through an agency. Arranging things was hectic enough and the agency took a long time to reply to my initial application, and things only started moving after a continuous string of phone calls to Vienna. In the end I heard from them just two weeks before I was set to go.*

Of course it is always possible to bypass the services of an agency, either by turning to the internet or keeping your ear to the ground after you arrive, which is what Ann Derry did when she grew dissatisfied with her agency placement:

After three months I moved to another family where things were much better. There was a lot more work, but the atmosphere was so nice that I didn't mind. To find this second job, I didn't use the agency. The 'au-pair grapevine' is very efficient, and when you start asking around, it is amazing how many people know families that need help.

If you want to make contacts who might know of families looking for an au pair, one suggestion is to try the English Church in Vienna on Jauresgasse. Ask if you can attend one of the vicar's weekly get-togethers where you may even get a free meal. Among the church stalwarts several are very familiar with the problems faced by au pairs and, according to Nicola Wenban, are full of advice.

Many possibilities for seasonal au pairing also exist in the mountain resorts of the Tyrol, especially during the winter. Qualified nannies can apply to tour operators like Esprit (185 Fleet Road, Fleet, Hampshire GU51 3BL (01252 618318; recruitment@esprit-holidays. co.uk) or Crystal Holidays (King's Place, Wood St, Kingston-upon-Thames KT1 1JY; 020-7420 2081; www.shgjobs.co.uk). TUI SHG recruits nannies with at least an NNEB or NVQ Level 3 for Thomson as well as Crystal.

If you are job-hunting in a resort, you can get started by babysitting. Ask for permission in the big hotels to put up a notice. Family positions can also be arranged privately as Camilla Lambert did:

I was offered a job as an au pair with a family whose father coached the Austrian ski team and needed extra help during the winter when he was away. This offer was in response to a small ad I had placed in the Tiroler Tageszeitung newspaper. This is the best way to find any kind of job in and around Innsbruck.

REGULATIONS

Au pairs from EU countries will have no trouble sorting out the paperwork in Austria. Officially au pairs from outside the EU must obtain both a work and residence permit *(Beschäftigungsbewilligung)*. Although this can be applied for inside Austria, the process is expensive and time-consuming and some avoid it. Alien au pairs are allowed to stay in Austria for no more then a year and must renew their permit a month before the first six months is up.

If a host family wants to try to obtain a *Beschäftigungsbewilligung* for their non-EU au pair from the US, Canada, Australia, New Zealand, Japan and a few others, they should apply to the local employment office (*Arbeitsmarktservice*) at least two weeks before the au pair is due to arrive. Before the permit can be approved and an *Anzeigebestätigung* issued, the authorities must see an agreement or contract (Ref: 10 Abs 3 FrG, signed by the employer and the au pair) and proof that health and accident insurance cover has been obtained by the au pair. A template of the contract is available on the Austrian Employment Service website (www.ams.or.at/download/aupair-vertrag.pdf). The agency should help with this process and tell the au pair where to take the documents to be stamped (for a fee). If your first language is not English, German, Spanish or Italian, you will have to prove your level of German in order to obtain a visa.

Maree Lakey from Australia, who went from Germany to Austria to au pair, was told by her Austrian au pair agency that she had no chance of obtaining the permit. She therefore took their advice and registered officially as a guest:

I simply did as most non-European au pairs do, which was to de-register myself after the first three months, which was for me at Christmas time when I left the country to visit friends in Germany. After my return in January, I registered again, and after completing another three months, the same procedure again. I never heard of anyone who went through the official procedure of applying for a work permit.

HEALTH AND INSURANCE

Au pairs pay no tax and cannot contribute to the state-run health and social security scheme. EU nationals should be sure to take with them to Austria a European Health Insurance Card (which has replaced the E-111). This can be taken to the Gebietskrankenkasse (regional health insurance office) where forms are available, allowing you to register with a doctor. If you wish to supplement the basic health cover, au pair agencies in Austria can recommend suitable private policies. In some cases families give extra money to cover the cost of insurance.

LEISURE TIME

At one time the Catholic agency Auslands-Sozialdienst ran an active social programme for au pairs in Vienna, which included a club, theatre trips, excursions and so on. Twenty-first century au pairs will have to find their own fun. Most agencies like Au-pair4You hold occasional get-togethers for au pairs and will provide a list of other au pairs in the vicinity with whom you can organise day trips to Salzburg for example, and ski weekends, though these often fall outside the budgets of au pairs.

Several universities and institutes run International Student Clubs which au pairs can enquire about joining. Membership would entitle you to use the bar, TV room and common room with foreign language newspapers. Nicola Wenban and her friend Laura attended one of the University of Vienna's discos and were disappointed to find the room full of middle-aged men from the Middle East. Some of the club's other activities sounded more promising, such as salsa evenings, discussion groups, etc.

Maree Lakey decided to take the initiative in building a social life after she had been in Vienna a short time
I was a very lonely person for the first six weeks in Vienna, until I placed a contact notice on the billboard of the British Bookshop in Vienna. This was a great idea and I got a number of calls, especially from Austrians which was a bonus as I would never have met any Austrians otherwise. It is so true that the Viennese are hard to make friends with, so I was lucky to have found some exceptions. The only trouble with such a contact notice was the unwelcome phone calls I received from a few annoying males, but the children in my family handled this problem quite well when they answered the phone. My social life was at its best during my last two months

> *in Vienna after I met another Aussie au pair at the agency's meeting (we are a rare breed!) and the two of us became regulars at one of the Irish pubs in the city. It didn't take us long to become part of a group mainly consisting of British blokes and we enjoyed many an amusing evening. I really hated to have to leave.*

No less than 17 Irish pubs are listed on the website www.irishabroad.com. There are now three branches of the British Bookshop: at Weihburggasse 24, Mariahilfer Strasse 4, and Albert Schweitzergasse 4A.

Language classes are held at the universities in Vienna, Salzburg, Innsbruck, Graz and Linz as well as various institutes such as the non-profit Internationales Kultur-Institut (www. ikivienna.at) and Goethe Institute in Vienna. Also the folk high schools or *Volkshochschulen* offer German classes throughout Austria. Most courses start either in September/October or January/February. Nicola Wenban was pleased with the IKI course in Vienna (Opernring 7; 1-586 73 21), both for the standard of German teaching and for the social contact. She attended five hours of classes on two evenings a week. The only drawback is that it is so popular with au pairs (especially Swedes) whose common language is English that you have to remain determined to practise German.

The organisation Campus Austria at the University of Vienna (Ebendorferstrasse 10, 1010 Vienna; 1-4277 24102; info@campus-austria.at) comprises 16 language schools all providing German language training. Some courses lead to Goethe Institute qualifications while others lead to the OESD (Austrian Diploma for German as a Foreign Language). Campus Austria publishes a clear pamphlet of the courses on offer and prices, with contact details of its 16 member schools.

Some au pairs have found that it is not as easy to make friends with Austrians as it is with foreigners in Vienna. The Viennese can give the impression of being aloof and image-conscious, even snooty, though they are probably just reserved like the British. Nightlife is expensive and Nicola found that the only night-clubs she could afford were frequented by 'wolf gangs' (men on the prowl).

A quite different form of entertainment can be enjoyed at the Vienna State Opera. Comparatively cheap standing room tickets are sold two or three hours before a performance, though you have to queue to get these.

Outside sophisticated Vienna, people will be friendlier. In the villages the people show a keen interest in any foreigners who choose to come and live in their tight-knit communities; in fact you may receive more attention from the young men of the village than you want.

TRAVEL

No frills airlines have made it much cheaper to fly to Austria than it was a decade ago. Ryanair (www.ryanair.com) now flies from Stansted to Salzburg, Linz, Graz, and Klagenfurt. Flybe connects regional British airports Southampton and Birmingtham with Salzburg as does Thomsonfly which flies from Bournemouth and Conventry. The only cheap airline to fly to Vienna is the German-owned Niki (www.flyniki.co.uk). Scheduled fares to Vienna on Austrian Airlines (0845 601 0948), Lauda Air or British Airways normally have a maximum validity of three months which isn't much use to an au pair. For a specialist travel agency try Austria Travel in Essex (01708 222000; www.austriatravel.co.uk).

Ökista Travel in Vienna ceased its involvement with au pair placement in 2001 and has more recently been taken over by STA Travel as the main youth travel bureau with several branches in Vienna and others in Graz, Linz, Innsbruck and Salzburg.

The under 26 coach fares quoted by National Express from London to Vienna are £79 single, £99 return, with an advance purchase promotional fare of £69 return with fixed dates. Open returns are more expensive (£109).

If you arrange to have time off for a holiday or at the end of your stint as an au pair, you might consider travelling east of Austria into Hungary, which is adjacent and still exceedingly cheap. Weekends in Budapest are entirely feasible. If you are on a tight budget and have some time, don't buy a through ticket to Budapest. It is cheaper to buy one to Hegyeshalom just across the border and then buy a local onward ticket. A more romantic way to make the trip is by boat along the Danube which takes five hours.

DIRECTORY REFERENCES

For agencies based in Austria, see: **Au-Pair4You** (Vienna) and **AuPair Austria** (Vienna). **Personal Touch** in Germany also places au pairs in Austria.

For agencies in Britain which deal with Austria, see: Academy, Nannies of St. James, People & Places, Quick Au Pair & Nanny Agency.

Other agencies abroad that send au pairs to Austria include:

Australia: JCR
Belgium: Services de la Jeunesse Feminine, Stufam
Canada: Le Monde Au Pair, Scotia Personnel
Czech Republic: Au Pair International CZ, British Contact, Student Agency
Finland: Allianssi
France: Accueil International, Euro Pair Services, Fée Revée, France Au Pair Eurojobs, Jeunesse et Nations, Inter-Séjours, Oliver Twist Association
Germany: AupairArk.de, Personal Touch
Greece: Nine Muses
Iceland: Studentaferdir
Italy: Au Pair International, Soggiorni All'Estero per la Gioventù
Netherlands: House-o-Orange Au Pairs, S-Au Pair Intermediate, Travel Active
Peru: Au Pair Peru
Spain: Actividad Au Pair Internacional, Agencia Intercambios, Interclass

Belgium & Luxembourg

Belgium is a country which is often ignored. Sandwiched between France and the Netherlands, its population can be broadly divided between the French-speaking people of Wallonia in the south and those who speak Flemish (which is almost identical to Dutch) in the north. Of course the large number of multinational companies, attracted by the presence of the European Commission in Brussels, creates a huge and fluctuating demand for live-in childcare, though it must be said that nursery provision is so good in the major cities that many families opt for crèches rather than nannies or au pairs.

Most au pairs who want to learn French think only of going to France, rather than to a French-speaking family in Belgium. The French-speaking Belgians (known as Walloons) live mainly in the south and west of the country. Belgian bureaucracy and its strict employment legislation (which insist that au pairs be paid high wages) have dealt a blow to au pairing (described below) and nowadays very few agencies are active in Belgium. The Belgian authorities take the language learning aspect of au pairing seriously and there are plenty of courses available (for monolingual Belgians as well as for foreigners). Like the Dutch, most Flemish people have an excellent grasp of English, which is much less true in French-speaking Belgium where people will expect you to communicate in their language.

There is a continuing demand for qualified nannies and au pairs especially in Brussels. The other main cities in Belgium where there is a reasonable demand for au pairs include Antwerp, Ghent and Ostend which are primarily Dutch speaking cities. Among expatriates in Brussels, English may well be the working language of the household.

> **Searching the vacancies on an internetsite like www.jobvertise.com will bring you to current vacancies posted by the** *Almondbury Agency.* **A typical one might read:**
>
> *An Australian/Thai family living in the city centre of Brussels seek an au pair to help care for their daughter aged 6 years old. Mother is a journalist and father is a diplomat. They live in a 3-bedroom apartment and own 2 gerbils. The au pair will have her own bedroom with shower room. All weekends are free. Although a driver is not needed the au pair will have use of a car if she can drive. The family wish to find an au-pair from the European Union who can provide good references.*

Au pairs are entitled to one week's paid holiday after six months work. Summer au pairs can be placed only infrequently so, as is the case throughout Europe, it is necessary to apply early for these posts, by the middle of May at the latest.

If Belgium is often neglected, Luxembourg is overlooked completely. Yet it is an independent country with a steady demand for live-in childcare. The main language is Luxemburgish, but both German and French are spoken and understood by virtually everyone.

FIXING UP A JOB

Very few agencies in the UK and continental Europe deal with Belgium. For example only one Belgian agency (WEP) is a member of IAPA and it does not place incoming au pairs. A better possibility is to make contact with one of the big Dutch agencies that place au pairs both in the Netherlands and Belgium, namely *S- Au Pairs Intermediate, House-o-Orange* and *Juno Au Pairs.* In addition to these Dutch agencies, all with entries in the Directory, IAPA member Au Pairs Worldwide in the Netherlands places au pairs in Belgium as well as Holland, Germany, etc. (Morgenster 13, Marum, 9363 LH; Postal address: PO Box 36, 9300 AA Roden (tel/fax +31 594-510 801; aupairww@worldonline. nl; www.aupairsworldwide.com).

Indigenous au pair agencies are placing fewer au pairs in Belgium than they once did, though it might be worth giving one of these a try:
Home From Home, Spillemanstraat 1, 2140 Antwerp (+32 3-235 97 20; fax + 3-235 97 19; info@homefromhome.be; www.homefromhome.be). Works in partnership with House-o-Orange Agency in the Netherlands, so that agency's au pairs in Belgium can participate in House-o-Orange Au Pair Club activities. Contact Lut Vereycken or Annemie Delfosse.
Services de la Jeunesse Feminine asbl, rue de Dave 174, 5100 Namur, Belgium (tel/fax +32 81-30 91 35). Belgian branch of Catholic organisation ACISJF/In Via.
Stufam V.Z.W, Vierwindenlaan 7, 1780 Wemmel, Belgium (+32 2-460 33 95; fax +32 2-460 00 71; aupair.stufam@scarlet.be; www.aupair-stufam.be). Contact Lieve Deschuymere.
Most Belgian cities are so accessible from southern England that anyone considering a live-in position with a Belgian family should considering travelling to meet them before signing a contract. The family might be prepared to travel to a Channel port to meet you part way. Despite having no relevant experience beyond having led a girl guide group, Annie Stevens was invited by a family resident in Brussels to an interview in Calais, where she could meet the children before accepting the job.

Belgium's English language weekly publication *The Bulletin* carries job adverts such as live-in positions (normally with English-speaking ex-pat families) and language tuition. The classified advertisements can be seen online at www.xpats.com/classifieds_main.shtml (click on 'Children') where some au pair vacancies are listed among the many more 'Jobs Wanted' advertisements. The magazine is published on Thursdays and can be bought from newsstands for €2.70. An example of a recent advert read 'Mature, reliable and fun au-pair is urgently required for British, single mother living in Brussels. You should be a trustworthy, dynamic and independent person, with a good standard of spoken English.'
Newcomer is a free bi-annual magazine-type supplement published by *The Bulletin* in

March and September. Aimed at new arrivals in Belgium, it carries useful sections called 'Getting to Grips with the Red Tape' and 'Job-Seekers' Guide'. The daily *Le Soir* (rue Royale 120, 1000 Brussels; www.lesoir.be) is also worth consulting for employment and au pair work. The free French-language newspaper *Vlan* is an effective advertising medium for prospective au pairs under the heading 'Garde Malades & Enfants' (www.vlan. be/emploi).

The Federation Infor Jeunes Wallonie-Bruxelles is a non-profit making organisation which co-ordinates 12 youth information offices in French-speaking Belgium. These can give advice on work as well as leisure, youth rights, accommodation, etc. A leaflet listing the addresses is available from the Federation whose Brussels office is at rue Van Artevelde 155, 1000 Brussels (70-233444; www.inforjeunes.be). Among Infor Jeune's services, they operate holiday job placement offices (*Service Job Vacances*) between March and September.

REGULATIONS

The regulations governing the employment of au pairs in Belgium is more rigorous than in other countries in Europe, partly to protect the girls but also to discourage non-EU au pairs from staying on after their au pair stay is over. Rules differ slightly among the three main regions (Dutch-speaking Flanders, French-speaking Wallonia and Greater Brussels) but throughout the country the requirements are now so onerous that several long-established agencies such as WEP (Av. De Jette 26, 1081 Brussels 1081; www.wep.org) no longer bother with incoming placements. The reason the rules changed was that an estimated 80% of East European au pairs were staying on in Belgium after their maximum two years was up. The accession of Hungary, Poland, Lithuania, etc. to the EU in 2004 has alleviated some of the problem, but the strict rules remain.

For EU nationals, the usual rules apply: those arriving in Belgium intending to stay for a period of three months or more should register within eight days at the local Town Hall where the *Administration Communale* will issue either a temporary *certificat d'immatriculation* valid for three months or the one year certificate of registration (*certificat d'inscription au registre des étrangers* or CIRE). In Flanders, the government site with information about visas is only in Flemish (www.vlaanderen.be/werk.

Among the many regulations, the minimum monthly wage for an au pair has risen to €450 for a trifling 20 hours of work a week. Families must also pay for their au pair's health insurance policy (normally €45 a month) and travel expenses (often paid in installments of between €20 and €70 a month). If the au pair is not an EU national, she will need a work permit which costs €250, which is an extra expense for the family. All of these regulations mean that fewer families are choosing to take on the financial burden of employing an au pair.

But some non-EU citizens do tackle the bureaucracy with the help of an agency. They must obtain an authorisation of provisional sojourn from the Belgian Embassy in their home country before arriving in Belgium. The contract with their host family must be approved by the *administration communale* before a one year 'B' work permit can be granted by the regional Office National de l'Emploi (ORBEM in Greater Brussels, FOREM in French-speaking Belgium or VDAB in Flemish-speaking Belgium). To qualify, a document proving that the applicant has a working knowledge of either French or Dutch must be submitted or, alternatively, proof that he or she has registered in a language course in Belgium for a minimum of 15 hours a week, at least two hours every day (which makes it difficult for many to fulfil their childcare duties). Note that there is no obligation on the employing family to pay for the language course, though these tend to be relatively inexpensive in Belgium because of generous state-funding. Those who apply for a visa extension or want to change employers may find that the authorities check to make sure that these au pairs have been attending the required number of language classes. The school must issue a certificate of progress every three months.

Families are limited to no more than three au pairs in total. Au pair stays must begin in July/August or September and cannot last more than 12 months in total, even if the girl changes families in that time. Furthermore the authorities have been known to take five months to process the visas, by which time many families give up on the idea and find alternative childcare arrangements such as day nurseries or (in many cases) taking on an au pair without declaring her, probably an inevitable if unsatisfactory outcome in the circumstances. All the red tape affecting non-EU au pairs means that European girls with the automatic right to work in Belgium are in high demand.

HEALTH AND INSURANCE

According to Belgian law, long stay au pairs must be insured against accidents and illness by inclusion in their host family's insurance policy. This new requirement is as a result of the fact that au pairs were arriving with inadequate cover or policies that expired after two or three months. British au pairs should obtain an EHIC (which replaces the E-128) to cover European nationals for emergency treatment when working or studying abroad for extended periods. Some families obtain insurance from the local *Mutualité/Ziekenfonds* office rather than purchase a more expensive private policy, though this is not strictly permitted. There can be long delays while the insurance is being sorted out, so it is imperative to arrive with private insurance cover for the first few months.

LEISURE TIME

Even in larger Belgian cities, au pairs find it easier to meet the locals than in, say, Paris or Vienna. Annie Stevens found Belgians warm and generous to strangers, which compensated a good deal for her unhappy employment situation. Public transport is on the whole good, even to the suburbs, though suburban services tend to finish about 10pm.

The Orange Au Pair Club (run by *House-o-Orange* in conjunction with Home From Home in Antwerp) organises parties, trips to Paris, regular meetings, etc. Their activities are open only to au pairs placed by them, so it is not possible to bring along a friend to one of their trips or events.

If you are in Brussels and want to meet more English-speaking people, check the listings in *The Bulletin* for entertainments and meetings, as well as the adverts for pubs and discos frequented by the English-speaking community. *Newcomer: An Introduction to Life in Belgium* (mentioned above) is aimed at the affluent expatriate market, and contains some useful information such as a list of English-language bookshops, social clubs, children's library (which you are more likely to visit in working hours than in your leisure time) and French and Dutch courses, though with no indication of fees.

As mentioned, language courses are plentiful and affordable. The same cannot be said of a popular Dutch language text *Taal Vitaal* which costs €70. Try to find a second-hand copy by networking with other au pairs.

TRAVEL

Travel by air can be cheaper than other means. The Antwerp no-frills airline VLM has fares from London City Airport to Brussels and Antwerp starting at €23 one way (plus tax). Ryanair uses Charleroi Airport rather than Brussels International but was fined by the EU for unfair competition (because the municipality of Charleroi gave Ryanair huge incentives to use the airport, thus harming business at Brussels International). As a result Ryanair dropped its Stansted-Charleroi flights but still has a service from Glasgow. Richard Branson's Virgin Express (www.virgin-express.com) is based in Brussels and flies to many European cities, but none in the UK. Cheapest of all are the 'Tiny' promotional fares from BMI (www.flybmi.com) which start at an amazing £7 one way Heathrow to Brussels.

There is no longer a ferry or Hoverspeed service to Ostend or Zeebrugge, so if you take a Dover-Calais crossing you will have to make your way to your Belgian destination from there. The under-26 fare to Brussels on both the train and coach from London is about £40 one way, £60-£80 return.

For travel bookings in Brussels try Connections at 19-21 Zuidstraat (2-550 01 30; www. connections.be).

LUXEMBOURG

Agency placements in Luxembourg are rare. Most positions are found through word of mouth or advertisements in local papers. The online *Lux Bazar* (www.luxbazar.lu) lists as many as 100 jobs under the heading *Emploi: Babysitting* in the autumn, though these are undated. As a longshot you can also check the weekly French language *Le Jeudi* (www. le-jeudi.lu) aimed at foreigners living in Luxembourg.

Luxembourg Accueil Information (10 Bisserwee, L-1238 Luxembourg-Grund; +352 24 17 17; www.luxembourgaccueil.com) is a centre for new arrivals and residents which puts on courses and workshops and may serve as a good potential source of contacts for a job-seeking au pair or nanny. Ask if you can be added to their register of au pairs and babysitters, though they may expect you to show training or experience first. The office is open mornings only. Online au pair agencies may be your best bet. For example at the time of writing, Findaupair (www.findaupair.com) listed a dozen families in Luxembourg looking for live-in help.

The national employment service (Administration de l'Emploi, address below) may be able to advise on au pair, mother's help and nanny positions. A more promising source of leads is the youth and student office Centre Information Jeunes (CIJ, 26 place de la Gare, L-1616 Luxembourg; +352 26 29 32 06; fax +352 26 29 32 03; CIJ@info.jeunes.lu; www. cij.lu). In addition to running a special service for student summer jobs between April and August, it publishes information of interest to prospective au pairs and babysitters. In fact families sometimes contact the CIJ and job vacancies are posted in the reception area.

AFP Services (L'Action Familiale et Populaire) offers regular babysitting training sessions for about €10; contact AFP at 39, bd.Grande-Duchesse Charlotte, L-1331 Luxembourg; +352 46 00 04-1. They are likely to have contacts with families, particularly single mothers, looking for help.

Having previously ratified the European Agreement on Au Pair Placements, Luxembourg has recently renounced it since it has been revealed that young girls who applied for visas as au pairs in accordance with the provisions of the Agreement were forced into prostitution. Applicants for an au pair visa must regularise their status by submitting four copies of an 'Accord Placement Au Pair' to the national employment service, the Administration de l'Emploi (ADEM) at 10 rue Bender, L-1229 Luxembourg (352-478 53 00; www.adem. public.lu). The Accord amounts to a contract and must set out in detail the conditions of work and be signed by both the employer and the au pair. In the case of non-EU nationals, the Accord must be obtained before entry to the country. ADEM also operates a *Service Vacances* for students looking for summer jobs; contact the youth employment department for more information (800-24646; info.jeu@adem.public.lu).

Employing families in Luxembourg are obliged to register their au pairs with the social security system. After arrival, the employer should go to the Caisse Nationale d'Assurance-Maladie des Ouvriers (125 route d'Esch, L-1471 Luxembourg; +352 40 112 1; or a local branch) to fill out the appropriate declaration.

DIRECTORY REFERENCES

No agencies in Belgium included in the Directory arrange incoming placements. For au pair agencies based in the Netherlands that deal with Belgium, see: **House-o-Orange** (The Hague)**, Juno Au Pairs** (Schiedam) and **S- Au Pairs Intermediate** ('s-Hertogenbosch).

For au pair agencies based in Britain which deal with Belgium, see: Abacus, Academy, Childcare International, Hyde Park International, Jolaine, Konnex and Sunflowers Childcare.

Other agencies abroad that send au pairs to Belgium are:

Australia: JCR
Czech Republic: Au Pair International CZ, Student Agency
Finland: Allianssi
France: Inter-Séjours, Soames
Germany: Felicity Nannies, In Via
Greece: Nine Muses
Italy: Roma Au Pair
Spain: Interclass
Switzerland: Pro Filia
USA: goAuPair

Canada

Far more people dream of living and working in Canada, whether temporarily or permanently, than can ever fulfil their dreams. In reaction to the high levels of immigration in the past and a worrying rate of unemployment, the Canadian government has actively promoted a 'Canada-only' policy when it comes to employment. Working for families is one of the few exceptions and provides one of the most straightforward ways of acquiring the chance to live in Canada. Some estimates indicate that as many as half of foreign nannies apply for residency at the end of two years.

Although there is a demand for British and European nannies among the professional classes, particularly in Toronto, Vancouver and Calgary, that demand is not as great as it was ten years ago. This is on simple grounds of expense. About five years ago, the federal government of Canada abolished the licensing system for nanny agencies which has meant that many new agencies have come on the scene, some operating solely on the internet, specialising in bringing in nannies from developing countries, especially from the Philippines. Because the agents are unregulated, they can charge nannies thousands of dollars and therefore charge their client families much less. It has become less profitable for agencies to confine their placements to European nannies who are not willing to pay high registration fees. Client families are unwilling to pay the high fees necessary to cover costs plus a profit for the agencies if they can get a Filipina nanny for a third of the cost.

Yet many families are so affluent that they are prepared to shoulder the extra expense of hiring a European nanny and in a few cases may even offer extra incentives, such as free air fares, to nannies with special skills or experience. Your living quarters are usually spacious and comfortable and you will probably enjoy a relatively high standard of living. Like American employers, Canadians are usually very friendly and open and unhierarchical with their live-in staff. Carol Dredge was a 19-year-old secretary when she decided to go to Canada for a year:

> *I was bored and desperately needed a change. When I met the family, we just sort of clicked and quickly became more like friends than employers. The parents were very easy-going and informal though the children were a bit spoilt. Really it was one of the best years of my life.*

With any luck you should be able to develop as relaxed a relationship with the parents as with the children. There are very few cases of nannies breaking their one-year contract due to a failure to get on with their families, which must be a good sign.

> **Another nanny confirms that employers take a laid-back attitude provided you can cultivate a good relationship with the children:**

> *It was probably my childcaring experience and love of kids that got me the job: I am a rotten cook and a fairly pedestrian housekeeper, but the family put up with all that because the kids liked me. The job wasn't bad; when the kids were at school, I had hours to myself to potter round, do some cleaning and prepare dinner. More often than not, I read or watched TV waiting for the kids to come home at 3.30pm.*

Many of the expectations will be similar to those encountered in the US; for example there is a very strong preference for non-smokers, swimmers and car drivers. A large proportion of Canadian families own (or rent on an annual basis) a lakeside or mountain holiday home, usually referred to in Canada as a 'summer cottage'. One ex-nanny described her spare time, 'hiking, water-skiing, cycling, ice skating and skiing - Canada is made for the outdoors lover.'

The federal government sets out guidelines for hours, time off, salary and deductions which most families and all agencies in Canada abide by. As of 2005/6, the legally enforced minimum hourly wage varied among the provinces from $6.25 in Newfoundland to $8 in British Columbia. For example most nannies working in Ontario earn the minimum wage of $7.45 for the first 40 hours plus some extra for babysitting. One of the agencies gives an example of a nanny earning about $1,550 a week less deductions for board and lodging of $370. Further deductions will be made for taxes, unemployment insurance and pension amounting to about $230, leaving a net wage of $950. Note that if you leave Canada, you can claim for a partial refund of pension and other contributions. The net salary of a nanny in Canada will fall into the range $800-$1,200+ which allows a careful nanny to save.

Working as a nanny in Canada has more status attached to it than au pairing in the USA, and the conditions of work reflect this. The wages are higher too, especially now that the Canadian dollar has strengthened against the US dollar over the past few years. Canadian au pairs (a rare breed) earn about C$100 a week, which is far less than the US$139 earned by au pairs in America. Canadian nanny salaries are based on a 40 or 44-hour week depending on the contract. Extra babysitting should be paid as overtime, usually time and a half, for example C$12. The offer of employment which you and your employer signed at an early stage of the recruiting procedure, normally serves as a contract setting out hours and duties. Most of the families who employ nannies comprise two working parents, so you normally have sole charge during the day and weekends off. There is usually a reasonable amount of flexibility about how you handle the children and what you do in your time off. You are entitled to two weeks paid holiday a year.

There are fewer jobs available for British nannies in Montreal or other French-speaking areas, since Québecois agencies and families tend to look to France for their live-in helpers. However there are pockets of French-speakers throughout Canada, and it is a good idea to ascertain the language of the household before accepting a family. This is something which Pam Robb signally failed to do:

Just prior to Christmas, a family in Edmonton offered me a position since their previous nanny had left suddenly and they needed a replacement immediately. During my first evening I was to discover a very important fact which had not been evident from our correspondence: French was the dominant language spoken in their house. The twin girls of 4 years spoke only in French; luckily 8-year old Oren spoke English, French and Hebrew. That first week was tough with Rachel, Naomi and me struggling to understand each other. (The twins learnt English quicker than I learnt French!) Joining the family in the living room in the evenings was difficult, since the time was spent trying to make conversation in French, listening to the stereo in French, or listening to Mr. Kaufman play his guitar... often in French!

Pam obviously was landed with an atypical Canadian family. Not only were they French-speaking and strict observers of the dietary rules of Judaism (something else of which Pam had not been forewarned), but they disapproved of television and didn't own one.

FIXING UP A JOB

Fewer agencies in Britain are prepared to try to place nannies in Canada than was once the case. Two agencies that you might try are *Childcare International* and the *Janet White Agency* (run by Janet White, herself a Canadian) though in recent years the latter has been asked to supply far fewer nannies to Canada than a few years ago (for the reasons given above). Agencies in Canada accept direct applications, though it is probably more reassuring to have an agent who is familiar with the visa application process in your country.

A search of the internet will take you to some Canadian agencies though some are more experienced in bringing in nannies from countries like the Philippines and Hong Kong rather than Europe. In all cases, nannies must satisfy the government's Live-in Caregiver requirements. For example try www.Canadiannanny.ca, an online database that links nannies and au pairs with parents looking for experienced part-time or full-time child care in their home.

Here is a small selection of agencies in addition to the ones in the Directory of Agencies:

Able Nannies (New Westminster) Ltd. Royal Square, P.O. Box 51032, New Westminster, British Columbia V3L 2P6 (604-540-7453; fax 604-540-7459)

Calgary Able Nannies Unlimited, 350, 604 First Street SW, Calgary, Alberta T2P 1M7 (403-266-2890; fax 403-265-3287)

Global Nannies & Caregivers Association, Employment & Marketing Consultants, 112-1151 Mt. Seymour Road, North Vancouver, BC, V7H 2Y4 Canada (604-464-5707; fax 604-464-5759; globalna@shaw.ca). Contact Radu Podoleanu or Evelyn Gawat.

Home Helpers Placement Services, Carlton Street, Suite 1403, Toronto, Ontario M5B 1J3 (416-596-0855; info@homehelpers.com)

International Au-Pair, 1334 West 7th Avenue, Vancouver, British Columbia V6H 3W5 (604-734-0188)

International Nannies & Homecare Ltd., 204 - 402 West Pender Street, Vancouver, BC Canada V6B 1S5 (604-609-9925; fax 604-609-9927; info@internationalnannies.com; www.internationalnannies.com). Local offices throughout Canada: Kamloops, Kelowna and Nanaimo in British Columbia; Calgary, Edmonton, Saskatoon, Winnipeg, plus Barrie, Toronto, Windsor, London and Ottawa in Ontario; and Montreal in Quebec.

Paragon Personnel Ltd, Suite 1, 2nd Floor, 4529A Hastings Street, Burnaby, British Columbia V5C 2K3 (604-298-6633; fax 604-298-6655; paragon@smartt.com). Member of Better Business Bureau for 22 years.

Nannies on Call, 308 – 788 Beatty St, Vancouver, BC V6B 2MI (604-734-1776; fax 604-648-8362; info@nanniesoncall.com; www.nanniesoncall.com). High-end agency serving Vancouver and region.

Nanny Finders Directory Agency, 204-8055 Anderson Road, Richmond, B.C. V6Y 1S2 (604-272-1622; fax 604-272-1627; hire@nannyfindersbc.com; www.nannyfindersbc.com)

Nanny Providers Canada, 45 Sheppard Ave East, 9th Floor, Ste.12 (416-628-8388; canada@childcare.net; www.canada-nanny.com). Part of Be International Recruiting which also operates *Au Pair Canada* from the same address (see entry).

Selective Personnel International, 12 Irwin Avenue, Toronto, Ontario M4Y 1K9 (416-962-5153; selective@on.aibn.com). Placement agency in business since 1967 that recruits and markets caregivers, nannies, nurses and housekeepers from all over the world.

Trafalgar Personnel, Miller Mews at 323 Church St., Unit 17, Oakville, Ontario, L6J 1P2 (905-849-6520; fax 905-849-6921; mmartin@interlog.com; www.trafalgarpersonnel.com). Contact Marna E Martin. In business since 1979.

It is possible to arrange a job on your own via contacts or advertisements. Pam Robb found her job in Edmonton by answering a magazine ad. Advertised jobs are likely to be in smaller towns where agencies are less accessible.

Many domestic jobs are advertised in Canadian papers as Miss T. Lye from Malaysia discovered when she was in Toronto:

After looking through the classifieds in the Toronto Star, the main tabloid, I called up several numbers for nannying. Most were unwilling to employ me without papers, but I found one job nannying and housekeeping for a good wage. As I didn't pay taxes or rent, my wage allowed me to save a considerable amount of money.

The *Vancouver Sun* also has a classification 'Domestic & Daycare Jobs' as does the *Province*, the other main Vancouver paper. Check the Classified section online (http://workingvancouverjobs.canada.com) and search for 'Childcare/Nannies'.

Myriam Nguyen, resident in France, struck off independently to find a family in Canada, with the help of the free *Vancouver Courier*:

I was really broke but I found out that the Courier was offering a free ad to anyone who would bring three cans of food to be donated to a food bank. Of course it was just a temporary offer but it really saved my life. Two days later I received the first call and I took the job, though I did get about five other phone calls later. The family was very nice. They asked me whether I wanted to be declared or paid under the table. I chose not to be declared and was paid $7 an hour, and worked 25 hours a week looking after a sweet two year old girl, no housework required. Three months after I started, I moved in with the family which meant I didn't have to pay $300 rent for my basement apartment.

I got my second job after responding to an ad, again in the Vancouver Courier. I was still paid minimum wage, however the duties were much more demanding: two children who bit and screamed at first, and 50% housework including two loads of laundry every day. I was also offered to clean the three bathrooms but they paid me an extra $40 each time which, I think, is pretty generous. Basically, I am very satisfied with my stay in Vancouver. Childcare jobs are quite easy to find, either through agencies or newspapers. After you get to know some people, you often hear about jobs available.

RED TAPE

The 'Live-in Caregiver Program' exists in Canada because there is a shortage of Canadian citizens to fill live-in positions with Canadian families. In order to be eligible to apply, prospective nannies must meet three basic criteria. They must have sufficient ability in English or French to be able to communicate effectively in an unsupervised setting. They must have successfully completed a course of study which is equivalent to completion of Canadian secondary school (normally five GCSEs). Finally, they must have sufficient formal training or sufficient relevant work experience. Formal training means they must have successfully completed a relevant course of at least six months duration comprising full-time classroom study. Relevant work experience means at least one year of full-time paid employment as a nanny (or nurse, teacher, etc.) including at least six months of continuous employment with one employer within the previous three years. Note that the training need not have been consecutive and may include courses taken at school, though it must include first aid and CPR.

The fourth requirement is that you must have an offer of employment which has been validated by a Human Resources Department Centre in Canada (equivalent of a Jobcentre). This means that unless you have made personal contact with a Canadian family who want to hire you, it is necessary to go through an agency.

For details of the Live-in-Caregiver Program, write to the Immigration Section of the Canadian High Commission (38 Grosvenor St, London W1K 4AA); mark 'LCP' in the top right hand corner of a large self-addressed stamped envelope. Otherwise check details on the website of Citizenship & Immigration Canada (www.cic.gc.ca/english/pub/caregiver). Note that anyone with a job fixed up in Quebec must comply with separate and additional Quebec immigration procedures (see www.immigration-quebec.gouv.qc.ca/anglais/immigration/temporary-worker/caregiver.html).

Despite rumours a couple of years ago that Canada was going to allow a limited number of Europeans to enter Canada on an au pair basis, no new programme has been implemented. Europeans who want to live with a Canadian family in exchange for some childcare and domestic duties will have to do so on a tourist visa. The alternative for Britons, Australians and New Zealanders is to enter Canada with a working holiday visa. In the UK the British Universities North America Club provides the easiest route to spending a year in Canada. BUNAC (16 Bowling Green Lane, London EC1R 0QH; 020-7251 3472) offers three programmes: for students, gap year students and non-students. Work Canada is for both full-time tertiary level students aged 18-30 (departures mostly in summer) and for non-students aged 18-35, and Gap Canada is for candidates with a confirmed place at university who depart between October and December. All must prove that they intend to return to the UK. Early application is advised because of the quotas set by the Canadian government. The great majority of participants go to Canada without a pre-arranged job and spend their first week or two job-hunting.

The majority of working holiday makers work in hotels and tourist attractions, especially in the Rockies, though there is no reason why the visa cannot be used by an au pair or nanny. The Montréal agency *Le Monde Au Pair* invites applications from incoming au pairs though it mainly sends Canadian au pairs abroad. At one time *Au Pair Canada* did try to match foreign applicants with Canadian families but its activities now are all in the other direction.

Once a live-in caregiver has been matched with a family, probably via an agency in Europe or Canada, she will be sent details of the family and a validated offer of employment. A copy of this will also be sent to the Canadian High Commission in the country of residence then the High Commission will send on further instructions on submitting the application accompanied by proof of training/experience. The fee for processing applications is C$150.

When your application has been approved, you will be sent instructions about the compulsory medical examination. You cannot choose just any doctor but must go to one of the private doctors specified by the High Commission; depending on where you live, there may be no choice. This will incur a further expense of £100-£150 and add up to three months to the processing time. The examination is very thorough including blood tests and chest X-ray so there is not much point in applying unless you are in excellent health. Once the certificate of good health has been sent to the High Commission, you should receive the work permit within a month.

This means that the whole process takes on average three to four months. Because there can be unexpected delays, it is unwise to buy a ticket with fixed dates before you receive the permit. Kathryn Halliwell, who was applying from New Zealand, made this mistake:

The red tape was supposed to take no more than six weeks. In actual fact I had to pay for a private courier service to get my passport and work permit back from the Canadian Consulate in Sydney in time to catch my flight. This was after repeated phone calls to Sydney to remind them that I existed.

In the long waiting period, you should keep in touch with your host family and try to learn as much about them as possible. You might also want to take driving lessons, since being able to drive is almost as essential a skill in Canada as it is in the US.

The employment authorisation will be valid for one employer, though it can be changed within Canada as long as your subsequent job is as a live-in child-carer. If you leave your job prematurely on good grounds, you should be eligible for unemployment benefit while you look for another job, since you will have been paying into the scheme. The authorisation can be renewed within Canada for a further year (again for a fee). After completing two years, you are eligible to apply for an open work permit (one which allows you to take any job in Canada) and eventually landed immigrant status, i.e. permanent residence.

HEALTH AND INSURANCE

Eventually you will become eligible to participate in the subsidised or free health scheme which operates in your province. For example the British Columbia Medical Plan and OHIP (the Ontario Health Insurance Plan) cost $50-$60 a month. Live-in child-carers in Alberta are eligible to join the Alberta Health Care Insurance Plan as long as they apply within 90 days of arrival in the province; the monthly premium for a single person is $44; ring 403-427-1432 for details. In some cases you are eligible as soon as you arrive; however there is usually a time lag of up to 90 days when it is a good idea to have private cover. If you fail to fix up something ahead of time and there is going to be a period when you will not have any cover, you can buy emergency cover after arrival. The ETFS brokerage in North Bay Ontario (1-800-526-7420; www.ecanadianinsurance.com) sells a 'Visitors to Canada' policy offering any amount of cover from a budget $10,000 to the maximum $150,000, for a reasonable cost for those under 30. Blue Cross also offer daily cover; pick up an application form in any drug store and apply within five days of arrival. These may work out cheaper than taking out a travel insurance policy before you leave home, but will cover only medical emergencies.

LEISURE TIME

Once you get on the nanny circuit you should have no trouble building up a social life. Most agencies in the major cities are active in running a social programme for nannies. In some cases an agency newsletter informs nannies of upcoming events (e.g. skiing trips, new arrivals' tea parties, etc.) and also advises on practical matters such as how to obtain a provincial driving licence (which is compulsory after residing in the province of Ontario for three months), recipes popular with Canadian children, etc. Local community centres sometimes organise regular coffee mornings for nannies and their charges.

Even without the help of a local agency, you will eventually bump into other nannies from a range of countries and other expatriate Britons. One nanny who arranged her job independently felt lonely and cut off until she met another nanny. This came about when she boarded a city bus and the driver introduced them.

According to government guidelines, all nannies must get a minimum of two weeks of paid holiday a year plus 1½ or 2 days off a week (quite often on weekends), plus statutory holidays. This allows a reasonable amount of time for seeing some of the country and perhaps taking up a new sport such as skiing or skating.

Most nannies want to cross the border into the US at some point. British citizens can purchase a visa at the border for US$6 (payable only in US currency).

TRAVEL

A sample return fare between London and Toronto for travel outside the peak season will be as low as £200 plus £70 in taxes, however a bargain fare on Air Canada with a 12-month validity would probably be about £150 more than that. One-way fares start at £120 plus £40 tax. It is always worth checking the fares of the Ottawa-based airline Zoom Airlines (www.flyzoom.com) though very few flights are available to Toronto for less than £300 (including tax). If you can't afford the flight, ask your agency about the possibility of borrowing the sum from your future employers, and repaying it out of your first few months' salary.

DIRECTORY REFERENCES

For agencies based in Canada, see: **ABC Nannies Canada Inc** (Vancouver, BC), **Au Pair**

Canada (Toronto Ont), **Donald Fraser Foreign Nanny Placement Agency** (Montréal, Québec), **Helping Hands Caregiver Agency** (Newmarket, Ont), **Le Monde Au Pair** (Montréal, Québec), **Opti-Mum Childcare** (Vancouver), **Nannies and Seniors Caregivers Inc** (Vancouver, BC), **Philglobe International Inc** *(*Montréal, Qué), **QC Home Support Services** (London, Ontario), **Sapphire Personnel Inc** *(*Barrie, Ont) and **Scotia Personnel Ltd** (Halifax, Nova Scotia).

For nanny and other agencies in Britain which deal with Canada see: Academy Au Pair & Nanny Agency, Childcare International Ltd, Eden Childcare, Janet White Agency, Sunflowers Childcare.

Other agencies abroad that send nannies to Canada are:

Australia: Au Pair Australia, Childcare Team, JCR Au Pairs and Nannies
Belgium: Services de la Jeunesse Feminine
Czech Republic: Au Pair International CZ
France: Inter-séjours, Nacel, Nurse Au Pair Placements
Germany: Aupair-Ark.de, Experiment E.V., Personal Touch Au Pair Service
Ireland: Job Options Bureau
Italy: Celtic Childcare, STI Travels
Netherlands: House-o-Orange Au Pairs
New Zealand: International Nannies, International Working Holidays

France

The demand for foreign au pairs in France is strong and, as throughout Europe, the supply of au pairs from Eastern Europe has increased to fill the demand. In France there are no qualifications equivalent to the British ones like CACHE and some in the industry have suggested that childcare in France has a low status, with many people assuming that if you look after children, you do it because you cannot find a better job.

One advantage for prospective au pairs who do not have a whole year to spare or simply want a taste of the French way of life, is that summer placements are very common, some for as short a period as four weeks. Demand for experienced nannies to work for tour operators is booming and anyone with a childcare qualification or references should be able to fix up a job for the summer or winter season (see Introduction). Even au pairs can sometimes find seasonal resort jobs. Lucy Sumner looked after the children of a hotel-owning family from December to May in Monetier-les-Bains near the Italian border:

> *My job involved two hours cleaning the family apartment and baby-sitting from 5pm until M. and Mme. returned from the hotel which they ran ... often after midnight. In addition to free afternoons, I was entitled to 1½ days off which they scrupulously adhered to, and so I had plenty of time for skiing. As I was willing to make the effort, I soon got to know the locals and became completely absorbed in the village life. I thoroughly enjoyed every aspect of my time in France.*

French people are less often bilingual than Germans or Scandinavians (which may or may not prove that they are as culturally chauvinist as they are often reputed to be) so, unless your French is fairly good, you will feel excluded, especially at the beginning of your stay. In any case a basic knowledge of French is usually essential for agency placements of any duration in France.

> **On the other hand, many au pairs eager to improve their French are frustrated in their attempts, as Natalia de Cuba was:**
> *I found that the French I learned with the kids was limited to 'Stop' and 'Come here' and 'What are you doing?' while the mother was fluent in English. I learned a great deal more with friends I met outside work.*

Inevitably some families expect too much work from their au pairs, but (statistically-speaking) the French do not seem to be as demanding as some other nationalities and are less interfering in how the children are treated and the housework done. If your charges are of school age, you may find that they won't have many idle hours for you to fill since the French educational system keeps them occupied with their studies for much of the time (though in some regions school children have Wednesdays off for extra-curricular activities, when they may well be your sole responsibility).

Although many urban French families live in rented flats, au pairs are normally given their own room. It is common, especially in Paris, to be given the garret room, formerly the maid's quarters (called *une chambre de bonne*) with a washbasin and perhaps a hotplate. This arrangement suits many au pairs since it provides a certain level of privacy. Kathryn Kleypas's response is not atypical when she reported that 'the parents were very very reserved and had a hard time communicating things to me; I was often expected to guess what they might be trying to say'.

Despite problems, the joys of living in Paris are self-evident (even in the wake of the immigrant riots of 2005). With luck your employers will allow you to take the children (especially if they are under school age) on excursions to the Eiffel Tower, the Georges Pompidou Centre, the Musée d'Orsay, the Luxembourg Gardens (where you will find au pairs of every nationality walking the children) and so on. One problem often encountered by au pairs hoping to experience Paris is that they find themselves living in a distant suburb. Quite a few foreigners are too hasty in arranging what seems at the outset a cushy number and only gradually realise how little they enjoy the company of children and how isolated they are. At least with a *carte orange* (see the section on Leisure Time below), trips into central Paris are cheap, if time-consuming. Unless you actively like small children, it might be better to look for a free room in exchange for minimal babysitting (e.g. 12 hours a week).

Matt Tomlinson went into his au pair job in the country near Paris with his eyes open:

I'd heard too many horror stories from overworked and underpaid au pair friends to be careless, so chose quite carefully from the people who replied to my notice on the upstairs notice board of the British Church (just off the rue de Faubourg St Honoré). My employers were really laid back, in their mid-20s so more like living with an older brother and sister. The little boy was just over two whilst the little girl was three months old, and they were both completely adorable. On the whole it was great fun. Baking chocolate brownies, playing football and finger-painting may not be everybody's idea of a good time but there are certainly worse ways to earn a living (and learn French at the same time).

Although it is still more difficult for men than women to find au pair placements, France seems to be streets ahead of some other European countries in this respect.

> **Iain Croker confirms this:**
> *I have had a thoroughly rewarding and enjoyable year as an au pair in France - so much so that I'm going back again in September for another year. Certainly in France there are quite a few male au pairs - four in my village near Fontainebleau alone. In my experience the boys tend to get placed in families with a lot of energetic children or families that have traditionally had a large turn-over of au pairs. After*

> *a year in the sticks with four kids I feel I have proved myself and my agency have offered me one of their best placements in Paris, one child and my own apartment. By the way, my agency (Soames International) is great.*

The pocket money for au pairs in France is well regulated and is at least €60 a week plus in most cases a weekly contribution of €20 to pay for language classes. Mothers' helps should earn at least €200 a week and a nanny with a qualification €300. In addition, au pairs in or near Paris are normally given the *carte orange* (travel pass) which is worth about €52 a month (valid for travel on the métro and RER system).

The standard working week for au pairs consists of 5½ hours per day Monday to Saturday, with variations of course, as reported by Tracie Sheehan (who nevertheless greatly enjoyed her job near Geneva):

The law stating that an au pair should not work more than 5½ hours a day definitely does not apply to me, or for that matter any of my au pair friends. My day is usually 8.30am to 7.30pm, though I only mind one little boy who goes to school, so I always have my afternoons free. But the housework is not too taxing and when the weekend comes the mother (a single parent) literally forbids me even to clear up after breakfast. She takes a genuine interest in my life here and in Ireland and includes me on any family outings. I have been very lucky. I know one au pair who has to mind five kids, do all the cooking and only gets Sunday afternoons off. She is treated like a servant by the kids, and the parents are not very family-like towards her.

As usual it is impossible to generalise about the kind of treatment you can expect.

For girls who want to concentrate on their studies and not commit themselves to a full au pair workload, there are positions available for demi pairs. In exchange for 12 hours of work per week, demi pairs receive room and board but no pocket money.

FIXING UP A JOB THROUGH AN AGENCY

Au pairing has always been a favoured way for young women to learn French and, increasingly, for young men too. Dozens of agencies in all European countries can arrange placements and some specialise in France. One of the first places you should turn is Frenchaupairs.com. With a postal address in the UK (PO Box 68, Whitchurch, Shropshire) and a fax number (0012069 849698), they mainly work over the internet, bringing French au pairs to the UK and placing au pairs of all nationalities in France as well as Belgium, Switzerland, etc.

The majority of European agencies listed in this book make placements in France, and you may want to compare the services offered by several. While some agencies charge nothing to applicants who apply directly, others do charge a registration fee which can be steep (€160+). Some au pair services are incorporated into language schools which make their in-house language course compulsory.

A small number of established agencies are members of UFAAP, the Union Francaise des Associations Au Pair, an umbrella group set up in 1999, based at present at *Euro Pair Services* in Paris. Contact details for the member agencies are included on their website www.ufaap.org. In addition to the more than a dozen agencies with entries in the Directory, the following are active both in Paris and the provinces:

Acatel (Association Culturelle Artistique Touristique d'Enseignement et de Loisirs), 82 Bd du Général de Gaulle, 06340 La Trinité, Nice (4-93 54 64 54; fax 4-93 27 28 91; acatel@ aol.com). Au pair opportunities in the south part of France.

Alliance Culturelle Internationale (A.C.I.), 4 Av, Félix Faure, 06000 Nice (4-93 13 44 13; fax 4-93 92 58 85). Has been placing au pairs mainly in Provence and Cote d'Azur since 1963.

Alliance Francaise Marseille Provence, 310 rue Paradis, 13008 Marseille (4-96 10 24

60; fax: 4-96 10 24 69; info@alliancefrmarseille.org; www.alliancefrmarseille.org). Language course at Alliance Francaise are compulsory.

Apitu, La Gaverière, 35270 Combourg (2-99 73 22 36; apitu@apitu.com; www.apitu.com). Member of UFAAP. Minimum stay of 2 months to study French and live with a family in Brittany, Normandy, the Loire or Paris. Partner agency with Good Morning Europe (see entry).

Atout France International – Lyon, 9 rue Roger Lenior, 69100 Villeurbanne (Lyon) (4-72 65 91 15; fax 4-72 65 93 02; www.atout-fr-international.com).

Au Pair South of France, Av De Rimiez 183, 06100 Nice (6-12 67 80 55; gerald@webstore.fr). Contact Gerald Lhonneux.

Bretagne Au Pair, 15 rue Jeanne d'Arc, 35480 Messac (2-99 50 88 25; bretagneaupair@aol.com)

Les Enfants d'abord, 4 avenue Berthelot, 69007 Lyon (4-72 73 11 46; info@lesenfantsdabord. fr; www.lesenfantsdabord.fr). Most host families live in eastern France near the Swiss border and Lyon. Placements from Christmas to Easter in alpine ski resorts.

Goelanguse, 26 rue Vignon, 75009 Paris (1-43 12 55 99; fax 1-43 12 50 81; goelangues@goelangues.org; www.goelangues.org)

Mary Poppins, 4 place de la Fontaine, La Fontanil, 38120 St Egrève (Geneva) (4-76 75 57 33; mary.Poppins@wanadoo.fr; http://assoc.wanadoo.fr/marypoppins.aupair). UFAAP member with placements in Rhône Alpes, Auvergne and Provence.

Ouest Au Pair, 68 Boulevard des Belges, 44300 Nantes (2-51 89 96 75; ouest.au.pair@tiscali.fr; www.ouestaupair.org). Au pairs placed in Brittany, the Loire and Poitou Charentes. Member of UFAAP. Contact Morgane Bernard.

Perlangues, 1 Impasse De La Boissee, 91080 Courcouronnes, 91080 (1-60 77 35 00; fax 1-60 79 11 34; perlangues@wanadoo.fr; www.perlangues.com). IAPA member.

The most exotic address of any French au pair agency must surely be Guadeloupe which is where the Lingpair Agency is located (211 Résidence les Sylphides, 97139 Abymes, Guadeloupe; tel/fax +590 91 04 55; http://perso.wanadoo.fr). They have been known to place au pairs, au pairs plus and mother's helps in the Caribbean islands of Guadeloupe and Martinique as well as in Europe; however there is some doubt over whether these activities continue.

If you have a specific destination in mind contact the nearest bureau, though most do not confine themselves to the local area. Until recently there seemed to be a shortage of agencies in northern France, however several of the agencies listed above now deal with families in Brittany and Normandy.

Almost all agencies require a medical certificate and a basic knowledge of French, though the latter requirement is flexible. Agencies will try to accommodate applicants with a weak knowledge of French by placing them in bilingual families, families with infants, or ones where mainly cleaning is needed. Requirements vary; for example, some will place applicants aged between 25 and 30 while others confine their placements to younger candidates. The deadline for summer placements is usually the end of March, though some agencies accept applications for summer jobs until early May. The preferred summer period lasts from the end of June to the middle of September. For shorter summer placements, au pairs are often given no more than a couple of days notice of their destination. August is the month for holidays throughout France, so there are some short-term placements for the month, usually in the country or by the sea.

It is also possible to fix up an au pair job through an agency on the spot, though not during the summer months (when au pair agency employees, like everyone else, take holiday). *AFJE* says that they can generally place a girl in central Paris within a fortnight of arrival, and will help her find affordable accommodation while she is waiting. Being on location while your agency is trying to place you has the usual advantage that you can meet the parents and children before committing yourself to a job with them. If you are considering this method, ascertain from your agency before travelling to France how prompt placement normally is, since it may be difficult part-way through a term.

Qualified and/or experienced nannies can easily find resort jobs for both the summer and winter seasons via tour operators in the UK and France. Links to many of these are available on the specialist ski recruitment websites like www.natives.co.uk mentioned in the introductory section on Working for Tour Operators and the French specialist Ski Staff (www.skistaff.co.uk).

Powder Babies is a new childcare service based in Morzine in the Portes du Soleil which was set up in 2005/6. They hire qualified nannies with first-aid training and a current CRB certificate to work from mid-December to the end of April. The job entails looking after children of all ages in clients' chalets, picking them up from ski school, cooking their lunch, evening babysitting, etc.; further details are available by ringing 07739314253 or emailing info@powderbabies.co.uk.

Some tour operators active in France who hire nannies for the winter and sometimes also summer season include:

Cheeky Monkeys Morzine, Chalet le Roncherai, 1650 Route de la Manche, 74110 Morzine, France (01273 729297; jobs@cheekymonkeysmorzine.com; www. cheekymonkeysmorzine.com).

Chilly Powder, BP 116, 74110 Morzine, France (UK: 020-7289 6958; France: 4-50 74 75 21; fax 4-50 79 01 48; enquiries@chillypowder.com; www.chillypowder.com). Ski operator offering crèche facilities.

Esprit Holidays Ltd, 185 Fleet Road, Fleet, Hants. GU51 3BL (01252 618318; recruitment@ esprit-holidays.co.uk; www.esprit-holidays.co.uk). Nannies should have NNEB, NVQ3, BTEC or RGN qualification.

First Choice Holidays, Kings House, Wood St, Kingston, Surrey KT1 1JG (Recruitment hotline 0845 055 0255; www.shgjobs.co.uk). 150 children's reps and nannies are hired for flexible periods between March and October. Must have NNEB, BTEC or NVQ level 3 in Childcare, a Diploma in Nursery Nursing or an equivalent UK qualification.

Kids Etcetera, No. 8 Arolaz 1, 73550 Meribel Les Allues, Savoie, France (tel/fax 4-79 00 71 39; shirls@kidsetc.co.uk; www.kidsetc.co.uk). Contact Shirley O'Neill who employs nannies in Méribel.

Mark Warner, tel 0870 033 0760; www.markwarner.co.uk/recruitment. Employs nannies in Corsica between April and October, and in French ski resorts between November and April.

Merinannies, Birch House, Birtley Coppice, Market Harborough, Leics. LE16 7AS (07860 925 055; www.merinannies.co.uk). About 10 private nannies for Méribel. Must be over 21 and have NNEB, NVQ level 2/3, BTEC or any other childcare related qualification.

Neilson, Locksview, Brighton Marina, Brighton, BN2 5HA (0870 241 2901;skijobs@ neilson.com or for summer positions recruitment@neilson.com). Nannies for summer and ski seasons.

Powder Byrne, 250 Upper Richmond Road, London SW15 6TG (020-8246 5342; www. powderbyrne.com). Upmarket company employing nannies to manage resort crèches.

Simon Butler Skiing, Portsmouth Rd, Ripley, Surrey GU23 6EY (01483 212726 and 0870 873 0001; www.simonbutlerskiing.co.uk). Qualified nannies (minimum age 20, EU nationality) needed for 5 months in France.

Ski Beat Ltd, Metro House, Northgate, Chichester, Sussex PO19 1BE (Ski@SkiBeat.co.uk). Nannies hired for Les Arcs, La Plagne and La Tania.

Ski Famille, Unit 10 Chesterton Mill, French's Road, Cambridge CB4 3NP (tel/fax 0845 64 437 64; www.skifamille.co.uk). 20 qualified or experienced nannies and playroom assistants to work for between 3 weeks and 5 months in Les Gets and Morzine. Male applicants welcomed. Salary £480 per month plus accommodation and travel.

360 Sun and Ski, 306 route de Serveray, 74300 Les Carroz d'Arâches (0870 068 3180 in UK or tel/fax +33 4-50 90 31 80; www.360sunandski.co.uk). Childcare assitants/nannies for British holidaymakers for winter season. €100 per week plus off-site accommodation, meals, lift pass, ski insurance, equipment and travel from Geneva. All the major campsite tour operators like Eurocamp (01606 787525; www.holidaybreakjobs.com) and Canvas Holidays (01383 629018; www.canvasholidays.com) employ children's couriers to run activity programmes, mainly for children over four.

FIXING UP A JOB INDEPENDENTLY

Although Mig Urquhart had not intended to take up au pairing, she could not resist (some years ago) the range of possibilities which her first reading of the *Lady* magazine on a train to France opened up for her:

Several jobs caught my eye and I applied for one that suggested more cleaning and cooking than looking after kids (since I'm not particularly keen on children). I got the job because I phoned up a week after writing and caught Jenny unawares. The phone number wasn't in the ad. I got it from directory enquiries. She had received about 30 letters and decided not to hire anyone because she couldn't choose between them. I must have sounded OK on the phone and, because I was able to get to the house easily, we met and she decided to take me on.

There are 32 regional *Centres d'Information Jeunesse (CIJs)* which may be of use to the newly arrived job-hunting nanny or au pair. They can advise on cheap accommodation, local jobs, the legal rights of temporary workers, etc. The main Paris branch is CIDJ (*Centre d'Information et de Documentation Jeunesse*) whose foyer notice board is a useful starting place in Paris. It can also provide leaflets on topics of possible interest such as becoming an au pair, though these are not always updated very frequently. 'Going to France as an Au Pair' can be read online at www.cidj.com/contents/309092003160631.pdf.

Expatriate grapevines all over Paris could prove helpful for finding a family placement. Many people find their jobs as well as accommodation through one of the city's many notice boards *(panneaux)*. Again, the one in the foyer of the CIDJ near the métro stop Bir-Hakeim is recommended for student-type jobs and live-in positions. The American Church at 65 Quai d'Orsay (01-40 62 05 00; métro Invalides) is a well-established mecca for job and flat-hunters. Official notices are posted on various notice boards inside and out; the cork board in the basement is a free board where anybody can stick up a notice. You will bump into lots of other people studying the board here, and so it is a good place to make contacts. Obviously it is necessary to consult the notices in person; they are not available by phoning the church or on the internet.

The American Cathedral in Paris at 23 avenue George V (www.us.net/amcathedral-paris; métro Alma Marceau or George V) has a notice board featuring employment opportunities and housing listings. Also check the two British churches: St Georges Anglican at 7 rue Auguste-Vacquerie in the 16th arrondissement and its sister church St Michael's at 5 rue d'Aguesseau in the 8th (métro Madeleine).

The British Institute at 11 rue de Constantine has a notice board with occasional live-in tutoring and au pair jobs. Although the notice board at the Alliance Française (101 Boulevard Raspail; métro Notre Dame des Champs) is for the use of registered students of French, you may be able to persuade a student to look at the adverts for you, many of which are exchanges of room for some babysitting and/or teaching.

Most expat places like WH Smith's Bookshop near the Place de la Concorde and the Virgin Megastore on the Champs Elysées distribute the free bilingual newsletter *France-USA Contacts* or *FUSAC* (www.fusac.org) which comes out every other Wednesday. *FUSAC* comprises mainly classified adverts including some for live-in childcarers and tutors which are best followed up on the day the paper appears. It is possible to place an ad before your arrival in France. An advert under the heading 'Work Wanted in France' costs US$24 for 20 words, and can be e-mailed to franceusa@aol.com or sent in the US to France Contacts at PO Box 115, Coopers Station, New York, NY 10276; 212-777-5553/fax 212-777-5554).

Other possible sources of job and accommodation leads and adverts can be found in the weekly free ads paper *J'Annonce* (www.jannonce.com) or in *Paris Voice* which calls itself the 'magazine for English-speaking Parisians' (http://parisvoice.com). The free ads online website http://paris.kijiji.fr carries some ads for au pairs though far more from residents offering their services as nannies, etc.

Long-stay expatriates favour the western suburbs of Louveciennes, Bougival, Chatou, Croissy, Marly-le-Roi, Le Pecq and St. German-en-Laye. Therefore these areas have a demand for English-speaking live-in staff, so it might be worth putting up a notice on a local supermarket (e.g. Prisunic) or English-language bookshop notice board.

You can also introduce yourself at one of the many crèches or *garderies d'enfants* in the cities, where you will meet au pairs, nannies and mothers, all of whom may have some suggestions for fixing up a job with a family. If you want to meet parents, you could start by doing occasional babysitting; see the CIDJ leaflet *Garde d'enfants* or check the Yellow Pages.

It is possible to find an au pair job in a ski resort on-the-spot, though if you don't succeed straightaway, you will find the cost of living very high. Matt Tomlinson noticed a range of possibilities in Courchevel:

The standard deal for nannies seems to be flight, uniform, board and lodging, skipass, skipack plus a weekly wage. For that you work six days with maybe a couple of evenings of babysitting. You don't get to ski all that much, but most do it for the ambience and camaraderie. An NNEB and some experience seems to be a standard requirement, but I was offered a job on the basis of experience, references and, surprisingly enough, being a guy. It seems that positive male role models to take the little lads snowballing and sledging are quite sought after. I met quite a few people who had been hired mid-season as there is a fair amount of turnover. One girl rang up the operator on spec and was on a plane 36 hours later.

RED TAPE

Since 2004, EU nationals living or working long-term in France are no longer obliged to obtain a *carte de séjour* (residence permit). Some people have gone ahead and applied for one anyway as a useful piece of identification, though it is a palaver. As a European *stagiaire aide-familiale*, a designation sometimes used for au pair meaning 'trainee home help,' you are entitled to apply for a *carte de séjour* at the local police station *(préfecture)* or town hall *(mairie)*. Take your passport, four photos and some proof of your local address (e.g. letter from your host family). The list of requested documents differs from place to place and in some cases you will be asked to show an officially translated and authenticated copy of your birth certificate, which must show your parents' names. The website of the French Consulate in London does not provide much information for prospective au pairs (www.consulfrance-londres.org) though nationals of countries requiring a visa for France can download an application form for a short stay visa or obtain it from the Service des Visas Department at 6A Cromwell Place, London SW7 2EW.

By law au pairs coming to France from outside the EU must be women or men aged between 17/18 and 30, have some knowledge of French and have pre-registered in a language course in France which entitles them to obtain a student visa before arrival. The requirements for an au pair visa for Americans (for example) are two long stay visa application forms, au pair contract from the host family approved by the local Direction Départementale du Travail (DDTEFP), i.e. employment office, proof of studies in the US, letter of enrolment in a French language school and the visa fee. The process takes at least three months and sometimes more than four. Non-EU au pairs with student visas should apply for a *carte de séjour* within eight days of arrival in France. (This does not apply in the case of summer stays.)

A Paris organisation, Centre d'Echanges Internationaux (CEI) has a Work in France department which can assist higher education students over 18 (or occasionally new graduates) from outside Europe to obtain temporary work permits *(autorisation provisoire de travail)* to work in France for up to three months starting any time. Those participating in training programmes may stay for up to one year. All candidates must be conversant in French. The basic placement fee for independent job-seekers is €330. Details are available from CEI Paris, 1 rue Gozlin, 75006 Paris (01-40 51 11 81, fax 01-43 29 06 21; wif@ cei4vents.com; www.cei4vents.com).

The Cultural Services section of the French Embassy in the USA collates information of use to Americans who wish to study or intern in France (972 Fifth Ave, New York, NY 10021; fax 212-439-1455; www.frenchculture.org). Their web page www.info-france-usa. org/culture/education/france/go/pair.html covers the topic of au pairing in France and lists some of the major agencies (addresses all included in this book). The Studies Office of the Embassy can provide a list of language schools.

The French American Center in Montpellier (4 rue St. Louis, Montpellier 34000; 04-67 92 30 66; www.frenchamericancenter.com/english/aupair.asp) arranges au pair placements for Americans aged 18-25 with families in the Languedoc region, plus internships in local businesses. Americans and other non-Europeans in Paris regularly fix up informal au pair positions via notice boards and the grapevine. Despite the absence of residence and work permits and a contract, the arrangement seems to work out in most cases. Beth Mayer describes her situation compared to a British friend:

> *I have lived here with no papers with no problems for over a year. They never stamped my passport when I entered the country nor when I travelled in Europe. They don't seem to care that I'm here, but unfortunately the case is different for Africans and many other foreigners - maybe even for a black American. It's the way things are here.*

HEALTH AND INSURANCE

By law, French families are supposed to make social security payments to the local URSSAF office on behalf of their au pairs staying longer than three months. The monthly contribution *(cotisation)* ensures that the au pair will receive social security benefits in the case of illness or accident. French families are told to expect to pay at least €150 per month. EU nationals should rely on their EHIC (European Health Insurance Card) perhaps topped up by private insurance for the first three months or for a summer stay. Most agencies urge their families to register the au pair immediately, though they cannot enforce this.

Even if your family does pay contributions to cover illness and accident you are still responsible for obtaining third party or 'civil liability' insurance *(l'assurance responsabilité civile)*. In some cases agencies will organise this on your behalf or offer a supplementary insurance policy at a reasonable price (€19-€35 per month). It is worthwhile getting maximum cover in France since the procedures for reclaiming health costs are time-consuming and may result in reimbursement of only 70% of costs.

Information is available from the local Caisse Primaire d'Assurance Maladie. If you need medical care, be sure to go to a *médecin conventionné*, i.e. one whose fees are in accordance with the state insurance authorities, and make sure you get a receipt *(feuille de soins)* which should enable you to apply for reimbursement later.

LEISURE TIME

Complaints that the French are a snobbish, contemptuous and untrustworthy race usually emanate from Britons who go to France with negative preconceptions and who stay for a short time. The experience of au pairs usually contradicts these clichés and most return from their sojourn in France filled with admiration for the French way of life. One of the most basic differences is the reverence with which the dinner table is regarded, resulting not just in a higher standard of cuisine but in transforming it into a social centre. French families will linger round the table for hours of conversation and wine, and au pairs are nearly always included in the conviviality.

If you want the companionship of other foreigners, it is easy enough to find them at your language school, au pairs in your neighbourhood, strolling round the Luxembourg Gardens and so on. Alexandra Wheeler found friends in Paris through all these avenues as well as looking up former penpals, students who had been to Britain on school exchanges, etc. Irish pubs are a good place to meet other young English-speakers.

As usual it is easier to make friends in smaller towns. Tracie Sheehan's positive experiences in the affluent town of Annemasse (10km from Geneva) provide a useful antidote to the clichés:

There are many au pairs in the area, though all my friends are local. It appears that English-speaking people (especially female!) are objects of fascination here, so a good way to make introductions is to grab an amiable looking person and ask for directions, e.g. to the tourist office or simply proclaim extreme loneliness and invite them to go for coffee. Actually people here have been so nice to me that it's like being in Ireland.

To get the most out of Paris, a *carte orange* is essential. In most cases the family will provide one, but if not you should invest in one. This transport ticket gives unlimited travel on public transport (métro, bus and R.E.R.) within specified zones of greater Paris, and is much better value than buying a *carnet* (book of ten tickets), which in turn is much cheaper than buying tickets singly.

Most au pairs are keen to improve their French and sign up for a language course. If you want to select a course in advance, request the list *Cours de Français pour Etrangers* from the Service Cultural section of the French Consulate (21 Cromwell Road, London SW7 2DQ). Unfortunately many courses are expensive, though some tailor-make courses for au pairs, like the Institut de Langue Française (see below). Prices outside Paris are somewhat cheaper, but the very cheapest ones may conflict with working hours. Beth Mayer arrived speaking only a few words of French and urgently wanted to sign up for a French course. She searched for an inexpensive school, and found that most prices started at the same monthly fee as au pairs earn in pocket money (for 2½ hours of lessons a day). Eventually she found a great school (which didn't ask to see a visa or any papers) for considerably less, i.e. ASSOFAC Centre in the 20th arrondissement (93 rue Alexandre Dumas, 75020 Paris; 1-43 70 17 37). She met people from all over the world in her classes, from Iraq to Vietnam.

Here is a list of some well known courses in Paris:

Alliance Française: 101 Boulevard Raspail, 75270 Paris Cedex 06 (1-42 84 90 00; www.alliancefr.org).

Ecole Etoile, 38 Bd. Raspail, 75007 Paris (1-45 48 00 05; www.ecole-letoile.com).

France-Langue: 2 rue de Sfax, 75116 Paris (1-45 00 40 15; www.france-langue.fr).

Institut Catholique: 21 rue d'Assas, 75270 Paris (1-44 39 52 00; www.icp.fr).

Institut Franco-Nordique, 28 rue Vignon, 75009 Paris (1-42 68 10 07; ifn-paris@wanadoo. fr). Affiliated to au pair placement agency Accueil Franco-Nordique at the same address (1-47 42 45 04). Timetable of 4 classes per week designed to suit au pairs, e.g. no classes are scheduled for Wednesday when most au pairs will be looking after their charges.

Institut Parisien: 87 boulevard de Grenelle, 75015 Paris (1-40 56 09 53; info@institut-parisien.com). Special courses for au pairs.

Institut de Langue Française: 3 av. Bertie-Albrecht, 75008 Paris (1-45 63 24 00; www.inst-langue-fr.com).

Paris Langues: 30 rue Cabanis, 75014 Paris (1-45 65 05 28; www.parislangues.com).

Université Sorbonne: 47 rue des Ecoles, 75005 Paris (1-40 46 22 11; www.ccfs-sorbonne. fr).

Depending on your location, you might want to investigate others. If you are not specifically interested in studying the French language, you might want to consider the courses on French art and civilisation offered by the Sorbonne, which are popular with foreigners residing in Paris.

Although you can make preliminary enquiries by post, most schools will expect you to register in person and in many cases pay the full fee in advance. If you cannot afford to register in a course, it is possible to become an *auditeur/auditrice libre* at any French university, which can be a most enjoyable way to learn something that interests you and to meet local students. But it won't help you if course registration is a requirement for your visa.

As has been mentioned, language courses are not available during the summer, and in fact the au pair's leisure time dwindles radically when accompanying a family on vacation. Several agencies warn that it is impossible to distinguish between work and leisure during the summer. Leah Wilmoth, an American au pair in Montpellier in 2005, advises newcomers to arrive with a copy of the *Language Survival Guide: France,* a visual phrasebook and dictionary from Harper-Collins. She kept a copy handy in her handbag and found it a life saver.

Older au pairs and mother's helps with a university education often supplement their pocket money by doing occasional English language tutoring fixed up locally (through notice boards or contacts of your family).

TRAVEL

Fares to Paris are very competitive, with ferry companies trying to outdo the direct rail service through Eurotunnel. Several coaches depart from Victoria London daily bound for Paris, charging less than £35 for a youth fare. Watch the travel press for promotional airfares or check out flights on easyjet (Luton to Charles de Gaulle, Paris) which cost from £30 (£45 with tax). Ryanair has opened up many regions of France and their flights can be ideal for an au pair or nanny who is not bound for Paris. The earlier you can book ahead the more negligible the fare will be.

In France the equivalent of the Young Person's Rail Card is called the Carte 12-25, available to anyone under 26 years old from French Railways (SCNF) and applicable to all routes except Paris suburban lines (RER). This card costs €45 and entitles the holder to 25% off all rail journeys and 50% off some for a year. Details are available online at http://12-25sncf.com or from Rail Europe in London on 08705 371371.

DIRECTORY REFERENCES

For agencies based in France, see: **AFJE - Accueil Familial des Jeunes Etrangers** (Paris), **Accueil International Services** (St. Germain en Laye), **Association Familles et Jeunesse** (Nice), **Au Pair Azur** (Villeneuve Loubet near Cannes), **Butterfly et Papillon** (Annecy), **Euro Pair Services** (Paris), **Fée Rêvée** (Suresnes, Paris), **France Au Pair Eurojob** (St-Palais-sur-Mer), **Good Morning Europe** (Paris), **Institut Euro'Provence** (Marseille), **Inter-Séjours** (Paris), **Jeunesse et Nations Au Pair** (Rueil-Malmaison), **Nacel** (Rodez), **Nurse Au Pair Placement /N.A.P.P.** (Paris), **Oliver Twist** (Pessac), **Soames Paris Nannies** (Levallois-Perret) and **Solution Au Pair** (Marcq-en-Baroeul, near Lille). Almost all au pair agencies in Britain and Western Europe that have an outgoing programme make placements in France. **Almondbury, Anglo Nannies** and **Regency Nannies** all maintain offices in France. All the North American au pair placement organisations send au pairs to France (see list in Introduction).

Germany

Au pair placements in Germany normally follow the European Agreement on Au Pair Employment, so any exploitation which au pairs encounter should be reported to the relevant agency. On the other hand, most au pairs in Germany find that expectations are high and there is little tolerance for idleness. Au pairs whose primary intention is to learn German sometimes get a nasty shock when their host family sets out their schedule of tasks, so if possible check on this before accepting a post. Maree Lakey from Australia regretted that she had not stood up for herself more vigorously:

> *I was all too willing to make my job in Frankfurt work, and basically that meant that when the mother said 'jump', I nodded obediently and asked 'how high?' She realised this of course and took full advantage. The notion that au pairs work an average of 5 hours a day, 30 hours a week with 2 evenings of babysitting is a total farce. I never heard of anyone who stuck by these guidelines. On the whole I was working double this amount.*

The monthly pocket money for an au pairs in Germany is fixed by the government at €260 per month (since January 2006). Most families pay for a monthly travel pass (to allow you to attend language classes) and make a contribution towards the cost of the course, up to €100 per semester. Some agencies ask their families to make a contribution to your fare home if you stay for the promised period of nine or ten months, typically up to €150. Although the extra perks are not as generous as in neighbouring Switzerland, it is customary to be given a paid fortnight's holiday after six months of work. In return they will expect hard work.

> **The job usually involves more housework than au pairs normally do, as Maree Lakey describes after her year as an au pair in Frankfurt:**
> *I found that Germans do indeed seem to be obsessed with cleanliness, something which made my duties as an au pair very hard. I also found that from first impressions Germans seem to be unfriendly and arrogant, however once you get to know them and are a guest in their home, they can be the most wonderful and generous people. The Germans I met were sincerely impressed by my willingness to learn their language and at the same time genuinely curious about life in Australia, my home country.*

The stereotype of the obsessive cleanliness of the Germans also held true in Frances Thirlway's experience. Her Munich employer took such exception to the way Frances did the ironing and other chores that she would take over the job herself, leaving Frances to look after the baby (which defeated the purpose of the mother's having given up her job to stay at home).

Munich, Hamburg and Berlin are among the most popular destinations, though the main placement organisations have offices throughout the country including the eastern *Länder* (for example *IN VIA* has offices in Magdeburg, Leipzig, Dresden, Rostock and Anklam in the former East Germany). They will try to accommodate any geographical preferences you might have, though there are still far fewer opportunities in the east than the west part of Germany.

The vast majority of available jobs are for the duration of the school year. The school terms differ between northern and southern Germany, which will affect the starting dates of most jobs. Northern school children return to school in mid-August and carry on till late May, while southern schools do not resume classes until late September and disband at the end of June. Summer placements are uncommon in Germany because there is so little demand from families.

A basic knowledge of German is a requirement for most placements. Without any grounding in the language, it will be easier to find a job with a service family, who often provide generous terms of employment, e.g. paid travel, German lessons, etc. After qualifying as an NNEB nanny, Carol Rowan arranged a job at a US base near the French border. She stayed several years, moving easily between families (once by putting up a notice in the base post office). When she decided it was time to leave Germany, she found work with an American family who were planning to return to the States, and she accompanied them.

In addition to the language requirements, proof that the applicant has a basic knowledge of housekeeping is also often requested. Fortunately a letter from your mother will suffice (and most mothers are prepared to perjure themselves in such a cause).

You should be prepared for a certain amount of culture shock if you work in a German family. For example, breakfast may be a more formal occasion than you are used to, with a carefully set table and everyone eating together. Manners may be more formal than those to which you are accustomed, as Emma Colgan found:

The northern Germans are actually very formal and at first I was always forgetting to stand up when someone entered the room, or I used 'Du' instead of 'Sie'. I also had to get used to the continual shaking of hands.

In fact Prussian stiffness is mostly a thing of the past and your chances of being placed with a welcoming and fair-minded family are as good in Germany as anywhere else.

According to the professional nanny agency *Felicity Nannies* in Munich, live-in nannies in Germany earn between €1,515 and €1,817 net per month while live-out nannies earn €1,700-€2,400.

FIXING UP A JOB

Among the longest established agencies is the non-profit Roman Catholic agency *IN VIA* whose full title is Katholische Mädchensozialarbeit, Deutscher Verband e.V. with branches throughout Germany and one in England *(German Catholic Social Centre)* and one in Paris (Foyer Porta, 14 Pierre Demours, 75017 Paris; 1-45 72 18 66). Its Protestant counterpart is *Verein für Internationale Jugendarbeit* (VIJ) also with offices throughout the country. Both place both male and female au pairs for a preferred minimum stay of one year.

Dozens of secular agents have popped up all over Germany, many of them members of the Aupair-Society e.V. (www.au-pair-society.org) which has three offices in Germany and more than 40 member agencies. Commercial au pair agencies do not charge a placement fee to incoming au pairs. The Directory of Agencies in this book includes information about 18 German agencies, all of which invite direct applications from individuals abroad to meet the healthy demand for English-speaking au pairs.

Here is a selection of other agencies to try, most of which are IAPA members:

Astur Plus, Sturmiusstrasse 2, 36037 Fulda (+49 661-92 80- 221; fax 661-92 80 223; aupair. info@astur-gmbh.de; www.astur-gmbh.de). IAPA member.

Au Pair Agentur Eichhorn, Mühlengasse 10, 40213 Düsseldorf (+49 211-674860; AgenturEichhorn@aol.com; www.au-pair-eichhorn.de)

Au-Pair Agentur International Maria-Theresia, Abt-Danner-Strasse 12, 85406 Zolling (+49 8168 963144; fax +49 8168 963145; aupair.maria-theresia@t-online.de; www. aupairmaria-theresia.de). IAPA member.

Au-Pair Vermittlung Föry e.K., Reisigstrasse 54a, 76768 Berg (+49 727 391 9812; fax +49 727 391 9813; au.pair@t-online.de; www.au-pair-info.de). IAPA member.

Dr Frank Sprachen & Reisen, Siegfriedstrasse 5, 64646 Heppenheim (+49 6252 9332 22; fax +49 6252 9332 60; s.schaefer@dfsr.de; www.dfsr.de). IAPA member.

Eur-o-Pair, Leitnerstrasse 6b, 83727 Schliersee, Bavaria (+49 8026 4298; fax +49 8026 209874; eur-o-pair@t-online.de). IAPA member.

Family-Concept, Herzogstrasse 7, 80803 Munich (+49 89-3610 5828; fax +49 89-3610 5829; info@family-concept.de; www.family-concept.de). IAPA member.

PME Familienservice GmbH, Lindwurmstrasse 35, 80337 Munich (+49 89-5447 9419; fax +49 89-5447 9435; aupair@familienservice.de; www.familienservice.de). IAPA member.

RDAV (Ring Deutscher AuPair Vermittler), Finkenweg 48, 88048 Friedrichshafen (+49 7541-500743; fax +49 7541-500742; kontakt@rdav.org; www.rdav.de)

Salut! Au Pair Agency (Regina Schlecker), Grüner Weg 3, 88719 Stetten (+49 7532-495052; fax +49 7532-495053; info@aupair-salut.de; www.aupair-salut.de)

It is also possible to find a job independently through advertisements, notice boards and so on. The Saturday edition of *Suddeutscher Zeitung* carries plenty of adverts, though many are aimed at German women to work for families abroad. Local English-language papers and websites might prove useful such as www.munichfound.com (click on 'Jobmarket' then 'Private Jobs' Offered).

REGULATIONS

As an EU country, Germany is a straightforward destination for European au pairs, males as well as females, who flock there in their thousands every year to gain fluency in the second most popular language on the continent. Furthermore, au pairing is a possibility for young people of all nationalities who wish to improve their German, and formalities are minimal for Americans and nationals of EEA countries. The age limits for au pairs in Germany are 18 and 24 (though older candidates from the EU can be placed, up to 27 or 30). It is a general requirement that au pairs have some knowledge of German, though exceptions are made in the case of native English speakers.

All au pairs must register within a week of arrival with the local authority *(Einwohnermeldeamt),* taking with them four photos and a letter from the host family. After having done this it is possible to apply for a residence permit *(Aufenthaltsgenehmigung)* from the aliens' authority *(Ausländerbehorde/Ausländeramt)* probably located in the *Rathaus* or the *Kreisverwaltungsreferat* (Area Administration Centre). As of 2005, EU nationals no longer need to obtain the *Aufenthaltsgenehmigung,* only register locally (as do German nationals whenever they move house).

Prospective au pairs from outside the EEA and the US must apply for a special visa before leaving their home country, since it cannot be issued after arrival. The process requires them to submit documents to the German Consulate in their country including an *Annahmebestätigung* or official confirmation of placement as well as an invitation letter including written confirmation that the host family will pay for a medical check-up on arrival. They must be registered with a licensed agency. Processing will take two to three months, so candidates who wish to work for the normal stint of an academic year should apply by the preceding May. The paperwork is so extensive, that agencies normally stipulate that au pairs requiring a visa stay for a minimum of ten months. Maree Lakey found the process fairly nerve racking when she applied for the visa in Melbourne Australia:

> *Despite applying three months in advance, the visa didn't come through until a few days before I was due to fly, and only then because I phoned my host mother in Germany and asked her to enquire personally from her end. The Consulate told me they assumed the delay was due to the large number of applications in Frankfurt. The initial visa needed to be extended after three months, which involved an enormous amount of paper work and legwork on my part. On the whole I feel very envious of my many Australian friends who have a British passport and have no such restrictions with regards to travel and working overseas.*

On arrival, non-EU citizens will be issued with the key document, the *Aufenthaltserlaubnis* (residence permit). This will be extended for up to a year, provided the mandatory medical certificate *(Gesundheitszeugnis)* has been obtained from the local health department *(Gesundheitsamt)* at a cost of about €75 (more from a doctor), a cost which the family is usually prepared to bear. A work permit *(Arbeitserlaubnis)* will also have to be obtained from the local labour exchange *(Arbeitsamt)*.

German bureaucracy is notorious, so be prepared to surrender your passport for extended periods and to queue for permits during limited opening hours.

HEALTH AND INSURANCE

Although only non-EU au pairs have to obtain a *Gesundheitszeugnis*, most of the German agencies insist that all applicants provide a medical certificate translated into German before arrival.

State health insurance is compulsory for all long-stay categories. Good information is available on the website www.justlanded.com. Au pairs from the EU should obtain an EHIC before arrival which they can then exchange for local health insurance by registering with a local health insurance office such as *Allgemeine Ortskrankenkass* (www.aok.de), *Betriebskrankenkasse* or *Techniker Krankenkasse*. They will issue a settlement form called an *Abrechnungsschein* and, upon request, a list of contracted doctors and dentists who practise within their scheme. If you require hospitalisation, you must get the permission of your insurance company first (except in a genuine emergency).

LEISURE TIME

One of the great bonuses for au pairs in Germany is the opportunity to attend subsidised classes at the *Volkshochschulen* (VHS) which exist in nearly every town of the republic. In addition to offering 'German for Foreigners', they offer a range of evening classes in drama, handicrafts, sport, languages and so on. Most bookshops sell the prospectus of courses available, though you can make direct enquiries if you prefer. Terms begin in September and January, though you can usually join at any time.

> **Emma Colgan was delighted with the *Volkshochschule* which she attended in Hamburg twice a week:**
> *Our class resembled a United Nations meeting with representatives from Iran, Libya, Turkey, France, Spain, Denmark, Israel, Thailand, etc. The lessons were naturally conducted in German and helped me to maintain my written German. At the end of the course in May, I sat the Mittelstufe Prüfung II as set by the Goethe Institute and passed with 'gut'. Unfortunately nobody seems to have heard of this exam in England.*

Nevertheless Emma was pleased with her own achievement. It is not necessary to study for a qualification since the *Volkshochschule* courses are primarily designed for enjoyment.

Serious language students might prefer to register in the German classes conducted on most university campuses. These usually get underway in October and April. Private language schools also proliferate and some offer special discounts for au pairs. Some au pair contracts require the family to pay for all study expenses. It might be worth noting that the purest German is spoken in the north, but even if you are living in Bavaria where there is a pronounced accent, the teaching will be of standard German.

Your agency should be able to advise on clubs and social events. In major centres au pair clubs organise outings, concert trips, etc. Once your German is proficient, you can join any neighbourhood class or club to meet the local people. Despite the difficulty of following instructions in aerobic exercises in German, Emma Colgan found the classes fun.

Despite the difficulties Maree Lakey had with rude and hostile behaviour from her 5 and 11 year old charges and the huge burden of housework she was assigned, she found many compensations in her extracurricular life:

My language skills did improve, with relatively little effort and through language classes I not only gained a certificate to testify to my ability but made many friends who helped make life a little easier. I was disappointed to find the nightlife in Frankfurt not terribly appealing: techno-music dominated the discos and over-friendly unsavoury characters crowded the pubs. My favourite pastime was going to the cinema with my Swedish pal; we saw about 60 films over the course of the year, both in German and English. Frankfurt has many cultural outlets such as concerts and opera, however these were out of my budget.

Making friends with the locals was of course quite difficult. I found that with a bit of luck and effort I was able to strike up conversations with neighbours, people in the park or in shops, all of which helped me gain a sense of belonging in the community. Sometimes a simple conversation resulted in a dinner invitation or outing which I really enjoyed. I took full advantage of the fact that everybody seemed to be interested in meeting an Australian. As a bonus I met my current boyfriend in Germany, who was previously my penfriend for some years.

TRAVEL

The cost of flights compares very favourably with the train to major cities in Germany including northern cities like Cologne and Hannover. Check out Ryanair (of course) which flies from the UK to Dusseldorf, Frankfurt, Hamburg, Berlin, Karlsruhe, Friedrichshafen and Leipzig. Actually the airfields at which Ryanair flights land are famous for being a long way away from the city they serve like Hahn (not really Frankfurt at all) and Weeze rather than Dusseldorf. For Munich, try easyjet. Other discount airlines are Air Berlin (www. airberlin.com), Germanwings (www.germanwings.com) and Hapag Lloyd Express (www. hlx.com) which serves Edinburgh, Manchester and Newcastle. For discounted flights on Lufthansa, try the German Travel Centre, 85 Bridge St, Pinner, Middlesex HA5 3HZ (020-8429 2900; www.german-travel-uk.com). Cities in northern Germany like Aachen and Düsseldorf can be reached fairly cheaply by train or coach.

One of the best travel bargains anywhere is the 'Länder-Ticket' which can be bought online or at any staffed station. For a flat fare of €27, up to five people can travel anywhere in a single German state, provided they travel on regional rather than express trains. The deal also covers most local bus, tram and U-bahn connections. The Happy Weekend ticket is a few euros more.

DIRECTORY REFERENCES

For agencies based in Germany, see: **A'nF Au Pair & Family** (Berlin), **APAB Agentur Berger** (Bochum), **AuPair2000** (Edingen), **Aupair-Ark.de** (Holzgerlingen), **Au-Pair Interconnection** (Landsberg am Lech**), Au-Pair Service Dr. Uwe Krenz** (Mannheim), **Au Pair Service Silke Sommer** (Hemdingen), **Au Pair Vermittlung Sigmar Bassmann** (Friedrichsdorf), **CP Au-Pair Agentur** (Duisberg), **Family Au Pair Service** (Berlin), **Felicity Nannies** (Munich), **GSAP** (Bunsoh), **IN VIA** (Freiburg and throughout Germany), **Inwox** (Wörrstadt), **Multikultur international Exchange Programs** (Aschaffenburg), **Munichaupair** (Munich), **Only 4 Me** (Frankfurt), **Perfect Partners** (Arnstein), **Personal Touch Au Pair Service** (Buchbach), **VIJ (Verein für Internationale Jugendarbeit)** Bonn and throughout Germany.

For agencies based in Britain which deal with Germany, see: Abacus, Academy, Angels International, Au Pair Agency (Edgware), Au Pair Search, Bloomsbury Bureau, Childcare International, The Childcare Solution, Delaney International, German Catholic Social Centre, Hyde Park International, IAPO, Johnson's Au Pairs, Konnex, Lloyd's, Nannies of St. James, Nanny & Au Pair Connection, Peek-a-boo, People & Places, Quick Au Pair &

Nanny Agency, Solihull, Sunflowers Childcare, UK & Overseas.

Other agencies abroad that send au pairs to Germany include:

Australia: Au Pair Australia, Australian Nanny & Au Pair Connection, Charlton Brown Group, JCR Au Pairs & Nannies, People for People

Belgium: Services de la Jeunesse Feminine, Stufam

Canada: Au Pair Canada (Alberta), Au Pair Canada (Toronto), Globetrotters, Le Monde Au Pair, Scotia Personnel

Czech Republic: Au Pair International CZ, British Contact, Kiddykare, Student Agency

Finland: Allianssi

France: Accueil International, A.F.J.E., Au Pair Azur, Butterfly et Papillon, Euro Pair Services, Fée Revée, France Au Pair Eurojob, Inter-Séjours, Jeunesse et Nations, Nacel, Nurse Au Pair Placement, Oliver Twist Association, Soames International, Solution Au Pair

Greece: Nine Muses

Hungary: Au Pair Kft

Iceland: Studentaferdir

Italy: 3 Esse, ARCE, Au pair International, Celtic Childcare, Euroma, Intermediate, International Study Vacation, MB Scambi Culturali, Roma, Soggiorni all'Estero per la Gioventu, STI Travels

Netherlands: House-o-Orange Au Pairs

Peru: Au Pair Peru

Slovakia: SAPA

South Africa: Mary Poppins

Spain: Actividad Au-Pair International, Agencia Intercambios Culturales y Au Pair, Centros Europeos Galve, Interclass, Servihogar, Spanish Teachers

Switzerland: Pro Filia

USA: Au Pair USA/Interexchange, goAuPair

Greece

Anyone who has had a holiday in Greece or even just ogled the brochures might want to consider living with a Greek family for an extended stay. Yet working hours in Greek families tend to be much longer than in other countries and you may have only one full day off a week in which it will be difficult to do much touring or sightseeing. Fortunately Greeks are proud of their country and understand that their au pairs will want to use their time off to travel, and some will be flexible enough to allow for several days to be taken off in a row.

There is relatively little demand for 25- or even 30-hour-a-week au pairs. Since very few people want to learn modern Greek, au pairing (strictly speaking) is rare. The majority of positions are for women who are willing to work long hours, up to 60 hours a week. The line between au pairs and mother's helps is more blurred in Greece than elsewhere, and mother's help positions are sometimes available to people without a background in childcare but with an outgoing personality, self-confidence and a willingness to devote virtually all their time to working for the family. Most Greek children do not go to bed before 10pm, so evening work is commonplace.

The average rate of pocket money for a 30-hour-a-week au pair is €60, though most families pay more in exchange for longer hours (at least 50 a week plus babysitting, sometimes averaging four evenings a week). Qualified applicants are paid up to €150 a week. You can expect to be paid at the end of each week, at least one week in arrears. If you leave after less than four weeks or without giving the agreed one or two weeks' notice, you are likely to forfeit at least one week's wages. On the other hand if you complete a year's contract, there is a chance that the family will pay your return airfare.

Family placements are usually for six to twelve months, though summer positions are available, preferably from the second week of June to the second week of September. Hours are especially long in the summer, of course, when children are out of school. The two main centres for jobs are Athens and Thessaloniki, both of which are so hot in the summer that many families repair to an island or mountain retreat. Yacht trips for summer au pairs are not unusual, though the cramped conditions (which often involve sharing sleeping quarters with the children) detract somewhat from the romance. Many families insist that their summer au pairs be able to swim.

As is true throughout the Mediterranean, extended families in Greece are closely knit and will often warmly welcome a foreign girl into their family circle. This has potential disadvantages, especially for those who value their privacy. The cultural difference between British reserve and Greek gregariousness can be charming when you are on holiday, but more problematic when you are living in a family. It is not uncommon to be expected to share a room. Even if you have a room to yourself, both the children and parents are likely to disregard the door as a barrier. Claire Robson found herself having to resist night after night invitations to join the family in front of the television which was of course all Greek to her. There is also a tendency to assume that your property is communal; teenage girls are apparently very partial to any CDs or cosmetics you might own; the latter are expensive in Greece.

A minority of Greek women work and so in many cases, mother's helps work alongside the mistress of the house. It is not unusual for fathers to remain working in the cities while their families escape to cooler altitudes, and the motivation of some Greek women for requesting a summer au pair is for companionship. This can be a little wearing unless the mother's English is good. Vivienne Wood had a wonderful two months working for a family comprising an American mother, Greek father and bilingual children, and found not only could she enjoy the company of the family more since they all spoke English, but she didn't have to work as hard either. If the family does not speak good English, the language barrier is extreme.

Anyone who has spent time in Greece and noticed the outside steps being scrubbed daily may have inferred that standards of cleanliness are high in Greece, and a lot of housework including cooking may be expected of a mother's help. On the other hand many Greek families employ cleaning staff too. Personal hygiene is of paramount importance and you may have to adjust your habits accordingly. Because such a high percentage of Greek adults smoke, there is a higher level of tolerance of the smoking nanny in Greece than elsewhere, and of course the non-smoking nanny will have to show tolerance of smokers.

Greeks are almost idolatrous when it comes to their children and so you may often encounter the spoiled brat phenomenon. In the words of one agency, many have been largely raised by a 'dotting grandmama'. It is customary to be asked to provide English tuition for the children, since speaking English is a skill greatly prized in Greece. This can usually be done on a completely informal basis. In fact informality is a key to successful au pairing in Greece where rules are less important than personal rapport.

The restrictions on the au pair's freedom imposed in conservative countries like Greece are illustrated in this extract from a Greek family's letter of introduction to their new au pair from Finland:

Another very important matter I should mention is that the activities of the au pair in her free time and personal life have to comply with the rules and principles of the house. This mainly refers to being careful which places one visits and the quality of people one keeps company with. The au pair should not drink or smoke and the time of return at night should be not later than 2am.

FIXING UP A JOB

Greece has no representation on the International Au Pair Association (IAPA) and very few agencies elsewhere in Europe claim to be able to make placements in Greece. One Athens agency has received praise from partner agencies and from the au pairs and nannies it has placed. *Nine Muses,* which has recently moved premises to the Athens suburb of Nea Smyrni (located on a trolley bus route from Syntagma Square) accepts postal applications from young European and North American women and also can place candidates after arrival in Athens. The agency is run by Popy Raekou who charges no fee to incoming au pairs. They distribute occasional newsletters, arrange social gatherings for their au pairs and provide a friendly and personal service to au pairs including in a crisis. She is also affiliated to a Greek language programme for people interested in studying the language and culture of Greece. The agency prides itself on the after-placement service it offers. Among her satisfied au pairs is Riitta Koivula from Finland who, from an unsatisfactory situation on Kos (described in the introductory section on 'Culture Shock'), moved with Popy Raekou's help to a much better one in Athens:

> *When I arrived in Athens, I went to Popy Raekou's agency and she soon arranged a new family. I fell in love with Athens and its people right away. My new family was the best and we are still very close. I learned so many things, even to read and write and speak Greek because we took Greek lessons during the spring with Popy. I have many happy memories of Athens and friends who are still dear to me.*

Trained nannies might consider applying to UK tour operators like Mark Warner (www. markwarner.com) which employs nannies at their resorts in Greece. *Weigan Nannies* recruits a few nannies for Mediterranean resorts on behalf of a tour operator.

For many years the Athenian Nanny Agency run by Maritsa Skinitis placed nannies and mother's helps in well paid high level positions around Greece. Its descendant, the Athenian Domestic Agency, was seen advertising for nannies in 2005 but has not been traced since. The ad claimed that the agency was looking to hire qualified nannies from the USA, Canada, Australia and South Africa. If you want to play detective, the last whereabouts of this agency were at K. Kotta 28, Neo Psyhico, 11525 Athens (tel/fax 210-672 3974; ezelda@otenet.gr).

With so little agency-led traffic to Greece, many prospective au pairs and nannies turn to on-line matching services.

A sample vacancy listed by www.eaupair.com
FAM Ref 248187 - Last Name : Papanikolaou. 2 Children Aged 7 and 4. Country of residence – Greece. Languages spoken - English, French, German, Greek. Religion - Greek Orthodox. Weekly salary offered - €100. Expected weekly hours - 40 hours. Gender of au pair – female. Dates required – January 1st - June 1st. Minimum needed – 3 months. Maximum needed – 18 months.

It is sometimes worth checking the Situations Vacant column of the English daily *Athens News* (3 V. Lada str, 102 37 Athens; 210-333 3733; an-classified@dolnet.gr). You can check the classified ads on the internet (www.athensnews.gr) which are renewed every Tuesday. Some adverts are for live-in jobs in private households, and range from the distinctly dodgy to the legitimate. Vaughan Temby was sorry he replied to one ad which landed him with a 'hideous valet/houseboy job' from which he fled after only two days. You could also try placing your own advertisement in the column 'Situations Wanted'. The minimum charge for placing an advert is €11 for 15 words.

Mig Urquhart arrived in Athens on a Friday in September, got the *Athens News* on Saturday, had an interview on Sunday and started a live-in job a week later, even though she had hoped to avoid that option. Live-in jobs of course cut out the hassle and cost of finding accommodation. Although Mig liked the children and the father well enough, she didn't enjoy being treated more like a servant than a member of the family by the mother. The last straw was being told she was hanging up socks on the washing line the wrong way and being faced with piles and piles of ironing, so she too quit.

Julie Richards had registered with several British agencies which came up with nothing. She decided to go to Athens in any case and was offered five jobs in the first few days. The main advantage of waiting until you get to Greece is that you can meet your prospective family first. When considering live-in jobs, take your time and thereby you will be adapting to the Greek pace of life. Try to visit the family, drink coffee with them and bargain amiably about wages, duties and time off.

RED TAPE

Residence permits should be applied for by anyone intending to stay in Greece for longer than three months. To get a residence permit in Greece, take your passport, proof of support (which normally consists of a contract or letter from your host family) and a medical certificate to the local police station or, in Athens, to the Aliens Department *(Grafeio Tmimatos Allodapon)* at Sofokleous 70 & Pireos Street; 210-523 5671. The bureaucratic procedures are still fairly sluggish and frustrating and some au pairs have opted for renewing their three-month tourist visa when it is due to expire by popping over a border and re-entering on another tourist visa.

Non-EU nationals who find employment are supposed to have a 'letter of hire' sent to them in their home countries. Although there is a chance that an English-speaking nanny with qualifications and experience from North America, Australia or South Africa might be granted a permit, in reality most work without a residence permit. In its desire to conform to EU policies, the Greek government has increased the fines for illegal workers, though live-in child-carers are unlikely to be traced. So much of the work undertaken in Greece (including by Greeks) is done 'black', many long-stay foreigners encounter few problems.

Detailed information sheets on the procedures for EU nationals intending to work in Greece and on the social security system can be requested from the Economic & Commercial Section, Embassy of Greece, 1a Holland Park, London W11 3TP (020-7727 8860; commercial@greekembassy.org.uk).

HEALTH AND INSURANCE

It is mandatory for Greek employers to register their nannies (and any employees) with the Greek National Health Insurance scheme (IKA) and pay employer contributions. You should go with your employer to the local IKA office in order to apply for an IKA book 60 days after starting to pay contributions; thereafter you are entitled to free medical treatment and reduced cost prescriptions on production of the book. Most IKA payments are now done on-line and further information regarding the Greek Social Insurance scheme can be found at www.ika.gr. IKA offices will give you a list of participating doctors who treat IKA patients free of charge.

LEISURE TIME

Greek society is still very conservative and, as throughout the Mediterranean, a wild social life for au pairs is not really a possibility (even in Faliraki). Although public transport is excellent during the day, services are severely curtailed in the evenings making late night socialising difficult as well as unpopular with families. Certainly it will be very unlike holidaying on the Greek islands, where topless sunbathing and discos are the norm.

Girls will be expected to join in most family events such as trips to the taverna (which normally include the children) or to festivals at the local Greek Orthodox church (for which modest attire is needed). Cinema is popular in Greece and most films are subtitled rather than dubbed into Greek.

The rich Athens suburbs of Kifissia and Politia are full of families who hire au pairs so if you happen to find a job there, it should be easy to make friends. The suburbs of Pangrati and Filothei are also well-heeled enough to support a large au pair community, as is the more central suburb of Kolonaki.

The Mediterranean sun makes up for many drawbacks, though be sure to take plenty of cold weather clothes if you are going to spend the winter there. Greek hospitality is justly famed and if you have a chance to explore the countryside on your own you will be offered food and invited into people's homes. Although *kafeneions* (cafés) are a decidedly male preserve, women visitors seldom experience any hostility. They may even be bought a drink.

If you do want to learn Greek, the state offers free language courses in some places. In Athens, you can investigate the courses offered at considerable cost by the Athens Centre (48 Archimidous St; 210-701 2268; www.athenscentre.gr). Most courses start in October and finish before the summer.

TRAVEL

Flights on easyjet from London Luton or Gatwick are available for £50 plus tax of about £15, which means that flying to Athens is about half the price as it was two or three decades ago. It is advisable to have a return ticket (preferably with a return which can be changed or refunded if your plans change) since it is difficult to obtain cheap fares to London from Greece. Air Scotland (www.air-scotland.com) links Glasgow with Athens.

Travel within Greece is relatively cheap (particularly the ferries) so it should be possible to see some of the country with the money you save from your family placement. On the other hand, girls who have long working weeks may find themselves envying the thousands of free spirits who converge on Greece every year simply to travel and party.

For travel deals, it is worth checking with Busabout (020-7950 1661) who offer a three- or four-island ferry pass ('Greek Island Explorer') which includes Paros, Naxos, Ios and Santorini. Busabout also offers ferry links from Venice or Ancona in Italy, across to Patras, on the Greek mainland.

DIRECTORY REFERENCES

For agencies based in Greece, see **Nine Muses** (Athens).

For au pair and nanny agencies in Britain that deal with Greece, see: Angels International, Nannies Abroad and Weigan Nannies.

Other agencies abroad that send au pairs to Greece are:
Australia: JCR
France: Euro Pair Services, France Au Pair Eurojob, Jeunesse et Nations
Germany: In Via, Munichaupair
Italy: 3 Esse

Ireland

Several of the au pair placement services in Ireland included in this book are offshoots of English-teaching centres in Dublin as is evident from their names: for example *Dublin School of English*, the *Swan Training Institute* and the *Linguaviva Centre*. These schools are only secondarily au pair referral services, run for the benefit of students enrolled in their own English courses. By contrast, *CARA International* in County Mayo and the *Job Options Bureau* in Cork are primarily au pair and nanny placement agencies, which can place young women in families all over Ireland.

Au pairs who are placed through the Dublin agencies are normally obliged to study at the associated school. The *Dublin School of English* charges au pairs €800+ for a three-month course of English (nearly £550) while the *Au Pair Study Centre* charges a more competitive €100 a month (for a minimum of three months). These courses tend to be exam-oriented with a wide range of options available, from Cambridge Certificate to commercial English. Most are open to full-time foreign language students as well as au pairs (who must necessarily study part-time) and so most run a lively programme of discos, outings and other social events.

The preferred minimum stay is six months, but most of the agencies undertake to make three-month summer placements. The recommended pocket money is on a par with that in Britain, no less than €80 a week for 30 hours of duties. There is also a strong demand for au pairs plus willing to work 40+ hours a week, and their weekly wage is about €115 in Dublin. One important difference between Irish and English agencies is that the ones in Dublin can charge a placement fee to incoming au pairs, though this may be waived in the case of girls applying through a European agent or subsumed in the cost of the compulsory language course. Experienced nannies placed through agencies like *Cara International* and *Job Options Bureau* usually earn at least €250 a week, while less experienced mother's helps earn wages based on the Irish minimum wage of €7.65 an hour (less allowable deductions for board and lodging).

Agencies not included in the Directory may be worth trying:

Au pairs 4 Ireland (incorporating Au pair and Horse Job)s, The Coach House, Leinster Stud, Maynooth, Co. Kildare (48-44615105 or 86-1645485; jkidd@horsejobs.freeserve. co.uk). Also at: 62 Glencairn Cresent, Leopardstown, Dublin 18 (1-294 0515 or 87-235 0141; Aupairs4Ireland@eircom.net; www.aupairs4ireland.com).

First Choice Au Pairs Ireland, 14 Old Connell Weir, Newbridge, Co. Kildare (tel/fax 45-436854; info@firstchoiceaupairs.com). Closed at the time of writing but hoping to resume activities.

Shamrock Au Pair Agency, 'Magheree,' Kilmoroney Athy, Co. Kildare, Ireland (+353 598 625533 fax +353 598 625534; info@aupairireland.com; www.aupairireland.com). Independent au pair placement agency not affiliated to a language school. Non-refundable placement fee of €190 for long stays and summer stays of 8+ weeks.

The organisation MEI ('Marketing English in Ireland') has a web page that lists 16 language schools that offer au pair programmes (www.mei.ie/mei/Main/AuPair.htm). Many European young people are more drawn to Ireland than England as a venue for learning English because of the reputation of the Irish for being hospitable and family-oriented (not to mention Roman Catholic which is a factor for many girls from Spain, Italy, etc.). The rise in Ireland's fortunes over the last 15 years has been astonishing and the standard of living has gone up at the same time as the cost of living has. Dublin, Cork and Galway are buzzing European cities which attract au pairs and nannies from all over the continent and further afield.

RED TAPE

The Republic of Ireland is a member of the EU so work permits are not needed by EU or EEA nationals. British citizens intending to nanny in the Republic of Ireland do not even require a passport. Although some agencies claim to be able and willing to place all nationalities, in practice most placements are of European nationals who come to Ireland to learn English, especially from the new accession countries of Hungary, Poland, etc. Those intending to stay for more than three months should apply for a residence permit; enquire at the police station. The language learning requirement is enforced more seriously in Ireland than in Britain and visa extensions will normally be given only after a certificate of attendance at a language course is submitted. All language schools in Ireland are private, but fees are somewhat lower than in Britain.

American, Canadian, Australian and New Zealand students who would like to consider working as nannies in Ireland are eligible to apply for an 'Exchange Visitor Program Work Permit'. Americans are permitted to stay for up to only four months whereas the others can stay for 12 months, starting at any time of the year. Participants must be students between the ages of 18 and 30 and have the ability to fund themselves while looking for work. Once participants from the US and Canada are in Ireland, the youth and student travel agency USIT can advise on job opportunities (19-21 Aston Quay, O'Connell Bridge, Dublin 2; 1-602 1777; www.usit.ie). Although they do not normally deal with live-in childcare jobs, their crowded notice board carries some au pair adverts.

The only option for other nationalities is to enter Ireland on a student visa. From 2005, full-time foreign students are permitted to work for up to 20 hours per week in term and full-time in the vacations, but only if their course lasts at least one year and leads to a recognised qualification.

The employment service of Ireland is FAS (Foras Aiscanna Saothair) with about 70 offices throughout the country which EU nationals may consult. Mig Urquhart ended up staying in Dublin for two years and found the FAS very useful if only because she used their phones to follow up leads. She also found the Dublin City Council Community & Youth Information Centre in Sackville Place off O'Connell St helpful for consulting the papers and using the internet free of charge.

HEALTH AND INSURANCE

An EHIC card brought by EU nationals enables holders to apply for a medical card which gives entitlement not only to free health care but also dental treatment at appointed clinics. As in Britain, Irish families do not make national insurance contributions for au pairs, so non-EU residents should consider making private provision.

DIRECTORY REFERENCES

For agencies based in Ireland, see: **Au Pair Study Centre** (Dun Laoghaire, Co. Dublin), **Cara International** (Castlebar, Co. Mayo), **Dublin School of English** (Dublin), **European Au Pair Agency** (Dublin), **Job Options Bureau** (Cork), **Kidz Au Pair Agency** (Cork), **The Linguaviva Centre** (Dublin), **Native Speaker** (Sligo), **Pace Language Institute** (Wicklow), **Swan Training Institute** (Dublin).

Several UK agencies actively place au pairs and nannies in Ireland, including 3 to 4 Agency, Angels International, Anglocontinental (mainly hotel placements), Bloomsbury Bureau and Occasional & Permanent Nannies.

Other agencies abroad that send au pairs to Ireland are:

Australia: Au Pair Australia

Belgium: Stufam

Canada: Scotia Personnel

Czech Republic: Au Pair International CZ, British Contact, Student Agency

Finland: Allianssi

France: Accueil International, AFJE, Au Pair Azur, Butterfly et Papillon, Euro Pair Services, Fée Revée, France Au Pair Eurojob, Inter-Séjours, Jeunesse et Nations, Nurse Au Pair Placement, Oliver Twist Association, Soames

Germany: A'nF, Au Pair Interconnection, Au-Pair-Vermittlung Sigmar Bassmann, CP Au-Pair Agentur, IN VIA, Munichaupair, Personal Touch

Iceland: Studentaferdir

Italy: Agenzia Alla Pari, ARCE, Au Pair International, International Study Vacation, MB Scambi Culturali, Roma, Soggiorni All'Estero per la Gioventù, STI Travels, Welcome Agency

Netherlands: House-o-Orange Au Pairs, S-Au Pair Intermediate, Travel Active

Spain: Actividad Au-Pair Internacional, Agencia Intercambios Culturales, Centros Europeos Galve, Crossing Limits, Interclass, Spanish Teachers

Switzerland: Pro Filia

Israel

Israel is not a happy country. The conflict between the Israelis and Palestinians often seems beyond resolution. Predictably, as the Peace Process has unravelled, Israel has lost much of its appeal for travellers, and the number of young people choosing to head for what was a generation ago a favourite travellers' destination is drastically down. Personal security is bound to be a consideration but the statistics should be reassuring, that tourists and other foreigners are rarely the targets of violence. However, a general clamping down on foreigners in the country has resulted in a great loss of opportunities, including for au pairs and nannies, which at one time flocked to Israel.

The prospects for finding work are also much gloomier than they used to be, mainly because the government has made the visa situation much more difficult. A couple of years ago the Immigration Authority mounted a controversial ad campaign against employing foreign workers without permits. These ads implied that foreign workers harmed the Israeli economy, society, morality and even security. (It was later taken to the High Court of Justice for inciting racial hatred so the campaign has since been toned down.)

But the attitude of the authorities has changed utterly. For example, the owner of a long-established au pair agency in Rishon-le-Zion south of Tel Aviv reported that she had been forced to close her agency (Hilma's Intermediary) in 2004 due to the ferocity of the clampdown on all foreigners working in the country. Her account is strongly worded and very discouraging:

Due to government regulations and severe actions against foreigners working here, there is NO WAY for any agency or individual to work in Israel as an au pair, mother's helper, etc. Basically it comes down to the fact that no one should even try to work on a tourist visa, because many people are just sent back at the airport. If they do receive a tourist visa, they may be able to stay for only two weeks or at most three months. No family wants a mother's helper for that short a period. Besides this, there is now a special police force that goes after anyone working that does not have a working permit and many people are being stopped in the streets or sometimes picked up from their homes (when a neighbour gives information!). Israel is at the moment a no-go country for those who want to work as nannies, au pairs or housekeepers. It is sad to see a foreigner getting into trouble and many Israelis are against this situation. But for the time being at least, I advise no one to come.

Not everyone takes such a negative view. The co-owner of a Tel Aviv hostel wrote in 2005 to say that, although it is not as easy as it once was, casual work is still available. But he agrees that 'the problem is the immigration police, because people who hire illegal workers risk big fines.'

Other Israeli au pair agencies once mentioned in this book have fallen by the wayside, and Israel has no member agency in the International Au Pair Association. In fact not a single agency in the directory claims that it can make placements with Israeli families. The only possibility seems to be internet matches, though anyone who makes contact with a family this way should ask some probing questions about the legalities. One vacancy posted on an au pair site mentioned that the au pair candidate must either be Jewish or have a work permit already, which implies it is easier for people of Jewish ancestry to get permission to work in Israel. The site www.greataupair.com normally has a smattering of vacancies in Israel.

The following gives a flavour of the kind of job that might be on offer:
We are a lively and social family looking for an English-speaking au pair to help

> *us with our four dynamic children. We moved from the US to Israel 13 years ago. All our children are native English speakers, but go to school in Hebrew. We have private English lessons for all of them, and would love to have an Au Pair who can sit and read English-language books with them. Zichron Yaakov is a seaside tourist town with about 15,000 residents and a 30-minute train ride from Tel Aviv. We have a number of friends here with au pairs living with them, typically young women from Australia, the US, Canada, Scandinavia, Holland, etc. They all seem to be happy here and have active social lives. We are Sabbath observant Jews. This will have little impact on you, except you will see a lot of colourful activities! We do not mix milk and meat and have two separate sets of dishes. The ideal au pair for us would be a young woman, after high school, perhaps in college, somewhere between the ages of 18 and 25, a native English speaker from an English speaking country, who loves children, either already loves Israel or is curious about the country, and wants to take a break and see the world a bit for a year, before proceeding with their life and career goals. We know that such a year off is a once-in-a-lifetime experience, and we will do everything that we can to ensure that it is a positive experience.*

This reference to a group of au pairs in a town of 15,000 indicates that the situation cannot be as dire as some would suggest. Assuming you do brave the visa situation and accept a live-in job, it is likely that a considerable amount of housework will be expected, especially if you happen to be around in the period leading up to Passover in April, when practising Jews like to have their houses immaculate. In addition to the daily routine, you can be asked to do up to four evenings of babysitting per week. Miss L. E. Wallace was glad to have the backing of Hilma Shmoshkovitz's agency (now no more, as mentioned):

> *Some of the families here in Israel tend to be very assertive about what they require and expect. Girls I have spoken to say that households can be very hectic and boisterous, and the children given a lot more freedom and so can be difficult to cope with. It is difficult for some girls to stand up to the family in discussions about working conditions, etc.*

In return for all this hard work, wages are moderately high, normally in the range of US$200-$300 per week (compared to the US$139 paid in the US) for the same length of working week, i.e. up to 45 hours. Those who stay for an entire year are entitled to request a fortnight's paid holiday and/or reimbursement of travel expenses to your home country.

The English language *Jerusalem Post* (Jerusalem Post Building, Romena, Jerusalem 91000; www.jpost.com) carries job adverts and from time to time might have vacancies for childcare help. Friday is the best day. The classified ads can be searched online.

If you are looking for a summer placement, bear in mind that Israel can be exceedingly hot in the summer. The hottest part of the country is the Red Sea resort of Eilat which is much less crowded in the summer than in the winter. If you are lucky, you might find yourself looking after one child on the beach all day. Eilat is also a very popular harbour for yachtsmen and women who sometimes need someone on board to look after their children for short or long periods. You will probably have to hang around for a while before you hear of such an opportunity.

In some cases culture shock can be compounded by a language barrier, as Helen Aspinall found in her first live-in post in Israel which lasted nine months:

> *I worked from 6.45am to anything from 4pm (rare) to 8-9pm (normal). I had to clean the whole house, do all the laundry and ironing, cook for the two little girls and entertain them. The girls spoke only Hebrew so out of desperation and necessity I began to attempt to learn the language from whatever source was available: radio, TV, friends, the children, a phrasebook, etc. I was expected to teach these two averagely-able little*

madams to converse in the Queen's English. This never happened of course as I had 101 other things to see to. For all this I was paid less than the average wage and, regrettably, had no contract. The family treated me as an employee; the wife clearly expected me to be Julie Andrews and Mrs. Doubtfire rolled into one.

In Helen's next job, she earned $150 more a month for a 40-hour week rather than 60, but best of all she found herself in a warm busy family.

Another variant on au pairing is looking after children on a kibbutz. In the early days of the kibbutz movement, most children lived in a communal house rather than with their parents. Although this practice is no longer carried out, foreign volunteers on a kibbutz are sometimes assigned the task of looking after children during the day. Anyone interested in working on a kibbutz should contact Kibbutz Representatives at 16 Accommodation Road, London NW11 8EP (020-8458 9235; fax 020-8455 7930; enquiries@kibbutz.org.uk; www.kibbutz.org.il).

REGULATIONS

Like most countries, Israel officially insists that anyone in employment must obtain a work permit, which is virtually unobtainable to those working as au pairs and mother's helps. Whereas at one time, many foreigners worked on a tourist visa with impunity, the situation has changed dramatically.

When you arrive in Israel, be prepared for a potentially gruelling interview at immigration, when you may be asked to show an outbound air ticket and/or enough funds to support yourself. Even if you have a pre-arranged family placement, request a tourist visa at immigration control which will be valid for three months. When asked to give your contact address in Israel, write down a youth hostel or hotel. If you do give the name of your host family, you should claim that they are friends who have invited you to stay as their guest. After emerging from Ben Gurion airport, take the hourly bus 222 into central Tel Aviv. The tourist visa can be renewed either by applying to the Ministry of the Interior with 'proof' that you are doing something worthwhile (like studying Hebrew or doing voluntary work). Others who want to stay longer in Israel take a trip to Jordan, Cyprus or Egypt and get a new tourist visa on re-crossing the border.

HEALTH AND INSURANCE

A comprehensive private insurance policy is essential, since Israel has no reciprocal arrangements with Britain or the US. For the purposes of travel insurance, Israel counts as Europe since it borders the Mediterranean. If you wait until you arrive, you should be able to insure yourself against accident and medical expenses; the Kibbutz Program Center in Tel Aviv sells a 12-month policy to kibbutz volunteers for a modest $80. Some families will ask prospective employees to show a medical certificate which indicates that they are free of HIV and hepatitis.

LEISURE TIME

Israel is a fairly compact country with a great range of landscapes, from the mountains in the north which even have a few ski resorts to the Negev Desert in the south. Internal travel is very cheap, even if you don't resort to hitch-hiking.

The families who employ home helps tend to be concentrated in a few prosperous suburbs (e.g. North Tel Aviv) and so you will usually meet up with your fellow au pairs locally. According to Bianca Tonkin, the au pair community is very close and shares all the gossip about bad families, etc.

Anyone who wants to study Hebrew seriously can do so at an Ulpan. Ulpan courses are run throughout the country, usually in conjunction with the Jewish Agency, to give students thinking of settling in Israel a working knowledge of Hebrew and an understanding of the Jewish way of life and history.

Italy

Because Italian is such a beautiful and satisfying language, Italy is a popular destination for *alla pari,* also known in Italian as 'babysitters'. Even if you arrive without having studied much of the language - and this is quite common - you should be able to understand the basics after a relatively short stay. Italians are famous for their garrulousness, so your ear will soon become attuned, especially if you spend time with children of talking age. Italian family life is justly known for its closeness and vitality and many au pairs have greatly enjoyed their experiences.

If learning Italian is your main objective you may be disappointed to find that many Italians are eager to practise their English on you. Many also want to get their money's worth out of their English-speaking au pair by having her speak English to the children or even give unscheduled English lessons each day if the children are of school age (which may not be very popular with the children). For this reason there is a tendency for agencies to prefer well-spoken and educated girls, and some job descriptions specify girls from Southern England. This can of course provide useful teaching experience, especially if exaggerated later on a CV. What the expectations will be in this regard should be established in advance, especially if you are planning to pursue Italian studies at home.

Wages in Italy are average or above for Europe, normally around €60-€70+ for au pair hours (30 per week) and €80-€100+ for mother's help hours (40 per week). Demand is strong for experienced or trained nannies and nanny/governesses; the agency *Europlacements* specialises in this market (see entry) and quotes a monthly salary of €500-€800 for mother's helps and up to €1,200 for top nannies.

Often families have other domestic staff to do all the cleaning, leaving you free to spend time looking after and teaching the children. Louise Rollett, who spent a summer working for a fabulously wealthy Florentine family, appreciated the opportunity to live in a style which would be otherwise impossible and to spend time on the Tuscan coast and other glamorous resorts. But she did not enjoy the social no man's land between servants and employers. However she found her employers formal and forbidding and overall found the life very lonely.

As is true throughout the Mediterranean, children tend to be spoiled by their parents and other relations, so be prepared to cope with more wilful and attention-seeking behaviour than you may be used to.

> **Dustie Hickey, who fixed up a job as a junior nanny in Rimini through a British agency, describes her charges:**
> *A lot of the time the children (girls aged 6 and 8) I look after only want attention, and they do the strangest of things to get it. They don't show much respect for their parents because they more than often get their own way. If they are told off they become mad and hit their mother, which makes it difficult for me, as when I ask them to do something they ignore me. One minute they can be your best friend and the next they're trying to hit you!*

But in general, Dustie had few complaints about her placement since she had a light workload (about five hours a day plus occasional babysitting), good pay and more days off than stipulated in her contract. If you get on well with your employers, you may find yourself the recipient of spontaneous acts of generosity in the form of gifts and treats. On the other hand many families frequently bend the rules, for example by expecting the au pair/mother's help to supervise the children's evening meal on top of daytime duties. This can be a significant burden since Italian children almost never go to bed before adults. Joanne Moscrop from Grimsby found her two charges' schedule hard to cope with when she au paired in Milan:

> *Both the boys would sleep from around 3pm to 7pm when they would wake for their evening meal. Rather silly time for children to sleep in my opinion. Then the three year old began going to sleep later and waking at 8pm or 8.30pm so the children wouldn't go to sleep at night which caused tempers to rise.*

Italy is not ideally suited to the shy and retiring. Some have found Italian behaviour too flamboyant for their taste, particularly in Southern Italy, and have (wrongly) assumed that a raised voice denotes real anger. It took Frances Thirlway a little while to get used to the flaming rows which occasionally engulfed her employers (usually ending in patently ridiculous accusations of infidelity). But she soon realised that this was the way they functioned and that the next day normality would be restored. At extended family gatherings in a Calabrian village, one or other member would often flounce out of the dining room after a shouting match, ostensibly in a rage, but really because they didn't fancy the next course; at least that was the conclusion Frances drew. In fact after a few months Frances felt so at home that she began to indulge in the odd bit of shouting herself. But not everyone will find it possible to adapt to behaviour which is so alien and unEnglish.

Away from the big cities it will be difficult to find people who speak much English, as Angie Copley found in Sardinia:
I thought it would be easy to learn the language, make friends, etc. but the first two months were the most difficult of my life. Nobody spoke English in the town, and at times I felt very lonely and isolated. It was frustrating not to be able to make friends until I had a basic knowledge of Italian. My work involved mainly speaking English to the two-year old boy and playing with him. In the summer we spent every day in the swimming pool. I was free for four hours in the afternoon and every evening after 8pm. But once I picked up the language, I had the best summer of my life. I could go out, meet lots of people and have beach parties at night. Basically it was one big holiday.

Apart from the language barrier, another alienating factor which au pairs have come up against is the extreme security consciousness of some families, not to mention a tendency to hypochondria. Many of the families which employ home helps in Italy tend to be more wealthy than in northern Europe. Although some wealthy families are looking for qualified nannies and governesses, many simply want a well-behaved English-speaking au pair. Working in an extremely privileged environment has several repercussions, good and bad. It often means that the mother does not go out to work. Also anxiety about burglars and terrorists can verge on paranoia. Some families even hire bodyguards once their children start school. They want you to amuse the children at home rather than take them out onto the dangerous streets. At the very least you may find yourself spending a good part of your day locking and unlocking windows and doors.

Susie Walton deeply resented that her wealthy Neapolitan employers would not entrust her with the keys to the several layers of doors and gates at their seaside villa. Whenever she went out she had to rely on someone being at home to let her back in. Such families are also very reluctant to allow their au pairs to bring friends into their homes. Susie was told that she was not allowed to meet than two friends on the beach at any one time.

The advantages of working for a wealthy family are more obvious than the drawbacks. Many families have villas by the sea or in the mountains where they can escape from the summer heat and tourist crowds of Rome, Florence, Venice, etc. In fact even if you are working in a more modest household, chances are you will accompany the family to their holiday retreat. Families with two houses often repair to their country retreat on weekends which can cut into your social life as Joanne Moscrop soon found:

The family had a house on Lake Garda (for the week) and a house on Lake Como (for the weekends). This meant bringing clothes and toys backwards and forwards, and I found the children extremely naughty while we prepared them. Also this packing up cut into what was supposed to be my free time. Most of the friends I made were in Lake Como, but we spent more time at Lake Garda which was deserted out-of-season.

Summer-only positions are readily available, though holidaying with a wealthy family may not prove as idyllic as it sounds, as recounted by one reader of this book:

My first job as an au pair in Italy was with a family who were staying in the middle of nowhere with their extended family. It was a total nightmare for me. I could just about say hello in Italian and couldn't understand a word of what was going on. After three weeks I was fed up, homesick and ready to jump on the next plane to England. But a few days later we moved back to town (Modena) and from then on things improved dramatically. I was able to go out and meet other au pairs and nannies at the park, etc. and we all socialised together. I ended up learning Italian quite well, making lots of friends (partly through my language school, which was free) and visiting most of the Italian cities. The only part that I didn't like in that job was going away with the family to their holiday houses for skiing, etc. You end up working twice your usual hours for the same pay, have no social life as you don't have any friends there, can't go skiing as you are minding the baby and then they tell you to cheer up because you're on holiday.

Writing in 2005, Anna Paravia of *Au Pairs Recruitment* in Turin wanted prospective au pairs to be forewarned of possible culture shock in Italy:

The au pair must be aware that she will be homesick, so she has to be sure she wants this experience, as at the beginning it might be hard. The au pair has to be mature enough to adjust to the new habits and ways of life, very different from hers, without feeling shocked by the cultural differences.

Even stronger language is used on the specific subject of au pairing in Sicily on the interesting non-commercial website www.bestofsicily.com/jobs.htm#au_pairs in which expat foreigners express their personal opinions:

One should distinguish between au pairs and full-time nannies or housekeepers. Most of the au pairs here in Sicily are young women (under 25) from England, Scandinavia or Germany. A typical work term lasts about six months. We must stress that a candidate should only search for such a position through a reputable international agency, of which there are rather few in this generally unregulated field. Recommendations through friends are not always a reliable approach. In any event, it is extremely important to know the host family reasonably well (personally rather than merely through correspondence) before coming to live with them. The dynamics of family life in Sicily (even 'typical marriages') may differ considerably from that to which a young woman is accustomed in her own country. Obviously, the candidate should feel perfectly comfortable in this environment before considering becoming an au pair, even for a brief period. This is a highly individual choice, but unless all these conditions are met, being an au pair here in Sicily (or perhaps anywhere) is generally discouraged.

FIXING UP A JOB

A considerable number of European au pair and nanny agencies deal with Italy, so British and other European au pairs should have little trouble arranging a job. If you want to work directly with an agency in Italy, choose one which is based in the city or region where you hope to work, for example *ARCE* for Genoa, *Au Pairs International* in Bologna, *Celtic Childcare* in Turin, and so on. There can sometimes be substantial delays between submitting your application and receiving details of a family, but on the other hand you may be given as little as a fortnight to get yourself organised for departure once the family's details are sent.

Angie Copley fixed up her job in Sardinia through the now defunct British agency Au Pairs-Italy:

After finding the address of a specialist agency in your book, I wrote to them and before I knew it they had found me a family. When I arrived, the family met me and took me to their house. Some house. It wasn't just a house but a castle where the Italian royal family used to spend their holidays. What was even better was that the family had turned it into a hotel, the best possible place for meeting people.

An agency in the UK that specialises in Italy is the *English-Italian Agency* though, like so many British agencies, it is now more active in bringing au pairs to Britain rather than sending them abroad. An agency with a consistently high number of vacancies in Italy is *Totalnannies.com* which publicises many of its choice jobs on the free monthly electronic newsletter *Jobs Abroad Bulletin* (www.jobsabroadbulletin.co.uk).

You can of course work directly with an Italian agency, since most of them will speak English, but make sure first that you won't be liable to pay a hefty registration fee. *ARCE* is a long established agency which makes placements free of charge throughout the country. Two agencies to try in Florence are:

Au Pair Florence, Via di Valiano 2/a Molino del Piano, 50065 Florence (tel/fax +39 055 8364663; Mobile: +39 3337213107; aupairflorence@virgilio.it; www.aupairflorence. com). IAPA member.

Euro Au Pair, Via Ghibellina 96/R, 50122 Florence (055-242181; tel/fax 055-241722). Contact Laura Pini.

Quite a few Italian agencies, often attached to English language schools, arrange only for Italian girls to go abroad, for example *MB Scambi Culturali, STI* and *Soggiorni all'Estero per la Gioventù*; the latter arranges paying guest but not au pair stays for foreigners coming to Italy. Similarly the Italian branch of the Experiment in International Living (Istituzione Culturale Senza Scopo di Lucro, Via A De Gasperi 2, 14100 Asti; www.experimentitalia.it) runs only an outbound au pair programme.

If you are already in Italy you can check the classified adverts in English language journals many of which are published online such as *Wanted in Rome* (www.wantedinrome. com) aimed at the expatriate community. Try notice boards in English language bookshops, for example the Lion Bookshop at Via dei Greci 33/36 in Rome, churches for expats like the Church of England on Rome's Via del Babuino and the student travel agency CTS (Centro Turistico Studentesco e Giovanile) where the staff may be able to advise. CTS is the main student travel agency in Italy which does far more than arrange flights and travel, e.g. its website www.cts.it has links to language courses *(corsi di lingua)* as well as to its offices *(sedi)* throughout Italy.

Language school notice boards are always worth checking. For instance at the Centro di Lingua & Cultura Italiana per Stranieri where Dustie Hickie took cheap Italian lessons in Milan, there was a good notice board with adverts for au pairs, dog-walkers, etc. Every region has a Youth Information Office *(Centro Informazione Giovani)* which is in a position to advise on holiday work, for example in Bologna the Informagiovani is at Piazza Maggiore n°6 (informagiovani@comune.bologna.it). Links to all the youth information centres throughout Italy can be found at www.comune.torino.it/infogio/cig/ecr.htm.

The links between Italy and the US are very strong and often an Italian family will notify friends in the US to find them an au pair. Janet Renard saw a notice on the bulletin board of her university in Illinois and arranged to be interviewed by a friend of the employer. Even after confessing that she had little experience with children, could not speak Italian and had no idea where Sicily was, the family invited her to come.

Alternative summer employment is available with tour operators. Mark Warner employ nannies at their Mediterranean Beach Club Hotels in Italy and Sardinia; further details from the Resorts Recruitment department on 0870 033 0760 (www.markwarner.co.uk/recruitment).

RED TAPE

Au pairs from the European Union who intend to stay in Italy longer than three months should apply at the local police station *(questura)* for the correct documents to allow them to stay. You should take a letter from the family for whom you will be working and apply for a residence permit *(Permesso di Soggiorno)*. The situation for au pairs from outside Western Europe is much more difficult and the main sending agencies in North America, for example, warn of a long and tedious process.

Australian and New Zealand citizens aged 18-30 have recently become eligible for a 12-month working holiday visa in Italy, though the numbers are not great (1,500 at present). After obtaining a *Permesso*, an Australian working holiday visa holder is required to obtain a work permit, to be issued by the *Direzione Provinciale del Lavoro* (Provincial Labour Office which is a branch of the Ministry of Labour in each provincial capital). The work permit will allow a maximum of six months of working within 12, and for no more than three months with the same employer (which mirrors the limits placed on working holiday makers in Australia).

In general, non-EEA nationals without a working holiday visa are not eligible for the *Permesso di Soggiorno* and should obtain a student visa which permits them to work up to 20 hours per week (live-in or live-out). To obtain a long-stay visa, non-EU au pairs will need to enrol in and pay for an Italian language course at an approved school or college. The school registrar will issue a certificate which must then be stamped by the local police. The visa will be valid only for the length of the course. You must also show sufficient insurance cover, a return air ticket, proof of accommodation stamped by the police and a contract specifying dates, pocket money and benefits stamped by the provincial labour office and/or the police.

All working foreigners including au pairs should register at the local registry office *(Ufficio Anagrafe);* in Rome the address of the Central Registry Office is Via Luigi Petroselli 50 (behind Piazza Venezia). This must be done before foreigners are allowed to do certain things, such as open a bank account.

EU nationals who take jobs as summer au pairs need not worry about the *permesso* if they intend to stay less than three months. The only requirement for them is that they register within three days of arrival in the country, which is compulsory for all foreigners, including tourists, who normally do it through their accommodation.

HEALTH AND INSURANCE

All the usual EU regulations for social security and health insurance apply to au pairs in Italy and EU nationals should be sure to take an EHIC. This should be presented to the local Health Department *(Unità Sanitaria Locale* or USL) on arrival where you will be given a certificate of entitlement and a list of participating doctors and dentists. Au pairs from non-EU member states should take out private insurance since medical costs are very high in Italy. You can always purchase a policy after you arrive in the country, such as from any office of S.A.I., one of the major Italian insurance companies.

LEISURE TIME

The majority of au pairs enrol either in an Italian language course or, especially in Florence, in a course on art and civilisation. As usual most of these close down for the summer. There is usually no problem fitting classes in during the school year, since in most cities, children are at school from 8am to 4pm. Course fees are expensive, but they normally guarantee a good social life. You may be able to negotiate some free Italian lessons in exchange for helping with English classes.

In fact most things in Italy are expensive. For example Dustie Hickey used to go swimming in Rimini but found the entrance charges exorbitant (and she had to buy the compulsory hat and flip flops). Most au pairs find no difficulty in making friends, though of course every situation differs. For example Frances Thirlway had a wonderful social life in a fairly isolated village near Naples. Although her duties did not finish until 9.30pm or 10pm most nights, she simply strolled out into the square where she was sure to bump into some of the local teenagers she knew. With relatively little money, she appreciated that their social life seemed to be conducted over ice creams rather than alcohol, though this is changing in the bigger towns and cities. This obviously does not work for everyone since Janet Renard's village in Sicily (Mondello) is a seaside resort which flourishes in the summer but was deserted while she was there.

Italian families can be among the most warm and welcoming of any in the world. For every family which treats you as a servant, dozens of others will treat you as one of the family and will spurn protestations of gratitude for any generosity.

> **Being treated as one of the family may have its drawbacks as Janet Renard found in Sicily:**
> *I had my own room but quickly learned that a closed door was considered an affront; for nine months, I gave up privacy. On free afternoons when I wanted to read or write, Marcella would often ask if I could watch the baby for 'just five minutes' which meant half an hour or much more. They said it was their way of making me part of the family.*

If you are treated like a daughter, you may find your social life being a little cramped, since outside the major cities (and especially in Calabria and Sicily) it is not the 'done thing' for respectable young women to go out unescorted in the evenings. In some places the compulsory evening activity is the *passiagata* when everyone dresses up and promenades up and down the main street for several hours.

Susan Powell spent a thoroughly enjoyable year working for a family (again in Sicily), who disapproved strongly of her plans to go off alone to sightsee on the island. They insisted on driving her wherever she wanted to go and organised family excursions for her benefit; she greatly appreciated this, but if she hadn't been getting on with them so well, it would have been a real nuisance.

The problems which young women alone encounter on the streets of Italy are legendary, as recounted by Janet Renard:

Going places was also difficult because my friend (another American 'babysitter') and I were so often followed by men whom we didn't want following us. Whether we were shopping, going to the opera in Palermo or riding bikes, we were followed. In the end we curtailed activities outside the neighbourhood and relied on each other's company... Until I met a Sicilian boyfriend who lived three hours away in a small town. My visits there on Sundays (by bus) introduced me to the best aspects of Sicily, the people, the countryside, the sea.

In big cities it is an advantage to live close to public transport routes so as to cut down on long unaccompanied walks. The house in Rome where Emily Hatchwell stayed for six months was a ten-minute walk from the end of the bus line. Every time she walked this route, at least three cars would stop to ogle and hassle. Emily felt confident and fearless for the first couple of months which she thinks is the best protection (just as in New York City). But after a conversation with a scaremongering Englishwoman, she lost her nerve and had several unpleasant incidents, when men got out of their cars and grabbed her arms on either side; fortunately she managed to break free both times. So perhaps employers are not entirely misguided when they take an over-protective attitude to their au pairs.

TRAVEL

No-frills flights abound to various Italian destinations and more than one au pair has flown on Ryanair to Genoa, Trieste, Pescara or Palermo for about £30 (£25 of which will be taxes). Altogether Ryanair serves 15 airports all over Italy. Meanwhile a new airline Fly Globespan links Edinburgh and Rome between March and October (www.flyglobespan. com), and Thomsonfly serves Pisa from Coventry. Off-peak fares are quoted at £9 in each direction but the taxes and surcharges bring the total fare to over £60. Flying is almost always cheaper than going by train or coach.

DIRECTORY REFERENCES

For agencies based in Italy which place incoming au pairs, see: **Agenzia Alla Pari** (La Spezia), **Amicizia** (Genoa), **Angels Staff Services** (Rome), **ARCE** (Genoa), **Au Pair International** (Bologna), **Au Pairs Recruitment** (Turin), **Celtic Childcare** (Turin), **Euroma** (Rome), **Europlacements** (Milan), **Intermediate** (Rome), **Mix Culture** (Rome), **Roma Au Pairs** (Rome), **STI Travels** (Bologna), **Welcome Agency** (Turin).

For au pair agencies based in Britain that deal with Italy, see: Abacus, Academy, Angels International, The Au-Pair Agency (Edgware), Care Agency, Childcare International, The Childcare Solution, Delaney International, Edgware, English-Italian Agency, Hyde Park International, IAPO, Johnson's Au Pairs, Jolaine, Konnex, Nannies of St. James, Nanny & Au Pair Connection, People & Places, Poppins Nannies, Quick Au Pairs, Richmond & Twickenham, Solihull, Sunflowers Childcare, Totalnannies.com, and UK & Overseas.

Other agencies abroad which send au pairs to Italy are:
Australia: Au Pair Australia, Australian Nanny & Au Pair Connection, Charlton Brown Group, Childcare Team, JCR Au Pairs & Nannies
Austria: Au-Pair4You
Belgium: Stufam
Canada: Globetrotters, Le Monde, Scotia Personnel
Czech Republic: Au Pair International CZ, Student Agency
Finland: Allianssi
France: Accueil International, AFJE, Au Pair Azur, Butterfly & Papillon, Europair Services, France Au Pair Eurojob, Institut Euro'Provence, Inter-Séjours, Jeunesse et Nations, Nurse Au Pair Placement, Oliver Twist Association, Soames, Solution Au Pair
Germany: APAB Au-Pair Agentur Berger, Aupair2000, Au-Pair Interconnection, Felicity Nannies, In Via, Munichaupair, Personal Touch
Greece: Nine Muses
Netherlands: S-Au Pair Intermediate, Travel Active
Spain: Actividad Au-Pair Internacional, Agencia Intercambios Culturales y Au Pair, Centros Europeos Galve
Switzerland: Pro Filia
USA: goAuPair

Netherlands

Despite the fact that the state provides excellent day care facilities for working mothers, the demand for au pairs seems to be growing, so that an increasing number of agencies make placements in the Netherlands; for example the major au pair sending organisations in Poland, Peru and South Africa send au pairs to Holland.

Au pairs in Holland usually enjoy favourable working conditions, especially now that the Netherlands Au Pair Organisation or NAPO (www.napoweb.nl) has been established. As the Dutch chapter of IAPA, NAPO members strive to implement uniform standards, in conjunction with the government. For example the maximum number of hours an au pair can work is 30 per week. More than that, the person counts as a paid employee who has to pay taxes and social security contributions. Since 2004 the immigration authorities have operated a hotline for au pairs to report abuse of the system, e.g. complaints about an excess of domestic work, number of hours or the way in which they are treated. The telephone number in the Hague is 70-370 3888.

NAPO agencies insist that their client families and au pairs draw up an au pair agreement at the beginning of the arrangement. Au pairs are entitled to be paid €300-€340 a month and to be given two days off a week plus one full weekend off per month. Most families also pay for or at least make a contribution to the cost of a language course of up to €230 a year which is generally enough to cover the cost. In most cases travel costs are paid for by the family when the au pair completes her agreement.

The Netherlands has a strong tradition of social liberalism and egalitarianism, so you are unlikely to be treated as a skivvy, but will be considered part of the family. In fact the progressive policies and attitudes of the Dutch are what attract many young people from all over the world to spend time in the country. Although most au pairs are located in the western part of Holland, especially Amsterdam, Rotterdam, Den Haag & Wassenaar, Utrecht & 't Gooi, many families are also looking for au pairs in the regions of Deventer, Maastricht, Groningen, Nijmegen and Den Bosch.

Even without any knowledge of Dutch, you shouldn't encounter too many problems with communication, since the standard of English is remarkably high, except in rural areas. Of course it is expected that you be willing to learn some Dutch.

Jurata Ogorkis from Poland, who was an au pair in Holland for a year up till April 2005, was enthusiastic about her Dutch host family:
It was really worthwhile to go abroad as an au pair to Holland. I brought back thousands of good memories, made lots of new friends, saw many nice places. It's actually a great chance to learn more about yourself, improve a foreign language and see how you survive in a totally different world. I would take the same decision and go to Amersfoort and have a great year with the Oostroom-van der Kleij family! I had a very good relationship with the children. We spent lots of time together: playing, singing, dancing, cycling, camping or simply doing some crazy things. My host father is a musician, so I had a chance to meet personally all his band members, at the same time I could see Martien playing in concerts and get very close to the stage. My host mother, Nina, was a person to whom I could talk about anything. She was like a mother, sister and friend all in one person! Besides she is a very lively person, full of positive energy, always helpful, caring and optimistic. What I liked most about this family was that everybody had a great sense of humour and I really loved the atmosphere in their house. Maybe this is one of the reasons that I fell in love with Dutch people! I really think 'Nederlanders' are great!

FIXING UP A JOB

In 1999 the major au pair organisation Au Pair Discover Holland merged with *Travel Active* which now runs a large inbound au pair programme as well as an international Work, Study Language and Exchange programmes. Another major agency is *S-Au Pair Intermediate*. Activity International is an agency which used to make placements with Dutch families but they have stopped their inbound activities, handing on many of their families and applicants

to Travel Active.
Jill Weseman from the United States enjoyed her experiences as an au pair in a village of just 500 people 30km from Groningen:

After graduation I accepted an au pairing position in Holland, mainly because there is no prior language requirement here. I really lucked out and ended up with a family who has been great to me. Though the situation sounds difficult at best - four children aged 1½, 3, 5 and 7, one day off a week and a rather remote location in the very north of Holland - I have benefitted a great deal. The social life is surprisingly good for such a rural area.

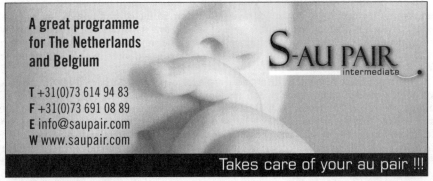

A great programme for The Netherlands and Belgium

S-AU PAIR
intermediate

T +31(0)73 614 94 83
F +31(0)73 691 08 89
E info@saupair.com
W www.saupair.com

Takes care of your au pair !!!

Among the bonuses which Jill received from her host family was the chance to spend the summer on their yacht on the south coast of France and then a return airline ticket to Japan to allow her to visit a friend.

Two good sources of links for au pairs are the webpages http://aupair.pagina.nl and 'Aussies in Holland' at www.coolabah.com/oz/hollandsite/employment.html. Among agencies to try in addition to the ones in the Directory are:

*Au Pairs Worldwi*de, PO Box 36 9300 AA Roden; street address: Morgenster 13, Marum, 9363 LH (tel/fax +31 594-510 801; aupairww@worldonline.nl; www. aupairsworldwide.com). Contact Anita Elema Places au pairs in Holland, Germany, Belgium, etc. Partner agency in Peterborough, UK.

Dutch Family Care Inc, De Frisia 71, 9207 CP Drachten (tel/fax +31 512-54 91 40; Info@ dutchfamilycare.nl; www.dutchfamilycare.nl).

Go Childcare, Kloosterlaan 61, 4551 BB Sas van Gent (+31 115-450863; fax: +31 115-450813; info@gochildcare.nl; http://home.hetnet.nl/~gochildcare)

Sana Au Pair Agency, Kloosterlaan 162, 1216 NT Hilversum (Postal address: PO Box 2306, 1200 CH Hilversum); +31 35-6284567; fax +31 35-6236052; sanaa000@planet. nl; www.sana-au-pair.com). Specialises in placing au pairs and nannies from South Africa, Eastern Europe, Australia and the Philippines.

Save-Way Consultancy, Klein Hoefblad 32, 1422 KH Uithoorn (297-522044; tel/fax 297-522045; pbaillet@freeler.nl; www.save-way.nl). €100 registration fee for incoming au pairs who are mainly from Eastern Europe, Indonesia, Nepal, etc.

World Wide Au Pair & Nanny, Burg. Hogguerstraat 785, 1064 EB Amsterdam (20-411 6010; fax 20-611 0330; www.worldwideaupair-nanny.com). Specialises in placing Peruvians among others.

In fact several agencies in the Netherlands specialise in bringing in au pairs from a specific country such as Yes Au Pairs (Koedijk 142, 7241 CL Lochem; +31 573 255184; info@ yesaupair.com) has a partner agent in the Philippines; Select Care (Vossenlaan 12, 3633 AN Vreeland; +31 294-234883; info@selectcare.nl) is run by a Romanian; while Indopool (Jacob Cabeliaustraat 19, 1067 AL Amsterdam; +31 20-68 97720; info@indopool.nl) recruits au pairs primarily from Indonesia and Poland. The Nanny Company (Postbus 2260, 5600 CG Eindhoven; +31 40-222 2834; www.nannycompany.nl) is a placement agency for professional nannies, but its website is only in Dutch.

RED TAPE

Until 20 years ago the Dutch legal system did not recognise the au pair arrangement since it was felt that it was inherently exploitative. However due to the lobbying of various youth and student organisations, au pairs are permitted to come to the Netherlands, provided the Council of Europe guidelines are complied with and the main purpose of the au pair stay is to learn about the Dutch language and culture rather than to work full-time.

Au pair positions are available to young women and men aged between 18 and 25 who can commit themselves to stay at least six months or, in the case of non-EU au pairs, 12 months, which is also the maximum length of stay. A few opportunities for summer stays are available. In addition to the statutory time off, the au pair must be given free time to attend a course (not necessarily the Dutch language), and must have health insurance provided by the family.

Citizens of EU/EEA countries do not need any special permits. Au pairs from Switzerland, Australia, Canada, Japan, New Zealand and the USA do not have to apply for a visa (MVV) in their country of residence but will have to obtain a residence permit (VVR BEP) after arrival. Note that a working holiday scheme operates for Canadians, Australians and New Zealanders aged 18-30 who can spend up to a year in the Netherlands working in any capacity. Nationalities that can come as au pairs without an MVV should register at the City Hall *(gemeentehuis)* within three days of arrival in the municipality *(gemeente)* where they will be au pairing. Once the forms are in order, a residence permit (VVR BEP, Vergunning Verblijf Regulier voor bepaalde tijd) should be granted for up to 12 months.

All other nationalities need both documents. The visa for a temporary stay or MVV *(Machtiging tot Voorlopig Verblijf)* must be applied for in Holland by the family, who normally pays the fee (currently €433) on behalf of the au pair. Application must be made to the Dutch immigration authorities (Immigratie & Naturalisatie Dienst) known as the IND; ring 0900-1234561 or consult www.ind.nl. This process can take up to three months. Without an MVV, the non-European au pair will not be able to obtain a VVR BEP. The residence permit will restrict you to remaining in the Netherlands only as an au pair, though it is possible to change host families. Satisfying the bureaucrats requires a lot of time and patience.

HEALTH AND INSURANCE

The residence permit will be granted only after the authorities are satisfied that you have adequate medical insurance. Nationals from outside Europe and some other countries are required to have a tuberculosis test.

All families in the Netherlands will pay for the au pair's insurance and the Dutch agencies will back their au pairs in this. For example *Travel Active* has a special department for au pair insurance (www.travelactiveinsurance.nl).

LEISURE TIME

The cultural and café life of the Netherlands is very vigorous and au pairs should have no trouble amusing themselves. Public transport is good so that even travelling to a nearby town for entertainment should pose few problems. Jill describes some of the good times:

Discos are packed on weekends and Americans are pretty rare here, so my company is a novelty. When I feel like catching the train or borrowing the family van and going to Groningen, a booming university city, I am always rewarded. There are a couple of other American au pairs there, and we always have a great time in the incredible discos and 'gezellig' (cosy) pubs. The energetic students give Groningen the reputation as the liveliest Dutch city next to Amsterdam. The nightlife doesn't die down until 6am (especially on Thursday nights).

The density of au pairs and nannies is in some areas too low for au pairs to rely on each other for their day-to-day social life; however most Dutch young people speak fluent English so you shouldn't feel too socially isolated. Travel Active runs the Travel Active Au Pair Club which all their au pairs in Holland are invited to join. It organises several group outings a year, for example trips to Volendam, Amsterdam, Utrecht and even a weekend trip to Paris. They also organise a Sinterklaas celebration: Sinterklaas is an important Duch celebration held on December 5th, precursor of some of the traditions associated with Santa Claus like gift-giving.

Another important agency, *House-o-Orange,* also runs a club for the au pairs it has placed in Holland and Belgium. The Orange Aupair Club organises a different activity each month.

Language classes are widely available, mostly for the benefit of aspiring migrants to Holland. A list of language and other education courses can be obtained from most agencies.

Holland is a compact country with such a well developed network of cycle tracks that cycling is a highly recommended way to spend your free time. Anyone considering staying for six months or more should consider buying a bicycle, which shouldn't cost much more than £60 second hand. Alternatively you can hire them cheaply from railway stations or your family might buy one for you.

TRAVEL

The cheapest way to get to the Netherlands is by coach from London Victoria. Expect to pay about £35 one way, £50 return if you are under 26. Fares on the train are comparable: the *Dutch Flyer* is a train and ferry service run jointly by One Railway, Stena Line and Netherlands Railways from London's Liverpool Station. The advantage of overland travel rather than flying is that you end up in the city centre not a distant airport.

Flights to Amsterdam on easyjet (www.easyjet.com), Thomsonfly from the Midlands (www.thomsonfly) and bmibaby (www.bmibaby.com) can sometimes match these fares despite the addition of very high taxes and charges (currently between £40 and £50). Ryanair services Eindhoven in the south of the country from Stansted (return fares from £35) and the Dutch no-frills airline Transavia (www.transavia.com) links London Stansted with Rotterdam. KLM (www.klm.com) serves a large number of regional British airports but its cheapest fares are normally about £100 return.

DIRECTORY REFERENCES

For au pair agencies based in the Netherlands, see: **Au Pair Interactive** (Naarden), **Happy Family Au Pairs** (Rotterdam), **House-o-Orange Au Pairs** (The Hague), **Juno Au Pairs** (Schiedam), **Mondial/Kryspol Au Pair Agencies** (Amsterdam), **S- Au Pair Intermediate** ('s-Hertogenbosch) and **Travel Active** (Venray).

For au pair agencies based in Britain that deal with the Netherlands, see: Academy, Angels International, Childcare International, Nannies of St. James, Nanny & Au Pair Connection, People & Places, Sunflowers Childcare.

Other agencies abroad which send au pairs to the Netherlands are:
Australia: Au Pair Australia, Charlton Brown Group, JCR
Austria: Au-Pair4You
Belgium: Services de la Jeunesse Feminine, Stufam
Canada: Au Pair Canada, Club Aventure, Le Monde, Scotia Personnel
Czech Republic: Au Pair International CZ, Student Agency
Finland: Allianssi
France: AFJE, Butterfly & Papillon, Inter-Séjours, Oliver Twist Association, Soames

Germany: A'nF, Felicity Nannies
Hungary: Au Pair Kft.
Iceland: Studentaferdir
Italy: Celtic Childcare, Intermediate
Peru: Au Pair Peru
South Africa: Mary Poppins
Spain: Agencia Intercambios Culturales y Au Pair
Switzerland: Pro Filia
Turkey: Yakin Bati
USA: Au Pair USA/Interexchange, goAuPair

Scandinavia

The demand for English-speaking au pairs is not vast but remains steady, especially in Denmark, where a certain number of young women over 18 are placed with families for 10-12 months through agencies. Another possible source of au pair vacancies is the searchable online database www.aupairforum.com, which has a selection of current family listings in Scandinavia whom interested candidates can contact directly. Searches take into account religious affiliation, and in Scandinavia there is a much higher proportion of requests for Protestant than Catholic au pairs (and almost none for atheists). Weekly wages vary a lot but many are around €100.

Another possibility is the Scandinavian Au-Pair Service Center (scandinavian@aupair.se; www.aupair.se) whose website provides contact names, phone numbers and email addresses for its headquarters in Helsingborg (Sweden) and offices in Oslo and Hamar (Norway) and Aalborg (Denmark) among others. The youth exchange organisation *Allianssi* in Finland claims to make au pair placements in Sweden, Norway and Iceland but not Finland.

Denmark, Sweden and Finland are full members of the European Union though only Finland has adopted the Euro as its currency. Norway and Iceland have decided to stay outside the Union but are part of the European Economic Area (EEA) and therefore permit the free movement of goods, services and labour from the EU. European citizens are now entitled to enter any Scandinavian country for up to three months to look for work.

Although there are many thousands of Swedes, Danes, Norwegians and Finns working as au pairs throughout Europe, the reverse is not true. A trawl of the internet will turn up plenty of au pair agencies in Scandinavian countries but they are mainly concerned with placing Scandinavian au pairs abroad rather than foreign girls with families in Scandinavia. The au pair system might be more extensive were it not that these countries tend to have excellent state provision of childcare. Also there is limited appeal for foreign young people to learn the Swedish, Danish, Norwegian, Finnish or Icelandic languages. On the other hand, the numbers of incoming au pairs are increasing especially in Denmark, Norway and Sweden. *Au Pairs International* in Copenhagen has expanded from making placements in Denmark to Norway and Sweden, and the *Scandinavian Au Pair Center* is active in the whole of Scandinavia. Au pairing is one of the few ways to afford an extended stay in this very expensive region of the world.

DENMARK

FIXING UP A JOB

Conditions for au pairs in Denmark are generally congenial. On top of the monthly pocket money of at least DKK 2,500, you should be given health insurance and are entitled to join free language courses in Danish.

The main au pair agencies in Denmark are *Au Pairs International* in Copenhagen and the *Scandinavian Au Pair Center Denmark* located in the north of the country but mainly working online with partners in Norway and Sweden. They do not charge a fee to incoming au pairs. *Au Pairs International* prefers applications to be sent through a partner IAPA agency in the applicant's own country.

Twenty-two year old Aracelli Miranda Pereira from Brazil was more than satisfied with the services of the Scandinavian Au Pair Center website (www. aupaircenter.dk) and wrote from Denmark in 2005 of her experiences:
My mother is married to a Danish man, and he told me a lot of about Denmark. I was very curious to know the famous land of LEGO. Currently I live with a sweet, funny and energetic family. They are mother, father, two daughters, 15 and 8, and one boy age 11. My work is cleaning, laundry, tidying up and helping with dinner, and also to entertain the youngest child after she gets home from school. I work 30 hours a week, have weekends off and the pay is approximately 2700 Danish kroners per month. In my spare time I'm an eager member of a local health club, and I enjoy participating in spinning-classes. I'm going to Danish lessons too, and sometimes I go clubbing. I am very pleased and satisfied with the agency. I would advise to any people who thinks about being an au pair in Denmark, to contact them.

If arranging a placement independently, place a free advertisement in English or Danish in the twice-weekly Copenhagen paper *Den Bla Avis* (meaning 'The Blue Paper'), a member of the Free Ads Paper International Association; it comes out on Monday and Thursday. The free Copenhagen paper *Sondagsavisen* carries a good number of ads for casual work and is distributed on Sundays. If you know a Danish speaker, check adverts in the jobs *(erhvervs)* section of the Sunday and Wednesday editions of *Berlingske Tidende* and *Politiken* newspapers. Advertisements in English are accepted by these papers. There is usually a fair sprinkling of adverts for au pairs and home helps.

Any temporary resident in Copenhagen should take advantage of the youth information centre Use It, Rädhusstraede 13, 1466 Copenhagen K (33 73 06 20/fax 33 73 06 49; useit@ kff.kk.dk; www.useit.dk). Their primary function is to help young foreigners get their bearings in Copenhagen and find affordable accommodation but they can also advise on a range of other topics. They distribute information about red tape procedures and can share realistic tips on finding a job or studying Danish. New arrivals can visit Use It to consult their files, newspapers and *fagboden* (Yellow Pages) and check their notice board. The helpful staff will even translate ads on request, though Use It is a tourist information centre for budget travellers, not an employment agency, and cannot offer or arrange employment.

REGULATIONS

The website of the Danish Immigration Service (www.udlst.dk) has a section in English about au pairing in Denmark. EU nationals who intend to stay longer than three months should apply for a residence certificate from the local authority *(statsamt)* after arrival. The website lists the countries whose nationals can enter the county as tourists, and then change their status afterwards. This allows a prospective au pair to meet the family before signing a contract.

Citizens of EU accession countries and all other nationalities must apply to a Danish representative abroad for an au pair residence permit, normally from their country of residence. Applicants should allow at least six to eight weeks for the permit to be issued. This will be valid for one year in the first instance but can be extended up to a maximum of 18 months and in special cases up to two years. The guidelines stipulate that residence permits will be granted to an au pair only when the applicant can demonstrate that she or he has the language and cultural qualifications to benefit properly from an au pair stay in

Denmark. For example the prospective au pair must speak a Nordic language, English or German to a reasonable standard. Another restriction on non-Schengen applicants is that they will not be granted a visa if they have previously stayed in Denmark as a student or trainee. The office of the Immigration Service *(Udlaendinge Styrelsen)* is at Ryesgade 53, 2100 Copenhagen Ø; 35 36 66 00.

Au pairs are not eligible to apply for a work permit because they are not in employment. The authorities are keen to avoid a situation in which au pairs are exploited as cheap childcare. According to the regulations, au pairs must be accepted as a member of the host family, be given free room and board, work no more than 30 hours a week, and they may not look after any other children apart from the ones belonging to that family. The family must submit a written contract on an official Immigration Service form. The minimum pocket money is 2,500 kroner (DKK 2,500) a month gross which is equivalent to rates paid in Britain i.e. £225 a month. 'Au pairs plus' is not a valid term in Denmark and if the family expects more than 30 hours household work a week the au pair has a right to change her family or go home instantly. Of course European nationals may legitimately work longer than au pair hours. Those who work 35 hours a week earn about DKK 700 a week; mother's helps earn DKK 700-900 and qualified nannies earn DKK 1200+. It is customary for au pairs to be given at least one week's paid holiday after six months. Au pairs from Europe are expected to pay for their own travel expenses whereas those from outside Europe have the right to ask the employing family to pay the return travel at the end of the agreed period of work.

After being granted an au pair visa and after arrival in Denmark, the au pair has a right/duty to get a CPR-number (Civil Registration Number or *personnummer)*. The au pair should take her passport to the Folkeregister at the local town hall. Eventually, this ID will entitle you to open a bank account, use the Danish health service and to enroll in free or subsidisd Danish classes. The CPR-number is issued instantly and after six weeks the au pair receives a health insurance card.

Nannies and mother's helps are liable to pay taxes on their earnings plus on board and lodging. Board and lodging are assessed as an income of DKK 2,033 per month and the tax-free threshold is approximately DKK 3,000 per month. That means that nannies are taxed on approximately DKK 1,500 a month (at a rate that averages 30%-35%).

SWEDEN

One domestic agency that mainly sends Swedish au pairs abroad will try to place British and other girls as au pairs in Sweden and Norway; see entry for *Au-Pair World Agency Sweden* in Trollhättan. The Scandinavian Institute for International Work and Study in Malmö (Box 3085, Drottninggatan 1J, 200 22 Malmö; 40-93 94 40/fax 40-93 93 07; info@ scandinavianinst.com) has in the past made a few au pair placements in Swedish families and throughout Scandinavia, though its website describes only its programmes in the USA for Scandinavians.

Other possibilities include:

Aupair & Language Center of Sweden KB, Nedre Långvinkelsgatan 36, 252 34 Helsingborg (+46 42 12 60 47; fax +46 42 12 60 25; aup@aupaircenter.com; www.aupaircenter. com).

Scandinavian Au Pair Service Center, Ultunagatan 62, 256 67 Helsingborg (+46 42 20 44 02/fax 42-32 82 39; scandinavian@aupair.se/ www.aupair.se).

Once you arrive, it is worth checking university notice boards for baby-sitting openings. A large proportion of Swedes speak English so, in general terms, you should have no trouble making your desire to find a live-in position known. The young American woman Woden Teachout found jobs as a domestic clearner this way and the last family for whom she cleaned gave her free room and board in exchange for acting as a companion to their ten year old daughter.

Au pairs are subject to the same regulations as all other foreign employees so non-EU nationals must obtain a work permit before leaving their home country. All the requirements are set out in the admirably clear English-language website of the Swedish Migration Board: Migrationsverket (www.migrationsverket.se/english.jsp). Immigration queries should be addressed to Migrationsverket, 601 70 Norrköping, Sweden (0771 19 44 00; upplysningen@migrationsverket.se; www.migrationsverket.se). Since 2004 it has been possible to apply for au permit permits electronically, provided you have the necessary documents including a job offer from a family (showing hours and pay), a certificate of intended studies in Swedish and two photos. You can also pay the fee of SEK1000 (£70) by credit card. The Swedish Migration Board stipulates that au pairs must work no more than 25 hours a week, must be serious about studying Swedish and must earn at least SEK3,500 a month before tax (currently £245).

The addresses of employment offices *(Länsarbetsnämnden)* around Sweden can be found on the website of the Swedish Employment Service (www.ams.se). The job centre in Stockholm might be worth visiting at 45 Kungstensgatan. Once you find work, you must register at the local taxation office *(Skattemyndigheten)* and get a *personnummer;* full information is in English on the taxation website http://skatteverket.se/english/index.html.

NORWAY

In Norway the situation is promising for au pairs of all nationalities, provided they speak some English, though the red tape is still considerable for non-Europeans. *Atlantis Youth Exchange* (Rådhusgata 4, 0151 Oslo; www.atlantis.no) runs a programme for up to 200 incoming au pairs who must be aged 18-30 and willing to stay at least six months but preferably 8-12 months. The first step is to contact one of Atlantis's partner organisations for application forms. Atlantis charges a sizeable registration fee of NOK 1,000, a quarter of which is non-refundable if the placement doesn't go ahead. Au pairs from an EEA country can obtain the residence permit after arrival.

All applicants must comply with terms of the Norwegian au pair programme as set out by the Department of Immigration on www.udi.no (search 'Au Pair'). When a family has been found for someone from outside Western Europe, the co-operating agency in Norway obtains an agreement of which four copies are forwarded to the au pair, together with an invitation letter. A standardised contract of employment (ref. GP-7030/1 B/E) is available in English and Norwegian from Politiets materielltjeneste, Nordre Ålsveg 18, 2770 Jaren, Norway (+47 61 31 80 00; fax + 47 61 31 80 11; pmtpost@pmt.politiet.no). The contract must be the original and must be signed by the applicant and the host family, and stamped/ signed by a recognised organisation (e.g. Atlantis).

These must be presented to the Norwegian Embassy in the applicant's home country, together with an original birth certificate. At least three months should be allowed for these procedures. The application fee for the work permit is currently €100/US$115.. Upon arrival in Norway, it is necessary to register with the local police within a week.

The monthly pocket money in Norway is NOK 3,000-4,000 which will be reduced by deductions for tax of 20%+ though families pay contributions into the health insurance fund *(Trygdekasse)*. The majority of families are in and around Oslo, Bergen or the other cities in southern Norway, although applicants are invited to indicate a preference of north, south, east or west on their initial application. Virtually all employers will be able to communicate in English. Au pairs are given a travel card worth NOK 400 a month.

People serious about pursuing a full-time university course in Norway might like to investigate the LEAPS (Language Education by Au Pair Stays) programme administered by AA-Adequate Assistance A/S (Gamle Algarheimsvei 140, N-2050 Jessheim, Norway; +47 94 13 86 57; aa@adequate-assistance.com) which in turn is part of an employment recruitment company. After spending one or two years as an au pair perfecting the language, the programme then provides for participants to study at a Norwegian university for several more years.

Agencies elsewhere in Scandinavia such as *Au-Pair World Agency* Sweden and *Au Pairs*

International in Denmark routinely place foreign au pairs with families in Norway. The Oslo Yellow Pages contain several au pair agency addresses, though these are primarily for Norwegians wanting to go abroad as au pairs.

Jill from Maryland decided to become an au pair in Norway after she was already in Europe and could not make her status official. In any case she headed north to stay with a family in Mosjoen north of Trondheim. She found that she didn't really have enough to do (since Norwegians receive paid maternity leave for up to a year and so the mother was at home), but she did enjoy hitching and exploring the local area, especially Bodo and Kjerringøy.

The Council of Europe regulations are scrupulously observed in Norway since Norway is one of the few countries to have ratified the agreement (principally to protect their au pairs abroad). So au pairs in Norway are normally not asked to work more than six hours a day, are covered by social security which the family arranges and so on.

Another programme administered by Atlantis is not specifically for au pairs but is based on a similar principle. The Norwegian Farm Guest Programme allows young people to spend between two and six months living with a farming family free of charge in exchange for helping around the farm. The programme is open to people aged between 18 and 30 of any nationality, provided they can speak English though the maximum stay is three months for non Western Europeans. The pocket money is not high relative to the Scandinavian cost of living, i.e. NOK 825 for a maximum of 35 hours a week. British applicants should apply through Gwendalyne (0800 804 8380; www.gwendalyne.com) whose fee is set at £320 for two months, £520 for six months.

Neil Tallantire worked for a number of winter seasons in Lillehammer, a ski resort 150km north of Oslo. He observed that there is some demand for seasonal live-in help in resort areas and recommends chatting to as many people as possible, for instance on the ferry if that is your chosen mode of transport:

Talk to people. Norwegians are friendly. You should get some job offers; I was offered work on a pig farm and an au pair type job, teaching English to some kids. Both were in resort areas and would allow plenty of time to ski.

As in Denmark there is a youth information centre known as Use It at Møllergata 3, N-0179 Oslo (22 14 98 20; mail@ung.info). It can recommend cheap accommodation and restaurants and can advise young people on practical problems. The Use It website (www.use-it.no) is in English and has lots of concrete tips for living and working in Oslo. Use It also distributes an informative booklet called *Streetwise*.

FINLAND

Au pair placements are rare in Finland, probably because very few people want to learn the Finnish language which is unlike all other European languages. However a new agency run by a husband and wife team *Snow Au Pairs* began placing foreigners in Finnish homes in 2005.

Finland offers about 1,800 short-term paid training opportunities to foreign students every year and it is not inconceivable that young people pursuing a career in childcare could participate. The International Trainee Exchange programme in Finland is administered by CIMO, the Centre for International Mobility (PO Box 343, 00531 Helsinki, Finland; +358 1080 6767; http://finland.cimo.fi); their website is in English. British students and graduates who want on-the-job training in their field (teaching, etc.) lasting between one and 18 months should apply directly to CIMO. Short-term training takes place between May and September, while long-term training is available year round. Applications for summer positions must be in to CIMO by the end of January.

Note that the longstanding Finnish Family Programme whereby young people at one time spent some months living with a family, helping with the children and speaking English is now open only to foreign students studying at Finnish universities.

Since so few agencies handle vacancies in Finland, the obvious alternative is to fix up something privately. Some years ago Natasha Fox exploited the Scandinavian desire to improve their English:

> *I found work as a nanny in Finland simply by placing advertisement cards in a few playgroups. The best area to place them in Helsinki is Westend, Espoo, about 15 minutes bus ride from the city centre. This is the most affluent area of the capital and I found a nanny job paying £110 a week for working 8am-4pm Monday to Friday. Most Finnish parents want their children to learn English so you may get hired on the strength of this.*

Natasha goes on to recommend asking some locals to translate newspaper advertisements for you. The main daily *Helsingin Sanomat* carries details of several domestic vacancies each day, and it is worth ringing up and asking if they would like an English-speaker for the benefit of the children.

If you advertise yourself, try to write it in Finnish, so you won't give the impression of being an arrogant foreigner. (You probably won't have to speak a word of it in the job.) This is the text of the advert Natasha used:

> *Haluaisitko `vaihtaa vapaale', lasten hoidon lomassa? Iloinen, vastuullinen Englandtilais-tytto antaa sinulle mahdollisuuden! Olen vapaa useimpina päivinä/ iltoina.*

This translates as, `How would you like a break from the kids? Responsible cheerful English girl will give you the chance! I am free most days and evenings.'

Immigration queries can probably be answered by looking at the English language website of the Directorate of Immigration (UVI), PO Box 18, 00581 Helsinki or in person at Lautatarhankatu 10 in Helsinki (09-476 5500; www.uvi.fi).

ICELAND

Interest in au pairing in Iceland is increasing, especially on the part of North Americans who can participate in the programmes run by *Scotia Personnel* in Canada. Exit-IS is a leading exchange agency in Iceland, the only agency certified to bring foreign au pairs to Iceland. The Au Pair in Iceland programme accepts au pairs aged 18-25 for periods of 9-12 months starting in August/September or for 6, 8 or 12 months from January. Details from Stúdentaferdir, (Bankastraeti 10, 101 Reykjavik, Iceland; +354 562 2362/fax + 354 562 9662; info@exit.is; www.exit.is). Families undertake to reimburse one-twelfth of the cost of your flights up to a maximum of ISK 5,400 after 12 months. The rate of weekly pocket money in Iceland since January 2005 has been a minimum of ISK 10,000 (£92) a week for a 30-hour week. Babysitting may be requested up to three times a week but will be paid extra. Note that the study of Icelandic is compulsory on this programme. The agency promises close supervision, opportunities to meet other au pairs, access to an Au Pair Club and hiking and riding trips offered at a discount.

The private employment agency Ninukot (Skeggjastadir 861, Hvolsvöllur; +354 487 8576; ninukot@islandia.is; www.ninukot.is) originally specialised in agricultural jobs throughout Iceland but has branched out to other spheres, and now includes a handful of jobs in childcare each year. Live-in childcarers are promised a minimum of €1,335 a month gross, with a deduction of €20 a day for room and board. After completing six months, the family pays for one way airfare to Iceland and after 12 months return.

TRAVEL

Travel to Scandinavia is less expensive than it was a few years ago when there was much less competition among airlines. Destinations served by no-frills airlines from the UK or in some cases Ireland are as follows:

Ryanair (www.ryanair.com): Aarhus and Esbjerg in Denmark; Gothenburg, Malmö and Stockholm in Sweden; Oslo and Haugesund in Norway; Tampere in Finland.

BMI (www.flybmi.com): Copenhagen, Esbjerg, Gothenburg, Stockholm, Oslo and Stavanger; mainly from Scottish and Northern British airports.

Norwegian Shuttle (www.norwegian.no): Bergen, Oslo, Trondheim (to Stansted and many other cities in Europe)

An alternative to flying is to take the DFDS Seaways ferry from Harwich to Esbjerg or Newcastle to Kristiansand in Norway (08705 333000; www.dfdsseaways.com) though the 18-hour journey Newcastle to Kristiansand is bound to cost more than a flight. Much of Scandinavia is accessible by ferries; route and fare information is available from the Color Line (www.colorline.com).

DIRECTORY REFERENCES

For au pair agencies based in Scandinavia with incoming programmes, see: **Allianssi** (in Finland but placements in Norway, Sweden and Iceland), **Atlantis** (Norway), **Au-Pair World Agency Sweden** (Sweden), **Au Pairs International** (Denmark), **Inter Au Pair** (Norway), **Scandinavian Au Pair Center Denmark** and **Scandinavian Au Pair Center Norway**, **Snow Au Pairs** (Finland), **Studentaferdir** (Iceland).

For agencies in Britain which deal with Scandinavia, see: Hyde Park International (to Scandinavia), Poppins Nannies (to Norway)

Other agencies abroad which send au pairs to Scandinavia are:

Austria: Au-Pair4You (to Denmark & Sweden)

Belgium: Stufam (to Denmark & Norway)

Canada: Le Monde Au Pair (to Denmark & Norway); Scotia Personnel (to Denmark and Iceland)

Czech Republic: Au Pair International CZ (to Denmark, Norway & Sweden), Student Agency (to Denmark, Norway & Sweden)

France: AFJE (to Finland), Inter-Séjours (to Denmark & Sweden), Oliver Twist Association (to Sweden), Soames (to Norway)

Germany: Au-pair Interconnection (to Norway), Munichaupair (to Finland), Personal Touch (to Denmark & Norway)

Greece: Nine Muses (to Denmark & Finland)

Hungary: Au Pair Kft. (to Norway & Iceland)

Italy: ARCE (to Finland)

Netherlands: House-o-Orange Au Pairs

Peru: Au Pair Peru (to Norway)

Spain: Actividad Au-pair Internacional (to Denmark & Norway)

Switzerland: Pro Filia (to Denmark & Norway)

USA: goAuPair (to Denmark, Norway & Sweden)

Spain & Portugal

WORKING IN SPAIN: PROS AND CONS

Spain's demand for au pairs and mother's helps is booming. The number of agencies inside Spain and of European agencies which have added Spain to their list of destination countries continues to increase. At the beginning of the 21st century, the popularity of Spanish studies continues to increase in Britain and beyond. The last two decades have seen unprecedented economic growth in Spain, which has fuelled a huge demand for the English language. Many Spanish families want more than an au pair; they want a young English speaker to interact with their children on a daily basis. The emphasis on conversational English means that a certain number of families are happy to consider young men for live-in positions.

Gone are the days when all the live-in positions in Spain were taken by Irish girls because of their Catholicism (though the Associacion Catolica Internacional Servicios Juventud Femenina continues to be involved in au pair placement in some Spanish cities). An amusing and vivid account of what it was like to be a 'governess' in Spain in the 1920s and 30s is provided in the book *No More than Human* by Maura Laverty, in which she claims that a whole generation of aristocratic Spanish children grew up with Irish accents.

The chances of being able to arrange an au pair placement in Spain, even at short notice, are good. In many cases requirements are minimal, e.g. a knowledge of Spanish or experience of childcare may not be necessary. The majority of jobs are in the cities and environs of Madrid and Barcelona, though jobs do crop up in glamorous resorts like Marbella, Majorca, Tenerife and elsewhere.

Despite the efforts of the many agencies and youth organisations active in Spain, the rules of au pairing are probably less strenuously enforced in Spain than in most other countries and hours tend to be on average longer than in other countries. Some au pairs report that they have ended up working the same hours as a mother's help but for au pair pocket money (which is normally paid on a monthly basis in Spain). The minimum pay for a standard au pair at present is €55/€60 per week, though agencies urge families who live in suburbs some distance from the city centre to pay a little more. No perks are built into the arrangement, so au pairs can't count on getting any paid holidays, subsidised fares or a contribution towards their tuition fees except at the discretion of their employers.

As noted, many families will want you to speak English, making it more difficult to learn Spanish. Another possible pitfall for serious linguists is that in some areas, principally around Barcelona, the dominant language is Catalan, which is incomprehensible to most speakers of Spanish. The Catalan language migrated to various corners of Spain including Majorca and Valencia, so if you are keen to learn 'pure' Spanish, make sure you are going to a family that speaks it. Basque is spoken in the north around Bilbao; however, since only 2% of the population of Spain are Basques, you are unlikely to encounter the language much.

Society remains fairly conservative in both Spain and Portugal (as throughout the Mediterranean) and a relatively small proportion of women go out to work. Good daughters stay at home helping their mothers, and there may be a certain level of intolerance of independent behaviour. One advantage of the traditional closeness of the extended family is that there is often an aunt or grandmother on hand to help with the childcare if the au pair wants some time off.

On the other hand many city families are as liberal as their counterparts elsewhere in Europe.

Judith Twycross had no complaints about her situation in Seville which had been arranged through a British agency:
The family treated me very well; they treated me as an equal with consideration for my need for privacy and free time. I was free to come and go as I liked during my spare time. Lunch was the main family meal of the day and I was expected to be there for it. I was rarely needed to babysit but, on the times I was needed, I was asked in advance. I also dog-sat a couple of weekends when the rest of the family went away. I was very lucky because the family had a maid and the only domestic duties I had were to tidy the girls' rooms and prepare breakfast for them in the mornings and a light tea when they got back from school. I had to give an hour's English class to the younger daughter and spoke to the elder daughter, who was already fluent, only in English. I was able to practise my Spanish with the parents

> and the maid, so didn't mind speaking English to the children, to whom I continued
> to give lessons for the rest of my stay in Spain, even after I stopped au pairing and
> began teaching English.

An extreme social elite remains in Spain and they are likely to maintain their distance from their home helps. Sally Stanley found this to be the case with her employers who ran a top hotel in Marbella and seemed to be out most evenings attending charity balls:

Although we were living together in a small flat, the mother's world remained completely remote from mine. There was no attempt to make me feel like part of the family, and I couldn't help but bristle whenever her treatment of me as paid help became especially glaring. Fortunately I got on fairly well with the three children (though they were terribly spoiled) who all spoke English, as they had had English nannies since birth - it was that kind of family.

FIXING UP A JOB IN SPAIN

Au pair placement is undertaken by many English language schools in Spain. Placing an English speaker in the household of a young Spaniard learning English benefits everyone. One of the biggest and longest established agencies in the field with partner agencies around the world is *Club de Relaciones Culturales Internacionales*, which is a non-profit club allied to the Ministry of Culture and the Ministry of Education and member of IAPA. Club RCI has many openings throughout the year. Although Noel Kirkpatrick wasn't really an au pair, he found them very helpful:

RCI helped me tremendously during my time here in Madrid e.g. finding students for me to teach and a family with whom to live this summer.

It is advisable to check out your agency quite carefully if the following extract is to be believed (from an article which appeared some time ago in the now-defunct newspaper *Overseas Jobs Express*):

The choice of au pair agency is important. We were lucky to find Centros Europeos Galve of Madrid which, for a reasonable registration fee, placed us in a good location and followed up to make sure we were acclimatising. I met another girl who had paid ten times what I had, and other au pairs whose agencies had turned a cold shoulder at the first sign of problems.

Although more a cultural exchange organisation than an au pair agency, Castrum (Ctra. Ruedas 33, 47008 Valladolid; 983-222213/ www.castrum.org) makes family placements of foreigners aged 18-30 in Castille and Leon. The arrangement involves participants spending three or four hours a day speaking English with members of the family and enrolling in a Spanish course for at least five hours a week. The cost of this student-teacher exchange is about €250 for 15-45 days.

Michelle Manion from Australia was happy with the language exchange arranged for her by Elena Garcia Perez of Castrum:

I would recommend the programme to anyone in my situation, i.e. anyone not entitled to a work permit who wants to live in Spain but not just as an au pair. I was placed with a family with two boys aged 11 and 14. In the morning I went off for my Spanish lesson and then gave a lesson to the boys in turn. Spanish boys are notorious for being spoilt and impossible to control, but also for possessing wonderful personalities and great senses of humour. Carlos and César were typically Spanish and always managed to be both delightful and infuriating. Anyone interested in undertaking this venture should try to ascertain the children's level of English before arriving in Spain and to bring textbooks, magazines and children's books to work with, since English books are difficult to find in Spain. Also, when you arrive in Spain try to make as many friends and take up every opportunity you're given as this is the best way to learn Spanish.

Madrid certainly does not have a monopoly on au pair agencies. Barcelona is an increasingly attractive destination; try the Barcelona agencies listed in the Directory: *Interclass, Actividad Au-Pair Internacional* and *Kingsbrook*. The Balearic and Canary Islands are also possible; families in Mallorca are registered with the *Agencia Intercambios Culturales y Au Pair* and with *ABB Au Pair Family Service*, both in Palma de Mallorca.

Other agencies to try include:

Adayss (Agencia de Au-pair y Servicios Sociales), C/ Jesús de Monasterio, 8 - 5° Ctro., 39010 Santander (tel/fax +34 942-375364; adayss@telefonica.net; www.adayss.com). Agency established in 2003.

Babel Idiomas, Calle Larios 4, 2°, 29005 Malaga (+34 952-608487; boelo@babelidiomas. com/ www.babelidiomas.com). Au pairs must stay minimum of 3 months and have intermediate Spanish.

B.E.S.T., Calle Solano 11, 3°C, Pozuelo de Alarcón, 28223 Madrid (+34 91-518 7110; www.bestprograms.org). Au pair placements for Americans and Europeans; fee $970 for 3 months.

Easy Way Association, C/ Gran Via 80, Planta 10, oficina 1017, 28013 Madrid (91-548 8679; www.easywayspain.com).

Globus-Idiomas, C/ Gomez Cortina, 5, 2B, 30005 Murcia (+34 968-29 56 61; fax +34 968-29 75 25; globus@ono.com; www.globusidiomas.com). IAPA member.

Hemingway Instituto, Bailén n° 5 - 2° dcha, 48003 Bilbao (+34 94-416 79 01; +34 94-416 57 48; info@institutohemingway.com; www.institutohemingway.com).

Info Inter, Mayor 32, 28013 Madrid (+34 91-366 3037; infointerspain@yahoo.es)

Juventud y Cultura, Edificio Bellas Artes, Calle Alcala 42, 5-14, 28014 Madrid (+34 91-531 28 86; fax +34 91-532 79 71; juvycult@juvycult.es; www.juvycult.es). IAPA member.

NuevasLenguas, Avda. Eduardo Dato 23, Local Interior, 41018 Seville (+34 954 422 879; masinformacion@nuevaslenguas.com; www.nuevaslenguas.com). Free placement of au pairs with families in Andalucia (Seville, Granada, Cadiz, Huelva, etc.). Bonuses for staying longer than 6 months.

Planet Au Pair, C/Los Centelles 45-6-11, 46006 Valencia (+34 96-320 6491; info@ planetaupair.com; www.planetaupair.com). Accept Europeans, Americans, Canadians, Australians and New Zealanders. Programme fee €232 for stays of less than 3 months, €319 for longer stays.

For links to other agencies, check the website www.azzoomi.com/eng_chldcare_home.htm (sic) which lists about 20 agencies in Spain. If you deal directly with a Spanish agency, you may have to pay a placement fee though mostly the agencies charge large fees for outgoing placements.

Au pair arrangements can of course be made without a mediating agency. The many language institutes and schools in every town and city can prove a good source of local families looking for an English-speaking live-in helper. If you want to make informal contacts and meet expatriate families who might be looking for live-in childcare, you could visit a mothers' and toddlers' group like the one held every week in Madrid at the British Embassy Church of St. George at C/ Nuñez de Balboa 43.

One English nanny wanted a live-in position but her status as the single mother of a two-year old boy made her quest more complicated. She used her initiative and contacted vegetarian/vegan societies around Europe, asking them to put her details in their newsletter, and several of the replies she received were from Spain.

Trained nannies looking for seasonal work in resorts should try British tour operators that specialise in Spain. For example Minorca Sailing Holidays (58 Kew Road, Richmond, Surrey TW9 2PQ; recruitment@minorcasailing.co.uk) employ nannies to work between May and September in crèches at their holiday centre in the Bay of Fornells on the north coast of Minorca.

Another possible way of fixing up a job ahead of time is to advertise in the free ads paper *Segundamano* (equivalent to *LOOT* in London). One summer Nan Bevan from California tried this means of fixing up an au pair position and described the responses to her ad as 'more than fruitful'. If you are on the spot, check local advertisements in the English language press. For example the *Majorca Daily Bulletin* and the weekly *Costa Blanca News* published in Alicante (www.costablanca-news.com) carry job adverts which occasionally include requests for au pairs. You can place your own advert, though newspapers may be reluctant to accept 'Employment Wanted' ads from outside Spain.

LEISURE TIME

State schools offer Spanish language instruction more cheaply than private schools, though of course they will be closed in the summer. Prices vary wildly among schools, so it is worth comparing several, since it is possible to spend over half your monthly pocket money on fees. A couple of internet searches via sites like www.spanish-living.com or www.quality-courses.com will quickly lead you to language schools. After arrival you can contact the library of the Cervantes Institute to find local courses.

Of course many other things can be studied in Spain apart from language. Learning some of the traditional dances is the aim of some au pairs who have the chance to learn Sevillanas, Malagueras, the Pasadoble or even the very difficult Flamenco.

> **Judith Twycross did not have to depend solely on her Spanish classes at a local institute twice a week for her social life**
> *I took Saviana classes in the afternoons for a month before the Seville feria. I went out at night three or four times a week to the cinema or bars where it was easy to meet other people, both Spanish and other foreigners. In the summer I was given a free swimming pass for the local swimming pool. I made the acquaintance of quite a number of other au pairs and found that while a number of us had a lot of freedom, others were working all night and day (often in families with pre-school children) for next to nothing.*

In Madrid, Barcelona and tourist-exploited areas, it may be difficult to break the ice with the locals. The impact of tourists (over 40 million of them per year) from the more permissive societies has prompted some Spanish men to turn their backs on their own over-protected women and consider foreign women fair game. This is all very well for the good-time girls who have set their sights on one of those beady-eyed Spanish waiters, but unfortunate for those interested in harmless friendships. As in Italy, you will have to learn how to repel unwelcome advances.

WORKING IN PORTUGAL

European au pairs are much less common in Portugal than nannies and childminders from former Portuguese colonies like Mozambique and Brazil, as well as other developing nations. Virtually no British agencies undertake placements there, partly because so few people are interested in learning Portuguese. However there are such sizeable expatriate British communities in the two main cities of Lisbon and Oporto as well as on the Algarve (the south coast) that there is some demand for English-speaking nannies and mother's helps in these households. The best chance is to network with expat families, possibly by advertising in an English-language paper. Each week the *Portugal Resident* carries six pages of classified advertisements including jobs and situations wanted, with live-in childcare positions advertised from time to time. It is published every Thursday (www.

portugalresident.com; Lisbon edition: 214-421 221).

The International Au Pair Association has only one member agency in Portugal: Babete & Avental Serviços Domésticos Lda, Rua dos Remolares 6-4 Dto, 1200-371 Lisbon (+351 21 324 72 50; fax +351 21-340 30 30; aupair@babeteavental.pt; www.babeteavental.pt). This domestic agency was established in Lisbon in 1999.

Another possibility is the APAI (Portuguese Association of Intercultural Learning, Rua Wanda Ramos, Lote 13 – Lojas 1900-917 Lisbon (+351 218-479 104; fax +351 218-479 109; apai2mw@mail.telepac.pt; http://apai.planetaclix.pt). Information is scarce and it may be that they organise only an outgoing programme for Portuguese au pairs.

A few positions may be advertised on the internet with expat families. Summer openings are most likely to occur in the school holidays between the end of July and end of September.

REGULATIONS IN SPAIN & PORTUGAL

EU nationals no longer need to apply for a residence card *(Tarjeta de Residencia)* although if you intend to stay in Spain for a long period, it may be useful to take up the option of applying for one from the local police headquarters *(Comisaría de Policía)* or to a Foreigners' Registration Office *(Oficina de Extranjería)*. The documents necessary for the *residencia* are a contract of employment, three photos, a passport, a medical certificate and a police clearance certificate.

As soon as you start any job you should also apply to the police for an NIF (national insurance number) which serves as a form of identity and will allow you to open a bank account, etc. Further details are available from the Ministry of the Interior website (www. mir.es/sites/mir/extranje/index.html) in Spanish only or can be checked with the Labour & Social Affairs Counsellor's Office of the Spanish Embassy (20 Peel St, London W8 7PD; 020-7221 0098; www.conspalon.org/indexeng.html); and with the British Consulate-General in Spain (Paseo de Recoletos 7-9, 4º, 28004 Madrid; 91-524 9700; www.ukinspain. com).

The red tape for non-EU applicants is so daunting that most Spanish agencies limit their placement services to Europeans. No special au pair visa exists. If a non-EU national wants to come for less than 90 days, they can come on a tourist visa. If they want to stay longer then a student visa will be needed (because a regular work permit is very complicated, takes six months to process and no family wants to wait that long). In order to obtain a student visa, non-Europeans will need a raft of documents including the offer of a full-time place at a recognised language school (at least 15 class hours), a recent medical certificate, police clearance certificate and contract from the family. The application must be made before leaving the country of residence. The right to remain in Spain will be extended only for periods of three months at a time, so this procedure will have to be repeated every three months. Non-EU au pairs and nannies who come to an informal arrangement with a family in Spain will have to leave the country every three months in order to renew their tourist visa on re-entry. The main Canadian agencies like *Scotia Personnel* can assist North American au pairs get to Spain.

Portugal has the reputation for being more lenient towards au pairs who, like live-in English tutors and governesses, traditionally worked without worrying about obtaining a work permit. So few au pairs go to Portugal, it seems, that the *Ministerio do Trabalho* does not concern itself too much with live-in childcarers from developed countries. Those who wish to apply for a residence permit in Lisbon must go to the *Servico de Estrangeiros e Fronteiras* (Rua Conselheiro José Silvestre Ribeiro 4, 1649-007 Lisbon; 217-11 50 00).

HEALTH AND INSURANCE

An employing family should register their au pair with the Instituto Nacional de la Seguridad Social or INSS and obtain a list of participating doctors (which are more widely scattered than is convenient). Some of the agencies in Spain recommend that the families registered with them arrange insurance cover for their au pairs but this can by no means be relied upon.

All EU passport and European Health Card holders are entitled to receive treatment at Portuguese health centres (*Centro de Sáude*) and state hospitals, though varying charges will be made which would be better covered by a comprehensive private insurance policy.

TRAVEL

With Ryanair serving 13 Spanish destinations plus Oporto and Faro, you should have no trouble booking a cheap flight to Spain. As usual the cheapest flights may not take you right to the city that is your destination. For example, the cheapest option for getting to Madrid is to fly with Ryanair to Valladolid and then take a bus from there. Easyjet has about the same number of destinations, but tends to be a little pricier. Bmibaby (www.bmibaby.com serves the Mediterranean resorts of Faro, Murcia, Malaga, Alicante and Palma. Also compare Monarch's scheduled and charter flights (www.flymonarch.com). No-frills and charter airlines plus specialist discount operators sell low-season return flights for reasonable fares, which are much cheaper than coach or rail fares. If you are prepared to leave at short notice, ask any travel agent for last minute bargains.

DIRECTORY REFERENCES

For agencies based in Spain, see: **ABB Au Pairs** (Palma de Mallorca), **Actividad Au-Pair Internacional** (Barcelona), **Agencia Intercambios Culturales y Au Pair** (Palma de Mallorca), **Centros Europeos Galve** (Madrid), **Club de Relaciones Culturales Internacionales** (Madrid), **Crossing Limits** (Seville), **English World Language School** (Madrid), **G.I.C.** (Jávea in Alicante), **Interclass** (Barcelona), **Interlink** (Zaragoza), **Kingsbrook Languages & Services** (Barcelona). **O'Neill School of English** (Vizcaya), **Servihogar** (Cádiz), **Spanish Teachers** (Madrid).

For au pair agencies in Britain that deal with Spain, see: Abacus, Academy, Angels International, Au Pair Agency (Edgware) including Majorca, Au Pair Connections (specialises in Spain), Bloomsbury Bureau, Childcare International, The Childcare Solution, Delaney International, Edgware, Hyde Park International, IAPO, Johnson's Au Pairs, Jolaine, Nannies Abroad, Nanny & Au Pair Connection, People & Places, Quick Au Pair & Nanny Agency, Richmond & Twickenham, Solihull, UK & Overseas, Weigan Nannies (to Spain and Portugal).

Other agencies abroad that send au pairs to Spain include:
Australia: JCR Au Pairs & Nannies
Austria: AuPair4You
Belgium: Services de la Jeunesse Feminine, Stufam
Canada: Au Pair Canada (Toronto), Globetrotters, Le Monde Au Pair, Scotia Personnel
Czech Republic: Au Pair International CZ, British Contact, Kiddykare, Student Agency
Finland: Allianssi
France: Accueil International, A.F.J.E., Au Pair Azur, Butterfly et Papillon, Euro Pair Services, Fée Revée, France Au Pair Eurojob, Institut Euro'Provence, Inter-Séjours, Jeunesse et Nations, Nacel, Nurse Au Pair Placement, Oliver Twist Association, Soames, Solution Au Pair
Germany: A'nF, APAB, AuPair2000, Au-Pair Interconnection, Au-Pair Service Dr. Uwe Krenz, CP Au Pair Agentur (to Portugal), Felicity Nannies, IN VIA, Munichaupair, Personal Touch
Greece: Nine Muses (also to Portugal)
Hungary: Au Pair Kft.
Iceland: Studentaferdir
Ireland: The European Au Pair Agency
Italy: 3 Esse (to Spain and Portugal), ARCE, Celtic Childcare, Euroma, MB Scambi Culturali, Roma Au Pair, Soggiorni All'Estero per la Gioventù, STI Travels

Netherlands: Au Pair Interactive, House-o-Orange Au Pairs, S-Au Pair Intermediate, Travel Active
Switzerland: Pro Filia
USA: Au Pair USA/InterExchange

Switzerland

Anyone who wants to spend a complete year abroad to learn French, German or even Italian should certainly consider au pairing in Switzerland where working conditions are very favourable. The enthusiastic literature from Karin Schatzmann, proprietor of the *Perfect Way Au Pair Agency*, is probably not far off the mark when she says Switzerland is the best country in which to be an au pair. The 'pocket money' is strictly controlled by government directives and differs between the French and German areas. The pocket money in German cantons starts at SFr590 net for 30 hours of work up to SFr740 for 40 hours; in the Geneva area the monthly minimum is SFr760 (€500). The gross salary starts much higher than this (i.e. SFr1340, SFr1415 and SFr1490) but the allowable deductions for full room and lodging is SFr900 a month plus monthly earnings are further reduced by compulsory deductions (see section below).

Other perks for Swiss au pairs are unheard of elsewhere. For example you are entitled to five weeks paid holiday during your year if you are 20 years old or less, and four weeks if you are over 20. When on holiday you get not only your weekly net salary but also financial compensation for the meals which you are not eating with the family. So if you took two of your four weeks off to tour the French Alps, visit Bavaria, travel home to England or whatever takes your fancy, your holiday earnings would go a long way to offsetting the cost of the travel. The cost of living in Switzerland is among the highest in the world so unless you lead a fairly spartan life you probably won't be able to save much from your wages. But becoming an au pair is one of the easiest ways of being able to afford an extended stay in Switzerland.

Families are required to pay at least half your language school fees which will be (in total) between SFr500 and SFr1,000 for six months of three or four lessons a week. After completing a 12-month contract, they should pay for a return ticket to your home.

An au pair stay in Switzerland is not necessarily a bed of roses however. The Swiss national character, with its very hard-working and orderly approach to life, is not to everyone's taste. Many families comprise two working parents, in which case the au pair will be in sold charge for much of the time. A streak of chauvinism can be detected in many Swiss which can lead to a certain smugness and even xenophobia. It is certainly a conservative country where women did not get the vote until 1971 and certain kinds of political activity are banned from university campuses. After au pairing for the winter season in Wengen, Mary Hall ended up agreeing with the clichés about the Swiss, that they are very organised, particular, money-mad and hard to befriend.

You may find yourself hemmed in by rules, for example being asked to keep all the receipts for any expenditures you make on behalf of the children or for shopping. The bumph from one of the agencies states that au pairs 'should not simply take fruit without asking first', or in fact help themselves to anything in the fridge, larder or pantry.

Most reports indicate that farming families tend to be warmer and more welcoming than city families, though equally hard-working.

> **Gillian Forsyth, who applied through the Landdienst-Zentralstelle described below, found her family placement hard work since she had to muck in with both farm and domestic duties**

> *The farm was extremely isolated and the only chance to leave it was on market day, when I sold the cheese we made. Life was very primitive - no electricity for example. However as we got up at 5am, we went to bed before dark. My duties included milking the goats, feeding the animals and making hay, as well as cleaning and looking after the baby. As far as improving my French was concerned, the job was not ideal as I was often alone with the goats or the baby.*

Another disadvantage for budding linguists is that Swiss German is very different from high German and can be unintelligible to students of German who have never been exposed to it before. *Hochdeutsch* is taught in schools in Switzerland and so most Swiss Germans can speak it if required. If you are placed in a family working at one of the many international organisations with headquarters in Geneva, you may find that the language of the household is English.

FIXING UP A JOB

A search for au pair agencies in Switzerland will turn up a handful, though be aware that a few of these specialise in placing Swiss young people rather than foreigners. Young German-speaking Swiss girls and boys (aged 15-17) often choose to have a *Welschlandjahr* when they live with a family in the French-speaking part in order to master Switzerland's other language, and vice versa for French-speaking teenagers. For instance Oui Si Yes (www.aupair.ch), the au pair placement wing of the Reformed Church of Switzerland, specialises in such placements as does Swiss Au Pair (Quai Maria Belgia 8, 1800 Vevey (www.swissaupair.ch) which co-operates with the Catholic church.

It is necessary to look elsewhere for agencies that are set up to invite foreigners into Switzerland. Note that IAPA has no member agencies in Switzerland. *Pro Filia* is a long-established Catholic au pair agency with branches throughout Switzerland. It charges incoming au pairs a fee of SFr300 which may be prohibitive for some, though it can be paid out of the first month's salary. Petite Pumpkin/Petite Fourni at 125 bis route de Saconnex d'Arve, 1228 Plan-les-Ouates, Geneva (+41 22-771 1302; Mob: +41 79 694 6588; Christine.breiteneder@lapetitefourni.com; www.lapetitefourni.com) works with its British counterpart Petite Pumpkin, 45 Nelson St, Buckingham MK8 1BT (01280 824745; susan@petitepumpkin.co.uk). The au pair traffic is in both directions.

Two agencies that have strong links with Canada may be able to assist other English-speaking nationalities:

Can Au Pair, Geissbuelstrasse, CH-8704 Herrliberg (+41 1-915 26 81; fax +41 1-915 26 56; office@canaupair.ch; www.canaupair.ch). Arranges au pair contracts in Switzerland for Canadian women aged 18-28.

Wind Connections, Erlenbach (+41 44-915 4104, fax: +41 44-915 4105; info@ windconnections.ch; www.canadalink.ch). Specialises in placing au pairs from Canada, Australia and the UK with Swiss families. All candidates must be interviewed.

Note that Compagna (formerly Freundinnen Junger Machen) is no longer involved with placement of au pairs in Switzerland.

It is possible to become an au pair in France with a family living within commuting distance of Geneva (about 40,000 people cross the border on a daily basis). At the other end of the country is the Italian-speaking canton of Ticino in which Agenzia Inter Au-Pair is located. The owner of this company (Mrs. Betté) reported at the end of 2005 that there was very little demand from au pairs these days, partly because people who want to learn Italian would be better off going to Italy than to the Italian-speaking province of Ticino. However she is willing to do her best for any individuals who have a particular interest in going to this region; contact Agenzia Inter-Au Pair at Via Pezza Venerdi 5, CH-6616 Losone, Ticino (+41 91-791 66 75); the agency has been in business since 1981.

Seasonal au pair jobs do exist, especially in ski resorts, where there is a demand for casual babysitters as well. Mark Stephenson noticed 'reams of requests for au pairs and nannies' in the tourist office of a French-speaking ski resort. While cycling from Scandinavia to Spain, Mary Hall (a nurse by training) decided to stop off in the Swiss Alps for the winter and look for work:

I arrived in Interlaken at totally the wrong time, since it was in between seasons at the beginning of November when all the hotel managers have gone on holiday. I went round all the hotels which were open without success. A friend advised me to get a phone card, the Yellow Pages and ring around. He also said to speak with a smile which seemed to work as I got a couple of offers straightaway. I accepted the first one and ended up in Wengen looking after the spoilt daughter of some hotel owners. They asked me to name a price; I had no idea what the going rate was and named a figure that was obviously too low because they accepted it immediately. They said that they would pay for my work permit and train pass (which never happened) but they did hire me skis for the season. I can't say I enjoyed the job or my relationship with the child and her parents, though they were fair with wages and days off.

You may see notices posted in resorts (check at tourist offices) or in places where expatriates tend to meet, such as the American Library and Church in Geneva (3 rue de Monthoux) which has a notice board where live-in jobs are often posted. Alternatively you can post your own request for a family placement. You may also read the *Petits Annonces* online at www.lausanne-famille.ch/aupair.aupair.htm which at the time of writing included 11 families looking for au pairs in the Lausanne area.

The Swiss office for Voluntary Farm Work (Landdienst-Zentralstelle/Service Agricole, Mühlegasse 13, Postfach 728, 8025 Zürich (1-261 44 88; www.landdienst.ch) can fix up young people who know some German with a job on a Swiss farm lasting from three to eight weeks starting in early August. Female participants in the programme often find that their duties are closer to those of an au pair than a farm assistant, though there is no guarantee of this when you apply. Participants are paid SFr20 a day and pay a registration fee of SFr80.

RED TAPE

Switzerland is not a member of the European Union. However a bilateral agreement with the European Union has been concluded and the main obstacles to free movement of persons were removed in 2004. The category of seasonal worker has been abolished. Now the system is more in line with the rest of Europe so that EU job-seekers can enter Switzerland for up to three months (extendable) to look for work. If they succeed they must show a contract of employment to the authorities and are then eligible for a short-term residence permit (valid for up to one year and renewable). This normally takes about four weeks to be processed and in that time you are not supposed to start work. From 2007, Switzerland aims to allow the unfettered movement of workers.

The employment of au pairs in Switzerland is organised almost as precisely as their watches. Au pairing is not the casual arrangement it is in some other European countries but is carefully controlled by various rules and regulations. Deductions of roughly SFr100 per month will be made from your earnings for AVS/AI/APG (taxes, pension and unemployment insurance contributions) although in some cantons families are expected to pay half the compulsory health insurance and all of the au pair's accident insurance contributions. Further information about working conditions are available from the Hauswirtschaft Zurich, Klosbachstr. 10, 8032 Zurich (+41 1-383 53 22; www.hauswirtschaft.ch). A good source of information about au pair conditions in French-speaking Switzerland can be found at www. geneve.ch/ocirt/relation_travail/contrats_types.asp.

EU nationals do not need a work permit, only a residence permit. This can now be applied for online (www.arbeitsbewilligungen.zh.ch/content/internet/vd/awa/e_workpermits2/ en/home.html) where details of the requirements can be found for the canton of Zurich.

Otherwise, the application can be made by post to Migrationsamt, Postfach, 8090 Zurich. The permit will be for one year, though EU citizens are allowed to stay for up to two years as long as they are working for the same family.

The requirements for non-EU au pairs are more rigorous. In order to qualify for an au pair permit, you must be a national of Europe, the USA, Canada, Australia or New Zealand and be between the ages of 17 and 29 (18 is the minimum in Geneva; 27 is the maximum in Ticino). You must be prepared to be placed in a German-speaking family in order to learn German by attending at least three or four hours of language classes a week (and attendance may be checked). The minimum stay is 12 months and the maximum 18 months. Your one-year contract can be broken only in exceptional circumstances and you must give at least one month's notice.

> **If you are thinking of trying to find a live-in job without having the permit organised in advance, you will encounter problems, as described by an Australian woman on a travellers' website (ww.eurotrip.com) in 2005:**
> *If you only have your Australian passport and you're planning to find work in Switzerland - it's damn hard - unless you are extremely qualified in an area that they are running short of people in. Switzerland is EXTREMELY organised and strict with pretty much everything. Not only concerning the obvious environmentally friendly attitude that everyone's heard about, but also with opening bank accounts, getting credit cards and jobs. If you get caught working illegally in Switzerland, the fines are huge and it's a massive pain to deal with - so make sure you do everything legally because it's not worth getting caught.*

HEALTH AND INSURANCE

No reciprocal agreement on health care exists between the UK and Switzerland. Therefore au pairs have to be absolutely sure that they have valid private insurance or are covered by the Swiss system. This will turn out to be quite expensive but essential. Because of the high degree of regulation of the au pair system, agencies and families generally play by the rules.

Deductions of between 6% and 7% for insurance and contributions are calculated on the basis of the au pair's gross salary (SFr1340-SFr1490 depending on hours worked). Swiss health insurance does not cover dental treatment which is exceedingly expensive. You may also be liable for a cantonal tax, unless you are lucky enough to have an employer who shoulders these incidental expenses for you or if you have not yet reached your 19th birthday.

LEISURE TIME

Plenty of language courses are available in all Swiss cities and towns. One of the most important organisations is Migros which has schools throughout Switzerland (www.ecole-club.ch or www.klubschule.ch). Families normally pay half the course fees, though this is not compulsory in most cantons. Mary Hall did not find the Swiss very friendly or helpful, though she would be willing to work there again (as long as it wasn't as a nanny!):

On the plus side, I learnt how to ski. Wengen and the Jungfrau region is absolutely gorgeous. There has never been such a good stress-reliever as sitting in the sunshine with my employer's fat out-of-condition dog for company. Oh I also learnt (kind of) how to play the organ at the local church since they were desperate for any kind of effort, regardless.

Despite the high cost of domestic travel by train and postbus, you should have the chance to visit some of Switzerland's more scenic corners. In some cantons, the cost of local travel can be reduced by acquiring a *carte d'indigène* from the *Fremden-polizei* (aliens police) (for which permit-holders are eligible) which allows you to travel on public transport at a subsidised local rate and also to buy a cheap seasonal ski pass if you happen to be working over the winter in a ski resort.

TRAVEL

You can find no-frills flights from a variety of UK airports. The only Swiss airline to try is Helvetic (ww.helvetic.com) which flies from Luton to Zurich. Quoted return fares are very low (e.g. £20) but taxes and surcharges raise this to a much less impressive £110. Flybe (www.flybe.com) links Norwich, Birmingham and Southampton with Berne and Geneva, while easyjet serves Geneva from many regional British airports and Basle from Luton and Stansted.

The easiest rail destination in Switzerland is Basel, which is on the principal Calais to Milan route. Many Swiss families will pay their au pair's fare home (within Europe) on completion of a one-year contract, though this should not be taken for granted.

DIRECTORY REFERENCES

For agencies based in Switzerland, see **Heli Grandjean Placements** (Colonge-Bellerive), **Perfect Way** (Brugg), **Priorité Enfant Sarl** (Geneva), **Pro Filia** (throughout the country) and **Sunshine Au Pair Agency** (Mies/Geneva).

For au pair agencies in Britain that deal with Switzerland, see: Abacus, Academy, Au Pair Search, Lloyd's, Nannies of St. James, Poppins Nannies, Quick Au Pair & Nanny Agency, Sunflowers Childcare, UK & Overseas.

Other agencies abroad which send au pairs to Switzerland are:
Australia: Au Pair Australia, Charlton Brown Group
Belgium: Services de la Jeunesse Feminine, Stufam
Canada: Au Pair Canada (Alberta), Le Monde Au Pair, Scotia Personnel
Germany: AuPair-Ark.de, Au-Pair Interconnection, Au-Pair-Vermittlung Sigmar Bassmann, Felicity Nannies, IN VIA, Personal Touch
Greece: Nine Muses
Iceland: Studentaferdir
Italy: ARCE, Celtic Childcare, Europlacements Italy
Netherlands: Au Pair Interactive, S-Au Pair Intermediate

Turkey

The pocket money quoted for Istanbul is about on a par with the average paid in the UK and in some cases a little higher. Mothers' helps and experienced nannies are sometimes paid very handsomely, are promised as much as £300 for 45 hours a week, though these posts are not easy to land. The high salaries quoted sound very attractive, though the reality can be less so. Many nannies encounter problems, partly due to cultural differences for which a good agency should try to prepare you.

While on her 'Overseas Experience' in London, 23 year old New Zealander Rachel Becroft came across an ad for nannying in Istanbul and jumped at the chance. In an interview for Turkey's English language paper *The Daily News*, she identified one of the positive differences:

What surprised me most was the warmth of the people, the real sense of family. There's a sense of community here with aunts, uncles, grandparents all together, whereas in New Zealand it'd be Mum, Dad, the two kids.

Of course all these family gatherings and constant socialising with family can make the nanny or au pair feel homesick for her own relations.

You must expect to give up some of your freedom and independence which can be difficult for qualified nannies in their 20s. The structure of society may also be difficult to accept, as Claire Slater recounts:

Turkish culture is very different from our own. It is a divided society with a small middle class. It is not uncommon to see a horse and cart next to a brand new sports car. It is commonplace for the families who have nannies to have maids and drivers in the home. They work very long hours for very little money, which is something that can take a little getting used to. We are used to doing domestic tasks for ourselves but that doesn't happen here. Working in Istanbul has been a great character building experience for me. You need to be adaptable in all areas and not expect the same kind of working life you have previously experienced. This is due to the very different ideas of child raising that Turkish people have. Turkish children are used to constant attention so you have to be prepared to be on the go at all times. Ideas regarding health and hygiene are also very different. Some of it might seem strange but it's what they are brought up with.

Despite noticing many of these same cultural differences, C. Martin enjoyed her stint in Turkey
Children are often idolised in Turkish families and are the centre of attention at family get-togethers. Usually you feel accepted straightaway even if people do not ask you a lot of questions about England. It's best to go with the flow. In Turkish (and all Muslim) culture, kitchen hygiene, child bathing and washing generally are very important. It is important to be flexible and open-minded. But the people are friendly, and working as a nanny in Turkey has been a good experience for me.

One persistent problem is that it is generally not acceptable for young women to go out alone in the evenings. But Turkish families are normally very generous and allow their live-in childcarers to share in family life on equal terms, even in their free time.

An experienced nanny working for *Anglo Nannies* identified the worst problem she had with culture shock was the Turkish attitude to time. In her experience Turkish people are either very late or too early; they do not tell you anything beforehand (such as what house guests there will be so she shocked a guest by wandering a corridor in her nightdress), they always have to go somewhere in the next five minutes and then change their minds and keep you hanging around for at least an hour.

FIXING UP A JOB

Anglo Nannies with offices in London and Istanbul is run by a Turkish woman Omur Yeginsu who has been praised by many of her nannies for offering plenty of support. Every month the agency hosts a 'Nanny Circle', usually on a Wednesday which is a day off for many nannies, at which problems can be aired and shared. The agency organises various social and educational events for its 60 or so nannies in Istanbul.

The Ankara agency *ICEP (International Cultural Exchange Programmes)* regularly places English-speaking women aged 18-28 as au pairs with families for short or long periods. These young women receive two full days and four evenings off per week and then two weeks of paid holiday after six months. The families mostly live in Ankara, Istanbul, Izmir and Antalya. Summer posts may also be available through ICEP as well as through *Anglo Pair*. Only a few agencies in Britain, and even fewer on the continent, have links with Turkey.

As usual the website www.greataupair.com can be helpful. At the time of writing there were 32 vacancies listed for Turkey, 25 of which were in Istanbul with a scattering in other towns and cities. Most of these indicated that they were expecting to pay less than US$100 a week for up to 45 hours a week.

Qualified nannies can try to get a job with a tour operator with operations in Turkish resorts like Marmaris and Bodrum. Mark Warner hire nannies for their beach hotels in Turkey (020-7761 7340; www.markwarner-recruitment.co.uk). A Turkey specialist that also hires nannies is Tapestry Holidays, The Glassmills, 322B King St, London W6 0AX; for overseas positions contact Jo@tapestry.com.tr.

RED TAPE

Although Turkey is an Islamic country, its sights are set on Europe and on some day joining the European Union. These aspirations, together with a remarkable expansion in tourism, mean that the privileged classes are very keen to learn English. This in turn has contributed to an increase in the demand for foreign nannies. Au pair-type jobs in Turkey normally involve more tutoring of English than domestic chores. Parents are desperate to give their children every possible advantage in the fierce competition for university places in Turkey. So English-speaking nannies are all the rage among the wealthy of Istanbul (of whom there are a considerable number) and to a much lesser extent Ankara.

Many jobs begin as three-month summer jobs which, if successful, develop into longer contracts. British nannies normally work on a three-month tourist visa which will have to be renewed every three months, usually by leaving the country and obtaining a fresh tourist visa after paying £10 (in cash) at the point of re-entry; the employer should be asked to arrange and pay for these visa trips. Alternatively you can apply for an extension at an immigration office, where you will have to show that you have the means to support yourself. Your host family might be prepared to vouch for you in the capacity of 'friend'.

With no bilateral agreement on health provision, it is essential for nannies to have their own private insurance.

DIRECTORY REFERENCES

For agencies based in Turkey, see: **Anglo Nannies** (London and Istanbul) and **ICEP** (Ankara).

For agencies in Britain that deal with Turkey, see: Anglo Nannies, Anglo Pair, Hyde Park International, IAPO, Jolaine, Nannies Abroad, Quick Au Pair & Nanny Agency and Weigan Nannies (on behalf of a UK tour operator).

United Kingdom

Tens of thousands of people are employed in the UK looking after the children of working parents. Foreign au pairs, the overwhelming majority of whom are from Central and Eastern Europe, comprise as many as 40% of the total. This chapter is primarily aimed at foreign young people who want to come to Britain as au pairs, mother's helps or nannies.

Working with families in Britain is not the sole preserve of foreign women and men. British school leavers and others may want to spend six or twelve months working as a mother's help to gain their first experience of employment and more specifically of childcare, or perhaps just to see a different part of Britain. Some may find it difficult to find other work depending on what part of the country they come from and many choose to move south as mother's helps to spare themselves the trauma of trying to find accommodation in the London region. Those who are unemployed should enquire at their local Jobcentre about the possibility of claiming travel expenses to the home of the family who hires them.

One of the important changes since the last edition is that the British Au Pair Agencies Association (BAPAA) has been formed to promote high standards of service and care to families and au pairs. Prospective au pairs abroad can be confident that BAPAA agencies will look after them well. Using the services of a respectable and well established agency means that there is somewhere to turn in the event of exploitation or other problems.

WORKING IN BRITAIN: PROS AND CONS

The demand for English tuition is strong among young people from around the world, tens of thousands of whom aspire to learn the language *in situ*. Language schools have noticed a marked increase in the numbers coming from China and Russia (whose citizens, of course, cannot become au pairs), but the supply of language learners from continental Europe, particularly from former Eastern Bloc countries, remains strong. Many come for intensive summer courses but often find that they spend most of their time socialising and therefore their English improves little. Coming as an au pair gets round the problem and most find that their English improves dramatically.

The demand for live-in childcare continues to increase and any woman aged 17-27 from one of the approved countries (listed below) should have no trouble fixing up a placement for six or nine months. Since Poland, Slovakia and eight other countries joined the EU in May 2004, there has been a greater supply of au pairs prepared to stay for a full 12 months which means that summer-only vacancies crop up less often than they once did. Yet, summer stays can usually be arranged if the interested au pair applies in plenty of time. Belaf Study Holidays (Banner Lodge, Cherhill, Calne, Wiltshire SN11 8XR; 01249-812551; fax 01249-821533; www.belaf.com/en) specialises in this arrangement, placing about 200 au pairs in families in Southern England for at least six weeks in the summer.

Most agencies abide by the Home Office guidelines, that au pairs should work no more than five hours a day for five days a week, not counting some evening babysitting. The work of an au pair consists of childcare and light housework duties. In cases where families are asking for more than this, the au pair should first bring the Home Office directives to the attention of the host family and, if that fails, seek the help of her agency.

The weekly pocket money has been rising steadily over the past few years (unlike the US weekly au pair wage which has remained unchanged for a decade). The Home Office recommended minimum is now £55 a week, which is broadly in line with the rest of Europe, and that is what the majority of families pay. Note that it is not a legally enforceable minimum. When the national minimum wage was introduced in the UK in April 1999, it first appeared that it covered au pairs which at a stroke would have doubled their wages and rendered them unaffordable by many families. However after some heated debate, au pairs were declared exempt from minimum wage regulations because of their special status as guests rather than employees.

Au pairs plus who work longer hours because both parents work earn at least £65-£70 a week. Full-time live-in helpers earn much more than this. They should be entitled to the national minimum wage which is £5.05 (2006). Realistically mother's helps are paid in the broad range of £120-£200 a week. Qualified live-in nannies seldom earn less than £200 a week net and the super qualified earn double that. Some families offer extra perks such as a contribution to the cost of a language course or a couple of driving lessons for an au pair who arrives with an International Driving Permit but who want a little guided practice on the busy English roads. It is reasonable to try to negotiate ten days off with pay after working for the same family for 26 weeks. Few British families contribute to travel expenses nor to course fees.

One disappointment for many au pairs is that they must live a considerable distance from central London. One agency goes so far as to say that almost no English-speaking families live in the city centre these days. There are of course plenty of middle class suburbs within easy reach of London with a high au pair population, but there is also a great demand in the Home Counties of Surrey, Essex, Hertfordshire, Buckinghamshire and Berkshire where access to London is not necessarily difficult but can be expensive.

If you are less interested in the London region than in one of the more scenic areas of

Britain, sift through the agencies in the Directory section and find one based in the area which interests you, for example *Abbey Au Pairs* on the Dorset coast, *Lloyd's* in South Wales, *Au Pair & Nanny Connection* in Bolton (Lancashire), *UK Nannies and Au Pairs* in Cambridgeshire and *People & Places* in Cornwall. Unfortunately there are not many in Scotland; one exception is the IAPA agency *Select Au Pairs* in Paisley near Glasgow. Other English agencies in the Directory specify Scotland including the *3 to 4 Agency* in Bristol and *Premier Au Pair Agency* in Worcestershire. Another Scottish agency to try is Aupair2u (Luciandra, West Ednie, St. Fergus, Peterhead, Aberdeenshire AB42 3BX; 01779 838082; aupair2u@aol.com; www.aupair2u.co.uk).

British families differ as much from one another as French, German or Israeli ones, but a characteristic reserve and a jealous attitude to privacy are noticed by many au pairs, especially at first. Barbara Henson, an ebullient American, soon learned that her employers in South London did not expect her to share their evenings, and so she either had to take her dinner up to her room or go out. This is not typical, but English people do on the whole find it harder to share their homes with strangers than other nationalities do.

Children's feelings and preferences are easier to interpret than their parents'. Another problem Barbara encountered (and one which is particularly noticed by North Americans) is how to gauge the tone and intention behind the polite facade. For example, 'help yourself to the chocolates/drinks cupboard/fridge at any time' may mean, 'have one if you must'.

British children do not always conform to the stereotype of the well-behaved English child of story books. On the other hand, British children do tend to be less spoiled than, say, Italian or American children and most are relatively obedient. After a couple of years of working for American families, Carla Mitchell took a temporary job with an English family and recalls her amazement when the children dutifully trooped off to bed after a single request.

And if British parents expect a lot from their children, they will not be very tolerant of slack discipline in their live-in helpers. Deserved or not, they are reputed to be demanding employers; for example one large French agency warns applicants that the English are *très exigeantes*. Whether or not any of these generalisations is useful is another question, and one which may well have been answered by the English poet William Blake who wrote that to generalise is foolish, whereas to particularise is the distinguishing feature of mankind.

FIXING UP A JOB

Au pair and nanny agencies proliferate in Britain and by law none can charge a placement fee for placing staff in Britain. They are no longer required to be licensed under the Employment Agencies Act of 1973; however they must still comply with the provisions of the Act. As described in the Introduction, there is very little regulation in this field of employment, which was the impetus behind the launch in 2003 of BAPAA, the British Au Pair Agencies Association, whose website (www.bapaa.org.uk) is an excellent starting

ANGLO CONTINENTAL

Suppliers of personnel for clients throughout the UK

Au Pairs/Mother's Helps/Home Helps & Babysitting Service
Hotel and Catering Personnel • Equestrian Staff

9 Wish Road, Hove, East Sussex BN3 4LL **T** 01273 27 12 81 **F** 01273 77 66 34
Email niki@anglocontinentalplacements.com

place for finding a British agency. Their office address is Lower Ground Floor, 10/11 Gray's Inn Square, London WC1R 5JD.

No single listing of all registered agencies exists. Some helpful search engines and specialist websites to use with links to established nanny and au pair agencies are www. bestbear.co.uk, www.findaupair.co.uk, www.all4kidsuk.com, www.seymourhouse. co.uk/Nannies and www.nannyjob.co.uk (the latter covers au pairs as well as nannies). The Childcare Approvals Scheme was introduced by the government in 2005 which is a voluntary register which qualifying nannies can join. Before acceptance individuals must provide evidence that they are over 18, have a relevant qualification or attended an approved induction course in childcare; have a certificate in first aid that is suitable to the care of babies and children and is not more than three years old at the time of approval; and have obtained an enhanced disclosure check from the Criminal Records Bureau to prove that there is nothing in their background that makes them unsuitable to care for children. Parents and agencies looking to recruit a nanny can check the status of the applicant online (see www.childcareapprovalscheme.co.uk), so professional nannies are advised to join; the current fee is £96.

The Professional Association of Nursery Nurses (PANN) does not think that this goes far enough and has been campaigning over many years for a single register for all childcarers to be set up in the UK as explained by the Senior Professional Officer at PANN to the *Independent on Sunday* newspaper in May 2005:

The DfES is responsible for childcare policy in England, Ofsted is responsible for inspecting nurseries and childminders, and individual nursery nurses are registered with local authorities. Until the introduction of the DfES's Childcare Approval Scheme, there was no system at all for registering individual nannies – anybody could (and still can) call themselves a nanny. Although PANN welcomes the new Childcare Approval Scheme, it applies only to England, is not mandatory, involves payment of a fee – which may be off-putting to some nannies – and does not verify whether a childcarer is suitable to work with a particular age group...A compulsory national register of all childcarers is the only way to protect children, parents and childcarers. It would mean those found guilty of bad practice could be struck off so they could no longer work with children. It would also stop unsuitable people moving around the country or between types of childcare to avoid detection.

Reputable nanny agencies may belong to REC, the Recruitment and Employment Confederation (www.rec.uk.com). The 22 British au pair agencies that belong to the International Au Pair Association (www.iapa.org) described in the introduction also belong to the British branch BAPAA. There is of course some overlap between the two, and some au pair and nanny agencies belong to all three of these trade associations. The following agencies all belong to BAPAA/IAPA; many others can be found in the Directory of Agencies. See also the advertisement above for Anglo Continental.

A Aupair & Nanny Agency Ltd, 200 High Road, Wood Green, London N22 8HH (020-8889 2010; fax 020-8889 7295; aaupair@aol.com; www.aaupair.uk)

A2Z Au Pairs, Catwell House, Catwell, Williton, Somerset TA4 4PF (08456 445506; fax 01984 639013; enquiries@a2zaupairs.com;www.a2zaupairs.com)

Angel Au Pairs, 8 Longfield Road, Ash, Surrey GU12 6NA (tel/fax 01252 675715; mail@ angelaupairs.com; www.angelaupairs.com)

Au Pairs Direct & Jobs UK Ltd, 7 Little Meadow Road, Bowdon, Cheshire WA14 3PG (0161-9415356; fax 0161-929 0102; enquiries@aupairsdirect.co.uk; www.aupairsdirect. co.uk)

Matchmaker Au Pair Agency, Rosewood, Leigh Gardens, Chelford Road, Knutsford, Cheshire WA16 8PU (01565 651703; fax 01565 631726; mmaupair@aol.com; www. matchmakeraupairs.co.uk)

Peter Pan Au Pairs LLP, The Greys, Erriot Wood, Lynsted, Sittingbourne, Kent ME9 0JW (01795 886475; fax 01795 886146; nickyprice.peterpan@virgin.net; www. peterpanaupairs.net)

Sunny Smiles Au-Pair Agency, PO Box 280, Sevenoaks, Kent TN13 1FU (01732 452282; fax 01732 452282; info@sunnysmiles.co.uk; www.sunnysmiles.co.uk)

Village Nannies Ltd, 74 Wentworth Road, Harborne, Birmingham, B17 9SY; 0121-684 9559; fax 0121-242 2667; info@villagenannies.co.uk; www.villagenannies.co.uk)

The Yellow Pages will reveal domestic agencies under the classification 'Nannies & Au Pairs' and can be consulted online from anywhere in the world (www.yell.com). Many are run as small businesses by one or two people, sometimes working from home, and these often provide a more personal service than the larger au pair 'factories', though naturally they will have a smaller choice of families on their books.

Certain nationalities should endeavour to apply directly to an agency in Britain rather than through an agency in their own country. France is one such country, since many French agencies charge large registration and placement fees, sometimes nearly €300. Nannying is an option that many young women from Australia and New Zealand choose, because it takes care of accommodation and pays a good wage. A number of agencies in London and southern England specialise in placing nannies from Australia and New Zealand who must have a working holiday or other relevant visa in place before they can register with an agency. Try *Family First International, The Childcare Company* or *Au Pair Connections*. A good way to meet a range of families in London is to do a lot of babysitting, possibly through an agency like *Babysitters/Childminders* who ask for childcare references. Another possibility for people based in London is to do some part-time nannying, which will pay £7-£10 an hour. For instance a company called After School Nannies (tel/fax 020-8871 2211; www.afterschoolnannies.com) recruits part-time nannies (who must have qualifications and relevant childcare experience) to collect children from school and look after them until the parents arrive home from work (approximately 3pm-6/7pm). Nannies with a driving licence are in great demand.

Many other ways of finding out about vacancies once you are in Britain can be pursued. Newspapers catering to wandering colonials often prove fruitful such as *TNT* (www. tntmagazine.com) which is distributed free on Mondays throughout London, e.g. outside travel agencies, tube stations, favoured pubs, etc. Many of the jobs will be in London but some will be in country areas.

> **An example taken at random from *TNT* gives a flavour of the opportunities advertised in their classified column as well as on dozens of other au pair/ nanny matching websites**
>
> *Mother's help needed for busy cheerful home in beautiful countryside near Guildford (40 minutes London) helping with horse, toddler and garden. Driver, swimmer, experienced rider, country lover, non-smoking, references essential. Previous childcare experience preferred but not essential for right person. Use of car. Own room and ensuite bathroom; cleaner employed.*

The first time Ms. T. P. Lye from Malaysia checked a notice board beside the Earl's Court tube station she found three possible live-in jobs, and accepted one of them taking one child to and from school in exchange for free board and lodging. (These days it seems to have more accommodation than jobs.)

Student Union notice boards are often a worthwhile source of positions. Simon Willis, an Australian on a working holiday visa, had the good sense to check one of the notice boards at London University and persuaded the advertiser (with difficulty) to take him on to look after two-year old Jessica. University news sheets are often used by academically-minded families looking for home helps. Anyone who keeps his or her eyes open is bound to come across openings of potential interest.

Nannies and au pairs in London might find *Angels & Urchins* online magazine of interest (www.angelsandurchins.co.uk) which invites nannies to place adverts free of charge. Among many other features, it has a good 'What's On for Kids' section.

REGULATIONS

Any national of a European Economic Area country may come to Britain as an au pair, mother's help, nanny or domestic, with few formalities and restrictions. In May 2004, ten new countries were admitted to the European Union which means that child-carers from Poland, Hungary, the Czech Republic, Slovakia, Slovenia, Latvia, Lithuania, Estonia, Cyprus and Malta are now free to come to Britain to look for work and accept jobs with families or in any capacity. Until the transition period is over, nationals of these new accession countries, as well as the permitted other nationalities, are obliged to register with the local police within one month of commencing work, regardless of the hours they are working or the wage they receive. The registration fee at present is £70. In London, au pairs must register at the Overseas Visitors Records Office, Brandon House, 180 Borough High St, London SE1 1LH (020-7230 1208).

People aged between 17 and 27 from 11 other countries are permitted to come as au pairs but not nannies or mother's helps: Andorra, Faroe, Greenland, Monaco, San Marino, Bosnia-Herzogovina, Bulgaria, Croatia, Macedonia, Romania and Turkey. People from the last six in the list must obtain a visa from the British Embassy or Consulate in their home country before they travel to the United Kingdom. The other permitted non-EU applicants will receive a visa at the point of entry to the UK. Note that Turkish au pairs must register within one week of arrival or risk a £2,500 fine and/or six months imprisonment and/or deportation.

The Home Office issues brief guidelines stipulating the acceptable standards for au pairs which can be seen at www.workingintheuk.gov.uk (search 'Au Pairs'). Au pair stays are available to single women and men between the ages of 17 and 27 who are entitled to work in the home no more than 25 hours a week (five hours a day with two days off per week). The maximum period which non-EU nationals are permitted to stay as au pairs is two years, whether consecutive or aggregated, and changing employer is permitted within that time limit.

The recommended pocket money for au pairs is £55 a week though some families, especially in London, pay £60. Higher wages and more hours would look to the Home Office like employment as a domestic servant which would require a work permit, tax registration and so on.

Citizens of the Commonwealth and the US may be eligible to work with families (see below) but not officially as au pairs since the au pair system presupposes the motivation of learning a language. Note that changing status after entry as a visitor is not permitted.

Many girls from other countries would dearly love to come to the UK as au pairs. Other European countries like the Netherlands have introduced measures for bringing in au pairs from around the world. Some consider the reasoning of the Immigration & Nationality Department's for the exclusion unconvincing:

By tradition the au pair arrangement of girls living in a family abroad to learn the language of their hosts and the way of life in that country has been a Western European arrangement. While the aspirations of girls from outside Western Europe are understandable, it was considered that those who came from further afield were more vulnerable to exploitation and that a number of girls were coming ostensibly as au pairs but in reality to do more substantial work, often with a view to long-term residence.

Often British families and non-European girls make an independent arrangement but both sides should be well-primed to avoid what happened in the following story. While a couple from London with a young baby were on holiday in Argentina they met Maria. They arranged to take her on as their au pair a few months later. She arrived at Heathrow with just $250 and a 12-month open return ticket, asking (in very poor English) to stay nine months. Questioning elicited from her a confession that she had arranged to work as an au pair. The employing mother (who speaks Spanish) was contacted by immigration and immediately drove to Heathrow where she was accused of trying to import slave labour. Maria was given permission to stay in England as a tourist for no more than 7 days and then had to return to Argentina. The whole episode cost the ill-informed employers £1,000.

In most cases, young people arriving from EU countries will automatically be given permission at entry to stay for six months in any capacity. If they intend to stay longer they should apply for a residence permit by submitting their passport and application form (available from any Jobcentre or police station) to the Home Office before the six months expire. EU nationals are of course entitled to reside in any Community country, so refusal is rare.

Citizens from countries on the approved list which are not in the EU must show the letter of invitation from the family at entry and be prepared for a grilling by immigration officials. In cases where the official is not satisfied, perhaps because the letter is too sketchy, the family or agency may be rung up and asked to corroborate the au pair's story. If the reply is satisfactory, permission is normally given to enter for the duration of the contract.

If a non-EU au pair wishes to extend her stay, she must apply to one of the Home Office's four Public Enquiries offices in Croydon, Birmingham, Liverpool or Glasgow. Any au pair who is confused about the regulations or her rights in any capacity might find it helpful to visit a Citizens Advice Bureau, manned by volunteers who will patiently sift through the regulations and try to interpret them.

Citizens of Commonwealth countries, principally Australia, New Zealand and Canada are entitled to apply for a working holiday visa, which will allow them to work in any casual capacity for a maximum of 12 months within a two-year period. The age limits are 17-30. Canadian students may participate in a Student Work Abroad Programme or SWAP (www.swap.ca) administered by the Canadian Universities Travel Service known as Travel CUTS. After paying the registration fee of C$440, eligible students are allowed to come to Britain to look for any kind of work including domestic work. Commonwealth citizens do not have to register as aliens.

There is a similar Work in Britain programme for American college students over 18. BUNAC USA (PO Box 430, Southbury, CT 06488; 1-800-462-8622; www.bunac.org) allocates 'blue cards' to about 3,750 applicants (for a fee of $290) which entitles them to enter Britain at any time of the year to work for up to six months.

HEALTH AND INSURANCE

The National Health Service offers emergency treatment to anyone and will also provide health care to EU nationals and anyone who is 'ordinarily resident' in Britain. Au pairs should register with a local doctor when they arrive, preferably the same one whose surgery the family attends. The standard fee for prescriptions at present is £6.40 with the exception of contraception which is free. Dental care by NHS-registered dentists is only partially subsidised; also very few dentists will accept new NHS patients onto their books since they are under no obligation to do so, and they earn more money from their private patients. As low-income citizens, au pairs may be able to obtain assistance with the cost of medical, dental and optical treatment if they complete form HC1 'Claim for help with health costs'. This is obtainable from medical centres, opticians and dentists.

Au pairs from countries outside the EU may find that there are reciprocal agreements between their country and Britain, however these are not really adequate to provide good cover. Au pairs should arrive with full travel insurance, to last for the total length of their stay. Affordable policies may be found through international student associations, universities or online.

Au pairs are not liable to pay National Insurance contributions, though they may make voluntary contributions if they wish to retain their rights to future benefits in their home countries. Further advice may be obtained from the Inland Revenue's Centre for Non Residents, Room BP1301, Benton Park View, Newcastle-upon-Tyne NE98 1ZZ (0845 915 4811; www.inlandrevenue.gov.uk/nic).

Contributions will be due for other positions however. Professional nannies must pay tax and contributions in the usual way and should present their P-45 form to a new employer. Anyone earning over £91 a week should pay National Insurance Contributions at a rate of 11% (to a maximum of £595). Anyone who earns more than £4,895 per year (about £94 a week) must also pay income tax at a rate of 20%. The employer must match these payments which can make it expensive for a law-abiding person to hire a mother's help; as a result many employers neglect this obligation, which may mean that their employees lose their entitlement to unemployment benefit, sick pay, maternity benefit and perhaps even their state pension. Occasionally nannies who do short stints for different families can claim to be self-employed which means that the employer does not have to pay contributions. Qualified NNEB nannies may want to consider a specialist insurance policy for nannies offered by Morton Michel Childcare Insurance Specialists (Alhambra House, 9 St. Michael's Road, Croydon CR93DD; 0845 257 0900; www.mortonmichel.com) whose premiums start at £60 a year and will protect nannies from lawsuits for negligence among other things.

All live-in child-carers are liable to pay council tax. Full-time students may be eligible for a discounted rate, normally 75%. Full-time is defined as 21 hours a week (including homework) for a year's course. It is also possible to claim a reduction on the basis of low income. If you are staying less than six months, there is every chance that your employer will not register you.

LEISURE TIME

In the London area most agencies can recommend social clubs, some specifically for au pairs. German-speaking au pairs might wish to frequent the *German Catholic Social Centre* in London which sends out a monthly programme of events (in German) including activities as diverse as special masses and pub crawls, as well as excursions outside London. Some long-established agencies (like Top Notch Nannies and Tinies Childcare) that at one time organised a social programme for their nannies have stopped this because the turn-out was so low, which must mean that nannies are happy to find their own entertainment.

In London, International Students House at 229 Great Portland Street, W1W 5PN (020-7631 8300; www.ish.org.uk) has a bistro with live music, bar, cybercafé and TV lounge. They put on an active sports and film programme and can advise on language classes. The student bar in Mary Trevelyan Hall is open most evenings (8pm-11pm) during term time. You might also make enquiries at the University of London Union on Malet Street which sometimes extends membership to non-students for a nominal fee. It has a pool, gym, bars, banks, discos, etc. and is a regular venue for concerts and dances. A student membership in the London Central YMCA might also be affordable for a term. Smaller au pair agencies often hold occasional au pair get-togethers, perhaps at Christmas or the end of the school year.

Of course it is not necessary to join a club to have a social life. English people can be surprisingly friendly in pub situations so it is a good idea to visit a few pubs in your local area until you find one with a congenial atmosphere or watch for posters advertising pubs with live music.

A wide range of language courses is available in almost every city in Britain over the academic year but not between June and September. Predictably state-run courses are significantly cheaper than private ones, so most au pairs prefer to investigate what is on offer at the local community college, adult education centre or college of further education. Most aim to sign up for two two-hour classes a week. Expect to pay roughly £4 per hour. It is necessary to enrol at the beginning of each term which run September to December,

January to March and April to June/July. Unfortunately local authority courses in London tend to be oversubscribed, so make enquiries as soon as you know your requirements.

There are of course plenty of private schools but their fees are usually beyond the means of au pairs. More intensive courses involve 15 hours of instruction per week which is generally more time than an au pair has available. In all cases the fees will be due in advance. Some families may be willing to lend you the money and deduct it from your pocket money.

The standard qualification is the Cambridge First Certificate, Advanced and Proficiency. Exams are held twice a year in December and June, though you must enter for the exam in the preceding October or March. Exam fees will be about £80.

Many au pairs supplement their weekly pocket money by offering themselves as a cleaner or babysitter in the neighbourhood where they are based. Often the host mother will know of local possibilities or the au pair can ask around in the school playground if she takes her charge to school. The hourly rate for a non-professional cleaner in southern England is £6 and for evening babysitting about £5.

DIRECTORY REFERENCES

The vast majority of au pair agencies in the UK and Europe place foreign applicants in British families and are far too numerous to list here. The majority of nanny agencies are able to place nannies only after a face-to-face interview, so foreign applicants should not contact these agencies before arriving in Britain.

United States of America

The only legitimate way for an au pair to work in the USA is on a J-1 visa obtainable through US State Department-designated agencies. The official au pair programme allows young women and men aged 18-26 with childcare experience to work for an American family for exactly one year. (The numerous conditions of participation will be dealt with in detail below.) Two changes were introduced in 2004: qualifying au pairs may now extend their stay for 6, 9 or 12 months, always under the auspices of their sponsoring agency in the US. Secondly, a summer-only au pairing programme is now a possibility.

Two separate programmes exist as sub-sections of the standard au pair programme. One is for qualified child carers/nannies, called variously the 'Au Pair Extraordinaire', 'Au Pair Elite' or 'Premier Au Pair' programme, depending on the agency. Candidates with the appropriate NNEB, BTEC, Diploma in Nursing or NVQ3 qualification are eligible to earn $200 a week plus a $500 study allowance. The other variation within the au pair programme was introduced in 2002 and named *Educare*, in which the emphasis is more on study and cultural exchange than on childcare (described below).

WORKING IN THE US: PROS AND CONS

The demand for au pairs in the US is massive and generally far outstrips supply. Upwards of 12,000 American families are interested in hosting a foreign au pair at any one time, which means that qualifying young people of any nationality have a very good chance of acceptance onto the programme. Most people are won over by the generosity of American families and by the way that they are treated as equals. The democratic habits of thought for which the US is justly famous carry over into the family situation where a spirit of egalitarianism normally prevails. British women are especially popular as a status symbol, a curiosity and as representatives of a culture which Americans subconsciously admire (without necessarily understanding it very deeply). The affection which American families develop for their au pairs and nannies seems to be more long-lasting than in any other country. It is not unusual for families to offer to sponsor their live-in helper for a 'green card' which entitles foreigners to settle in the US as 'resident aliens'.

> **Karin Huber, a young Austrian woman, spotted an advertisement in the Saturday edition of the German newspaper *Süddeutscher Zeitung* and after several months of corresponding accepted a job with a family living on Long Island:**
> *The minute we met at the airport, I knew I'd get on with them. After ten very enjoyable months, they offered to sponsor me, which means the family pays an immigration lawyer to try to get a green card on behalf of an employee. This can take two or three years, during which time you can't leave the US. I didn't want to go that long without seeing my family so I went home to Austria. But I still keep in touch with that family; in fact they phone me once a week.*

Susannah Walton's experiences echo Karin's and in her case, her Minnesota employer tried to persuade her to stay by offering to pay for her to take courses at the local university.

Many live-in helpers get the chance to travel around the US either on family vacations or sometimes just as a reward for services rendered, as in the case of Yvonne Standard who, after caring for the children single-handedly for a month, was sent to Florida for a week's vacation. There she was supposed to be chaperoned by the children's 75-year-old grandfather, though it was generally thought by the gossips in the hotel that he was Yvonne's sugar-daddy.

The fixed level of pocket money paid on official au pair programmes is in line with the US minimum wage and has not changed since 1997. The weekly payment is $139.05 in addition to room and board. Au pair programme participants are permitted to work up to 45 hours a week (which is nearly twice as many hours as the standard au pair in the UK). The perks of the programmes vary slightly but always include a free transatlantic flight plus one-way or return from New York to the family, up to $500 to cover fees for a course of the au pair's choice, and one or two weeks paid vacation. Sometimes, with the au pair's consent, a family vacation will count, though there are definite disadvantages to this (see *Leisure Time* below).

Problems do of course occur and it is not at all unusual for au pairs to chafe against rules, curfews and unreasonable expectations in housework, etc. The counsellors and advisers provided by the sending organisations should be able to sort out problems and in some cases can find alternative families.

Ann McCann found herself working in a horrific situation:

I was told by an agency in London that the family had five children, though by the time I got there a sixth had arrived! Both parents drank. The wife would call her husband at work and if he'd been drinking, she would start drinking so that when he came home they'd be equally smashed. The parents ate at the country club almost every night while the children had hot dogs and hamburgers, never any vegetables or fruit in the house. I lasted six months and then gave my notice.

This unhappy story is far from typical but the United States does have the highest divorce rate in the Western world (44%) and so your chances of working for people whose marriage is breaking up (or has done) are higher than elsewhere in the world. You might also find yourself working for what is sometimes known as a 'merged' family, i.e. couples on a second marriage with children from the first.

Another cliché about American life is its extreme mobility and you should not be unduly surprised to find that your employers aren't much more familiar with the town they are living in than you are, since they too may have arrived very recently. Another cultural difference you may encounter is the high profile which religion has in public and private life, so you should be prepared to exercise more tolerance than usual but not expect it in return.

Most nannies and au pairs who have worked for American families agree that it is possible to identify certain typical traits in American children. They tend to be noisy and rambunctious with a proclivity to interrupt adult conversation more often than would be tolerated in Europe. They are energetic, self confident and fearless. Their wishes tend to be indulged to an excessive degree which makes the task of imposing a workable routine difficult in some cases.

> **Carla Mitchell experienced an extreme version of this:**
> *Soon after I arrived the mother told me that I was not to use the word 'no' to the children (who were aged 3 and 6) because she didn't want them learning to say no. This made disciplining them virtually impossible. They would scream whenever thwarted and stop screaming only when the adults capitulated, which the parents did almost instantly. I took a tougher line at first but by the end they wore me down and I too started handing over chocolate biscuits on demand. When I tried to discuss the discipline problem with the parents they seemed surprised and offended that I should criticise their beautiful children.*

When Carla returned to England, she took up a temporary nannying job. When her new charges' bedtime was approaching, she found herself becoming tense and anxious, anticipating the inevitable battle of wills and nerves. This was a case of tilting at windmills since the English children sweetly said 'goodnight' and took themselves off.

Carol Rowan followed her American employers from a German army base back to their home in Colorado Springs to continue looking after 2½ year old Kelsey, whose behaviour was often impossible due to a lack of parental discipline. Her doting parents didn't even interfere and say No when she was teetering on a window ledge. One of her many acts of vandalism was to write on walls and so it was agreed with the parents that she not be allowed any pens. An hour later Carol found her writing on the wall. She confronted the father whose puzzling and inadequate reply was, 'But it's a green pen'. What use is an NNEB training in such circumstances? For a tragi-comic account of nannying for rich and selfish parents, read *The Nanny Diaries*, a novel by two ex-nannies in New York, Nicola Kraus and Emma McLaughlin. The innate snobbishness of your average New York socialite at an interview is well captured in this extract:

Nanny Fact: in every one of my interviews, references are never checked. I am white. I speak French. My parents are college-educated. I have no visible piercings and have been to Lincoln Center in the last two months. I'm hired.

FIXING UP A JOB
Prospective au pairs around the world must apply through a recognised sponsoring organisation which must follow the guidelines governing the programmes. The duration of the standard programme is 12 months, plus an optional 13th month is allowed for travel (at the au pair's own expense). The eleven authorised sponsors are listed below. However aspiring au pairs must find a partner agency in their home country, either by checking the relevant websites or by contacting the US office and asking for the nearest partner agency in their country or region. On the face of it there are not many differences between the sending agencies. *Au Pair in America* is the largest sender from the UK. *Cultural Care* has closed its UK office, though British applicants may contact the European headquarters in Lucerne (see entry).

At present the State Department has approved the following au pair programme sponsors, several of which have entries in the Directory of Agencies. The American Institute for

Foreign Study (whose programme is included in the Directory under *Au Pair in America*) is the largest one, sending between 4,000 and 5,000 au pairs to the States every year. Note that the current list and programme requirements can be read on http://exchanges.state.gov (search 'Au pairs').

Agent Au Pair, 1450 Sutter Street, #526, San Francisco, CA 94109 (415-462-1906; info@ agentaupair.com; www.agentaupair.com).

American Institute for Foreign Study, (Au Pair in America), River Plaza, 9 West Broad Street, Stamford, CT 06902 (800-928-7247/ 203-399-5000; info@aupairamerica.co.uk; www.aupairinamerica.com).

AuPairCare, Inc.(AYUSA International), California St, 10th Floor, San Francisco, CA 94108 (800-428-7247/ 415-434-8788 ext 501; www.aupaircare.com).

Au Pair International, Inc, 3163 S. Columbine St, Denver, CO 80210 (720-221-3563; fax 720-227-0682).

Au Pair USA/InterExchange, Inc, 161 Sixth Avenue, 13th Floor, New York, New York 10013 (800-287-2477/ 212-924-0446; aupairinfo@interexchange.org; www. interexchange.org).

Cultural Care Au Pair (Educational Foundation for Foreign Study), EF Center Boston, 1 Education St, Cambridge, MA 02142 (800-333-6056; aupair@culturalcare.com; www. culturalcare.com).

Cultural Homestay International, 104 Butterfield Road, San Anselmo, CA 94960 (415-459-5397; chimain@msn.com; www.chinet.org).

EurAuPair Intercultural Child Care Programs, 238 North Coast Highway, Laguna Beach, CA 92651 (800-713 2002/ 949-494-7355; euraupairwest@euraupair.com; www. euraupair.com).

Face the World Foundation, 1010 B Street, Suite 200, San Rafael, CA 94901 (415-257-4787 ext 204; www.aupairfoundation.org).

Go Au Pair - Exploring Cultural and Educational Learning, 151 East 6100 South, Suite 200, Murray, UT 84107 (801-255-7722; info@goaupair.com; www.goaupair.com).

USAuPair Inc, PO Box 2126,Lake Oswego, Oregon 97035 (503-697-6872; info@usaupair. com; www.usaupair.com).

All of the worldwide au pair agencies in the Directory that include the US as one of their destination countries are simply appointed interviewers for one of these licensed programmes.

After the tragic events of 1997, when British au pair Louise Woodward was convicted of murdering an infant in her care, the au pair programme requirements were tightened. The basic requirements are that you be between 18 and 26, speak English to an acceptable standard, be a non-smoker, have a full clean driving licence and provide a criminal record check. You must also show that you have experience of looking after children, e.g. babysitting, or helping at a summer playscheme or school. Whereas Au Pair in America asks to see evidence of 200 hours of childcare, other programmes may not be so specific in their requirements. Anyone wanting to care for a child under two must have 200 documented hours of experience looking after children under two. The majority of candidates are young women though men with relevant experience (e.g. sole care of children under five) may be placed. (It is still not unusual to have just a handful of blokes out of hundreds of au pairs.)

The job entails working 45 hours a week (including babysitting) with at least one and a half days off per week plus one complete weekend off a month. Successful applicants receive free return flights from one of many cities, a four-day orientation on arrival and support from a community counsellor. The time lag between applying and flying is usually at least two months. The counsellor's role is to advise on any problems and organise meetings with other au pairs in the area. Requirements differ among the agencies, but most applicants are required to pay a good faith deposit of $400-$500 which is returned to them at the end of 12 months but which is forfeit if the terms of the programme are broken.

All the programmes include free return flights. Most participants travel with groups of other au pairs on their programme, though some do travel alone. The most popular departure times are between January and March or between June and September, with the starting date of the majority of jobs coinciding with the beginning of the school year in September. All au pairs must attend on arrival at their point of entry (normally New York or California) a four-day training and orientation course in which they receive at least eight hours of child safety instruction, 24 hours of child development instruction plus some first aid including instruction in CPR (Cardio Pulmonary Resuscitation). The programme allows a thirteenth month of pure travel at the au pair's own expense. Those who choose this option will have their return flight arranged accordingly and their top-up insurance policy extended.

Interviews are a necessary stage in the application process. In addition to the interviews there will be a lot of form-filling, reference-gathering and letter-writing involved before you will be placed. You will probably have to prepare a standard autobiographical essay or an account of how you would amuse two children on a rainy winter day. (If you're short of ideas, see Appendix 4.)

Michelle Francis advises prospective au pairs not to take the information in the brochures too literally:

During my interview I discovered that it is not necessary to have any 'real' childcare experience; babysitting was quite sufficient as long as you could back it up with a good reference. I personally hadn't done any childcare for two years. The brochure also states quite clearly that au pairs are not allowed to choose their destination. However, once I'd arrived, I discovered that many au pairs (particularly those from the Continent) had requested a destination and/or ages/numbers of children preferred. Many got what they asked for. Some friends even asked to be placed together and were within a few miles of each other.

After your application has been accepted, it will be circulated among American families. The normal procedure is for any family who is interested in your application to ring you for a chat to see if you are vaguely compatible. If you are interested in them there may be a subsequent phone call when more specific details can be discussed.

Once you are in situ, follow-up is provided in both cases by community counsellors who meet about once a month with the au pairs in their region. These meetings are both social and of practical benefit since any problems can be aired here. The counsellors are also responsible for advising on local education facilities of which au pairs are expected to take advantage. In fact families pay up to $500 towards the cost of classes in whatever subject the au pair chooses to pursue for four to six hours a week from Tae KwonDo to American literature. The majority of au pairs from non-English speaking countries attend English classes.

With hindsight, Michelle makes the following recommendations to au pairs who are still at the stage of choosing a family on the basis of phone calls:
I would advise anybody considering embarking on such a trip to establish exactly what will be expected of them, how many nights babysitting at the weekends, do they believe in curfews and what restrictions would be put on the au pair regarding use of the cars and socialising. My situation was not as bad as other au pairs I met: one had a curfew of 10.30pm, another had to do all the housework, cooking and cleaning for a family of six, while another had to hoover the carpet in stripes and fold all the towels and underwear in a particular way. As it is really difficult to get to know somebody by just a telephone call, it's much better to ask as many day-to-day questions as possible.

Once you have applied and your application has been circulated by your agency in the US, you can be telephoned at any time by families who like the sound of you. It is recommended that you keep a list of questions handy by the telephone so that you will be prepared to clarify the expectations on either side.

Consider carefully the pros and cons of the city you will be going to. Emma Purcell was not altogether happy to be sent to Memphis Tennessee which she describes as the 'most backward and redneck city in the USA':

I was a very naïve 18 year old applying to be an au pair for a deferred year before university. During my eight months so far, I have experienced highs and lows. I have been very lucky with my host family who have made me feel one of the family. I have travelled the USA and Mexico frequently staying in suites and being treated as royalty since my host dad is president of Holiday Inn. On the bad side, I have lost numerous friends who have not had such good luck. One was working 60 hours a week (for no extra pay) with the brattiest children, so she left. Another girl from Australia lasted six months with her neurotic family who yelled at her for not cleaning the toaster daily and for folding the socks wrong. Finally she plucked up the courage to talk to her host parents and their immediate response was to throw her out. A very strong personality is required to be an au pair for a year in the States.

The penalties for breaking the terms of the contract are harsh. The hefty deposit is really a bond to guarantee that you don't flit and use your J-1 visa to take up other work. Not only will your bond (variously called deposit or completion bonus) be forfeit and your return ticket and insurance cancelled, but the US Immigration and Naturalization Service will be alerted, so the legal consequences can be serious.

The *Educare in America* programme is similar in many respects to the standard au pair programme, i.e. participants commit themselves to a minimum stay of 12 months and enter on a J-1 visa. The difference is that participants work fewer hours (normally the families have children of school age) and spend more time on their studies. Educare au pairs must be intending to return to full-time study in their home country. The main features are:

O   The number of working hours is 30 (rather than 45).
O   The weekly pay is $105 (75% of the standard weekly au pair wage of $139).
O   In addition to $100 placement fee, the programme fee is $750 (rather than $500) which covers flights to the US.
O   Up to 6 hours of study at an accredited US post-secondary college or university during term-time (instead of 3).
O   Families contribute up to $1,000 (instead of $500) towards course fees in any subject of interest to the participant.
O   Participants are called 'companions' rather than au pairs.

As mentioned, a three-month summer au pair stay is now allowed through *Au Pair USA/Interexchange*. The same eligibility requirements apply and summer au pairs earn the same weekly stipend as in the full-year programme plus a $250 educational stipend. Start dates fall between May 29 and July 10 and the programme finishes on September 15th.

This exhausts the official avenues for fixing up a family job in the States. Otherwise it is a question of going solo by following up advertisements on websites such as www.aupairs.co.uk or answering local ads.

Writing on the admirable payaway.co.uk site, 23 year old Nikki Prin contrasts being a participant on an official au pair scheme with her experiences freelancing:
After enjoying a year in Boston on the Au Pair in America programme, I have worked as an Au Pair for 3 other families all in the USA, but under very different experiences. I soon found out that although through an organised programme you

> *have the benefit of security, you also get the minimum of wage. I found it much easier and more agreeable to arrange my positions by myself (although, these positions usually are for shorter periods of time, due to visa restrictions). I found that through local papers in the area is a good way to go, along with advertising your availability or asking in local schools, or putting notices on notice boards at the local colleges and universities. Going it alone gives you the advantage of negotiating your pay and working hours. There are many positions that are available for part-time work, which is a good income if you want to study in the many universities and institutions in the USA.*

Many of the families advertising will not be aware of the visa difficulties and will almost certainly not be able to help you obtain legal status. The same is true of jobs posted on noticeboards both virtual - for example www.jobfind.com includes au pair vacancies in the Boston area while www.craigslist.com is recommended for the San Francisco Bay area - and actual, for instance at long stay backpackers' hostels.

There is a very active and helpful network of nannies outside the official programmes, and you may well benefit from their advice as Kim Wetherel did:

When the rich Dallas family I was working for announced that I would also have to look after their visitors' baby, I said I'd be leaving in a week. Fortunately I had made plenty of other nanny friends and their families were willing to put me up while I looked for another job. For two weeks I sunned myself, and through word of mouth went for interviews. Evenually I got a job with the nicest people I've ever met who ended up feeling like a sister and a brother-in-law.

Anyone with a nannying qualification or childcare experience would be welcomed by the directors of summer camps. Certain voluntary organisations working with children might also be interested in accepting people with a childcare background. For example Camphill Special Schools often need volunteers to help run their programme for children with disabilities. Volunteers willing to stay more than six months will receive room and board, a monthly stipend, car use, health insurance and will be helped to get a work visa. Details are available from Camphill Special Schools, 1784 Fairview Road, Glenmoore, PA 19343 (610-469-6993; Bvolunteer@aol.com; www.beaverrun.org).

Professional nannies who have a green card to work in the US will have no trouble finding a job which pays anything from $275-$600 a week. Pay for 'status nannies' in places like Manhattan and Silicon Valley has escalated dramatically so that they can command salaries of $80,000 and lavish perks for 40-hour weeks. Whereas ten years ago there were about 50 nanny referral agencies in the US, now there are 250, most of which will expect to see proof of eligibility to work in the US, including A Nanny Connection Inc (www.nannyconnection. com), Beacon Hill Nannies (www.beaconhillnannies.com), Northwest Nannies Inc (www. nwnanny.com) and the Nanny Authority (www.nannyauthority.com).

REGULATIONS

Information from the Visa Branch of the United States Embassy (5 Upper Grosvenor St, London W1A 2JB; www.usembassy.org.uk/cons_new/visa/niv/aupair.html) states that 'United States visa law prohibits anyone admitted into the United States as a visitor.... from working as an au pair, nanny or mother's helper even if only in exchange for room and board....Those seeking employment as an au pair are required to obtain an exchange visitor (J-1) visa through the sponsorship of an officially approved exchange visitor program.' By participating in an approved Exchange Visitor Program, au pairs of any nationality can obtain a J-1 visa valid for one year. These programmes are allowed to exist because of their purported educational value in the interests of international cultural exchange, and the au pair programme is no different. Its stated goal is to 'encourage intercultural understanding by living with an American family'. The conditions of the J-1 visa include not undertaking any paid work outside your job with a family and that you must return home at the end of your year's contract or, in the case of au pairs who are granted an extension, at the end of up to two years.

The sponsoring organisations listed earlier in this chapter are authorised to issue form DS-2019 which entitles you to apply for the coveted J-1 visa. This requires a personal interview by consular officials at the US Embassy in your country and a fee of $100. With tightening US security it is essential that you register with SEVIS (Student and Exchange Visitor Information System) for a fee of $35 which tracks the movements of all participants. For example if you intend to leave the country temporarily (e.g. to visit Canada), you have to register your intention at least two weeks in advance by sending your DS-2019 form to your sponsoring organisation.

Apart from the J-1, the only other visas which might be relevant in a few cases are the Q-visa 'International Cultural Exchange' and the H-2 'Temporary Worker' visa. For the H-2, the prospective employer in the US must file an application on Form I-129B ('Petition to Classify Non-Immigrant as Temporary Worker or Trainee') with their local Immigration and Naturalization Service (INS) office and present a strong case that a genuine effort has been made to fill the vacancy with an American citizen. While the application is being processed (usually between four and six months) there is no way of checking on the progress of the application. The Q visa is intended for foreign workers who will be providing practical training or sharing the history, culture and traditions of their country. Unfortunately this visa is not available to nannies, even one who wants to share her culture. A very good summary of the legal options for au pairs and nannies may be found on the ABC's of Immigration: 'Immigration Options for Nannies, Au Pairs and Child Care Workers' (www. visalaw.com.abcs.html, scroll down to Nannies & Au Pairs).

Inevitably there will be some people who cannot qualify for a visa but nevertheless want to work as an au pair or nanny in the US. In view of the publicity surrounding high-profile Washington politicians who have been caught employing illegal house staff as nannies and cleaners (mainly from Latin America), it would be wise to tread carefully. It is illegal for an employer to hire an alien. The nanny working illegally would therefore be putting her host family at risk. It would take only a nosy and hostile neighbour alerting the local INS before the authorities might start to investigate. Workers caught working illegally risk being deported and barred from travelling to the States for a minimum of five years.

Apart from the ongoing danger of being caught while you're working, the grilling you may get upon entry to the country is enough to put off many people. The suspicion has been that any young woman arriving alone from Britain or Ireland was coming to work with a family. Luggage may be carefully searched for incriminating evidence such as a letter of invitation from the family or summer clothing when you have claimed you are coming for just a short holiday in March. Unless girls have been tutored by someone familiar with immigration procedures, they can end up being turned back at the airport. Those who have been primed invent plausible stories often backed up by corroborating evidence such as a return ticket or a letter from a college or employer on headed paper stating that the bearer must return to England by a certain date. Your case will be strengthened if you are dressed smartly, have plenty of money and a return ticket (perhaps one which can be extended or refunded after arrival), and perhaps a list of people you intend to visit on your tour. (Do not invent these because if the immigration officer is suspicious, he or she won't hesitate to phone them.) Some girls go to extraordinary lengths, such as wrapping up a wedding gift to support their story that they have come to the States to attend the wedding of cousin Betty Lou.

Since the authorities are bound to be suspicious if you ask for a very long stay, be content with whatever they give you. It is possible to apply for an extension of your tourist visa from the local INS later. At entry Susie Walton was granted permission to stay for three months. She then got a six-month extension of her tourist visa from the INS in Minneapolis

- admittedly her employer did know a senator - and then applied for another one. After keeping her passport for two months (which serves the purpose of an extension in itself) her request was denied and she was given 15 days to leave the US, which she did. If you are staying on with an expired tourist visa, it can be difficult to cross borders into Canada or Mexico and then return again.

Most British citizens (and those of 27 other countries) do not need to apply for a tourist visa in advance. Tourists can wait until arrival to obtain a visa-waiver which is valid for one entry to the US for a maximum of 90 days. Individuals entering visa-free or with a visitor visa for business or tourism are prohibited from engaging in paid or unpaid employment in the US.

HEALTH AND INSURANCE

Everyone has heard horror stories of visitors to North America becoming destitute after having to pay enormous medical bills because they had insufficient insurance. All but the poorest Americans belong to health insurance schemes, and it is imperative that you be covered throughout your stay. All the agencies make insurance compulsory but some include it free and others charge. For example, *Au Pair in America* charges its participants $250 for medical cover of $100,000 ($200 deductible) and personal liability of $100,000 for 12 months. Some au pairs invest in an upgrade policy which provides extra cover, as well as $1,000 baggage and personal effects insurance for 13 months. If you intend to indulge in high-risk activities such as skiing you will need an even more expensive policy.

LEISURE TIME

The United States holds much fascination for people from around the world and it can be a great pleasure satisfying your curiosity and experiencing the real thing rather than the television version to identify truths and falsehoods about the Great American Myth. Of all the clichés about Americans, perhaps the one with the most foundation in truth is that they are open and friendly. It is very easy to meet Americans. They are not suspicious when foreigners address them, and they love to talk to strangers on buses and in restaurants. They are not critical or subtle and will accept overtures of friendship at face value. Americans of British, Polish, German or whatever ancestry will be especially delighted to befriend au pairs of that nationality. If you want to get on well with the locals try to be full of praise for the United States. Although many Americans have a hearty sense of humour, they seldom direct it at themselves or their country.

There may be a few impediments to developing a social life quickly, especially if you happen to start a job in the Midwest in the depths of winter. One is that you will probably be dependent on a vehicle. Most American families live in suburbs which can be many miles from the centres of nightlife. It is virtually impossible to get a live-in job in the US without being able to drive, and it is not unusual for the au pair or nanny to have unlimited access to a car.

But even with the use of a car, life in some American settings can be very dull. Barbara Schmuk travelled from Austria to take a job with a family in Vermont on the understanding that they would be moving to New York after a month. But this move never materialised so Barbara was left with hardly any company beyond that of her 2½ year old charge and the mother (even the father commuted into New York on a weekly basis). She didn't know what to do in her spare time, except ski, which was something she could do in Austria anyway. She stuck at the job three months before moving to New York where she found another job in Manhattan and so never again had to worry about how to fill her leisure time.

Au pairs who are used to the conviviality of British pubs might find the American counterpart a little disappointing. Social drinking in the States does not revolve around neighbourhood pubs; in fact there *are* no neighbourhood pubs since suburbia is almost devoid of bars. People tend to go to bars not for a quiet chat with friends, but for an expensive night out on the town, which can soon cut into the savings of a $139-a-week au pair. Nevertheless British au pairs and nannies are a familiar sight at certain singles bars in Boston, New York, Los Angeles and so on. You should bear in mind that the minimum drinking age in half the states of the Union is 21, though some British visitors have managed to acquire ID cards which exaggerate their age for this purpose.

Au pairs on the authorised programmes will be given a directory of all the participants, some of whom they will already have become acquainted with at the orientation. The Community Counsellor might also be able to suggest local clubs and sports centres where you can meet other people. The local YM/YWCA is always a good bet. Michelle Francis soon developed a busy social life in Seattle (too busy as it turned out): 'The au pairs who were already there (approximately 50) really did work to help me fit in, always telephoning me, introducing me to other people, clubs, bars, etc.'.

> **This experience was shared by 22 year old Beverley Smith from South Africa who had a 'fantastic experience' with a family outside Washington DC**
> *My first few weeks were a bit rocky. I was homesick and the kids were a bit difficult. But once we got to know each other we got on famously. The thing that was the biggest sanity-saver for me was having a big social circle of other au pairs in my area. We could call each other up to discuss problems (only a fellow au pair can fully appreciate these), arrange playdates (where the kids are occupied and the adults have company) and arrange weekend activities. My most important advice to prospective au pairs is (a) call up other au pairs as soon as you arrive; (b) get to know the lay of the land as soon as you can; (c) don't let initial homesickness overwhelm you and (d) if things are really not working out and you've tried all you could, do change families because going home will result in your losing out on what could have been the best year of your life!*

With two weeks of paid holiday and regular weekends off, you should be able to see at least some of the sights. As mentioned above, vacations with the family can be a real perk; however they are not necessarily a holiday for you if your duties continue. It had been one of Carla Mitchell's lifelong dreams to see Disneyland and she became excited when the family she was working for announced that as part of their visit to California (where they stayed in a hotel on Rodeo Drive in Los Angeles) they were going to visit Disneyland. But the day was spoiled for Carla by the presence of her two badly behaved charges who whined continuously. If there is something you are especially eager to see, it is probably wise to organise an independent visit.

If you are keen to enhance your childcare skills, appreciation for America or just meet some other au pairs, short courses tailor-made for au pairs are available at two institutes in New York State. Long Island University (516-299-2359; www.cwpost.liu.edu/cwis/cwp/aupair) is the venue for one of these and the other is at Silver Bay on Lake George (College of St. Rose; www.efaupair.org/silverbay).

TRAVEL

As mentioned above, anyone participating in the approved au pair programme will have their return flights organised and paid for. As soon as their 12 months of au pairing are up, they will be at liberty to travel round North America for up to one month before they are obliged to fly home under the terms of the programme. The agencies will be able to suggest ways to travel economically.

Incredibly, the price of flying across the Atlantic has been steadily decreasing over the past decade. Off-peak student returns to New York start at £150-£200 plus tax. Competition is fiercest and therefore prices lowest on the main routes between London and New York, Miami and Los Angeles. In many cases, summer fares will be twice as high as winter ones. One-way fares are also available to eastern seaboard cities like Washington for £100-£150. When comparing fares, always take the taxes into consideration since they now represent an extra £40-£70 in each direction.

Outside summer and the Christmas period you should have no problems getting a seat; at peak times, a reliable alternative is to buy a discounted ticket on one of the less fashionable carriers which fly to New York, such as Air India or Kuwait Airways. A one-year return London-New York on Air India might start at £265 plus taxes.

The USA and Canada share the longest common frontier in the world, which gives some idea of the potential problems and expense of getting around. One peculiarly American solution is to arrange a 'drive-away,' a term which refers to the widespread practice of delivering private cars within North America. Specialist companies find drivers, arrange insurance and arbitrate in the event of mishaps. You get free use of a car (subject to mileage and time restrictions) and pay for gas and tolls on the interstates. Usually a deadline and mileage limit are fixed, though these are often flexible and checks lax. Unfortunately for many young au pairs, you have to be over 21 or even 25 in some cases, as well as have a driving licence and enough money for the deposit (generally $300) which is refunded on successful delivery. Look up 'Automobile Transporters and Driveaway Companies' in the Yellow Pages of any big city.

A more conventional means of getting around is by bus or air, both of which are cheaper than in Europe. Bus passes (Ameripass) are a travel bargain for people who want to cover a lot of ground. Greyhound has no office in the UK but their US and Canada passes can be bought through STA and a few others such as Western Air Travel in Devon (0870 330 1100; www.westernair.co.uk). In 2006, Greyhound (www.greyhound.com) were offering 4, 7, 10, 15, 21, 30, 45 and 60 day passes in the low season to students and under 26s for £96, £118, £145, £166, £204, £224, £252 and £299. Once you are in the US timetable and fare information is available 24 hours a day on the toll-free number 1-800-231-2222.

Other forms of transport in the USA are probably more expensive but may have their own attractions, such as the trips run by Green Tortoise (494 Broadway, San Francisco, California 94133; 800-867-8647; www.greentortoise.com) which use vehicles converted to sleep about 35 people and which make interesting detours and stopovers. Trek America is a long established adventure tour operator based in the UK (0870 444 8735; www.trekamerica.co.uk) which markets its 1-4 week adventure tours specifically to au pairs.

DIRECTORY REFERENCES

The main au pair placement organisations in the USA are: **AuPairCare** (San Francisco), **Au Pair in America** (London office of AIFS), **Au Pair USA/InterExchange** (New York), **Cultural Care** (Boston), **Educare America** (AIFS programme administered in the UK by *Childcare International), **Euraupair** (UK agent in Shropshire); **go Au Pair Programme** (Utah). Two online nanny agencies based in the USA are **4nannies.com** and **Au Pair Connect**.

For au pair and nanny agencies in the UK that interview for US au pair programmes or agencies which deal with trained nannies, see for example: Almondbury, Annies Nannies, Au Pair Search, Cambridge Nannies & Au Pairs, Cherish Childcare, The Childcare Company, Childcare International, The Childcare Solution, IAPO, Janet White, Kensington Nannies, Konnex, Nannies of St. James, Nanny Search Ltd, Occasional & Permanent, Quick Au Pair & Nanny Agency, Regency Nannies, Simply Angelic, Solihull, Tinies Childcare.

Other agencies abroad which send au pairs to the USA are:
Australia: Australian Nanny & Au Pair Connection, Dial-an-Angel, JCR Au Pairs & Nannies
Austria: AuPair4You
Canada: Au Pair Canada (Toronto), Le Monde Au Pair, Opti-Mum Childcare, Scotia Personnel
Czech Republic: Au Pair International CZ, British Contact, Student Agency
Finland: Allianssi
France: A.F.J.E., Butterfly et Papillon, France Au Pair Eurojob, Good Morning Europe,

Inter-Séjours, Nurse Au Pair Placement, Solution Au Pair
Germany: A'nF, Aupair-Ark.de, Au-Pair Interconnection, Au-Pair Service Dr. Uwe
  Krenz, Au Pair Service Silke Sommer, Au Pair Vermittlung Sigmar Bassmann, Inwox,
  Multikultur International Exchange Programs, Munichaupair, Personal Touch
Greece: Nine Muses
Hungary: Au Pair Kft.
Ireland: Job Options Bureau
Italy: 3 Esse, Au Pair International, Euroma, Intermediate, International Study Vacation,
  MB Scambi Culturali, STI Travels
Netherlands: Activity International, House-o-Orange Au Pairs, S-Au Pair Intermediate,
  Travel Active Programmes
New Zealand: International Nannies, International Working Holidays
Norway: Au Pair Agency Norway
Peru: Au Pair Peru
South Africa: Youth Discovery Programmes
Spain: G.I.C., Interclass, Interlink, Kingsbrook
Switzerland: Perfect Way
Turkey: Yakin Bati

The Rest of the World

Occasionally vacancies crop up in other corners of the world outside the countries treated
individually above. Qualified or experienced nannies have a better chance of getting
unusual posts such as working for a Saudi sheikh, for a British diplomatic family abroad or
in fact anywhere where there are wealthy people. Another possibility is to arrange a live-in
position in which the primary duties are to improve the children's knowledge of English.
This is commonplace in Turkey, Egypt and elsewhere.

   Au pair and nanny agencies exist in some unexpected countries like Sri Lanka and Peru
(see entry for *Au Pair Peru* in the Directory of Agencies), but these invariably run outgoing
programmes only. International au pair databases like the ones operated by greataupair.com
and findaupair.com can sometimes turn up vacancies in farflung countries like Bermuda,
Guam and Qatar, normally with expat families. To take a couple of examples spotted at the
time of writing: a posting in the online *Jobs Abroad Bulletin* newsletter was made by an
Irish family based in Panama looking for someone to care for their four-year old daughter;
the advertiser worked for the United Nations and was offering an au pair the prospect of
extensive travels round Latin America and a possible stint in New York. Another exotic
possibility advertised on www.learn4good.com/jobs read (after being translated from
German):

   We live on a game reserve in Namibia called Kuzikus Wildlife Reserve 180 km from the
   capital Windhoek. We need someone to look after our three children (aged 8, 6 and 3)
   and to help with the horses. Would prefer a female about 25 years of age.

South African families may occasionally want to hire a foreign au pair or nanny, though
the visa situation is difficult. On the whole nannies from abroad can get only a six-month
visitor's visa, whereas the majority of families want a commitment of at least one year. The
norm is to hire live-out nannies with their own vehicles. Still, it is worth investigating JCR
Cultural Exchange in Johannesburg whose website (www.jcr.co.za) describes an incoming
au pair programme; see entry for *JCR Australia* for the South African address.

   In fact JCR Intercultural Exchange Programs Pty Ltd. in Australia (see entry for *JCR*

Au Pairs) with a large outgoing programme to many countries includes a live-in tutoring programme in Korea in which young women aged 18-30 can spend six months living with a Korean family, helping their children learn to speak English for 20 hours per week in exchange for free board and lodging. The scheme includes free airfares, insurance and pocket money of A$250 per week.

Anyone with a childcare or teaching background might consider working as a volunteer with underprivileged children in some distant part of the world from Central America to Central Europe. For example an orphanage in a remote part of Guatemala takes on volunteers in various capacities including caring for the pre-schoolers; details are available from the Casa Guatemala office in the capital (Angelina de Galdamez, 14th Calle 10-63, Zona 1, 01001 Guatemala City or Apdo. Postal 5-75-A; 502-232-5517; casaguatemal@ guate.net; www.casa-guatemala.org).

Another example would be to spend time volunteering for Mother Teresa's Missionaries of Charity in Calcutta (Administrative Office, 54A A.J.C. Bose Road, Calcutta 700016) caring for and feeding orphaned children, among others. Further information is available from their London office at 177 Bravington Road, London W9 3AR (020-8960 2644).

More than a decade and a half on from the fall of Ceaucescu, the orphanages and special schools of Romania continue to need voluntary input. For example Nightingales Children's Project operates a full-time volunteer programme in which volunteers spend from one to three months working with children who are disabled or have special needs (including with HIV); the orphanage is in Cernavoda near the Black Sea. Accommodation is shared with eight volunteers in a flat; volunteers contribute £2.50 a day to cover their rent and food. For further information contact the project on info@nightingaleschildrensproject.co.uk.

MIDDLE EAST

Specific vacancies are regularly advertised in the specialist press, i.e. *The Lady* and *Nursery World*. Of course the wealthiest families want professional Norland-trained nannies (or equivalent) but there are plenty of lesser nobility - the House of Saud alone numbers in the thousands - and other wealthy families eager to hire an English-speaking woman for reasons of prestige. Those who are attracted by the high wages paid in the Middle East should be warned that many nannies become unhappy due to the boredom and hardship of living in a strict Islamic society.

Trained and experienced nannies willing to live a relatively cloistered life should contact London-based international nanny agencies and watch the specialist press. Nanny agencies which make placements in the Middle East include *Eden Nannies, Anglo Nannies* and *Simply Angelic*.

EASTERN EUROPE

Under Communism the state provided such good childcare facilities for working parents that there is no tradition in the new democracies of Eastern Europe of live-in childcare (despite the huge demand for learning English). In general, the middle classes of Hungary, Czech Republic and Poland live in much more cramped accommodation than in western Europe and even if they could afford to take on an au pair, they could ill afford the space that she would require.

This is changing as individuals who have prospered in a market economy acquire more disposable income and bigger houses. Agencies in the UK which claim to have posts in Eastern and Central Europe are likely to be professional nanny agencies supplying nannies to expatriates earning international salaries in Moscow, Bratislava or any of the cities which have proved to be magnets for foreign businessmen.

Scores of au pair agencies exist throughout Eastern Europe, primarily concerned with the placement of their nationals in the rest of Europe and North America. The only incoming programme that has come to our attention is an au pair placement programme in Russia run by a Russian travel agency in the city of Izhevsk, 600 miles southeast of Moscow. SV charges a €150 fee; details on www.sv-agency.udm.ru/sv/aupair.htm. English-speaking au pairs will be expected to check homework and support children's creativity as well as help with the household. The average number of hours worked is 30 per week.

WORLDWIDE

Agencies whose operations extend beyond Europe or the USA tend to be professional nanny agencies filling high-level vacancies, often for expatriate families. The rise of the internet as a tool for matching nannies with families means that more agencies operate on a global scale than in the past.

Among UK-based agencies which claim to have clients all over the world are: Almondbury, Anglo Nannies, Eden Childcare, Hyde Park International, Kensington Nannies (excluding USA), Knightsbridge Nannies, Lloyd's, The London Nanny Company, Nannies of St. James (especially Hong Kong), Nanny Search, Occasional & Permanent, Regency Nannies International, Riverside Nannies, Simply Angelic, Star Nannies (excluding North America), Sunflowers Childcare, Tinies Childcare, Top Notch Nannies (excluding USA), Totalnannies.com, UK & Overseas (mainly Europe), Westminster Nannies International and Yorkshire Nannies (excluding USA).

PART III

Directory of Agencies

Alphabetical listing of 275 agencies
specialising in jobs for au pairs, nannies and
mother's helps in the UK, Europe
and overseas.

The information given in this section has been provided by
the agencies concerned. It should be checked personally
when applying for a placement.

3 ESSE AGENCY
Via Postcastello 7, 21013 Gallarate (VA), Italy. ☎+39 0331-771065. Fax: +39 01331-781682. E-mail: info@3esse.com. Website: www.3esse.com.
In business since 1993.
Placements: Italian au pairs sent abroad.
Jobs in: Europe (UK, France, Spain, Germany, Portugal, Greece), America and Australia (with compulsory course).
Male applicants can be placed in some countries, viz. England, France, Germany and Australia.
Minimum stay: 6 or 9 months in Europe; 12 months in USA; 3 months in Australia (combined English language course and staying with host family); Summer stays of 2-3 months are available in Europe.
Wages/pocket money: €65-€70 per week in Europe; A$100 per week for English + au pair programme in Australia.
Qualifications: must have basic knowledge of the language, childcare experience and be at least 18 years old. Maximum age varies with country (26, 27, 30 or 35).
Application procedure: within EU and Australia, need 2 references but no interview; average processing time is 15-60 days. For USA, need 3 references and interview; placement takes about 2 months.
Other services: full support service by partner agencies.
Fees: €180 for Au Pair in Europe. Enrolment fee for Australia is €55 plus cost of the language course (e.g. A$5,870 for 12 weeks).
Contact: Daniela Socci, Owner.

3 TO 4 AGENCY
71 Worrall Road, Clifton, Bristol BS8 2TX. ☎/fax: 0117-973 0466. E-mail: naomi@3to4-agency.co.uk. Website: www.3to4-agency.co.uk.
In business since 1990.
Placements: 300-500 au pairs, au pairs plus, mother's helps, nannies, maternity nurses, etc.
Jobs in: England, Scotland, Ireland and most European countries.
Nationalities placed: any that are allowed by immigration regulations.
Agency actively promotes male au pairs and places up to 5 per week. Also places couples.
Minimum stay: 1 month. Summer placements can be made.
Wages/pocket money: £55 per week au pairs; £65 for au pairs plus; UK minimum wage applies to mother's helps/nannies (£5.05 per hour in 2006).
Qualifications: ages 18-27. Childcare/driving experience useful for au pairs; childcare experience essential for mother's helps. Language is not a problem.
Application procedure: nannies and mothers' helps will have all references checked and will be interviewed if possible. Au pairs can be placed within a week.
Other services: au pairs are given contact lists, meeting places, welcome pack and school/college information. In the event of the arrangement breaking down, au pair is taken into owner's home until a new family can be found. Nannies are given advice on pay and tax and are offered a contract through employers. Helpline always available.
Fees: nil.
Contact: Naomi Rawlings, Director.

4nannies.com Inc
2 Pidgeon Hill Dr, Suite 550, Sterling, VA 20165, USA. ☎800-810-2611. E-mail: Support@4nannies.com. Website: www.4nannies.com.
In business since 1998. Member of International Nanny Association.
Placements: online nanny recruitment. Approximately 3,500 jobs listed per year.
Jobs in: primarily US.

Wages/pocket money: US nanny salaries range from $275-$800 per week depending on location plus nanny's education and experience as well as hours and numbers of children. $350-$500 per week is the mean.
Qualifications: must be over 18 and possess valid work authorisation.
Application procedure: applicants and families complete a detailed online form and are provided site membership within one business day.
Other services: online FAQ and help files.
Fees: nil.
Contact: Kathleen Webb, Managing Partner.

AAUPAIR & NANNY AGENCY LTD
200 High Road, London N22 8HH. ☎020-8888 8144. Fax: 020-8889 7295. E-mail: aaupair@aol.com. Website: www.aaupair.co.uk.
In business since 1999. Member of IAPA and BAPAA.
Placements: 700 au pairs, nannies, mother's helps and housekeepers.
Jobs in: worldwide, also UK. Network of 400 partners.
No male applicants are placed.
Minimum stay: 3 months; summer placements available.
Wages/pocket money: £55-£150 per week. Level of salary increases with amount of experience.
Application procedure: interviews required plus 'Dear Family' letter. Average processing time 7-14 days.
Other services: supporting services include advice on insurance, travel and language classes. Help au pairs in London to make contact with other au pairs. If a problem occurs, au pair can stay in agency's hostel until she is placed with another family.
Fees: £95 for summer placements. No fee for placements lasting 5-24 months.
Contact: Marcia Behseta, Manager.

AA AU-PAIRS UK LTD
11 Roy Road, Northwood, Middlesex HA6 1EQ. ☎/fax: 01923 450714. E-mail: AAAUPAIRS@aol.com.
In business since 2000.
Placements: 150 au pairs, mother's helps, nannies and housekeepers.
Jobs in: throughout the UK.
Nationalities placed: any with a valid visa including those from the Commonwealth on working holidays.
About 3% of applicants placed are male.
Minimum stay: 3 months in summer, longer during the year.
Wages/pocket money: minimum £60 per week for 25 hours of work.
Application procedure: applicants must provide 2 valid references and a police check. If au pairs are already in the UK, placement can sometimes to done in a day or two. If they have specific locations in mind, placement can take up to a month. Agency tries to match families and girls with similar interests.
Other services: supplies information about language schools, travel and contact details of other au pairs in the area.
Fees: nil.
Contact: Mrs. Savi Cockeram, Director.

ABACUS AU PAIR AGENCY
2 Byron Terrace, Byron Street, Hove, East Sussex BN3 5AY. ☎/fax: 01273 203803. E-mail: info@abacusaupairagency.co.uk. Website: www. abacusaupairagency.co.uk.
In business since 2000 (though owner has been placing au pairs since 1991).

Placements: around 300 au pairs per year. Now also placing Mother's Helps.
Jobs in: foreign applicants can be placed in positions throughout the UK. Also place overseas in France, Italy, Germany, Spain, Switzerland, Belgium, etc.
Nationalities placed: EU nationals plus other Europeans in accordance with Home Office regulations.
Male applicants also placed.
Minimum stay: normally 6 months although shorter stays considered. Summer jobs available (June to September).
Pocket money: minimum £55 per week for Au Pairs. Mother's Helps are paid according to hours/duties/experience, starting from around £120 per week.
Qualifications: Au Pairs should be 17-27 years with at least a basic level of the language. Should have some childcare experience that can include babysitting, working on summer camps or in a nursery/crèche, etc. The same conditions apply for Mother's Helps, although there are no age restrictions.
Application procedure: applicants can apply by post/fax or on-line. Agency requires a completed application form, 'Dear family' letter, minimum of 2 references, photographs and medical certificate. Placements usually take 1-2 weeks depending on when an applicant wishes to begin their stay. All applicants are reference-checked and interviewed where possible.
Other services: advice offered on insurance, travel and language classes. Details given of other au pairs/mother's helps in the area.
Fees: no charge to foreign applicants coming to the UK. £40 fee for applicants placed overseas, payable only when a placement is secured.
Contact: Deborah Bushell, Proprietor.

Abacus Au Pair Agency

Au Pair Agency

- Au Pair placements throughout England, Scotland and Wales
- We also offer placements throughout Europe – Spain, France, Germany, Italy etc.
- Male and female applicants required all year round for both short and long term positions
- Mothers Help positions also available

2 Byron Terrace, Byron Street, Hove, East Sussex BN3 5AY **Tel:/Fax:** 00 44 1273 203803
Email: info@abacusaupairagency.co.uk **Website:** www.abacusaupairagency.co.uk

ABB AU-PAIR FAMILY SERVICE
Via Alemania 2, 5°A, 07003 Palma de Mallorca, Spain. ☎+34 971-752027. Fax: +34 971-900153. E-mail: abbaupair@ono.com.
Placements: au pairs.
Jobs in: Mallorca, Spain. British au pairs can be placed throughout Spain.
Nationalities placed: European Union nationals. British au pairs in great demand.
Minimum stay: 2 months in summer. Minimum 6 month stays otherwise.
Qualifications: must be able to speak English.
Contact: Clara Mangin.

ABBEY AU PAIRS
8 Boulnois Avenue, Parkstone, Poole, Dorset BH14 9NX. ☎01202 732922. Fax: 01202 466098. E-mail: ursula.foyle@ntlworld.com.
In business since 1988. Originally licensed by the Department of Employment.

Placements: 100 au pairs.
Jobs in: England only.
Nationalities placed: mainly Swiss.
Very few males placed because of lack of demand.
Minimum stay: 6 months although summer stays are available.
Wages/pocket money: £55 for 25 hours of work per week.
Qualifications: ages 18-27. Basic knowledge of English and genuine fondness for children essential.
Application procedure: all families have been personally interviewed by owner of agency before placement. After all necessary documents and references are received, applicants can usually be placed within 2-3 weeks. Interviews arranged if candidate is in the country; otherwise telephone contact is arranged.
Other services: 'pastoral visits' are made after arrival; regular coffee mornings arranged. Advice given on language schools, activities and whereabouts of other au pairs.
Contact: Ursula Foyle, Proprietor.

ABC AU PAIRS
42 Underhill Road, Dulwich, London, SE22 0QT. ☎020-8299 3052. Fax: 020-8299 6086. E-mail: vivienne@abc-aupairs.co.uk. Website: www.abc-aupairs. co.uk.
In business since 1988. Member of IAPA and BAPAA.
Placements: 250 au pairs and mother's helps.
Jobs in: UK and France.
Minimum stay: 6 months; summer placements available.
Wages/pocket money: most families pay above the recommended minimum of £55, e.g. £60-£70 for 25 hours a week.
Qualifications: must have some experience with children (babysitting, work experience, etc.). Must have flexibility to fit in with family life, basic conversational English as a minimum, and be motivated to make the most of this cultural exchange.
Application procedure: files sent by partner agencies with references checked and criminal records checks, interview notes, etc. Average processing time of good applicants 2-3 weeks.
Other services: meetings, outings and social events arranged for au pairs. Welcome pack distributed with friendship contact information.
Fees: nil.
Contact: Vivienne Colchester, Owner.

ABC NANNIES CANADA INC
1630 - 701 West Georgia (Pacific Centre), Vancouver, BC V7Y 1K8, Canada. ☎+1 604-581-1018. E-mail: info@abcnannies.ca. Website: www.abcnannies. ca.
In business since 1996.
Placements: nannies as part of the Live-in Caregiver Program.
Jobs in: Canada only (Vancouver, Calgary, Edmonton, Winnipeg, Toronto, Ottawa).
Nationalities placed: all.
Male applicants cannot be placed.
Minimum stay: 12 months.
Wages/pocket money: C$850-$1,400 per month net.
Qualifications: 1-2 years of professional childcare experience, 6 months of which must be with the same employer. Fluent English, a clean driving licence, excellent health and a clean criminal record required.
Application procedure: it takes 1 week to process the application and 3-4 months to process the visa.

Fees: nil.
Contact: Jana McDermott.

ACADEMY AU PAIR & NANNY AGENCY
42 Milsted Road, Rainham, Kent ME8 6SU. ☎/fax: 01634 310808. E-mail: enquiries@aupair-select.com. Website: www.aupair-select.com.
In business since 1990. Member of REC.
Placements: au pairs, au pairs plus, nannies, mother's helps and housekeepers.
Jobs in: England, France, Germany, Spain, Italy, Netherlands, Belgium, Austria, Switzerland, Canada, Australia and occasionally other countries.
Nationalities placed: all that are legal.
Minimum stay: 6 months. Summer stays are available in Europe.
Wages/pocket money: £50+ per week for au pairs; £120+ for mother's helps; £200+ for nannies.
Qualifications: au pairs must speak language of chosen country. Non-smokers preferable. Nannies must be qualified. Mother's helps must have some sole charge experience.
Application procedure: medical certificates, photos, 2 references and life story. If within the UK, interviews are essential; telephone and letter contact otherwise. Applications processed within one week.
Other services: welcome pack sent on arrival. Advice on language classes and insurance available.
Fees: £40 upon acceptance (free if coming to the UK).
Contact: J. Bosworth.

ACCUEIL FAMILIAL DES JEUNES ETRANGERS - see A.F.J.E.

ACCUEIL INTERNATIONAL SERVICES
2a rue Ducastel, 78100 St. Germain en Laye, France. ☎+33 1-39 73 04 98. Fax: +33 1-39 73 15 25. E-mail: au-pair@easyconnect.fr or au-pair@easynet. fr. Website: www.accueil-international.com.
In business since 1983. Member of IAPA.
Placements: 450 au pairs principally, also au pairs plus.
Jobs in: all regions of France. Plus French women can be placed in Spain, UK, Ireland, Germany, Austria and Italy.
Nationalities placed: Western and Eastern Europeans and South Americans. Male applicants can be placed.
Minimum stay: 6 months. Summer stays: 1-3 months.
Wages/pocket money: €305 per month for au pairs (30 h.p.w. plus 2 or 3 evenings of babysitting). €400 for au pair plus (35 h.p.w. plus babysitting). All receive Paris transport card.
Qualifications: ages 18-30 years. Driving licence useful. Should be able to speak some French. Childcare experience essential for nannies.
Application procedure: placements are usually made 2-4 weeks after application, 2 character references and health certificate have been submitted. Office staff speak English as well as French.
Other services: agency recommends French schools in Paris and the suburbs.
Fees: on application.
Contact: Sophie Hertzog, Director.

ACE AU-PAIRS
27 Chickerell Road, Park North, Swindon, Wilts. SN3 2RQ. ☎/fax: 01793 430091. E-mail: info@aceaupairs.co.uk. Website: www.aceaupairs.co.uk.
In business since 1999.

Placements: 200 au pairs.
Jobs in: UK only.
Nationalities placed: all that are approved by Home Office.
About 10% of applicants placed are male. Males normally provide criminal record check.
Minimum stay: 6-week placements are possible though rare. Plenty of summer placements available lasting 2-3 months.
Wages/pocket money: £55 minimum per week (£60 in London) for au pairs.
Qualifications: ages 17-27. Proof of childcare experience required.
Application procedure: minimum 2 childcare references needed, the majority of which are checked by the sending agent abroad. Telephone interviews held with agency and with interested family to ensure level of English is satisfactory.
Other services: advice given on travel services and language classes. Agency tries to give as much pre-placement information as possible to avoid problems at a later stage.
Fees: nil if applying directly.
Contact: Mrs. V Huntley, Proprietor.

ACROBAT AUPAIRS
31 Ella Grove, Knutsford, Cheshire WA16 8UT. ☎01565 651883. Mob: 0798 440 5981. Fax: 01565 631029. E-mail: enquiries@acrobataupairs.com. Website: www.acrobataupairs.com.
In business since 1997.
Placements: approximately 100 au pairs.
Jobs in: England only.
Nationalities placed: all Europeans, especially au pairs from Czech Republic, Slovakia and Turkey.
About 5% of applicants placed are male.
Minimum stay: 1 month in summer.
Wages/pocket money: minimum £55 per week. Varies according to duties and the family.
Qualifications: ages 17-27. Childcare experience and reasonable level of English needed.
Application procedure: placement usually takes about 4 weeks.
Other services: list of other au pairs given as part of welcome pack.
Fees: nil.
Contact: Mrs. Andrea Fekete Valentine.

ACTIVIDAD AU-PAIR INTERNACIONAL
Paseo de Gracia 78-Atic 2°, 08008 Barcelona, Spain. ☎+34 93-215 72 47. E-mail: ainteraupair@jazzfree.com or bcnaupair@ya.com.
In business since 1973. Collaborate with the Generalitat (government) of Barcelona for the European exchange of au pairs.
Placements: au pairs. Also Spanish young people placed in British and Irish hotels.
Jobs in: Spain; outgoing programme to Britain, Ireland, France, Germany, Austria, Italy, Denmark and Norway.
Nationalities placed: any that are allowed by immigration regulations.
Minimum stay: 6 months, though 9-12 months preferred. Summer placements can be made.
Wages/pocket money: €250+ per month. 1 week paid holiday given after 6 months.
Qualifications: ages 18-28. Experience of routine housework and ability to look after children required. Basic knowledge of Spanish usually needed though some families will accept English or German speakers.
Application procedure: 2-3 childcare references needed. Personal interview held where possible.
Fees: nil but must send 12 international reply coupons to cover costs of processing application.
Contact: Vicky Vicente, Manager Co-ordinator.

ACTIVITY INTERNATIONAL
PO Box 694, 7500 Enschede, Netherlands. ☎+31 53-483 10 40. Fax: +31 53-483 10 49. E-mail: info@activity.aupair.nl. Website: www.activity.aupair.nl. Address for personal callers: Brammelerstraat 15, Enschede.
In business since 1986. Founding member of IAPA.
Placements: around 100 nannies and au pairs.
Jobs in: Europe, USA and Australia for Dutch girls; no incoming programme. Male positions are occasionally available.
Minimum stay: 6 months. Summer stays are occasionally available.
Wages/pocket money: from €200-€400 per month.
Qualifications: childcare experience normally required.
Application procedure: placement normally takes 2-3 months.
Other services: agency also organises international exchanges and work abroad programme for Dutch young people.
Fees: €200 for outgoing placement.
Contact: Ms. Janine Wegman or Bernice Spijker.

ADRIA RECRUITMENT
UK office: 54 Suite, 151 High Street, Southampton, Hampshire SO14 2BT. ☎023 80 254287. Croatian office: Zadvorska I odvojak 20, 10257 Brezovica, Zagreb; +385 91 588 1341; tel/fax: +385 1 6538596. E-mail: info@adriarecruitment. com. Website: www.adriarecruitment.com.
In business since 1992.
Placements: 130 au pairs, au pairs plus, mother's helps/nannies and hotel staff.
Jobs in: UK only.
Nationalities placed: all that are legal.
Very few male applicants can be placed.
Minimum stay: 6-24 months. Summer stays of 2-3 months are possible.
Wages/pocket money: from £60 per week for au pairs; £80 for au pairs plus; from £120 for mother's help/nannies.
Qualifications: ages 17-27. Knowledge of language and childcare experience are advantages.
Application procedure: medical certificate, photo, 2 references and letter to potential family must be submitted by au pairs. References are checked.
Other services: applicants can be put in touch with one another. Advice given on language schools. Agency tries to find different family or temporary accommodation if insoluable problems arise.
Contact: Irena Poje-Oxenham, Proprietor.

A.F.J.E.
Accueil Familial des Jeunes Etrangers, 23 rue du Cherche-Midi, 75006 Paris, France. ☎+33 1-42 22 50 34. Fax: +33 1-45 44 60 48. E-mail: accueil@afje-paris.org. Website: www.afje-paris.org.
Nearest métro: Sèvres-Babylone. In business since 1948. Member of IAPA. Also member in France of U.N.S.E. and Office National de Garantie des Séjours et Stages Linguistiques.
Placements: about 950 au pairs and paying guests.
Jobs in: France (Paris and Ile de France mostly, also university towns). Also French girls sent to Britain, Ireland, Germany, Italy, Spain, Netherlands, Finland and USA.
Nationalities placed: no restriction.
A few male placements are made.
Minimum stay: 6 months, though 9 months preferred (September-June). Summer stays of 1, 2 or 3 months arranged outside Paris between mid-June and mid-September.
Wages/pocket money: €267 per month plus Paris transport card.

Qualifications: ages 18-27 years. Some experience of childcare and some French needed. Driving licence welcome.
Application procedure: families in Paris area come to the office to choose files so that they can contact girls directly. Interviews arranged if candidates already in France. (In this case placements usually made within 2-3 weeks). Non-EU applicants must apply for a Long Stay Visa in their home country and allow 1-3 months for processing. Must submit the following documents: school and university diplomas (minimum Baccalaureat level), birth certificate and recent medical certificate, all translated into French by official translator. Must also send 2 references, hand written letter and photocopy of passport. Applications for summer stays should be sent before the end of March if possible.
Other services: civil liability insurance arranged, help with opening a savings account *(livret caisse d'Epargne)*, help given with visa procedures, 'Accord de Placement' and social security. Also addresses of language courses (e.g. Alliance Française, Institut Catholique, Sorbonne, Paris Langues, etc).
Fees: €65 for summer stays; €120 for year-long stays by EU nationals; €135 for non-EU nationals.
Contact: Brigitte Ferrier, Director.

AGENCIA INTERCAMBIOS CULTURALES Y AU PAIR
San Joaquin No. 17, 07003 Palma de Mallorca, Baleares, Spain. ☎/fax: +34 971-755124. E-mail: aicap@onon.com. Website: www.aicap.es.vg.
In business since 1987.
Placements: 500 au pairs.
Jobs in: Spain (mostly Majorca); plus France, England, Italy, Austria, Germany, Ireland, Netherlands, etc.
Nationalities placed: Europeans.
About 3% of applicants placed are male.
Minimum stay: 6, 9 or 12 months preferred. Summer stays are available.
Wages/pocket money: €50-€70 per week.
Qualifications: ages 17-30. Childcare experience needed.
Other services: can advise on local Spanish courses.
Fees: nil.
Contact: Catalina Garces, Director.

AGENZIA ALLA PARI
Via Piave 16, 19125 La Spezia, Italy. ☎/fax: +39 0187 20592. E-mail: info@speziallapari.it. Website: www.speziallapari.it.
In business since 2003.
Placements: 15 au pairs and mother's helps. Agency would like to set up new programme in Italy whereby young English-speaking foreigners receive free board and lodging in exchange for speaking English for 15 hours a week to the family. Minimum stay 2 weeks.
Jobs in: London and Ireland for Italian au pairs. Would like to start incoming au pair and live-in tutor programme in Italy.
Male candidates cannot be placed.
Minimum stay: 6 months; summer placements available.
Wages/pocket money: £55 a week in London, €75 in Ireland, €60 in Italy.
Qualifications: must have babysitting references and flexibility. Ages 18-30. Non-smokers and drivers strongly preferred.
Application procedure: references are always checked. Telephone interviews conducted or personal meetings if possible.
Fees: €250.
Contact: Chiara Cortese, Owner.

ALLIANSSI YOUTH EXCHANGES
Asemapäällikönkatu 1, 00520 Helsinki, Finland. ☎+358 20-755 2606. Fax: +358 20-755 2627. E-mail: aupair@alli.fi. Website: www.nuorisovaihto.fi.
In business since 1993. Member of IAPA.
Placements: 200 au pairs.
Jobs in: Britain, Ireland, Sweden, Norway, Netherlands, Germany, Spain, Italy, Iceland, France, Austria, Belgium and USA. No placements in Finland.
Nationalities placed: mostly Finns.
Minimum stay: 3 months in summer.
Wages/pocket money: £40 per week au pairs; £50-£55 for au pairs plus; £85-£130 for mother's helps.
Qualifications: minimum age 18. Must have experience of looking after children outside one's own family. Must speak English or language of target country.
Application procedure: at least one reference is checked in some cases (e.g. applications for placement in the UK). Interviews held for placement in some countries (e.g. Netherlands and the USA).
Fees: programme fee of €160.
Contact: Tiina Hokkanen.

ALMONDBURY AU PAIR & NANNY AGENCY
4 Napier Road, Holland Park, London W14 8LQ. ☎01803 380795 or 01288 359159. E-mail: admin@aupair-agency.com. Website: www.aupair-agency. com.
In business since 1994. Internet-based international agency with telephone contacts in France (+33 1 53-01-06-77) and the USA (718-732-2358).
At the time of writing, Almondbury's database included 10,234 registered au pairs and 967 families, 214 of them verified (i.e. repeat clients).
Placements: au pairs and mother's helps. Specialist nanny recruitment site is www.nanny-agency.com.
Jobs in: USA, UK and worldwide.
Nationalities placed: any that are allowed by immigration regulations.
Male applicants can register their details.
Minimum stay: variable. Many short-term and long-term placements.
Application procedure: applicants register on-line (free of charge) and can browse families looking for live-in care.
Fees: nil for au pairs; families pay £45 to register (membership lasts one year) and then an introduction fee starting at £85 for a one-month au pair up to about £230 for a 12-month placement.
Contact: Damian Kirkwood, Rosemary Riley.

AMBER AU PAIRS
Based in West Midlands – moving premises at time of writing. ☎01384 230429. E-mail: info@amberaupairs.co.uk or amberaupairs2@yahoo.co.uk. Website: www.amberaupairs.co.uk.
In business since 1999.
Placements: about 70. Mostly au pairs; some nannies including temporary nannies.
Jobs in: mainly incoming to UK; limited outgoing to EU countries.
About 10% of applicants placed are male.
Minimum stay: 6 months; 9-24 months preferred.
Wages/pocket money: £50 for 25 hours a week, £70 for 30-35 hours.
Qualifications: must have reasonable facility in English. Ages 19-26.
Other services: accommodation can be offered in an emergency.
Fees: nil.

Contact: Mrs. Lara Hammond, Manager.

AMICIZIA - MARIA DE ANGELIS
Via Andrea Doria 4/B/3, 16126 Genoa (GE), Italy. ☎/fax: +39 010-246 4428553 1096. Mob: 340-646 4191. E-mail: deangelismaria@tin.it. Website: www. mamicizia.it.
In business since 1970. Agency now operates mainly over the internet.
Placements: au pairs and mother's helps in Italy; au pairs and hotel workers in England.
Jobs in: UK and Europe for Italian au pairs.
Minimum stay: 6 months, preferably 12. Summer placements can be made.
Qualifications: minimum age preferred 19 years. Childcare experience needed.
Application procedure: visits by appointment.
Other services: agency also arranges paying guest stays in London and elsewhere in Europe.
Fees: €157.
Contact: Maria de Angelis, Owner.

A'nF – AU PAIR AND FAMILY
Argentinische Allee 110, 14163 Berlin-Zehlendorf, Germany. ☎+49 30-303 49 722. Fax: +49 30-303 49 723. E-mail: info@aupairandfamily.de. Website: www. aupairandfamily.de.
In business since 2005 (though part of another agency since 2003).
Placements: 50-100 au pairs.
Jobs in: USA, UK and Ireland primarily, also Iceland, Denmark, Spain, Netherlands and France. No incoming programme.
About 5% of applicants placed are male.
Minimum stay: 6 months; no summer placements.
Wages/pocket money: €50-€90 a week or US$140 in the US.
Qualifications: must have some experience with children.
Application procedure: interviews held to explain programme and references checked.
Other services: workshops lasting several days held to prepare au pairs, e.g. in cookery, childcare, play, first aid. In some countries, travel and insurance expenses are covered.
Fees: €50 service fee + €150 programme fee. Additional fees for USA programme.
Contact: Gudrun Strauss, Director.

ANGELS INTERNATIONAL AU PAIR AGENCY
Keystone Domestic Recruitment, 272-276 Pentonville Road, London N1 9JY. ☎020-7833 7788. Fax: 020-7833 7786. Website: www.keystone-jobs.co.uk.
Placements: au pairs, au pairs plus and mother's helps.
Jobs in: mostly UK (all areas but mainly London and surrounding areas), Ireland, Spain, Germany, Greece, Netherlands, Italy, etc.
Nationalities placed: all nationalities.
Males can be placed if they have experience with childcare or care-work and domestic duties.
Minimum stay: 2½ months for summer placements, 6 months all other times but preferably 1 year or longer.
Wages/pocket money: £55-£60 for au pairs (25 hours); £65-£100 for au pairs plus (35 hours); £150 for mother's helps (45-50 hours) or more if native English speaker.
Qualifications: ages: 17/18-27. Childcare experience not always necessary. Basic English. Happy, flexible and helpful attitude, honesty and willingness to communicate required. Mother's helps need good English, good experience with children (not necessarily professional), outgoing and willing personality.
Application procedure: request for information pack and application form can be done

by phone, fax, letter or email. Required documents include application form, 4 passport photographs and other snapshots, 2 references (one childcare, one character from a teacher, previous employer, etc., with contact details for referees), a 'dear family' letter and medical certificate.

Other services: 24 hour emergency help available. Welcome pack on arrival including bus and underground maps and agency ID card for emergency use. Agency checks to see that all is well during first few weeks of placement. Replacement family will be found as quickly as possible should au pair not be happy with host family.

Fees: none for those coming to UK.

Contact: Eraine Arnot, Branch Manager.

'ANGELS STAFF SERVICES' ASSOCIATION
Via dei Fienili 98, 00186 Rome, Italy. ☎+39 06-678 28 77. Mobile: +39 338 667 9718. E-mail: staffinitaly@yahoo.co.uk. Website: web.tiscali.it/angelsstaff.
In business since 1995.

Placements: nannies, mother's helps, English teachers, au pairs, housekeepers, butlers, secretaries, cleaners, etc. Live-in and live-out positions.

Jobs in: throughout Italy. Also place staff with Italian families in London.

Nationalities placed: all that are already legally in Italy, and applications considered if sent from UK, France, Australia, New Zealand, USA, Canada, etc.

Steady number of requests for male applicants to work with families with sons. About 3% of applicants placed are male.

Minimum stay: 10 months (Sept/Oct to June) or 12 months. Many summer placements of 1 or 2 months available in July and/or August.

Wages/pocket money: au pair earns €350 per month for working 25 hours a week, 5 hours a day, Mon-Fri. Mother's helps earn €500+ per month for 40 h.p.w., 8 hours a day, Mon-Fri. Nannies are paid €1,000+ per month for 55 working hours per week, 10 hrs a day Mon-Fri plus 5 hours on Saturday. All salaries are live-in.

Qualifications: ages 18-60. Some previous childcare experience is essential. No requirement to speak Italian.

Application procedure: average processing time 1 week to 1 month.

Other services: language school addresses are provided. Replacement family found if necessary and introductions give to other English girls.

Fees: nil.

Contact: Rebecca Harden, Recruitment Consultant.

ANGLO CONTINENTAL
9 Wish Road, Hove, East Sussex BN3 4LL. ☎01273 271281. Fax: 01273 776634. E-mail: sharon@anglocontinentalplacements.com. Website: www. anglocontinentalplacements.com.
Placements: Supplier of domestic staff to UK households.

Jobs in: UK.

Nationalities placed: all nationalities with an appropriate visa.

Contact: Sharon Wolfe or Niki Davis.

ANGLO NANNIES LONDON
Based in Wimbledon; moving offices at time of writing. ☎020-8944 6677. Mob: 07802 419781. Istanbul office: Bebek yolu Sokak, Ebru Apt, No 25/2, Etiler-Istanbul; +90 212-287 6898. Fax: +90 212-265 4340. E-mail: nannies@ anglonannies.com. Website: www.anglonannies.com. Also has office in Marseille, France.
In business since 1989.

Placements: nannies (about 60 in Istanbul), maternity nurses, governesses and teachers.

Nannies and Maternity nurses urgently wanted for best positions throughout London and Overseas.

Call now to register on
020-8348 4111
www.nanny-search.co.uk

"London's Leading Nanny Agency" Evening Standard

Jobs in: Turkey mainly, also Europe, Middle East and worldwide.
Minimum stay: mostly permanent positions (minimum 1 year). Summer jobs also available (June to September).
Wages/pocket money: £350-£600 per week for nannies; £400-£600 for governesses; £600+ for maternity nurses; £400+ for teachers.
Qualifications: childcare experience needed in most cases.
Application procedure: all applicants are interviewed personally.
Other services: Nanny and teacher circle in Istanbul which hosts monthly coffee mornings, theatre groups, lunches, etc. Owner travels frequently between London and Istanbul.
Fees: nil.
Contact: Mrs. Omur Yeginsu, Director.

ANGLO PAIR AGENCY
40 Wavertree Road, Streatham Hill, London SW2 3SP. ☎020-8674 3605. Fax: 020-8674 1264. E-mail: Anglo.Pair@btinternet.com.
In business since 1985.
Placements: 100 au pairs mainly.
Jobs in: UK, Turkey and France.
Nationalities placed: Europeans.
Male applicants very rarely placed.
Minimum stay: 6 months (3 months for Turkey). Short summer stays are sometimes available.
Wages/pocket money: £55 per week in the UK; roughly the same in Turkey. Qualified nannies earn far more (e.g. £300 per week) in Turkey, but these positions are rare.
Qualifications: ages 17-27 years. Childcare experience generally needed.
Application procedure: interviews generally required, plus 2 character references and a medical certificate. Agency arranges correspondence, phone conversation and when possible meeting between applicants and host family.
Fees: £40 for applicants going abroad; otherwise nil.
Contact: Mrs. G. Kirtley, Proprietress.

ANNIES NANNIES
83 Victoria Street, Victoria, London SW1H 0HN. ☎020-7078 6486. Fax: 020-7078 6030. E-mail: livein@annies-nannies.co.uk/ annie@annies-nannies.co.uk. Website: www.annies-nannies.co.uk.
In business since 1980. Agency has been inspected by PANN (Professional Association of Nursery Nurses).
Placements: specialise in live-in placements in London, UK and international, and in daily/nanny/mother's help positions in central/south and West London. Maternity/temps

and babysitting service provided. About 1,000 placements made per year.
Jobs in: UK and worldwide (including USA).
Nationalities placed: must satisfy legal requirements for working in the UK.
About 3% of applicants placed are male.
Minimum stay: temporary placements from 1 week to permanent placements requiring 1 year's commitment.
Wages/pocket money: £250-£400 live-in. Daily nannies earn £350-£450 per week.
Qualifications: minimum age 21. Must have some experience with children.
Application procedure: all candidates are personally interviewed and asked to produce 3 forms of ID including photo ID. Qualification in childcare or a minimum of 3 years' experience, with checkable references is essential. As many references are checked as possible (within reason.) All candidates are CRB checked. Agency also has a training centre where candidates can take first aid training and other childcare courses.
Other services: consultant visa specialist attorney for placements in the USA. In-house training for first aid skills and other childcare courses for unqualified nannies.
Fees: no registration fees.
Contact: Amanda Cotton, Director.

ANTOINETTES AUPAIR AND NANNY AGENCY
2nd Floor, 37 Meneage Street, Helston, Cornwall TR13 8RB. ☎01326 572660. Fax: 01326 572911. E-mail: antoinettes@btopenworld.com. Website: www. childcare-agency.co.uk.
In business since 1995.
Placements: 500+ au pairs, nannies, babysitters, mother's helps, maternity nurses, nursery nurses.
Jobs in: UK, Western Europe and Canada.
Nationalities placed: European.
Almost no male placements.
Minimum stay: average placement 12 months. Some families prefer 6 months and summer stays are 2, 3 or 4 months.
Wages/pocket money: £55 a week.
Qualifications: minimum age 18. Must have childcare experience in work setting and speak some English.
Application procedure: varies depending on placement. After completed application is received, vetting takes a couple of weeks and then a suitable position must be found.
Other services: complete after-placement service including English pack and au pair/ nanny network newsletter.
Fees: nil for UK placements. £47 for outgoing.
Contact: Toni Southern, Manager.

A-ONE AU-PAIRS & NANNIES
Top Floor, Union House, Union Street, Andover, Hampshire SP10 1PA. ☎01264 332500. Fax: 01264 362050. E-mail: info@aupairsetc.co.uk. Website: www.aupairsetc.co.uk.
In business since 1997. Member of IAPA and founder member BAPAA.
Placements: au pairs, au pairs plus and temporary and permanent nannies.
Jobs in: incoming to UK. Overseas placements via agents.
Nationalities placed: according to Home Office Guidelines for the UK. Au pairs plus must be from EU according to British law.
About 30% of applicants placed are male.
Minimum stay: 6 months during the year. Summer placements can be made.
Wages/pocket money: £55-£65 for up to 25 hours worked per week. Higher pocket money for au pairs plus. £3 per hour for extra hours over 25.

Qualifications: ages 18-27. Should have some childcare experience and be able to hold a basic conversation in the language of the host country.
Application procedure: placement time varies; longer for males than females.
Other services: language classes are available in every town. Agency telephones the au pair within the first few days to ensure that both parties are satisfied with the placement. 24-hour emergency telephone number provided to all au pairs. Welcome pack provided.
Fees: nil to job-seekers.
Contact: Mrs. Karen Hopwood, Proprietor.

APAB AU-PAIR AGENTUR BERGER
Lothringer Str. 28, 44805 Bochum, Germany. ☎+49 234-953 6884. Mob: +49 (0)171-328 8152. Fax: +49 234-953 6661. E-mail: office@au-pair-berger.de and office@au-pair-berger.com. Website: www.au-pair-berger.com.
In business since 1998. Member of Aupair-Society e.V.
Placements: 100 au pairs. Have specialist programme whereby au pairs with a background in riding can be placed in host families who have horses.
Jobs in: Germany; also German au pairs placed in Britain, France, Spain, Italy, etc.
Nationalities placed: all.
About 15% of applicants placed are male.
Minimum stay: mostly 1 year though 6 or 10 months also possible. Summer placements can be made.
Wages/pocket money: minimum €260 per month in Germany.
Qualifications: vary among countries.
Application procedure: applicants fill in very detailed application form and send two references (one childcare, one character), a medical certificate a 'Dear Family' letter, a CV and photos. Interviews conducted in person or by phone to assess knowledge of German language. After a family has been found, au pair communicates on phone or by email several times before arrival in Germany.
Other services: offer special au pair insurance policy to host families. 24-hour emergency contact number.
Fees: free for incoming au pairs. German au pairs going abroad are charged €102 for stay of up to 6 months and €154 for longer stays.
Contact: Jens Berger, Owner.

ARCE (ATTIVITA' RELAZIONI CULTURALI CON L'ESTERO)
Via XX Settembre 20/124, 16121 Genova, Italy. ☎+39 010-583020. Fax: +39 010-583092. E-mail: info@arceaupair.it. Website: www.arceaupair.it.
In business since 1948.
Placements: 120 au pairs and mother's helps in Italy; 100 sent abroad.
Jobs in: Italy; plus Italian au pairs sent throughout EU. Work and study programmes for Italian students in UK, Ireland, France Germany, Finland, Spain, Switzerland.
Nationalities placed: EU nationals plus Americans, Canadians and Australians with correct visas.
Male applicants can be placed.
Minimum stay: September to June preferred. Summer stays: June to September though some 2-month placements available.
Wages/pocket money: about €60 per week for au pairs, €95+ for mother's helps.
Qualifications: ages 18-30 and childcare experience.
Application procedure: must submit medical certificate, 2 references (including one attesting to previous babysitting experience), photo and presentation letter.
Other services: social activities arranged. Advice given on Italian language courses, e.g. at nearby language school Il Mondo, Via Settembre 8/15b, 16121 Genova + 39 010-582718; www.ilmondoweb.it). For applicants placed outside Genova, agency advises on schools

and cultural activities, and provides contact details for other au pairs.
Fees: nil incoming, €160 outgoing.

ASSOCIATION FAMILLES & JEUNESSE (AFJ)
4 rue Masséna, 06000 Nice, France. ☎+33 4-93 82 28 22. Fax: +33 4-93 88 12 86. E-mail: info@afj-aupair.org. Website: www.afj-aupair.org.
In business since 1984.
Placements: 400 au pairs and au pairs plus.
Jobs in: France (mainly French Riviera and South of France including Monaco and Corsica).
Nationalities placed: British, American, Canadian, Australian, New Zealand and South African.
Male applicants are welcomed.
Minimum stay: 6 months from January, though 9-12 months preferred. Summer placements of 2-3 months can be made.
Wages/pocket money: €75 per week for au pairs (30 hours per week); €84 per week for au pairs plus (35 h.p.w.).
Qualifications: ages 18-30. Childcare experience needed such as babysitting or camp counselling. First aid diploma useful and driver's licence a plus (must be able to drive standard transmission). Must have completed secondary education and studied French for at least 2-3 years.
Other services: hosts annual au pair meeting in September. Provides listing of other au pairs and French language courses in area plus guides and maps. End-of-stay certificate may be requested.
Fees: €105 enrolment fee (€45 non-refundable).
Contact: Mme. Birte Larsen.

ATLANTIS YOUTH EXCHANGE
Rådhusgt. 4, 0151 Oslo, Norway. ☎+47 22-47 71 70. Fax: +47 22-47 71 79. E-mail: atlantis@atlantis.no. Website: www.atlantis.no.
In operation since 1987.
Placements: 200 au pairs.
Jobs in: Norway, mainly in and around Oslo, Bergen or other southern cities.
Nationalities placed: no restrictions.
An attempt will be made to place male applicants, but it is very difficult.
Minimum stay: 6 months (8-12 month stays preferred).
Wages/pocket money: minimum NOK 3,000 per month less tax of up to 25%. Au pairs also receive a monthly travel card worth NOK 400 and holiday pay of just over 10% of their total wages at the end of their stay.
Qualifications: ages 18-30 years. Must be able to speak English well and have some childcare experience.
Application procedure: application must be made through a partner agency, as listed on the Atlantis website. Currently there is no co-operating agency in the UK. The partner in the USA is Interexchange (see entry).
Other services: agency helps with various stages of work permit application for non-EU au pairs.
Fees: varies with partner agency, e.g. Interexchange charges US$400.
Contact: Inbound Department or Michael Hagring, Director.

AUPAIR2000
Am Neckarufer 6, 68535 Edingen, Germany. ☎/fax: +49 6203-839427. E-mail: ghalasy@t-online.de or info@aupair2000.de.
In business since January 2000. Member of Aupair-Society e.V.

Placements: au pairs.
Jobs in: Germany; also outgoing programme to UK, Spain, France and Italy.
Nationalities placed: all.
About 5% of applicants placed are male.
Minimum stay: mostly 12 months, sometimes 6. No summer placements.
Wages/pocket money: €260 per month.
Qualifications: ages 18-24. Childcare references needed. Good or basic German language knowledge required.
Application procedure: average processing time is 1-2 months which includes checking of references. Phone interview arranged with family.
Fees: nil for incoming au pairs. Outgoing au pairs pay €154.
Contact: Gabriele Halasy, Manager.

AU-PAIR4YOU
Hasnerstrasse 31/22, 1160 Vienna, Austria. ☎+43 1-990 1574 or +43 676-493 86 50. Fax: +43 1-990 157412. E-mail: office@au-pair4you.at. Website: www. au-pair4you.at.
In business since 1999. Member of IAPA.
Placements: 200 au pairs and au pairs plus.
Jobs in: Austria; also outgoing programme for Austrians, Germans and Swiss to Britain, Italy, France, Monaco, Spain, Netherlands, Sweden, Denmark and USA.
Nationalities placed: EU, Swiss, Eastern European, American, Canadian and New Zealander.
About 1% of applicants placed are male.
Minimum stay: 1 month in summer.
Wages/pocket money: about €60 per week for 25 hours of work. At least €45 given per month for language classes and/or public transport.
Qualifications: ages 18-28. Applicants who speak English, Spanish, French or Italian do not require knowledge of German for Austria but other nationalities do. Outgoing au pairs need good knowledge of language of destination country.
Application procedure: interviews not required. Native English speakers can normally be placed within a few days.
Other services: au pair contact list is circulated; au pair meetings are organised.
Fees: €50 registration fee unless you come via partner agency.
Contact: Maria Waidacher, Manager.

THE AU-PAIR AGENCY
231 Hale Lane, Edgware, Middlesex HA8 9QF. ☎020-8958 1750. Fax: 020-8958 5261. E-mail: elaine@aupairagency.com. Website: www.aupairagency. com.
Established 1986.
Placements: au pairs, au pair plus and mother's help positions throughout Britain. Au pairs and mother's helps placed in Europe.
European placements are available in: France, Spain, Majorca, Italy and Germany.
Minimum stay: 9-12 months or longer. Summer holidays: 10 weeks minimum.
Wages/pocket money: in Britain £55 per week for au pairs, £75 for au pair plus, £150 net for mother's helps. In Europe, au pairs receive €50-€80 per week depending on country of choice.
Qualifications: reasonable conversational ability in language of chosen country plus proven childcare ability.
Application procedure: contact the agency for an application or apply on-line by visiting the website www.aupairagency.com.
Fees: nil to incoming applicants; £40 if outgoing from the UK.
Contact: Mrs. Elaine Newman, Proprietor.

AU PAIR AGENCY BOURNEMOUTH
45 Strouden Road, Bournemouth, Dorset BH9 1QL. ☎/fax: 01202 532600. E-mail: andrea.rose@virgin.net.
In business since 1977. Licensed by the Department of Employment.
Placements: 250 au pairs.
Jobs in: England only.
Nationalities placed: Europeans and other nationalities in accordance with legal requirements.
Very few male applicants are placed (less than 5%).
Minimum stay: 6 months normally but there are exceptions. Summer stays are available.
Wages/pocket money: £55 per week.
Qualifications: minimum age 18 years. Some babysitting experience needed plus knowledge of the language of the destination country.
Application procedure: 2 childcare references needed. Interviews are helpful but not essential. All potential families are interviewed by agency. Placements are sometimes made on same day application documents are received.
Other services: arranges social activities for au pairs and offers follow-up visits and after-care. Helps to arrange language courses. In case of difficulties, 24-hour help/advice available.
Fees: nil.
Contact: Ms. Andrea Rose, Proprietor.

AU PAIR AGENTUR SYLVIANE ZÜRNER
Läutenring 1, 85235 Pfaffenhofen (Glonn), Germany. ☎+49 8134-935 565. Fax: +49 8134-935 464. E-mail: sylviane@au-pair-zuerner.de. Website: www. au-pair-zuerner.de.
In business since 2003.
Placements: 36 au pairs.
Jobs in: Germany, plus France and Spain.
Nationalities placed: all.
About 1% of applicants placed are male.
Minimum stay: 2 months in summer.
Wages/pocket money: €205-€260 a month.
Qualifications: ages 18-24. Must have some knowledge of the host country's language.
Fees: €50.
Contact: Andreas Zürner.

AU PAIR AND STUDENT PLACEMENT AGENCY
Nation House, The Stable Block, Milwich Road, Stafford ST18 0EG. ☎01889 505544. Fax: 01889 505543. E-mail: info@hq-demon.co.uk. Website: www.uk-demon.co.uk/aspa.
In business since 1985. Member of CBI and SCCI.
Placements: 400 au pairs.
Jobs available: throughout UK.
Nationalities placed: all approved countries including UK, EU, Eastern Europe and Turkey.
Male applicants can usually be placed.
Minimum stay: 6 months.
Wages/pocket money: typical UK wage £55-£70 but depends on hours worked.
Application procedure: detailed application form and references required. Interviews arranged if possible in office in applicant's country. For contact details of partner agencies, contact above address. Placements usually made within a few weeks of receiving application form.

Other services: insurance and travel arranged. Freephone number in UK. Free accommodation in emergencies and if host family no longer requires an au pair. If problems, new family can be offered within 7 days. Free language school, collection from airport/ coach station, medical advice and immigration advice. Multilingual staff.
Fees: nil. The host family pays the fees.
Contact: Joanna or Paul.

AUPAIR-ARK.de
Glashauweg 9, 71088 Holzgerlingen, Germany. ☎+49 7031-677921. Fax: on request. E-mail: welcome@aupair-ark.de. Website: www.AUPAIR-ARK.de.
In business since 2003.
Placements: 50 au pairs mainly but also nannies.
Jobs in: Germany, Austria and German-speaking Switzerland. Also outgoing programme for German au pairs to Europe, UK (London area mainly), Canada, USA, Australia and (soon) New Zealand.
Nationalilties placed: all that do not require visas, i.e. from Western Europe plus (as of 2005) Israel and Japan.
15%-20% of applicants placed are male.
Minimum stay: 6 months, though most families prefer 8-12 months. Summer stays of 2-4 months are occasionally available.
Wages/pocket money: €260 a month. Families also pay for a monthly transport ticket and language lessons. 4 weeks paid holidays are part of 12-month contract, or 2 days paid leave per calendar month worked.
Qualifications: ages 18-24 for au pairs coming to Germany, Austria and Switzerland. Childcare experience welcome, but babysitting will do. Basic German language skills are definitely a plus but placements available for au pairs who do not know German, e.g. with families who may be raising their children bilingually and want their au pairs to speak English to the children. Police clearance required and good health.
Application procedure: placements in Germany can be made quickly since no visa is required. Longer lead-in times needed for other countries.
Other services: beginner German course offered (for a fee) at agency office to au pairs within the Böblingen/Stuttgart area. Families pay for health, accident and third party insurance for their au pairs. Some families are willing to contribute towards au pair's airfares. Change of family offered if match proves unsatisfactory. Au pair meetings and excursions arranged in some areas. Contact details of other au pairs are distributed. Agency stays in touch with au pairs via phone and email.
Fees: free for placement in German-speaking countries, and also in most Western European countries. Varying fees are charged for placement in Canada, USA and Australia (given on request).
Contact: Liane Kamin, Owner.

AU PAIR AUSTRALIA
PO Box 1164, Glebe 2037, Sydney, Australia. ☎+61 2-9571 6121. E-mail: info@aupairaustralia.com.au. Website: www.aupairaustralia.com.au.
In business since 2003. Au Pair Australia's quality standards are based broadly on those of IAPA with amendments where appropriate to suit Australian cultural requirements.
Placements: au pairs and nannies.
Jobs in: Australia. Outgoing programme to UK, France, Germany, Netherlands and Italy; and occasionally to Switzerland, Canada and Ireland.
About 5% of applicants placed are male.
Minimum stay: 6 month commitment required, preferably 8 months. Occasionally 4-month placements are available.
Wages/pocket money: A$180-$250 a week depending on the hours (typically 30-35 h.p.w.).

Qualifications: aged 20-30 (to be eligible for a 1-year working holiday visa). Driver's licence strongly preferred. First aid an advantage. Must be non-smoking and able to cook simple meals. Childcare experience essential; at a minimum babysitting. Must have love of children and good level of energy with patience, flexibility and openness to new challenges. 'High Intermediate' level of English required.

Application procedure: 2 good references needed (not from applicant's family). Police clearance certificate required. Placement in Sydney and Brisbane can be made after arrival, provided agency has been forewarned of arrival date and preparations can be made. After all documents are submitted, agency interviews candidate and arranges meetings with 2 or 3 families. The candidate then chooses. Process normally takes 3-4 days; au pair then starts immediately. For all other areas of Australia, pre-matching takes place before arrival. Families and applicants exchange information by phone and mail before an agreement is made; the process usually takes 2 months from first contact between the au pair and the agency.

Other services: agency helps prospective candidates with accommodation on first arrival. Replacement families found in case of problems. Contacts given of a network of other au pairs in the area.

Fees: nil for incoming au pairs and nannies. Small charge for outgoing nannies depending on destination country.

Contact: Pien Frissel, Director.

AU PAIR AUSTRIA
Mariahilferstrasse 99/2/37, 1060 Vienna, Austria. ☎/fax: +43 1-920 38 42 or +43 1-595 5745. E-mail: office@aupairaustria.com. Website: www.aupairaustria. com.
In business since 2001. Member of IAPA.

Placements: 200 incoming au pairs and au pairs plus. 30 outgoing au pairs.

Jobs in: Austria. Outgoing programme for Austrians.

Nationalities placed: all.

Minimum stay: 8 weeks for summer au pairs, 6 but preferably 9-12 months for academic year.

Application procedure: written application on agency forms and interview.

Fees: €100 for incoming, €180 for outgoing.

Contact: Gabriela Kummer, Chief Executive Officer.

AU-PAIR AZUR
155 avenue de Cireuil, 06210 Villeneuve Loubet, France. ☎+33 6-61 98 81 81. E-mail: aupairazur@aol.com. Website: www.aupairazur.com.
In business since 2003.

Placements: 40 au pairs.

Jobs in: France (especially the Côte d'Azur in and around Cannes). Outgoing programme to England, Ireland, Spain, Italy and Germany. About 1 male placement per year.

Minimum stay: 1 month; summer placements available.

Wages/pocket money: €80 a week.

Qualifications: must have experience with children and some knowledge of the language.

Application procedure: interviews and references checked.

Fees: €50 incoming, €200 outgoing.

Contact: Tatjana Hugelmeier, Director.

AU PAIR CANADA
15 Goodacre Close, Red Deer, Alberta T4P 3A3, Canada. ☎/fax: +1 403-343-1418. E-mail: aupaircanada@shaw.ca.

In business since 1993.
Placements: 30-40 au pairs.
Jobs in: outgoing programme mainly for Canadians to Netherlands, France, Germany and Switzerland.
Minimum stay: 5 months for regular au pairs; Most candidates leave for Europe late August/early September.
Qualifications: ages 18-30. Basic knowledge of language needed (French, German, or Dutch) plus desire to improve language skills. Must enjoy working with children and have relevant references. Should be highly independent, open-minded, flexible and hard-working.
Application procedure: applicants first send in a profile sheet with a photo from the email information package, then send initial registration fee. After application packet is received, telephone interview held and references checked. Matching via overseas partners normally takes 2-4 months. Visa processing takes time, so application deadlines fall early for late summer departures.
Other services: guidance through the maze of red tape involved in getting an au pair visa, orientation package sent; help with pre-registration in language course if wanted or needed for visa; help finding a replacement family if necessary. Agency maintains periodic contact with Canadian au pairs throughout their time in Europe. List of other au pairs in the vicinity is given.
Fees: C$75 non-refundable registration fee. C$500 application fee upon acceptance completion and acceptance of dossier. Agency will refund application fee if it does not fulfil its promises and responsibilities.
Contact: Clem Hebert.

AU PAIR CANADA
Division of Be International Recruiting Inc, Sheppard Ave East, Ste. 900, Toronto, ON M2N 5W9, Canada. ☎+1 416-590-7429. Fax: +1 647-439-4112. E-mail: office@aupair.ca. Website: www.aupair.ca.
In business since 2000; previously known as Canadian Work Opportunities. Member of IAPA.
Placements: 300 live-in caregivers in Canada.
Jobs in: Canada; also USA, Germany and occasionally France, Spain and UK. Only 1-2 males per year are placed.
Nationalities placed: all.
Minimum stay: 1 year.
Wages/pocket money: minimum C$750 net per month plus room and board plus medical insurance for 9 months + $1,000 tax refund at end of the year. Average $900 net + $1200 tax refund.
Qualifications: minimum age 18 with some childcare experience or training. Must speak English or French to a satisfactory level.
Application procedure: after application dossier has been processed, candidates are interviewed in person by a partner agency or over the phone. Most placements are finalised in 3-4 months, but agency expects applicant to remain available for up to 6 months for placement.
Other services: toll-free number support line, free medical insurance for 9 months (out of 12), tax return at the end of the year, re-match option in case of breakdown, free English and French classes.
Fees: US$750 Good Faith Deposit, refundable at the end of the year. Featured Candidate Fee (sometimes required according to qualifications and skills for marketability purposes). Monthly administrative fee of C$80.
Contact: Bogdan Enica, CEO.

AU PAIR CARE (USA)
600 California Street, Floor 10, San Francisco, CA 94108, USA. ☎415-434-8788 or 1-800-428-7247. Fax: 415-434-5415. E-mail: info@aupaircare.com. Website: www.aupaircare.com.
In business since 1991. Member of IAPA. Programme from Intrax (www.intraxinc.com).
Placements: approximately 1,700 au pairs.
Jobs in: USA.
Nationalities placed: all that have access to international recruiter for programme.
Male applicants can be placed (about 5% of total).
Minimum stay: 12 months.
Wages/pocket money: $139 per week.
Qualifications: secondary school graduate. Childcare experience. Ages 20-26. Good English skills. Experienced driver.
Application procedure: applicants must apply through partner agency in their own country e.g. Au Pair Care in Switzerland; ww.w.aupaircare.ch. Email headquarters to find your nearest representative abroad. Processing takes 4-12 weeks after interview and acceptance. Medical examination, photos and 3 references required.
Other services: health insurance, support of local field staff and $500 contribution for education.
Fees: $500 training fee (varies according to country and recruiter). $300 cancellation penalty after family match is made.
Contact: Heidi Woehl.

AU PAIR COMPANY
1 Bennett House, The High Street, Sutton Valence, Kent ME17 3AW. ☎01622 843285. Mob: 07810 814597. E-mail: ali@theaupaircompany.com. Website: www.theaupaircompany.com.
In business since 2004.
Placements: online service that has 1,000+ registered au pairs.
Jobs in: UK mainly, though site is global.
About 10% of registrants are male and 10% are couples (an upward trend).
Minimum stay: 3 months.
Wages/pocket money: £60-£80 a week.
Qualifications: must have some experience with children.
Other services: all queries answered within 24 hours. Telephone support given to those who need it. Au pair chat room facility and many appropriate links on website.
Fees: registration is free. Membership costs £35 for 100 days and allows au pairs and families to see the contact details of the total database.
Contact: Ali Kittermaster, Managing Director.

AU PAIR CONNECT
8370 W. Cheyenne Avenue #76, Las Vegas, NV 89129, USA. ☎702-839-2201. Fax: 702-395-8713. E-mail: support@aupairconnect.com. Website: www. aupairconnect.com.
Online agency. In business since 2002.
Placements: 2,000 au pairs and nannies.
Jobs in: worldwide.
Minimum stay: 1 month.
Application procedure: families and au pairs find matches themselves.
Fees: $29 to register details on website.
Contact: Pinar Caglayan, Operations Manager.

THE AUPAIR CONNECTION
3 Deacon Road, Kingston-upon-Thames, Surrey KT2 6LT. ☎/fax: 020-8287

5566. Mobile: 07711 672 959. E-mail: aupairconnection@aol.com. Website: www.aupairconnection.co.uk.

In business since 1998.
Placements: 100 au pairs and au pairs plus.
Jobs in: UK only.
About 10%-15% of applicants are male.
Minimum stay: 6-12 week placements made in summer.
Wages/pocket money: minimum rate £60 a week for a standard au pair working 25 hours per week. Higher wages may be paid to older or more experienced au pairs or to au pairs with special skills such as driving. Au pairs get paid extra for extra hours worked or receive paid time off.
Qualifications: minimum age 19. Some childcare experience required, for example babysitting, assisting in a school or children's summer camp. Applicants must have studied English for at least 1 year and have a 'Basic+' (strong basic) level of English. If their current level of English is assessed as below 'Good', they must be motivated to study and improve their English.
Application procedure: normally 2-4 days taken to process applications. 2 references needed to include full contact details of referees for checking, one of which should be a childcare reference. No references written by family members are accepted. Interviews, either in person or on the telephone are conducted with each candidate to assess their level of English, etc. If references are written in a foreign language, they should be submitted with a translation.
Other services: support services include making travel arrangements, assistance with finding suitable language classes, inclusion in a social contact list (to help au pairs meet other au pairs), and trouble shooting if the au pair has any difficulty.
Fees: nil.
Contact: Mary Andersen, Proprietor/Agency Owner.

AU PAIR CONNECTIONS

39 Tamarisk Road, Hedge End, Southampton, Hampshire SO30 4TN. ☎01489 780438. Fax: 01489 692656. E-mail: apconnect@ntlworld.com. Website: www. aupairconnections.co.uk.
In business since 1987, though agency started as Spanish Connections in the 1970s. British Council recommended.
Placements: au pairs, demi pairs, mother's helps and home helpers who work longer hours and sometimes undertake full housekeeping duties.
Jobs in: Europe (mainly southern France and Madrid and Barcelona, Spain); also UK for incoming au pairs.
Nationalities placed: all those permitted by Home Office. Agency also encourages candidates on working holidays from Australia, New Zealand and South Africa. Home helpers must be EU nationals.
Male applicants can sometimes be placed.
Minimum stay: 10+ weeks in summer; 6-12 months at other times.
Wages/pocket money: from £55 per week for au pairs. Home helpers can earn up to £100 per week.
Qualifications: ages 18-27 for au pairs. Childcare experience and some knowledge of target language needed. Older candidates are accepted as home helpers; driving licence compulsory for this position.
Application procedure: applications can be made through website. Agency works with more than 43 foreign partner agencies. Interviews where possible or phone conversation between candidate and family. References needed. Long stay au pairs are placed within 2 weeks (on average) and summer au pairs placed within 2 months.
Other services: advice on language classes given. Help-line available. Agency owner

speaks French, Spanish and Italian.
Fees: £40 to outgoing au pairs.
Contact: Denise Blighe, Director.

For the time of your life!

Au Pair
IN AMERICA

At the beach
The time of your life

Tel: +44(0)20 7581 7322
www.aupairinamerica.com

AU PAIR IN AMERICA
Dept. APN, 37 Queen's Gate, London SW7 5HR. ☎020-7581 7311 or 020-7581 7316. Fax: 020-7581 7345. E-mail: info@aupairamerica.co.uk (with address to request a brochure). Website: www.aupairinamerica.com.
Parent organisation AIFS (American Institute for Foreign Study; www.aifs.com) founded in 1967; Au Pair Programme authorised 1986.
Placements: 4,000+ au pairs. See entry for Educare in America for sister programme.
Jobs in: USA only.
Nationalities placed: all nationalities in whose country an established interviewer network exists.
Minimum stay: 1 year placements available year round with option to extend the J-1 visa for a further 12 months.
Wages/pocket money: $139.05 per week. Guaranteed 2 weeks paid vacation.
Qualifications: ages 18-26 years. Practical childcare experience, a full clean driving licence and a good command of English are essential.
Application procedure: must submit application forms, passport photos, references including at least one childcare reference, a personal essay, medical report, etc. Interview compulsory with local representative.
Other services: free return flights to New York from many cities around the world. A 4-day orientation near New York City. Legal J-1 visa and medical insurance are arranged by agency. All au pairs are placed in cluster groups with a local counsellor who arranges social and cultural activities. Participants are required to attend a local college for 3 hours a week during term time; host families contribute up to $500 for tuition fees.
Fees: $100 non-refundable placement fee. $500 programme fee which includes medical insurance. After successful completion of the programme, au pairs receive a $400 Completion Bonus.

AU PAIR INTERACTIVE
Frans Halslaan 5, 1412 HS Naarden, Netherlands. ☎+31 35-632 1190. Fax: +31 35-632 1191. E-mail: info@aupairinteractive.com. Website: www. aupairinteractive.com.
In business since 2002. Member of IAPA and co-founder of NAPO.
Placements: 150 au pairs, nannies and babysitters.
Jobs in: Netherlands. Outbound programme to UK, Spain, France and Switzerland. About 5 male applicants are placed per year.

Minimum stay: a very few 3-month stays in summer, otherwise minimum 6 months, 9 months preferred.
Wages/pocket money: €340 a month. Au pairs are entitled to a contribution of approximately €240 for a training course (including language courses).
Qualifications: ages 18-25. Must have a good command of English. Au pairs must enjoy working with children.
Application procedure: application form, medical report and au pair interview by partner agency are compulsory. Following interview, it usually takes 1-4 weeks to find a suitable family. Visa applications for non-EU candidates can take 3-6 months to be issued.
Other services: families pay premiums for health, accident and liability insurance for duration of stay in their homes.
Fees: nil for incoming; €175 for outbound au pairs.
Contact: Roswitha Heijmerink, Director.

AU-PAIR INTERCONNECTION
Staufenstrasse 17, 86899 Landsberg am Lech, Germany. ☎+49 8191-941 378. Fax: +49 8191-941 379. E-mail: susanne@caudera.de. Website: www. aupair-interconnection.de.
In business since 1987.
Placements: au pairs and mother's helps.
Jobs in: Germany, and also UK, France, Ireland, Spain, Italy, Switzerland and Norway. Sister agency GoAmerica e.V. (www.go-america.org; aupair@go-america.org) organises job and student exchanges in the USA.
Male applicants can be placed.
Minimum stay: 6 months. No summer stays.
Wages/pocket money: from €50 per week (£55 per week in the UK, €230 per month in France).
Qualifications: ages 18-26. Experience in childcare and basic knowledge of the host language needed.
Application procedure: average processing time within the EU is 1-2 months. Have 50 partner agents abroad.
Other services: help given with arranging insurance, travel and language classes. Trouble-shooting advice available.
Fees: €150 for Europe, €129 for North America.
Contact: Susanne Caudera-Preil, Director/Manager.

AU-PAIR INTERNATIONAL
Cherry Gardens, Nouds Lane, Lynsted, Kent ME9 0ES. ☎01795 522544. Fax: 01795 522878. E-mail: info@aupairinternational.co.uk. Website: www. aupairinternational.co.uk or www.countynannies.co.uk.
In business since 1981.
Placements: 450 au pairs, au pairs plus, mother's helps and nannies.
Jobs in: UK.
Nationalities placed: any that are allowed by immigration regulations. Male applicants can be placed.
Minimum stay: 6-12 months. Summer stays of 2-3 months also available.
Wages/pocket money: £55 per week for au pairs; £70 per week for au pairs plus.
Qualifications: ages 17-27. Some childcare experience and childcare references needed.
Application procedure: 2-3 childcare references and 2 character references needed. Personal interview held wherever possible.
Other services: social contact encouraged with other au pairs in area. Offer basic counselling and help to establish friendly working relationship between au pairs and families.

Fees: nil.
Contact: Benedicte Speed, Managing Director (speed@countynannies.co.uk).

AU PAIR INTERNATIONAL
Via Sante Vicenzi 46, 40138 Bologna, Italy. ☎+39 051-636 0145. Fax: +39 051-304601. E-mail: info@au-pair-international.com. Website: www.au-pair-international.com.
In business since 1990. Member of IAPA.
Placements: 150 au pairs and au pairs plus in Italy.
Jobs in: all regions of Italy; plus all EU countries (Austria, France, Germany, Britain, Ireland) and USA for Italian young people.
Male positions are sometimes available.
Minimum stay: 6 or 9 months. Many summer stays of 1, 2 or 3 months are arranged.
Wages/pocket money: €60-€65 per week for au pairs; €80-€85 for au pairs plus.
Qualifications: Ages 18-30. Childcare experience needed. Knowledge of Italian not needed; English language an advantage.
Application procedure: 2 childcare references, 1 character reference, medical certificate and collage of photos make up application dossier.
Fees: nil for incoming to Italy; €216 for up to 3 months outgoing, €252 for 3-24 months.
Contact: Valentina or Monica.

AU PAIR INTERNATIONAL CZ
Kuzmínova 336, CZ-278 01 Krapuly nad Vlt 1, Czech Republic. ☎+420 315-741 681 or +420 777 170 777. Fax: +420 315-741 682. E-mail: au-pair@kralupy. cz or au-pair@ipnet.cz. Websites: www.ap1.cz, www.au-pair-int.cz, www.au-pair-int.com, www.apb.cz, www.au-pair-box.cz.
In business since 1992. Czech co-ordinator for the American agency goAuPair (see entry).
Placements: 120+ au pairs, au pairs plus, mother's helps, caregivers, nannies and housekeepers.
Jobs in: Austria, Belgium, Canada, Denmark, England, France, Germany, Ireland, Italy, Netherlands, Norway, Spain, Sweden and USA. Possibility of au pairing in the Czech Republic in the future.
Nationalities placed: Czech, Slovak and EU nationals; also Americans and Canadians.
Males can rarely be placed as au pairs but are encouraged to join children's summer camps, voluntary workcamps, work and travel programmes, etc.
Minimum stay: 6 months; longer stays of 9-12 months preferred. 12 months for Canada and the USA. Summer stays are sometimes available.
Application procedure: varies from country to country.
Other services: agency sells travel insurance and coach tickets to most European countries.
Fees: variable.
Contact: Martin Tlustý, Proprietor.

AU PAIR KFT.
Váci utca 15, 2ⁿᵈ Fl, 1052 Budapest, Hungary. ☎+36 1-235-0889, +36 1-486-1987. Fax: +36 1-235-0890. E-mail: aupair@aupairkft.hu. Website: www. aupairkft.hu.
In business since 1996. Member of IAPA.
Placements: 400-500 au pairs and nannies.
Jobs in: Hungary. Outgoing programme to USA, UK, France, Holland, Spain, Germany, Norway and Iceland.
Nationalities placed: many. Outgoing au pairs mainly Hungarian and Romanian. Childcare

experience is a must (agency carries out au pair training).
About 5% of applicants placed are male.
Minimum stay: 9 months (no summer placements).
Wages/pocket money: €600 a month.
Qualifications: must have some experience with children.
Application procedure: screening and orientation, interview and, if necessary, au pair training (see below).
Other services: practical au pair training courses offered. If candidate wants to work with babies in the Au Pair in USA programme, 200 hours of relevant experience are needed, so candidates can log hours in agency's private babyhotel with babies aged 4 months to 2 years.
Fees: €100.
Contact: Nagy Livia, Managing Director.

AU PAIR NETWORK INTERNATIONAL
118 Cromwell Road, London SW7 4ET. ☎020-7370 3798. Fax: 020-7370 4718. E-mail: admin@apni.co.uk. Website: www.apni.co.uk.
In business since 1993. Founding member of IAPA. Member of BAPAA.
Placements: 300 au pairs, mother's helps and nannies.
Jobs in: UK only.
Nationalities placed: any that are allowed by immigration regulations, mainly Europeans.
Male au pairs are becoming more popular and can be placed.
Minimum stay: 3-12 months. Summer placements are available.
Wages/pocket money: £55 per week au pairs; £65 minimum for au pairs plus; £100-£180 for mother's helps, £200-£400 for nannies.
Qualifications: ages 18-27; 23+ for nannies. Good childcare experience and some English needed.
Other services: branch agencies in Stockholm Sweden and in Germany providing flights, insurance, orientation and counselling. Au Pair Club for au pairs in London plus excursions and monthly outings.
Fees: free
Contact: Mario Ristovski, Director, and Valentina Doncevic, Manager.

AU PAIR PERU S.R.L.
Avenida Benavides 768C, Miraflores, Lima 18, Peru. ☎+51 1-446 7766. Fax: +51 1-446 6966. E-mail: aupairperu@aupairperu.com. Website: www. aupairperu.com.
In business since 1995.
Placements: 400 au pairs.
Jobs in: USA, Germany, Austria, Holland, France and Norway.
Nationalities placed: mainly South American.
About 10% of applicants placed are male, and most of these are placed in German families.
Minimum stay: 1 year; no summer placements.
Qualifications: childcare experience and knowledge of English needed.
Application procedure: interviews are held.
Other services: support given throughout application process. Insurance and travel are covered by the programme.
Fees: varies according to country.

AU PAIRS BY AVALON
7 Highway, Edgcumbe Park, Crowthorne, Berks. RG45 6HE. ☎/fax:

01344 778246. E-mail: enquiries@aupairsbyavalon.com. Website: www. aupairsbyavalon.com.

In business since 1954. Incorporating Au Pairs of Surrey, European Au Pairs and Linden Bureau.

Placements: 90+ au pairs.

Jobs in: UK only.

Nationalities placed: all approved nationalities.

Minimum stay: 6 months.

Qualifications: age limits 18-27 years.

Application procedure: write or apply online for information and application. Photos, statement of medical fitness, references (including 1 from employer or school) and 'Dear Family' letter needed.

Other services: Welcome Pack supplied on arrival and Completion Certificate given at end of placement.

Fees: nil for au pairs.

Contact: Mrs. Wendy Gibbings or Mr. Gordon Gibbings, Proprietors.

AU PAIR SEARCH LTD
Stableford House, Alderford Street, Sible Hedingham, Essex CO9 3HX. ☎01787 463318. Fax: 01787 463318. E-mail: info@aupairsearch.co.uk. Website: www.aupairsearch.co.uk.

In business since 2004. Member of IAPA.

Placements: au pairs, au pairs plus and mother's helps.

Jobs in: incoming to UK and outgoing to Australia, Germany and Switzerland. About 2% of applicants placed are male.

Minimum stay: 3 months in summer.

Wages/pocket money: £55 a week for 25 h.p.w.

Qualifications: must have childcare experience and knowledge of target language.

Application procedure: questionnaire can be emailed. Matching normally takes 3-4 weeks.

Fees: nil.

Contact: Joanne Dearden, Managing Director.

THE AUPAIR SEARCH
Postnet Fourways Mall #88, Private Bag X033, Rivonia, 2128, South Africa. ☎+27 11 4642975. Fax: +27 11 4642973. E-mail: clients@aupair.co.za. Website: www.aupairsearch.com.

In business since 1997. International internet database of au pair vacancies.

Placements: thousands of au pairs and nannies make contact with families through the website above. Host families and au pairs interact directly with each other via the web.

Jobs in: USA and Europe.

Nationalities placed: any that are allowed by immigration regulations. About 25% of registrants are male.

Minimum stay: 1 month, though most families require 12 months. Summer placements can be made.

Other services: no support given. This is a do-it-yourself service.

Fees: free to applicants registering information and waiting for placement. Fee of $39 if they wish to manage their own placement.

Contact: Renee Varejes, Director.

AU-PAIR SERVICE DR. UWE KRENZ
N 7,8, 68161 Mannheim, Germany. ☎+49 621-799 4248. Fax: +49 621-799 4251. E-mail: info@au-pair-dr-krenz.de. Website: www.au-pair-dr-krenz.de.

In business since 1999. Member of IAPA and Aupair-Society e.V.
Placements: au pairs.
Jobs in: Germany; also outgoing programme to USA and occasionally to UK, France and Spain.
Nationalities placed: all nationalities placed in Germany.
About 5% of applicants placed are male.
Minimum stay: 90% of German families prefer au pairs to stay for a year. Some summer placements available.
Wages/pocket money: €260 per month in Germany. $500 per month in US plus $500 for college courses.
Qualifications: ages 18-24. Childcare experience and basic knowledge of German needed. For US programme, candidates must have had at least 5 years of English instruction at school plus childcare experience.
Application procedure: usual documents required (e.g. childcare reference) plus at least 2 photos of applicants with kids. Brief telephone conversation required before placement.
Fees: none for incoming au pairs. Outgoing au pairs pay €150.
Contact: Dr. Uwe Krenz.

AU PAIR SERVICE SILKE SOMMER
Steindamm 39, 25485 Hemdingen, Germany. ☎+49 4123-7749. Fax: 4123-7728. E-mail: aps.sommer@t-online.de. Website: www.aupairprofi.de.
In business since 1995. Member of Aupair-Society e.V.
Placements: 200 au pairs.
Jobs in: Germany; also outgoing programme to Western European countries and USA.
About 2% of applicants placed are male.
Minimum stay: 6 months. Little demand in Germany for summer au pairs.
Wages/pocket money: €260 per month.
Fees: nil for incoming; €130 for outgoing.
Contact: Mrs. Silke Sommer, Owner.

AU PAIRS INTERNATIONAL
Sixtusvej 15, 2300 Copenhagen S, Denmark. ☎+45 32 84 10 02. Fax: +45 32 84 31 02. E-mail: info@aupairsinternational.dk. Website: www.aupairsinternational.dk.
In business since 1994. Member of IAPA.
Placements: au pairs and au pairs plus.
Jobs in: Denmark, Norway and Sweden.
Nationalities placed: all nationalities, provided they speak good English or have knowledge of a Scandinavian language. Fluent speakers of German or French may also be placed but with more difficulty.
Minimum stay: normally 6 months; some summer placements available.
Wages/pocket money: monthly minimums are 2,500 Danish kroner, 2,700 Norwegian krone, and 3,400 Swedish krona,
Qualifications: Minimum age 20 (many families prefer applicants aged 20-25). Good references needed, especially references from non-relatives and related to working with children. Au pairs should be non-smokers, be good English speakers (or have knowledge of a Scandinavian language), have a driver's license, plus experience of and willingness to take care of babies and children under 5. Experience with cleaning also valuable.
Application procedure: agency prefers applicants to use its own form (available online). Emailed files accepted in pdf or other Word format. Applications sent by post should be sent in triplicate.
Fees: nil.
Contact: Vera Sørensen, Director.

AU PAIRS RECRUITMENT
Via Gaeta 22, 10133 Turin, Italy. ☎/fax: +39 011 660 2245.
In business since 1999.
Placements: 50 au pairs, mother's helps and nannies.
Jobs in: Italy mainly; also Europe.
Nationalities placed: Europeans, Australians, New Zealanders and holders of double citizenship due to visa restrictions.
About 5% of applicants placed are male.
Minimum stay: one month during summer.
Qualifications: experience with children required plus excellent spoken English, French or German.
Application procedure: agency begins family search as soon as dossier is assembled. Process can take between 1 week and some months depending on current availability.
Fees: nil.
Contact: Anna Paravia-Tosi, Proprietor.

AU PAIR STUDY CENTRE
10 Wellington Street, Dun Laoghaire, Co. Dublin, Ireland. ☎+353 1-284 4675. Fax: +353 1-284 5635. E-mail: apsc@eircom.net. Website: www.Aupair-Ireland.com.
In business since 1990. Partner of Bluefeather School of English in Dublin. Member of TANDEM International Language Schools, ATT (Association for Teaching Training in Ireland) and Recognised by the Department of Education.
Placements: 250-300 au pair-students.
Jobs in: Ireland (mainly Dublin and area).
Nationalities placed: EU nationals only.
Very few male applicants are placed.
Minimum stay: 6-9 months. 3-month summer placements can be made.
Wages/pocket money: Aupair Companion (30 hours per week + 2 nights babysitting) earns €90 per week. Aupair Minder (35 hours per week + 2 nights babysitting) earns €100. Aupair Plus (40 hours + 1 night babysitting) earns €115.
Qualifications: ages 18-27. Experience required but genuine liking for children is most important. Basic English required.
Application procedure: all families have been visited by agency. Telephone interview arranged with family.
Other services: all au pairs are enrolled in English course; maximum of 10 students in class. Students have direct contact with agency staff on a daily basis should they require any assistance.
Fees: placement fee is €200 for direct applicants or €85 if au pair comes through a partner agency. All au pairs must enrol in a 3-month language course at a cost of €100 per month.
Contact: Eva Obalat Mangrane, Director.

AU PAIR USA/INTEREXCHANGE
10th Floor, 161 Sixth Avenue, New York, NY 10013, USA. ☎212-924-0446. Fax: 212-924-0575. E-mail: info@interexchange.org. Website: www.AuPairUSA. org (for incoming to USA) or for outgoing: www.interexchange.org/ workingabroad.
In business since 1987. Member of IAPA.
Placements: approximately 1,500 au pairs per year.
Jobs in: Au Pair USA Programme places au pairs from around the world in families throughout the USA, and a Working Abroad programme places American, Canadian and European Union residents as au pairs in France, Germany, Netherlands and Spain.
Nationalities placed: all accepted for US placement including Western and Eastern

Europeans, Korean, Australian, African, Indian, Central and South American, etc. Positions available for both males and females.
Minimum stay: 12-month programme and a new 3-month summer-only programme.
Wages/pocket money: $139.05 per week ($164.05 with experience caring for children under 2) plus free room and board and 2 weeks paid vacation. 1½ days off per week and one weekend off per month.
Qualifications: ages 18-26. Childcare experience needed.
Application procedure: e-mail Interexchange to find a partner agency in the home country. 8-12 weeks needed to process applications and visas. Two childcare references, one character reference, a 'Dear Host Family' essay, photos, copy of secondary school education diploma, copy of driving licence and a criminal background check from local authorities must be included. Interviews carried out in home country by International Co-operators where applicable. Outgoing au pairs should apply at least three months before departure and arrange a telephone interview.
Other services: free round-trip flights to USA, up to $500 for tuition fees and free health insurance provided. Optional month at end of programme for personal travel, etc.
Fees: $200-$500 depending on country of departure. Fee for outgoing au pairs is $400.
Contact: aupair@interexchange.org for placements in the USA; workabroad@interexchange.org for placements in France, Germany, Netherlands and Spain.

AUPAIR-VERMITTLUNG SIGMAR BASSMANN
Limesstr. 13, 61381 Friedrichsdorf, Germany. ☎+49 17017 47135, +49 6 17579 6319. Fax: +49 1212-5-6529 8135. E-mail: aupairinfo@web.de. Website: www. aupairforyou.de.
In business since 2003.
Placements: 50 au pairs.
Jobs in: Germany. Outgoing programme to UK and Ireland.
Nationalities placed: EU, Switzerland, USA, Canada, Australia, New Zealand and Japan. About 2% of applicants placed are male.
Minimum stay: 6 months.
Wages/pocket money: minimum €260 per month in Germany and £65 a week in UK and Ireland.
Qualifications: ages 18-24 for non-EU nationals at the time of visa application; maximum age 30 for EU nationals. Must have a baasic knowledge of German and/or English, and experience in childcare.
Application procedure: average processing time at least 1 month. References and interviews required.
Other services: families pay for monthly transport ticket or provide transport to language classes, and also pay for the language course. Au pairs that stay for 12 months are given 4-week holiday or 2 working days per month.
Fees: nil to au pairs.
Contact: Sigmar Bassmann, Director.

AU-PAIR WORLD AGENCY SWEDEN
Box 299, 461 26 Trollhättan, Sweden. ☎+46 520-30953. Mob: +46 70-720 65 24. Fax: +46 520-311 89. E-mail: info@aupairsweden.com or interteamthn@swipnet.se. Website: www.aupairsweden.com.
Placements: au pairs.
Jobs in: Sweden, Norway and worldwide for Swedish au pairs.
Nationalities placed: most.
Wages/pocket money: 3,500 Swedish kronors per month in Sweden; 4,000 Norwegian kroners per month in Norway.
Qualifications: ages 17-27. Good childcare experience and some English needed.

Application procedure: 2-3 childcare references needed. Personal interview held where possible.
Contact: Anita Rundberg, Manager.

AUSTRALIAN NANNY & AU PAIR CONNECTION
404 Glenferrie Road, Kooyong, Victoria 3144, Australia. ☎/fax: +61 3-9824 8857. E-mail: info@australiannannies.info or rosemary@australiannannies. info. Website: www.australiannannies.com.au.
In business since 1989.
Placements: 100-150 nannies (mostly live-out), mother's helps and housekeepers. Not many au pairs.
Jobs in: Australia (especially Melbourne). Also outgoing working holiday programme for Australians to UK, USA, Italy, France and Germany. Specialise in international corporate jobs for elite Australian nannies.
Nationalities placed: many, especially British, Irish, Canadian, Dutch and Japanese on working holiday visas.
Minimum stay: 6 months. Short-term summer work sometimes available between December and February.
Wages/pocket money: live-out hourly wage is A$15-$22. Live-out nannies from overseas often stay in good value Melbourne backpackers' hostels long term. Pay is lower for summer placements which usually consist of accompanying a family to a summer house on the beach. Elite nannies receive airfares, health insurance and generous wage packages.
Qualifications: babysitting experience is minimum requirement. Minimum age 18 years. Medical certificate and knowledge of English needed. Native English-speaking nannies are the easiest to place. Driving licence preferred.
Application procedure: personal interview usually necessary. Minimum 3 references, preferably childcare ones and a detailed resumé.
Other services: recommends College of Adult Education for learners of English.
Fees: registration fee of A$100 for incoming overseas applicants; variable for outgoing.
Contact: Rosemary McCormack, Managing Director.

BABYSITTERS/ CHILDMINDERS
6 Nottingham St, London W1U 5EJ. ☎020-79345 4578; Childminders 020-7487 4587. E-mail: Perrec@aol.com. Website: www.babysitter.co.uk.
In business since 1967. Affiliated to the Nanny Service (see entry). Member of REC.
Placements: babysitters only. Also recruit nannies for holiday resorts abroad.
Jobs in: London, suburbs and Thames Valley. Recruit for tour companies operating in French, Austrian and Italian ski resorts as well as summer resorts in Greece, Turkey and Sardinia (for a minimum of 10 weeks).
Nationalities placed: EU nationals, Australians, New Zealanders, South Africans and all those eligible for working holiday visa or student visa.
About 5% of applicants placed are male.
Qualifications: minimum age 19 years. Must be fluent in English and have previous experience as nurse, nanny or teacher.
Application procedure: 2-3 childcare references needed. Personal interview held where possible.
Contact: Helen Robertson.

BLOOMSBURY BUREAU
3 Rokeby House, 86-90 Lambs Conduit Street, London WC1N 3LX. ☎020-7430 2280. Fax: 020-7430 2325. E-mail: bloomsburo@aol.com. Website: www. bloomsburyaupairs.co.uk.
In business since 1971.

Placements: au pairs and au pairs plus.
Jobs in: UK, Jersey and Ireland mainly. Placements also possible in Germany, France and Spain.
Nationalities placed: mainly Eastern European au pairs but all nationalities, including Australians, New Zealanders and Canadians with working holiday visas.
Males may apply but there is little demand.
Minimum stay: 12 months preferred, but shorter stays of 6 months possible at short notice. Summer stays of 2-3 months are available between June and September.
Wages/pocket money: £60 per week in return for 25-30 hours help. Hours in excess of this should be paid at minimum wage, i.e. £5+ an hour. In Germany monthly pocket money is normally €300 but families sometimes pay for language classes and fares.
Qualifications: ages 18-27. Should have some childcare experience, good knowledge of target language and be non-smokers. Driving licence often required.
Application procedure: must supply references showing practical experience in childcare, a recent medical certificate, a letter of motivation, 2 passport photos and some full length snapshots. Copies also requested of school leaving reports or work references and a police clearance report. Families always insist on a personal telephone interview with the applicant.
Other services: advice given on travel arrangements and language classes. Regular au pair meetings and group activities arranged in London and Dublin.
Fees: introduction fee required by agencies on the continent is €100-€150.
Contact: Marianne Dix, Principal.

BRITISH CONTACT AU PAIR AGENCY
Medunkova 62, 100 00 Prague 10, Czech Republic. ☎+420 2-7477 0637. Fax: +420 2-779749. E-mail: bcontact@volny.cz. Website: www.volny.cz/ britishcontact.
In business since 1991.
Placements: au pairs, au pairs plus, demi pairs, mother's helps (outgoing programme only).
Jobs in: UK including Guernsey and Jersey, Ireland, France, Germany, Austria, Spain and USA.
Nationalities placed: Czech, Slovak and EU nationals.
Males can be placed as au pairs or au pairs plus in UK, and very occasionally in Germany, Austria, Spain and the USA.
Minimum stay: 2 months; longer stays of 6-12 months preferred. 12 months in the USA. Summer stays are available (rarely for males) from 2 months in the UK, Austria, Germany and Spain.
Other services: coach tickets to European destinations and travel insurance available.
Contact: Pavel Kocanda, Proprietor.

BUCKS AU PAIRS
The Lodge, B57 West Drive, Harrow, Middlesex HA3 6TX. ☎020-8385 7665. Fax: 020-8385 7960. E-mail: enquiries@bucksaupairs.co.uk. Website: www. bucksaupairs.co.uk.
In business since 1994.
Placements: 100 au pairs.
Jobs in: UK, mainly Buckinghamshire, Hertfordshsire and Middlesex.
Nationalities placed: Slovakian, Czech, Romanian, Polish, Spanish, Italian, French and Hungarian.
About 5% of applicants placed are male.
Minimum stay: 2 months. Summer placements can be made. Usual stays are 6-12 months.

Wages/pocket money: £55+ per week.
Qualifications: ages 18-27. Some childcare experience and basic knowledge of English needed.
Application procedure: placement takes 1-3 weeks whether applicant applies directly or through partner agency abroad.
Other services: advice given on local language classes. Post-placement support and advice available if needed.
Fees: nil.
Contact: Joan O'Connor, Sole Proprietor.

BUNTERS LTD AU PAIRS AGENCY & BRIDGE NANNY AGENCY
The Old Malt House, 6 Church St, Pattishall, Towcester, Northants. NN12 8NB. ☎01327 831144. Fax: 01327 831155. E-mail: office@aupairsnannies. com. Website: www.aupairsnannies.com.
In business since 1962. Member of IAPA and founder member of BAPAA.
Placements: au pairs, nannies and parent helpers.
Jobs in: UK only.
15-20 positions for male applicants annually.
Nationalities placed: EU nationals and all others that are legal.
Minimum stay: au pair positions for 8-10 weeks over summer months; 6-12 months during the rest of the year.
Wages/pocket money: minimum recommended for au pairs £55 per week.
Qualifications: ages 17-27 for au pairs. Childcare/babysitting experience and some knowledge of English needed. Nannies require childcare qualification.
Fees: nil.
Contact: Mrs. Caroline Jones, Director.

BUTTERFLY ET PAPILLON
5 avenue de Genève, 74000 Annecy, France. ☎+33 4-50 67 01 33. Fax: +33 4-50 67 03 51. E-mail: jean-marc.butterfly@wanadoo.fr. Website: www.butterfly-papillon.com.
In business since 1992. Member of IAPA.
Placements: au pairs.
Jobs in: France (Alps near Swiss border); also Germany, Netherlands, Spain, Italy, UK, Ireland, Australia and USA.
Nationalities placed: all.
Males can rarely be placed.
Minimum stay: year long or short stays of 3 months (2 months in summer).
Wages/pocket money: €60 per week plus €20 contribution to language course.
Qualifications: ages 18-26 (maximum 30 for nannies). Childcare experience and references needed. Must have equivalent of A levels and some knowledge of French (for France). Driving licence preferred.
Application procedure: complete file of documents and phone interviews.
Other services: language school, homestays and student exchange programme. Advice on insurance and travel arrangements given. On-going back-up service provided.
Fees: nil for those coming via partner agency; otherwise €160.

CAMBRIDGE CONNECTION
Milford House, 134 High St, Cottenham, Cambridge CB4 8RX. ☎/fax: 01954 206489. E-mail: caroline@cambridgeconnection.co.uk. Website: www. aupairagency.co.uk.
Small agency in business since 1988.
Placements: au pairs.

Jobs in: England only (40 mile radius of Cambridge).
Nationalities placed: all allowed nationalities but has special link with France.
Minimum stay: 3-12 months.
Other services: au pair tea parties held in October and February and a garden party in July.
Fees: nil.
Contact: Mrs. Caroline Mackay, Proprietor.

CAMBRIDGE NANNIES & AU PAIRS
189 Musters Road, West Bridgford, Nottingham, NG2 7DQ. ☎0845 065 6665.
E-mail: jana@aupairs4you.co.uk. Website: www.cambridge-aupairs.co.uk.
In business since 1996.
Placements: 150 au pairs, au pairs plus, full and part-time nannies and mother's helps.
Jobs in: UK and USA.
Nationalities placed: any au pairs that are allowed by immigration regulations in UK. British, Australian and New Zealand nannies are placed.
About 10% of applicants placed are male.
Minimum stay: 6 months for au pairs, 10-12 months preferred. 12 months minimum for au pairs in USA and for nannies anywhere. Summer au pair placements of 2-3 months and temporary nanny positions sometimes available in Britain.
Wages/pocket money: £55 per week au pairs; from £65 for au pairs plus; from £250 net for full-time nannies.
Qualifications: ages 17-27. Childcare experience and references essential. Good knowledge of English preferred. Non-smokers and drivers preferred. NNEB, BTEC or equivalent qualification preferred for nannies; experience essential. Car owners preferred.
Application procedure: application forms available on-line. Au pairs need reference from an English teacher, medical certificate, photos, criminal record check, etc. Nannies must attend an interview and bring certificates, references, insurance certificate and driving licence with them. References will be checked. Processing of applications normally takes 2-4 weeks.
Other services: au pairs are given detailed guidelines about the work, local English courses and a list of au pairs living in the area.
Fees: nil.
Contact: Jana Robinson, Proprietor.

CANNECTIONS LIMITED
Cannections House, 5 Northfield Farm Mews, Cobham Surrey KT11 1JZ.
☎01932 868851. Fax: 01932 863844. E-mail: donna.barradale@cannections. com. Website: www.cannections.com.
In business since 2005. Member of IAPA.
Placements: 400 au pairs and nannies.
Jobs in: UK only (primarily London and the South of England).
Nationalities placed: specialises in placing applicants from English speaking countries, especially Canada, New Zealand, Australia and South Africa, i.e. those that are eligible for UK Working Holidaymaker Visa (INF15).
About 5% of applicants placed are male.
Minimum stay: 6 months; summer placements available occasionally.
Wages/pocket money: £80-£300 a week.
Qualifications: must have some experience with children.
Application procedure: telephone interviews and personal interviews where possible. Personal profiling exercises undertaken. Police checks and 2 references required and verified.
Other services: agency representative is assigned to individual au pairs/nannies. These reps

help applicants settle in with the family, help with any queries or concerns associated with the host family, arrange social outings and get-togethers and provide advice on travel.
Fees: nil.
Contact: Donna Barradale, Managing Partner.

CARA INTERNATIONAL
Chancery, Turlough, Castlebar, Co. Mayo, Ireland. ☎+353 94-903 1720. Fax: +353 94-903 1723. E-mail: info@carainternational.net. Website: www. carainternational.net.
In business since 1999. Member of IAPA.
Placements: 300-400 au pairs, nannies and Work in Ireland programme.
Jobs in: throughout Ireland.
Nationalities placed: EU.
Minimum stay: 12 weeks in summer.
Wages/pocket money: €75-€120 per week for au pairs, €150-€200 for au pairs plus and €250-€300 for live-in nannies.
Qualifications: ages 18-30 for au pairs; minimum age for nannies normally 25. Some childcare experience (2 references required). Fair command of English normally required.
Application procedure: Au pair application form available on website or on request from the agency. Placement is quick since they always have families looking for live-in help, and even quicker if au pair does not specify particular location. All girls are interviewed by agency and/or host family by telephone.
Other services: invitation letter provides travel details, language course information and contact details of other au pairs available from agency and/or host family. Agency maintains regular contact with au pair and family. Agency tries to mediate in event of problems; if they can't be sorted out, au pair can stay in an emergency room until replacement family is found or return flight is arranged.
Fees: none.
Contact: Caroline Joyce, Owner/Manager.

CARE AGENCY
The Red House, Stanford Place, Faringdon, Oxfordshire SN7 8EX. ☎/fax: 01367 243473. E-mail: careagency@ukonline.co.uk. Website: www.aupairbiz. co.uk.
In business since 1971; under present management since 1999.
Placements: au pairs.
Jobs in: UK mostly; some placements in Italy and France.
Nationalities placed: Swiss, Italian, German, Austrian, French, Hungarian and Czech. About 3% of applicants placed are male.
Minimum stay: 3 months.
Wages/pocket money: minimum £55 per week for 25 hours per week.
Qualifications: at least some basic language, plus household and childcare experience.
Application procedure: application documents provided followed by telephone interview.
Other services: agency can advise on language schools, au pair contacts and support throughout stay.
Fees: nil for au pairs; £25 registration fee for families plus placement fees of £85-£265.
Contact: Nora Roche, Proprietor.

CELTIC CHILDCARE
Via St Antonio Da Padova 14, 10121 Turin, Italy. ☎/fax: +39 011-533606. Mobile: +39 338 2642288. Fax: +39 011-533606. E-mail: info@celticchildcare. com. Website: www.celticchildcare.com.

In business since 1997. Member of IAPA.
Placements: 250 au pairs, nannies and mother's helps; also English teachers for children.
Jobs in: Italy. Outgoing programme to Ireland, England, Germany, Switzerland, Spain, France, Holland, Canada and the US.
Nationalities placed: all.
A few male placements are made of American and British au pairs to speak English and look after older children in Italy.
Minimum stay: 1-3 months during the summer to 12 months. Generally 6 months minimum.
Wages/pocket money: €90-€100 a week for au pairs, €250-€400 a week for nannies.
Qualifications: ages 18-26. Minimum childcare experience. No knowledge of Italian needed since agency's client families all speak good English.
Application procedure: interview by phone and thorough check made of references with the referees. If possible arrangements are made by Italian families to fly candidates out for an interview before starting job.
Other services: welcome guide to destination city provided on arrival as well as a list of other au pairs and nannies to contact. Also agency provides a list of public and private language schools, and a 24-hour mobile number for emergencies.
Fees: nil.
Contact: Elizabeth Lenihan, Director.

CENTRAL NANNIES
17 Lammasmead, Broxbourne, Herts. EN10 6PF. ☎/fax: 01992 470196; also 0870 606 4455. E-mail: lynne.centralnannies@ntlworld.com Website: www. centralnannies.net.
Shares 0870 number with Capable Nannies (117 Gwydir St, Cambridge CB1 2LG; 01223 464808; www.capablenannies.co.uk) and the Sussex Nanny Register, 56 Connell Drive, Brighton BN2 6RT; tel/fax 01273 308651; info@sussexnannyregister.com).
Placements: nannies (permanent and temporary), mother's helps and maternity nurses; no au pair placements made.
Jobs in: UK only (Hertfordshire, Essex, North London).
Nationalities placed: mainly British (due to requirement of providing CRB clearance).
Qualifications: must be formally qualified in childcare with checkable references, CRB disclosure and documents.
Application procedure: agency can apply for CRB clearance on nanny's behalf (takes about 6 weeks). Interviews required in all cases.
Other services: payroll service available.
Contact: Lynne Lecomber, Owner.

CENTROS EUROPEOS GALVE S.A.
Calle Principe, 12-6°A, Madrid 28012, Spain. ☎+34 91-532 72 30. Fax: +34 91-521 60 76. E-mail: centros-principe@telefonica.net.
In business since 1968.
Placements: 300 au pairs and a few demi pairs.
Jobs in: Spain (Madrid, Alicante, Pamplona, Valencia); plus France, Germany, Ireland, Italy and UK.
Nationalities placed: usually Western European. Agency will try to place non-EU au pairs.
Minimum stay: school year preferred, 6 months minimum. Minimum 2 months for summer placements.
Wages/pocket money: about €60 per week.
Qualifications: age limits 18-27 years. In Spain families prefer girls with good spoken English, French or German (to teach the children after school). A basic knowledge of

Spanish very useful.

Application procedure: school or work references required as well as a medical certificate. Personal interviews with Spanish girls only. Time needed to process application between 3 weeks and 2½ months.

Other services: agency organises other programmes, for instance homestays with Spanish families in Madrid, Valencia, Alicante, Segovia and Barcelona, and language exchanges between English, Spanish and French students. Affordable Spanish language courses at all levels offered in Madrid for 3-10 hours per week.

Fees: nil for foreign girls coming to Spain; otherwise €120+.

CHALFONT NANNIES
70 Kings Ride, Tylers Green, Buckinghamshire HP10 8BP. ☎01494 816660. Fax: 01494 816660. E-mail: mail@chalfontnannies.co.uk. Website: www. chalfontnannies.co.uk.

In business since 1997.

Placements: nannies, maternity nurses, mother's helps, temporary cover.

Jobs in: UK only.

Nationalities placed: English nannies primarily.

About 1% of applicants placed are male.

Qualifications: good interview with agency necessary. References must be first class, CRB, experience and qualifications and an up-to-date First Aid certificate all needed.

Contact: Carrie Philp, Proprietor.

CHARLTON BROWN GROUP
Level 16, 300 Adelaide Street, Brisbane, Queensland 4000, Australia. ☎+61 7-3221 3855. Fax: +61 7-3221 6855. E-mail: nannies@charltonbrowngroup. com.au. Website: www.charltonbrowngroup.com.au.

In business since 1990.

Placements: au pairs and nannies.

Jobs in: Australia. UK and (secondarily) to Netherlands, Germany, Switzerland and Italy; very occasionally to France and the United Arab Emirates.

About 15% of applicants placed are male.

Minimum stay: 10-12 weeks; no summer placements.

Wages/pocket money: on average $13 an hour.

Qualifications: minimum age 17. All candidates must have first aid and basic English; nannies also need childcare qualifications.

Application procedure: application with resumé should be forwarded to head office plus at least 3 references. Applicants will be contacted after an assessment of the application and contacting the referees. This usually takes 7 days.

Other services: agency handles all administrative and financial aspects of employment for any eligible candidate and will ensure that a worker is employed legally and protected from neglectful conditions. Charlton Brown also run a 12-week Nanny Award training course.

Fees: nil (charging job-seekers a fee is illegal).

Contact: Davey McBaron, Administration.

CHERISH CHILDCARE LIMITED
Pendelm House, The Croft, Aston Tirrold, Oxfordshire OX11 9DL. ☎01235 851090. E-mail: info@cherishchildcare.com. Website: www.cherishchildcare. com.

In business since July 2005.

Placements: 90 au pairs.

Jobs in: UK and outgoing to USA and occasionally Europe.

About 5% of applicants placed are male.

Minimum stay: 6 months; summer placements available.
Wages/pocket money: £50-£75 a week depending on hours worked, role and applicant's experience.
Qualifications: according to industry standards (according to IAPA).
Application procedure: families and applicants are met. Average time to recruit for family is 4-6 weeks. Average time to place au pair in the USA is 8 weeks including visa.
Other services: agency supports all au pairs whilst they are in the UK and meets as many as possible. Advice is provided regarding choice of language school. Get-togethers and trips are arranged for the au pairs. A contact list of other au pairs is provided.
Fees: nil.
Contact: Kathryn Powell, Director.

THE CHILDCARE COMPANY
Central Office, Emberton House, 26 Shakespeare Road, Bedford MK40 2ED. Also: 1 White`s Row, London E1 7NF; 15 Swaffield Road, London SW18 3AH; 7 Garth Road, Sevenoaks, Kent TN13 1RT; 23 Upper Havelock Street, Wellingborough, Northants NN8 LPN. ☎020-7377 2744, 0845 458 1551 and 01234 352688. E-mail: elizabethelder@thechildcarecompany.co.uk. Website: www.thechildcarecompany.co.uk.
Family-run business since 1981 but established company in 2005. Member of REC, IAPA and BAPAA.
Placements: au pairs from all designated areas placed throughout the UK and overseas, including Europe and USA. Also place nannies and nursery staff throughout the UK (including staff from overseas) and recruit resort staff in summer and for ski locations in winter.
Jobs in: UK, primarily the Southeast and East Midlands. Overseas mothers' helps placed throughout the UK.
Nationalities placed: British, European plus nannies from Australia, New Zealand and South Africa.
Application procedure: average processing time 2-3 weeks.
Fees: nil to au pairs and job-seekers.
Contact: Elizabeth Elder.

AMERICA ❖ AUSTRALIA ❖ CANADA ❖ EUROPE
NANNY – MOTHER'S HELP – AU PAIR

An opportunity to live abroad in a secure family environment, caring for children and helping in the home. Continuous agency support whilst overseas.

For further information please contact: **CHILDCARE INTERNATIONAL LTD**

Trafalgar House, Grenville Place, London NW7 3SA
Tel 020-8906 3116   **Fax** 020-8906 3461
E-mail office@childint.co.uk   www.childint.co.uk
Also Educare in America – see separate entry

CHILDCARE INTERNATIONAL LTD.
Trafalgar House, Grenville Place, London NW7 3SA. ☎020-8906 3116. Fax: 020-8906 3461. E-mail: office@childint.co.uk. Website: www.childint.co.uk.
In business since 1986. Founder member IAPA and BAPAA. Member of FIYTO. Member of REC.
Placements: nannies, mother's helps and au pairs.

Jobs in: Australia, Canada and Europe (Belgium, France, Germany, Italy, Netherlands and Spain). Recruitment agency for Educare America (see entry) and Au Pair in America in the UK.
Length of stay: 1 year for USA and 1 year plus for Canada. 3-6 months for Australia. 6-12 months in Europe. Short-term summer positions and winter ski au pair placements (December-April) available.
Wages/pocket money: depending on country, from £40 per week for au pairs in Europe to £200+ for mother's helps and nannies depending on position, age and qualifications. Au pairs in America receive $139.05 per week for 45 hours. Au pairs in Australia receive A$250-$300.
Qualifications: minimum age 18. Childcare experience and/or previous au pair experience required for Canada. Knowledge of language of country of choice an advantage for Europe. Driving licence essential for North America.
Application procedure: write or telephone agency for details and brochure.
Other services: full support and caring service of local agency in country of placement.
Fees: £47 (including VAT) for girls going to Europe. Programme fee for Australia.
Contact: Mrs. Sandra Landau, Director.

THE CHILDCARE SOLUTION LIMITED
Emberton House, 26 Shakespeare Road, Bedford MK40 2ED. ☎01234 352688. E-mail: centraloffice@thechildcaresolution.com. Website: www. thechildcaresolution.com.
In business since 1984. Has franchises covering Bedfordshire, Buckinghamshire, Northamptonshire, Sussex, parts of Kent and the Isle of Man. Member of IAPA and REC.
Placements: nannies, nursery nurses, mothers' helps and resort childcare staff.
Jobs in: UK and overseas.
Nationalities placed: Europeans in accordance with Home Office regulations.
Minimum stay: 3 months to 2 years. Resort nannies must be available for entire summer or winter season. One year for USA.
Other services: full agency support on all programmes.
Contacts: Elizabeth Elder, Jane Goodwin, Judy Kelly, Lesley Hanmore. Contact Central Office as above for nearest office, or check website www.thechildcaresolution.com/contact. htm.

THE CHILDCARE TEAM
Suite 2 7, Parkes St, Parramatta, NSW 2150, Australia. ☎+61 2-9891 4377. Fax: +61 2-9891 4366. E-mail: info@childcareteam.net. Website: www. childcareteam.com.au.
In business since 2002. Member of RCSA (Recruiting & Consulting Services Association).
Placements: 150 au pairs, mother's helps, live-in and live-out nannies.
Jobs in: Australia (throughout New South Wales and Brisbane area). Outgoing programme to Italy, England and Canada.
About 2% of applicants placed are male.
Minimum stay: longer stays (12 months) preferred, so that 3-month limit on any one job taken with a Working Holiday visa is difficult. Summer stays are possible.
Wages/pocket money: A$150-$250 a week, depending on skills and experience.
Qualifications: minimum age 18. Good communication skills, both written and oral are needed. Childcare certificates (NNEB or BA/Diploma/Certificate in Childcare) are not essential but highly desirable.
Application procedure: interviews in person or by telephone, reference checks and working with children check. It normally takes about a week between registration and placement or at least being sent out for interview by families.

Other services: can recommend a specialist nanny insurance policy.
Fees: A$495 incoming and outgoing.
Contact: Amy Scott, Junior Consultant.

CINDERELLA AU PAIR AGENCY
291 Kirkdale, Sydenham, London SE26 4QE. ☎020-8659 1689. Fax: 020-8265 2330. E-mail: aupairs@cinderella.co.uk. Website: www.cinderellaaupairs. co.uk.
In business since 1983. Member of IAPA.
Placements: au pairs and au pairs plus.
Jobs in: London and throughout UK.
Male au pairs occasionally placed.
Minimum stay: 3 month summer placements; otherwise 6-12 months.
Wages/pocket money: £55 per week for standard au pair in the UK. Contribution from family towards language school fees.
Qualifications: must have record of childcare jobs and references.
Application procedure: partner agencies abroad conduct careful screening.
Other services: advice given after placement, friendship list for au pairs and native speakers for most of the main languages available in the agency at least once a week to help the au pair settle in.
Fees: nil.
Contact: Trisha Waghorn, Au Pair Co-ordinator.

CLUB AVENTURE - AVENTURES JEUNESSE
757 Mont-Royal Est, Montreal, Quebec H2J 1W8, Canada. ☎+1-877-527-0999 or 514-527-0999. Fax: +1 514-527-3999. E-mail: info@aventuresjeunesse. com. Website: www.aventuresjeunesse.com.
In business since 1976. Formerly ELJA (Etudes Langues, Jeunesse, Aventure). International Work and Travel abroad programmes including English language assistants in Spain, live-in hotel/restaurant jobs in the UK and farm work in Australia.
Placements: 100 au pairs, language assistants, work and study interns, etc.
Jobs in: England, Scotland, France, Denmark, Iceland, Netherlands; no inbound programme to Canada, though French-speaking Canadians can be placed as au pairs with families in Western Canada (Vancouver, Calgary, etc.).
Nationalities placed: mainly French-speaking Canadians.
Minimum stay: 2-3 months during the summer or for the academic year.
Qualifications: minimum age 18; upper age varies according to country. Au pair applicants must be Canadian citizens, have completed secondary education, have basic knowledge of English or the language of the country and have recent childcare references and a criminal record check.
Application procedure: all applicants to apply at least 2-3 months in advance.
Other services: assistance with insurance, visa, tax refunds, etc.
Fees: C$325.
Contact: Elia Duchesne, Programme Co-ordinator.

CLUB DE RELACIONES CULTURALES INTERNACIONALES (RCI)
Ferraz 82, 28008 Madrid, Spain. ☎+34 91-541 71 03. Fax: +34 91-559 11 81. E-mail: spain@clubrci.es. Website: www.clubrci.es.
In operation as a non-profit club and youth exchange organisation since 1978. Member of IAPA and FIYTO.
Placements: 1,300 au pairs, mother's helps, nannies and demi pairs. Programme for Language Assistants whereby native English speakers live with families to improve their conversational English. Also arrange home stays and youth exchanges.

Jobs in: Spain, plus most countries for Spanish applicants.
Nationalities placed: no restrictions. Non-EU au pairs must register for a minimum of 15 hours of Spanish classes a week.
Males can be placed.
Minimum stay: 6-9 months preferred. Summer stays of 4-12 weeks easy to arrange. Live-in language assistants stay 3-12 months.
Wages/pocket money: €60 per week if family lives in the city centre, €70 if family lives on the outskirts. One week holiday given after 6 months, 2 weeks after 12 months.
Qualifications: age limits 18-27 years. Interest in and caring attitude towards children required. Knowledge of language helpful but not required.
Application procedure: application form, 2 references, medical certificate and telephone contact needed. Offer of host family often made within 24 hours.
Other services: Club RCI runs social programmes, Spanish courses at its own language centre and other summer courses in conjunction with Spanish universities. Also offers specially designed insurance policy, advisory service in the event of problems (including legal ones) and a travel service.
Fees: annual membership in Club de RCI.
Contact: Paloma Sierra.

COSY TOES NANNY AGENCY LLP
15 Church Green, Wickham Bishops, Witham, Essex CM8 3JX. ☎/fax: 01621 892080. E-mail: admin@cosytoesnannyagency.co.uk. Website: www. cosytoesnannyagency.co.uk.
In business since 2003. Member of Association of Nanny Agencies (www.anauk.org).
Placements: 30-40 full-time and part-time nannies, daily, live-in, temporary and permanent.
Jobs in: UK only.
Nationalities placed: mainly British.
About 1% of applicants placed are male.
Minimum stay: usual minimum is 1 year, though summer nannies sometimes requested by clients.
Wages/pocket money: full-time daily nannies earn between £250 and £300 a week. Part-time earn £50 to £60 a day.
Qualifications: recognised qualification or at least 2 years experience, an up-to-date CRB police check, first aid certificate and 2 forms of ID that match current address/name, etc. Also applicants need at least 2 previous employers who can be contacted for references.
Application procedure: after correct documents have been submitted as above, applicant has face-to-face interview. Minimum of two referees are contacted and certificates are also inspected.
Other services: supporting services like insurance available through Association of Nanny Agencies.
Contact: Belinda Hay and Suzanne Cropley, Co-owners.

CP AU-PAIR AGENTUR
Pilgrimstr. 4, 46053 Duisburg, Germany. ☎/fax: +49 203-3635 901. Fax: +49 203-3635 926. E-mail: christel.paul@cp-au-pair.com. Website: www.cp-au-pair.com.
In business since 2000. Member of Aupair-Society e.V.
Placements: nannies and au pairs.
Jobs in: Germany; also German au pairs sent to Great Britain, Ireland, Portugal and France.
No placement of male au pairs.
Minimum stay: 6 months.

Wages/pocket money: €260 per month.
Qualifications: European standard requirements (minimum knowledge of the host country language, health certificate, police check and at least babysitting experience all required).
Application procedure: interviews in person or by phone. Au pairs will not be accepted without references.
Other services: insurance and travel arrangements can be made. Information about language classes given.
Fees: on request.
Contact: Christel Paul, Director.

CROSSING LIMITS S.L
Av. República Argentina nº 22, Bis 8F (Los Remedios), 41011 Seville, Spain. ☎/fax: +34 95-40 83 931. E-mail: info@crossinglimits.com. Website: www. crossinglimits.com.
In business since 2004.
Placements: au pairs and nannies. Placement in conjunction with Spanish language course.
Jobs in: Spain. Outgoing programme mainly to UK and Ireland.
Nationalities placed: all.
No male placements.
Minimum stay: 1 month; summer placements available.
Wages/pocket money: €60 a week approximately.
Qualifications: minimum age 16. Must have childcare experience and some knowledge of Spanish.
Application procedure: CV and the payment of the management fees normally required 1½ months prior to start date. References are welcomed. No interview required.
Other services: range of complementary services includes insurance, translations, travel booking, etc.
Fees: €100 management fee and €150 programme fee.
Contact: Ana Vallejo, Co-Director.

CULTURAL CARE AU PAIR
EF Center, One Education Street, Cambridge, MA 02141, USA. ☎1-800-333-6056. Fax: 617-619-1101. E-mail: aupair@culturalcare.com. Website: www. culturalcare.com or www.ef.com/aupair. European HQ: Haldenstrasse 4, 6006 Lucerne, Switzerland; +41 41 41 74 512.
In business since 1967 as an educational travel organisation, au pair programme run since 1989. Member of IAPA.
Placements: 5,000 au pairs with host families in the US.
Jobs in: USA.
Nationalities placed: all. Cultural Care Au Pair currently recruits from Argentina, Australia, Austria, Bosnia, Brazil, Bulgaria, Colombia, Costa Rica, Croatia, Czech Republic, Ecuador, Germany, Hungary, Italy, Latvia, Mexico, Montenegro, Panama, Peru, Poland, Romania, Russia, Serbia, Slovakia, Slovenia, South Africa, Spain, Sweden, and Ukraine. It no longer has an office in the UK.
5%-10% of applicants placed are male.
Minimum stay: 12 months starting year round.
Wages/pocket money: $139.05 per week plus free return flights to family's address and free health and accident insurance. Family contributes up to $500 towards studies in the USA (including language classes).
Qualifications: ages 18-26. Must have completed secondary school, have a driving licence, previous childcare experience, conversational English and no criminal background.
Application procedure: application should be made to agent in home country 2-3 months

before intended departure to allow time for the matching and visa process. All applicants attend an information and interview meeting in their home country. Applicants must supply at least 3 non-family references.

Other services: free health and accident insurance. $500 given towards studies. 24-hour emergency service run from EF Au Pairs head office in Boston. Au pairs supported by local co-ordinators who hold monthly meetings for au pairs in their region.

Fees: varies among countries.

Contact: Gisela Nilsson, Director of Operations.

CZECH MATE AU PAIR AGENCY
8 Brown Street, Altrincham, Cheshire WA14 2EU. ☎0161-928 0023.

Placements: 50 au pairs.

Jobs in: UK.

Nationalities placed: all that are legal but specialise in Czech au pairs.

Minimum stay: 2 months to 2 years.

Wages/pocket money: £60 for 25 h.p.w.

Qualifications: ages 18-27. Some childcare experience preferred.

Application procedure: average processing time 2-3 weeks.

Other services: follow-up service to help au pairs to settle.

Fees: nil.

Contact: Eva Todd.

DELANEY INTERNATIONAL
Bramble Cottage, Thorncombe Street, Bramley, Nr Guildford, Surrey GU5 0ND. ☎01483 894300. Fax: 01483 894700. E-mail: info@delaney-nannies. com. Website: www.delaney-nannies.com.

In business since 1991. Member of REC.

Placements: nannies, mother's helps and European au pairs.

Jobs in: France, Germany, Italy and Spain; also incoming to England.

Nationalities placed: any that are legal.

Minimum stay: 1-3 months in summer.

Wages/pocket money: £60+ per week for au pairs; £200+ per week for live-in nannies.

Qualifications: should have some knowledge of relevant language.

Application procedure: free service for applicants who must complete an international application form and provide photos, a CV/letter about themselves, a minimum of two written references, a current medical and police clearance certificate.

Fees: none.

Contact: Marcia Delaney, Director.

DIAL-AN-ANGEL PTY LTD
Head Office, Suites 20 & 21, Edgecliff Mews, 201 New South Head Road, Edgecliff, NSW 2027, Australia. ☎+61 2-9362 4225. Fax: +61 2-9362 4001/9328 2654. E-mail: dialanangel@dialanangel.com. Website: www.dial-an-angel. com.au. Also 12 offices throughout Australia (see Australia chapter for list of contact details).

In business since 1967. Member of NAPC (National Association of Personnel Consultants) and AI Group (NSW).

Placements: au pairs, nannies and mother's helps.

Jobs in: Australia, UK and USA.

Nationalities placed: Australian nannies sent to UK and USA. Nannies and carers with good English skills can be placed in Australia.

Minimum stay: placements in UK and USA are for 12 months.

Wages/pocket money: varies according to age, qualifications and experience.

Qualifications: minimum age 21 for Australia. Ages 17-30 for UK and 18-26 for USA. NNEB or equivalent certification needed plus childcare experience. Linguistic skills an advantage. Carers with rehabilitation experience are in demand.
Application procedure: 2 work and 2 character references needed. Interviews essential. Placement can be almost immediate if references can be checked by phone or fax.
Other services: comprehensive insurance for staff Angels. Extensive agency back-up.
Fees: nil.
Contact: Norma Woodbridge, Manager, Nannies International & Dial-An-Angel, Lindfield (02-9416 7511).

DONALD FRASER FOREIGN NANNY PLACEMENT AGENCY
700 de Gaspé St., Suite 207, Montreal, Québec H3E 1H2, Canada. ☎+1 514-766-2025. E-mail: fraserlog@sympatico.ca. Website: www.frasernannies. com.
In business since 2004.
Placements: about 24 nannies a year.
Jobs in: Canada.
No male placements.
Minimum stay: 1 year.
Wages/pocket money: C$8 per hour for 40 hour week. $12 per hour in excess of 40 hours.
Qualifications: childcare experience. Early Childhood Care or Early Childhood Education diploma. Fluency in English.
Application procedure: recruit under the auspices of Canada's Live-in Caregiver agreement. Lead time from signing of contract to issuance of work permit by the Immigration Section of a Canadian diplomatic mission is approximately 6 months.
Other services: agency endeavours to have the parent-employers pay the travel expenses and interim health insurance as there is a waiting time of 3 months before the applicant is eligible for Medicare (i.e. free medical and hospital coverage).
Fees: nil.
Contact: Donald Fraser, President.

DUBLIN SCHOOL OF ENGLISH
10-12 Westmoreland Street, Temple Bar, Dublin 2, Ireland. ☎+353 1-677 3322. Fax: +353 1-679 5454. E-mail: admin@dse.ie. Website: www.dse.ie.
In business since 1968. Members of: MEI-RELSA, Dublin Tourism, FIYTO, ALTO, Dublin Chamber of Commerce, IBEC.
Jobs in: Ireland.
Nationalities placed: no restrictions.
Minimum stay: 3 months. Summer placements available.
Wages/pocket money: €70 per week.
Qualifications: age limits 18-24 years. Basic knowledge of English required.
Other services: language classes are included in Au Pair programme.
Fees: from €800 for 3 months.
Contact: Imelda Bird, Au Pair Placement Officer.

EDEN CHILDCARE
118 Piccadilly, Mayfair, London W1J 7NW. ☎0845 128 4279. Fax: 020-7569 6772. E-mail: enquiries@eden-nannies.co.uk or maternity@eden-nannies. co.uk. Website: www.eden-nannies.co.uk.
In business since 1998.
Placements: qualified and experienced nannies, maternity nurses, midwives, paediatric nurses, health visitors.

Jobs in: London and the Home Counties, worldwide including Europe, Asia, America, Canada, Middle East and Far East.

Nationalities placed: British, Irish, EU nationals, Australians, New Zealanders and South Africans.

Minimum stay: temporary and permanent.

Weekly salary: £200-£600 per week.

Qualifications: must have at least 3 years recent and relevant childcare experience or a recognised childcare qualification.

Application procedure: telephone screening followed by detailed application form (can register online). All candidates are personally interviewed. All references are verbally checked. Must have a CRB Enhanced Disclosure and up-to-date First Aid Certificate.

Other services: French spoken at agency. Free electronic fortnightly newsletter.

Fees: nil for candidates.

Contact: Julie Weir, Senior Consultant.

EDGWARE AU PAIR AGENCY
PO Box 147, Radlett, Hertfordshire, WD7 8WX. ☎01923 289737 Fax: 01923 289739. E-mail: info@the-aupair-shop.com. Website: www.the-aupair-shop. com

In business since 1963.

Placements: about 500-700 au pairs, nannies, mother's helps and demi pairs.

Jobs in: all over the UK with host families. 75 co-operating agents. Can place au pairs from country to country, e.g. Spain to Italy, France to Germany, etc.

Nationalities placed: Europeans in accordance with Home Office regulations.

Minimum stay: 6 months, preferably 1 year. Summer stays: 3 months.

Wages/pocket money: £55+ per week for au pairs; £180-£250 for nannies depending on age, experience and duties.

Qualifications: minimum age 18, maximum 26. Driving licence is a help. Childcare experience required for mother's helps and nannies.

Application procedure: application form, CV if available, 2 references from teachers and/or previous employers, medical certificate and photos. Interview necessary, plus copy of driving licence and, if possible, life-saving qualifications, first aid certificate or any evidence of childcare experience.

Other services: agency advises on schools, helps with medical or dental problems and encourages meetings with other au pairs.

Fees: nil.

Contact: Amanda Pampel, Proprietor.

EDUCARE IN AMERICA
Childcare International Ltd, Trafalgar House, Grenville Place, London NW7 3SA. ☎020-8906 3116 or 0870 77 47 475. Fax: 020-8906 3461. E-mail: office@ childint.co.uk. Website: www.childint.co.uk.

Parent organisation AIFS (American Institute for Foreign Study), 37 Queen's Gate, London SW7 5HR; 020-7581 7363/ fax 020-7581 7345; e-mail info@educareamerica.co.uk; www. educareinamerica.co.uk). AIFS (www.aifs.com) founded in 1967; Educare Programme was authorised in 2001 as a companion programme to Au Pair in America (see entry).

Jobs in: USA only.

Nationalities placed: nationalities in whose country an established interviewer network exists.

Minimum stay: 1-year placements with option to extend the J-1 visa for a further 12 months. Departures in July/August and December.

Wages/pocket money: $105 per week (for 30 hours of childcare). Guaranteed 2 weeks paid vacation.

Qualifications: ages 18-26 years Must be a current post-secondary student or a university graduate who intends to study on completion of the programme. Must have at least 200 hours recent practical childcare experience (e.g. regular baby-sitting for non-family members, helping at schools, youth groups and summer camps). A full clean driving licence and a good level of English are essential.

Application procedure: must submit application forms, passport photos, references including an academic, childcare and character reference, a personal essay, medical report, etc. Interview compulsory with local representative.

Other services: free return flights to New York from cities around the world. A 4-day orientation near New York City. J-1 visa is arranged with help of agency. All Educare Companions are placed in cluster groups with a local counsellor who arranges social and cultural activities. Participants are required to attend a local college or university for at least 6 hours per week during term time; host families contribute up to $1,000 for tuition fees.

Fees: $100 non-refundable placement fee and a $750 programme fee.

ELITE CHILDCARE
22 Rowena Crescent, London SW11 2PT. ☎020-7801 0061. Fax: 020-7801 0063. E-mail: elite.nannies@virgin.net. Website: www.elitenannies.co.uk.
In business since 1994.

Placements: nannies and maternity nurses.

Jobs in: worldwide but mainly UK.

Nationalities placed: must satisfy legal requirements for working in the UK. Qualified male applicants are very welcome. Agency tries to convince families of benefits of hiring a male nanny.

Minimum stay: temporary placements from 1 week; permanent contracts for minimum 1 year.

Wages/pocket money: live-in nannies £250-£350 net per week; live-out nannies £350-£450 net; maternity nurses approximately £700 gross per week. If a nanny is required to travel with a family, the employing family is responsible for making arrangements for nanny's travel and insurance costs.

Qualifications: minimum age 18. Childcare qualifications or minimum 2 years experience required with references that can be checked. Good spoken English essential.

Application procedure: all candidates are interviewed and references checked before introductions to families are made.

Other services: agency policy to speak to nanny and family during the first fortnight of a new placement to check everyone is happy.

Fees: nil.

Contact: Kim O'Shea, Proprietor.

ENGLISH-ITALIAN AGENCY
69 Woodside, Wimbledon, London SW19 7AF. ☎020-8946 5728. Fax: 020-8879 1660. E-mail: info@englishitalian.plus.com.

Placements: nannies, au pairs, mother's helps, governesses and housekeepers.

Jobs in: incoming to UK; placements in Italy and worldwide.

Nationalities placed: all.

Minimum stay: 6-12 months. Summer stays: 2-3 months. Also accommodation as paying guests with families can be arranged, short-term (from one week) or long-term.

Qualifications: minimum age 18. Childcare experience essential for nannies and mother's helps, babysitting for au pairs.

Application procedure: interviews not essential. Minimum 2 references, one related to childcare; also medical certificates and 2 passport-type photos.

Other services: agency puts you in touch with other girls in vicinity. Detailed job descriptions sent.

Fees: nil.
Contact: Agnes Coburn, Director.

ENGLISH WORLD LANGUAGE SCHOOL
4 Colombia Street, 28016 Madrid, Spain. Also: 9 Cronista Carreres, 46003 Valencia, Spain. ☎+34 609 246249. Fax: +34 91 443 0536. E-mail: ant@ yourenglishworld.com. Website: www.yourenglishworld.com.
In business since 1997.
Placements: au pairs (and language students).
Jobs in: UK only.
Nationalities placed: EU nationals, especially Spanish.
Minimum stay: 6 months; summer placements available.
Wages/pocket money: €60+ a week.
Qualifications: must have some experience with children and intermediate English.
Application procedure: personal interview, 2 references, family photos and in some cases telephone or email interview by family.
Fees: €70.
Contact: Andrew Thomson, Director.

EURAUPAIR
17 Wheatfield Drive, Shifnal, Shropshire TF11 8HL. ☎01952 460733. Fax: 01952 416850. E-mail: maureen@asseuk.freeserve.co.uk or info@euraupair. com. Website: www.euraupair.com.
In business since 1994. UK recruitment agent for EurAupair in the USA (250 North Coast Highway, Dana Point, CA 92629; 949-494 5500).
Placements: au pairs.
Jobs in: USA only.
Nationalities placed: British residents.
Male au pairs are not placed.
Minimum stay: 12 months.
Wages/pocket money: $139.05 per week.
Qualifications: ages 18-27. Babysitting experience needed; at least 200 hours of childcare experience needed if providing childcare assistance for infants and children under the age of two. Must be conversant in English.
Application procedure: personal interview required and 3 references. Minimum processing time is 8 weeks.
Other services: comprehensive medical, travel, personal liability and life insurance coverage, with no deductibles. Euraupair Community Counselors meet and help au pairs throughout their stay.
Fees: $500 fee will be refunded on successful completion of the 12-month stay.
Contact: Maureen Sanders, Organiser.

EUROMA
Viale Bruno Buozzi 19, A1, Int. 3, 00197 Rome, Italy. ☎+39 06-80 69 21 30. Fax: +39 06-80 66 67 85. E-mail: info@euroma.info. Website: www.euroma.info.
In business since 1990. Member of IAPA.
Placements: 150 au pairs, babysitters, language stays.
Jobs in: Italy; also France, UK, Spain, Germany and USA.
Male applicants cannot normally be placed.
Minimum stay: 6 or 9 months. Minimum 3-month summer placements can be made.
Qualifications: Childcare experience needed.
Fees: €130.
Contact: Mrs. Inès de Vendegies, Director.

EURO PAIR AGENCY
28 Derwent Avenue, Pinner, Middlesex HA5 4QJ. ☎020-8421 2100. Fax: 020-8428 6416. E-mail: info@europair.net. Website: www.euro-pair.co.uk.
In business since 1985.
Placements: 200 au pairs in UK.
Jobs in: UK for European applicants.
Nationalities placed: Europeans in accordance with Home Office regulations.
Minimum stay: 10 months from September; 2 months (July-August).
Wages/pocket money: £60 per week for 25 hours.
Qualifications: ages 18-27 with basic skill in English. Must like children and have experience looking after children.
Application procedure: email 2 months in advance.
Fees: nil.
Contact: Mrs. Christiane Burt.

EURO PAIR SERVICES
13 rue Vavin, 75006 Paris, France. ☎+33 1-43 29 80 01. Fax: +33 1-43 29 80 37. E-mail: contact@europairservices.com. Website: www.europairservices. com.
In business since 1986. Member of IAPA and UFAAP (Union Francaise des Associations Au Pair).
Placements: 300 nannies, au pairs and mother's helps.
Jobs in: France; also England, Scotland, Ireland, Germany, Spain, Italy, Greece, Austria, Iceland and Denmark.
Nationalities placed: EU nationals, Eastern Europeans, South Africans, Canadians, etc.
Minimum stay: 6 months. Summer stays: 2-3 months.
Wages/pocket money: €65 per week for au pairs (plus monthly transport ticket in Paris).
Qualifications: childcare experience and some knowledge of language needed.
Other services: au pairs in Paris put in touch with each other. Back-up services from partner agents in south of France, Lyon, Brittany, the Southwest, etc. Advice on language courses given.
Fees: nil.
Contact: Mme. Alison Davey.

THE EUROPEAN AU PAIR AGENCY
554 South Circular Road, Dublin 8, Ireland. ☎+353 1-453 4092. Fax: +353 1-454 5926. E-mail: eapa@indigo.ie. Website: none.
In business since 1994. Member of IAPA.
Placements: 200 au pairs (inbound).
Jobs in: Ireland. Outgoing placements to France and Spain (very few).
In 2005, agency placed 4 male au pairs in Ireland (a big improvement).
Minimum stay: 2-3 months. Limited number of summer placements.
Wages/pocket money: at least €85 a week.
Qualifications: must be over 18 and have EU nationality. Some experience with children needed (babysitting is acceptable) and knowledge of English.
Application procedure: usual requirements include application form, references, medical certificate, checkable references (which are checked) and photos. Agency meets the candidate when possible.
Other services: newly arrived au pairs are given a list of English schools. Agency contacts all au pairs and guides them through their stay if required. If a problem arrives and depending on the crisis, the agency will find another family for the au pair.
Fees: €150.
Contact: Sylvie Levasseur-Reilly, Director.

EUROPLACEMENTS ITALY srl
Via Felice Cavallotti 15, 20122 Milan, Italy. ☎+39 02-760 18 357. Fax: +39 02-763 96 711. E-mail: info@europlacements.it. Website: www.europlacements. it.
Nearest metro San Babila (red line).
In business since 1993.
Placements: 300-400 nannies, mother's helps, maternity nurses, babysitters, teachers and tutors.
Jobs in: Italy, Switzerland and internationally.
Nationalities placed: any with English as a mother tongue, especially Australians and New Zealanders.
About 1% of applicants placed are male.
Minimum stay: 12 months except for summer placements.
Wages/pocket money: salary between €500 and €1,200+ per month.
Qualifications: must have English as a mother tongue. Experience and qualifications needed by nannies and teachers. Ages 19-40.
Application procedure: application form, medical report, resumé, photos, 'Dear Family' letter, references, copies of qualifications/certificates and interview. Processing time between 1 day and 1 month.
Other services: back-up provided by Milan office.
Contact: Samantha Van Eldik (s.vaneldik@europlacements.it).

EXPERIMENT E.V.
Gluckstr. 1, 53115 Bonn, Germany. ☎+49 228-957220. Fax: +49 228-358282. E-mail: info@experiment-ev.de. Website: www.experiment-ev.de.
In operation since 1932. Member of Federation of the Experiment in International Living; Founding member of AJA (Arbeitskreis gemeinnütziger Jugendaustauschorganisationen) and UNESCO counseling member.
Placements: 50 demi pairs and other youth exchanges.
Jobs in: German demi pairs to Canada, New Zealand, Australia and Ecuador. No incoming programme.
About 5% of applicants placed are male.
Nationalities placed: Germans only.
Minimum stay: 3 months, year round.
Wages/pocket money: demi pairs work limited hours in exchange for free room and board and no wage. In New Zealand demi pairs received €60 a week.
Qualifications: ages 18-30. Good childcare experience (2 references), intermediate level of English (or basic Spanish for Ecuador).
Application procedure: approximately 12 weeks lead-in time. Interview carried out within 2 weeks.
Other services: all programmes offer comprehensive insurance including third party liability. Agency offers support 24-hours a day via emergency mobile number, pre-departure orientations, on-site counsellor, certified language courses and materials.
Fees: varies greatly according to language course booked (see website).
Contact: Ana Klähn, Programme Manager.

FAMILY AU-PAIR SERVICE
Gernsheimerstr. 38, 12247 Berlin, Germany. ☎+49 30-75 47 97 93. Fax: +49 30-75 47 97 92. E-mail: berlin@family-au-pair-service.de. Website: www. family-au-pair-service.de.
In business since 2000.
Placements: 35 au pairs.
Jobs in: Germany.

Nationalities placed: mainly Polish.
Male applicants can be placed occasionally.
Minimum stay: 6 months; summer placements available.
Wages/pocket money: €260 a month.
Qualifications: ages 18-25. Must be Christian in attitude. Some knowledge of German and childcare references needed.
Application procedure: average processing time 2-3 weeks.
Fees: €50.
Contact: Gabriela Scheffczyk, Owner.

FAMILY AU PAIRS LTD.
62 Newlands Avenue, Didcot, Oxon OX11 8PY. ☎/fax: 01235 819918. E-mail: liz@familyaupairs.com or admin@familyaupairs.com. Website: www.familyaupairs.com.
Placements: au pairs and au pairs plus only.
Jobs in: UK only.
Nationalities placed: must be from an EU country.
About 1% of applicants placed are male.
Minimum stay: 3-24 months, including summer placements.
Wages/pocket money: £55 a week for a standard au pair, £75 for au pair plus.
Qualifications: ages 19-27. Must have fair to good English and childcare experience consisting of babysitting, helping in kindergarten, orphanages, etc. or caring for younger brothers and sisters, nieces and nephews. Must be from an EU country.
Application procedure: depending on applicant's experience and level of English a placement can be found within 4 -6 weeks. References are required and agency will wish to speak to an English speaking referee.
Fees: nil.
Contact: Liz Walter, Manager.

FAMILY CONNECTIONS
7 Oak Court, Bowlas Avenue, Four Oaks, Sutton Coldfield, West Midlands, B74 2TT; or 5 Warstone Meadows, Bewdley, Worcestershire, DY12 1HT. ☎ (Head Office) 0870 888 3092; Worcs. office: 01299 402855. Fax: 0870 888 3093 / Worcs 01299 402855. E-mail: kate@familyconnections.co.uk, clare@familyconnections.co.uk, connections22@aol.com. Website: www.familyconnections.co.uk.
In business since 2002. Member of IAPA.
Placements: 300 au pairs, nannies, housekeepers, nursery nurses, babysitters and holiday rep nannies.
Jobs in: UK. Nanny positions in winter and summer resorts abroad with two major tour operators.
About 50% of applicants placed are male.
Minimum stay: 6 months; summer placements available.
Wages/pocket money: £65 a week.
Qualifications: must have some experience with children.
Application procedure: average processing time for au pairs 2-3 weeks, variable for nannies.
Fees: nil.
Contact: Kate Whitney, Director.

FAMILY FIRST INTERNATIONAL
10 Stoke Mill Close, Woking Road, Guildford, Surrey GU1 1QZ. ☎/fax: 01483 570305. E-mail: diana@nannyagencyuk.com. Website: www.nannyagencyuk.com.

In business since 1991.
Placements: nannies and mother's helps.
Jobs in: UK.
Nationalities placed: specialise in placing Australians, New Zealanders, South Africans and Canadians with working holiday visas, but others can be placed also. Male applicants can rarely be placed.
Minimum stay: 6-24 months. Summer stays of 2-3 months can be made.
Wages/pocket money: £200+ per week for mother's helps; £250+ for nannies (more in London).
Qualifications: ages 18-35. Must have impeccable references, medical certificate and solid childcare experience.
Application procedure: all applicants are interviewed either in UK or by partner agents in Australia, etc. References are checked. Police certificate required by foreign nationals. All applicants must submit medical certificates, photos, 2 references and life story.
Other services: maintain contact and offer advice.
Fees: nil.
Contact: Mrs. Diana Chadwick, Proprietor.

FAMILY MATCH LTD.
37-39 Southgate Street, Winchester, Hampshire SO23 9EH. ☎01962 855799. Fax: 01962 840246. E-mail: Karen@familymatch.com. Website: www.familymatch.com.
In business since 1992. Member of REC.
Placements: 300 nannies, mother's helps, housekeepers, maternity nurses and nursery staff.
Jobs in: UK (London and Southwest).
Minimum stay: most positions are permanent (full or part-time).
Wages/pocket money: £50-£60 net per day.
Qualifications: must have some childcare experience. 2 written references required, including one from most recent position. Nannies should have driving licence, diploma/certificates and first aid certificate if applicable. Overseas nannies must speak good English.
Application procedure: 1-hour face-to-face interview compulsory. Original documentation will be checked. Enhanced CRB check will be done (£34 fee).
Contact: Karen Dixon, Managing Director.

FAMILY MATCH AU PAIRS AND NANNIES
PO Box 6406, Kincumber, Sydney, NSW 2251, Australia. ☎/fax: +61 2-4363 2500. E-mail: info@familymatch.com.au. Website: www.familymatch.com. au.
In business since 1994. On-line service that matches au pairs/nannies with families in Australia and worldwide.
Placements: au pairs, mother's helps and nannies.
Jobs in: host families throughout Australia and worldwide.
Nationalities placed: any that are eligible for a working holiday visa or a student temporary residents visa. Applicants from the USA are eligible for a Special Program Visa 416. Male applicants cannot be placed.
Minimum stay: 3 months. Summer placements very common.
Wages/pocket money: live-in au pairs receive full board plus A$6 per duty hour. A$150-$180 per week for 20-30 hours of helping in the family home (normally Monday to Friday).
Qualifications: good childcare experience and knowledge of English needed.
Application procedure: online processing takes from 24 hours.

Fees: nil for au pairs.
Contact: Sheila, Amanda or Gerry Levy, Placement Co-ordinators.

FÉE RÊVÉE
6 rue de Bellevue, 92150 Suresnes, France. ☎/fax: +33 1-41 44 01 85. E-mail: contact@fee-revee.com. Website: www.fee-revee.com.
In business since May 2005. Intending to join IAPA.
Placements: au pairs.
Jobs in: France. Outgoing programme to England, Ireland, Spain, Italy, Germany, Austria and Scotland.
Nationalities placed: all.
Minimum stay: 6 months; summer placements of 1-3 months available.
Wages/pocket money: €70 a week for 30 hours and 2 evenings of babysitting.
Qualifications: ages 18-29. Must be capable of having a basic conversation in host country language. Must have childcare experience (babysitting, previous au pairing, etc.). Non-smokers preferred. Must be motivated to learn the language and have a cultural exchange.
Application procedure: 2 childcare references, 2 character references, a 'dear host family' letter, copy of any diplomas, copy of birth certificate and photos. Interviews in office or by phone. Placement normally takes no more than 2 months.
Other services: agency assists both family and au pair in administrative steps. List of French courses and recommended specialist insurance given to au pairs. Replacement family can be arranged if first one is unsuitable. Monthly meetings for all au pairs.
Fees: €60 to register for foreign applicants. French applicants pay the same plus a further €60 at the start of their placement.
Contact: Nathalie Chevallier, Administrator.

FELICITY NANNIES
Ina-Seidel-Bogen 69, 81929 Munich, Germany. ☎+49 89-999 49 644. Fax: +49 89-999 49 645. E-mail: info@felicity-nannies.de. Website: www.felicity-nannies.de.
In business since May 2004.
Placements: mainly fully qualified and experienced nannies; occasionally au pair placements.
Jobs in: 60% in Germany and neighbouring German-speaking countries. 40% in the rest of Europe, especially Switzerland, Italy and the UK, and also Spain, France, Belgium and the Netherlands.
Nationalities placed: British applicants are requested more often than othe English-speaking nationalities.
Almost no male applicants are placed.
Minimum stay: mainly permanent posts, but occasional temporary ones.
Wages/pocket money: average starting salary for qualified nannies (live-in, full-time 40 h.p.w.) from €1,515 per month net; salaries for live-out nannies start at €1,700 per month. Possible extra perks include use of car, mobile phone, own PC, separate bathroom, separate nanny flat and pension plan. Au pair's monthly pocket money is €260 plus a transport ticket and health insurance.
Qualifications: ideal candidate is in her mid-20s, has got a professional nanny training (NNEB or equivalent), and has worked for 2-4 years in a private household (preferably international) as a sole charge nanny. It is an advantage if the nanny can prove that she has stayed with previous employers for a few years, as most families look for a long-term solution. Further requests are: excellent, checkable references, sole charge experience, first aid certificate, driving license (international preferred), valid police-check, ability to swim well, non-smoker, overseas experience, and at least knowledge of one further language other than English. Newborn experience is very often requested. Nannies should be flexible

to the family requirements, open-minded and communicative.

Application procedure: applicants to fill in a comprehensive Nanny Profile. All references are checked personally by phone or in writing. Nannies will be expected to explain any gaps in their CVs. If the nanny is located in or around Munich (or willing to travel) an in–depth personal interview of about an hour is held. Occasionally personal interviews can be scheduled in the UK.

Other services: bilingual (German and English) staff. Ongoing support offered after employment has started and guidance for employees and employers in the event of any problems. Conflict management talks can be mediated by Felicity Nannies for both parties in the event of some internal irritations. If requested, agency offers a three-month-review after start date. Agency also organises Nanny Nights Out to facilitate the meeting of other childcare specialists in the Munich area. English-language orientation materials available for Munich including information about leisure activities for English-speaking people, explanation of the local public transport system and so on.

Fees: nil.

Contact: Mirja Lindberg, Manager.

FRANCE AU PAIR EUROJOB

B.P. 89, 6 allée des Saules, 17420 Saint-Palais-sur-Mer, France. ☎+33 5-46 23 99 88. Fax: +33 5-46 38 75 11. E-mail: contact@eurojob.fr. Website: www. eurojob.fr.

In business since 1996. Member of IAPA and UFAAP (Union Francaise des Associations Au Pair).

Placements: 1,000 au pairs and work placements (e.g. hotels and restaurants).

Jobs in: France; also outgoing programme to Europe (Spain, Italy, Germany, Austria, England, Ireland, Denmark, Sweden and Greece) and USA. Work placements for French young people in UK/Ireland.

Only 1% of au pairs placed are male.

Minimum stay: 6 months or 2 months in summer.

Wages/pocket money: €80 per week.

Qualifications: minimum age 18. 2 childcare references required. Must have studied the language of the country chosen for at least 2 years.

Application procedure: processing time normally 3 weeks.

Fees: on application.

GEMS

Unit 4F, Mayfair House, Redburn Road, Westerhope, Newcastle upon Tyne NE5 1NB. ☎0191-286 7210. Fax: 0191-286 5979. E-mail: gems@btconnect. com. Website: www.gemsservices.co.uk.

In business since 1986.

Placements: nannies, mother's helps, housekeepers and domestic helps.

Jobs in: UK only (mainly the North East).

Nationalities placed: any that are allowed by Home Office regulations.

No male au pairs have been placed, despite attempts to do so.

Minimum stay: 6 months. Summer placements can be made.

Qualifications: must have knowledge or experience of childcare with relevant qualifications.

Fees: nil.

Contact: C.L. Watts (Proprietor), Mrs. Nicola Jones (Secretary) or Cynthia Dobbie.

GERMAN CATHOLIC SOCIAL CENTRE

Lioba House, 40 Exeter Road, London NW2 4SB. ☎020-8452 8566. Fax: 020-8452 4114. E-mail: germancentre@germancentre.eclipse.co.uk. Website: www.germancentre.org.uk.

In operation since 1952; as a charity since 1976. The UK branch of In Via (see entry).
Placements: 250 au pairs.
Jobs in: England mainly, occasionally Germany and France.
Nationalities placed: mostly German au pairs placed in British families.
Minimum stay: 6 months from January; stays beginning August/September should be for 9-10 months. Summer stays are possible.
Wages/pocket money: £60 per week.
Qualifications: age limits 18-27 years. Childcare experience, basic knowledge of housework and basic knowledge of the language of the host country required.
Application procedure: applicants arrange placement by correspondence (including questionnaire, curriculum vitae, 2 references and health certificate). After arrival in Britain, they can stay in the hostel for a few days and visit the host family (who has enrolled personally with the agency beforehand).
Other services: agency organises social and cultural activities for au pairs, sends out bi-monthly newsletter in German with calendar of events in London, offers counselling services for au pairs and host families and advises on language classes. Lioba House operates as a hostel.
Fees: nil.
Contact: Marion Bettenworth, Director.

GIC EDUCATIONAL CONSULTANTS
Centro Comercial Arenal, Avda. del Pla 126, 2.22, 03730 Jávea (Alicante), Spain. ☎+34 96-646 04 10. Mobile: +34 666-74 53 43. Fax: +34 96-646 20 15. E-mail: ecsl@telefonica.net. Website: www.gic-spain.com.
In business since 1991.
Placements: 400 au pairs.
Jobs in: Spain (all regions); Europe and USA for Spanish au pairs.
Male applicants can sometimes be placed.
Minimum stay: 1 month in summer for au pairs in Spain, 6 months from January, July or September. 6 months for Spaniards in Europe, 12 months in USA. 2 weeks for language tutors.
Wages/pocket money: €55-€60 per week.
Qualifications: should have some childcare experience e.g. babysitting. Must be non-smoker.
Application procedure: if foreign applicants apply directly to agency, must submit an interview report as well as full application form. Otherwise all documents submitted by partner agency, e.g. in UK: The Childcare Solution (see entry). Average processing time is 2-3 months. Applicants should supply email address or fax number to speed up exchange of information. Agency receives phone calls between 10am and 1pm.
Other services: can arrange ISIS insurance policy. Welcome packet sent on arrival with information on language classes. Problems can be discussed at regular gatherings at university coffee shop in Valencia.
Fees: nil to foreign applicants. €250 to Spanish applicants, which covers up to three placements in different countries.
Contact: Pilar Garreta de Nombela-Cesari, Director.

GLOBAL-NANNIES
2/309 Lancaster Rd, Ascot, 4007, Brisbane, Australia. ☎+61 416 139 865. E-mail: admin@global-nannies.com. Website: www.global-nannies.com.
In business since 2004.
Placements: nannies and au pairs. Average of 11 registrations online a day for DIY matches. Also demi pair programme in Australia, in partnership with an international language school.

Jobs in: Australia and international.
Minimum stay: 3 months.
Wages/pocket money: A$150 per week in addition to full room and board.
Qualifications: must have childcare experience and knowledge of target language.
Application procedure: average processing time 2-3 weeks.
Other services: online nanny network chat so nannies can meet others in a new country and online forum for families. Access to tools to help families with the recruitment process e.g. interview questions, templates of working agreement, reference reports, etc.
Fees: US$45 monthly membership fee to access database and contact families and au pairs.
Contact: Helen Renisch, Managing Director.

GLOBETROTTERS EDUCATION CONSULTING INC.
1784 Rosebank Road, Pickering, Ontario, L1V 1P6, Canada. ☎+1 905-839-0090 or 416-839-4420. Fax: +1 905-839-0063. E-mail: laura@globetrotterseducation. ca. Website: www.globetrotterseducation.ca.
In business since 2003. Partner agencies are members of IAPA.
Placements: 50-100 au pairs, demi-pairs, mother's helps.
Jobs in: Spain, Italy, France, UK, Australia, Germany. No incoming programme to Canada.
About 10% of applicants placed are male.
Minimum stay: summer stays the most popular.
Wages/pocket money: £55+ a week.
Qualifications: normally 18-30 with knowledge of English (French study compulsory in France). Some childcare experience helpful. Nationality requirements vary with programmes.
Application procedure: all materials and references are verified. Interviews are required for some countries. Once eligibility is established, matching begins.
Other services: assistance given with travel preparations. 24 hour emergency assistance. Access to solid discounted health insurance.
Fees: US$250 per placement.
Contact: Laura Wood, Senior Education Consultant.

GLOGOVICH AU-PAIR AGENCY
Gransden Cottage, Tydcombe Road, Upper Warlingham, Surrey CR6 9LU. ☎01883 624842. Fax: 01883 624662. E-mail: info@au-pair-agency.com or glogovich.aupair@btinternet.com. Website: www.au-pair-agency.com.
In business since 1995.
Placements: au pairs, au pairs plus and mother's helps.
Jobs in: UK (especially Home Counties).
Nationalities placed: all European nationalities allowed, especially French, Romanian, Spanish, German, Croatian, Bulgarian, Czech, Slovak, Polish, Hungarian and Estonian. Male applicants cannot be placed.
Minimum stay: 3-month summer stays available only if applicants speak good English, have good references and apply early (by April/May). At other times, minimum stay is 6 months.
Wages/pocket money: £55 per week for au pairs working up to 25 hours; au pairs plus working 30 hours will get £70 and those working 35 hours will get £80. Mother's helps earn £90+.
Qualifications: minimum age 17 years. Must like children and be happy to help with housework.
Application procedure: all documents can be faxed, emailed or posted to the agency. Interested host family will then phone candidate and au pair can travel 7-14 days later or

when agreed.
Other services: welcome letter sent upon arrival containing telephone numbers of other au pairs in the vicinity. Free advice given on language classes.
Fees: nil.
Contact: Mrs. Laura Rainbow, Owner.

goAUPAIR
151 East 6100 South, Suite 200, Murray, Utah 84107, USA. ☎801-255-7722 or 1-888-AUPAIR1. Fax: 801-255-7782. E-mail: info@goaupair.com. Website: www.goaupair.com.
In business since 1984.
Placements: thousands of au pairs have been placed to date.
Jobs in: USA for non-US citizens. Outdoing programme for American citizens to Italy, Germany, France, Denmark, Sweden, Norway, Netherlands and Belgium.
Nationalities placed: all.
Minimum stay: 1 year in US; 3, 6, 9 or 12 months in other countries.
Wages/pocket money: US$139 per week in US for standard Au Pair Program; $170 per week for Au Pair Plus, $200 a week for Premiere Au Pair (for those that qualify for these). Wages vary among European countries.
Qualifications: aged 18-26 years. Must have childcare experience, knowledge of English and driving licence. Upper age limit is 29 for outgoing American au pairs.
Application procedure: applicants should check website or contact the US office directly.
Other services: arrange visa, health insurance, travel arrangements and provide year long support from a local counsellor.
Fees: vary.
Contact: Tanna Wilson, Director of International Relations (twilson@goaupair.com)

GOOD MORNING EUROPE LTD
Au Pair in Paris, 38 rue Traversière, 75012 Paris, France. ☎+33 1-44 87 01 22. Fax: +33 1-44 87 01 42. E-mail: aupair@good-morning-europe.com. Website: www.good-morning-europe.com.
In business since 1992. Member of UFAAP
Placements: 200+ au pairs,.
Jobs in: France (Paris and area); also UK and USA (for au pairs).
Nationalities placed: no restriction in France.
Male au pairs can be placed but special requirements apply (i.e. good language skills and childcare references, minimum stay 8 months).
Minimum stay: 6 months. Summer stays are available (May to end of September).
Wages/pocket money: €70-€80 per week for au pairs (plus transport pass)
Qualifications: ages 18-29 for au pairs. Must provide childcare references.
Application procedure: processing takes about 2 weeks for EU nationals coming to France, 6 weeks for non-EU to allow for visa applications.
Other services: in Paris, agency organises language classes and au pair club. Au pair meetings scheduled for some Friday evenings.
Fees: €115 for applicants from outside the EU; €75 for EU nationals.
Contact: Jackie Dawson, Director.

GSAP INTERNATIONAL EXCHANGE PROGRAMS
Bgm-Hasberg Str. 41, 25767 Bunsoh, Germany. ☎+49 4835 972790. Fax: +49 4835 972791. E-mail: greis@gsap.info. Website: www.gsap.info.
In business since 2000. Member of Aupair-Society e.V.
Placements: 150 incoming au pairs, 80 outgoing au pairs.

Jobs in: Germany. Outgoing programme to USA, England, Australia and Europe.
About 5% of applicants placed are male.
Minimum stay: 6-12 months; summer placements seldom arranged.
Wages/pocket money: €260 per month plus insurance.
Application procedure: references required. Average processing time 2-4 weeks.
Other services: all host families pay for insurance. All au pairs attend language schools. Au pair meetings and trips (including to Paris, Rome and Amsterdam) are organised. Serious back-up offered.
Fees: nil.
Contact: Angela Greis-Siebert, Managing Director.

HAPPY FAMILY AUPAIRS
Rotterdamse Rijweg 9, 3043 BE Rotterdam, Netherlands. ☎+31 10-478 1470. Fax: +31 10-476 0186. E-mail: info@happyfamilyaupairs.nl. Website: www. happyfamilyaupairs.nl.
In business since 2005.
Placements: au pairs.
Jobs in: Netherlands only.
Nationalities placed: all.
About 10% of applicants placed are male.
Minimum stay: mostly 1 year.
Wages/pocket money: €300 a month.
Qualifications: maximum age 25. Must have childcare experience and good knowledge of English.
Application procedure: agency interviews all families in their homes, meets the children and inspects the au pair's room. Most applicants come through partner agencies, but direct applications are considered. References checked and telephone interviews held (to check on level of English).
Other services: families pay for the au pair's full medical insurance for the duration of his/her stay (about €50 per month) as well as for a language course (to a maximum of €275, provided the au pair finishes the full course and stays with the family for a minimum of 6 months). Also families contribute to air/bus fare (negotiable with the family).
Fees: nil.
Contact: Lotty du Pont, Owner.

HELI GRANDJEAN PLACEMENTS AU PAIR
Chemin de Relion 1E, C.P. 4, 1245 Collonge-Bellerive, Switzerland. ☎+41 22-752 38 23. E-mail: grandjean@geneva-link.ch.
In business since 1992.
Placements: 10-20 au pairs.
Jobs in: Switzerland (French-speaking part), France (around Geneva) and England for Swiss au pairs.
Nationalities placed: Western European, Canadian and American.
Male applicants can sometimes be placed.
Minimum stay: 1 year normally; 6 months from January to June. 5-10 summer placements lasting 3-4 months are available.
Wages/pocket money: SFr500-800 per month.
Qualifications: ages 17-30.
Application procedure: application form, reference from teacher and/or previous employer, photos and 'dear family' letter needed.
Other services: written agreement setting out duties is sent to au pairs before they leave home. Assistance/advice with work permit and insurance given. All au pairs are contacted by agent after first fortnight to make sure all is well. New family is found if arrangement is

unsatisfactory. Agency provides list of addresses of other au pairs.
Fees: nil.
Contact: Heli Grandjean, Proprietor.

HELPING HANDS CAREGIVER SERVICES
309 Davis Drive, Newmarket, Ontario L3Y 2N6, Canada. ☎+1 905-853-4752. E-mail:helpinghandsagency@rogers.com.Website:www.helpinghandscanada.com.
In business since 2003.
Placements: nanny (childcare), au pair, caregiver (senior care). 2-5 placements per week.
Jobs in: Canada, especially York Region (near Toronto). A few outgoing placements on a request basis.
No male placements.
Nationalities placed: all that are eligible, especially Italian.
Minimum stay: 1 month; summer placements available.
Wages/pocket money: C$800-$1,300 net per month (after deductions for room and board plus taxes).
Qualifications: applicants must meet the requirements of the Live-in Caregiver Program.
Application procedure: application/resumé package includes a questionnaire found on agency website, a general personal letter to the employers, photos of the caregiver with and without previous charges, and copies of certificates and degrees. Once selection by a Canadian employer has taken place, it takes approximately 3-5 months to process the paperwork.
Other services: agency provides free in-house training (of up to 1 week) for those who feel they would benefit. Meals and accommodation provided free during training period.
Fees: registration fee C$250. Further fees vary according to length of work permit required, but on average C$1,500. No fees apply if candidate already has valid work permit and is currently working in Canada.
Contact: Mrs. Deryn Nicole Rizzi, Owner.

HOUSE-O-ORANGE AU PAIRS
Oostduinlaan 115, 2596 JJ The Hague, Netherlands. ☎+31 70-324 5903. Fax: +31 70-324 5913. E-mail: house-o-orange@planet.nl. Website: www.house-o-orange.nl. Co-operates with Belgian agency Home from Home in Antwerp (www.homefromhome.be).
In business since July 2000.
Placements: au pairs, au pairs plus and a few nannies inbound to the Netherlands and Belgium. Outbound placement of au pairs as well.
Jobs in: Netherlands and Belgium for incoming au pairs; UK, USA, Canada, Spain, France, Germany, Austria, Ireland, Australia, New Zealand and Scandinavia for Dutch au pairs.
Nationalities placed: inbound placement of EU nationals, South Africans, Americans (who must apply directly), Canadians, Australians, New Zealanders, East Europeans, Latin Americans and others.
Some placements available for male applicants.
Minimum stay: 1-3 months minimum but a longer commitment (9-12 months) is strongly preferred. No demand for summer au pairs.
Wages/pocket money: €340 minimum in Netherlands, €450 per month in Belgium (for 20 h.p.w.).
Application procedure: application form, 'dear host' letter, personal interview, references, reference check, clean criminal record, medical check and photos are generally required.
Other services: inbound au pairs are given contact details of other au pairs to contact and the agency hosts a message board for au pairs to make contact with each other. Every month the Orange Au Pair Club organises activities and meetings for au pairs in Holland

and Belgium. Only au pairs placed by House-o-Orange are members of the club. Nannies will be advised on how to obtain a sofi number and register with the tax office.
Fees: nil for incoming; €200 for outgoing.
Contact: Ellen Heesen-Hiemstra, Director.

HUTCHINSON'S
3rd Floor, 25 Thurloe St, South Kensington, London SW7 2LQ. ☎020-7581 0010. Fax: 020-7581 1011. E-mail: info@hutchinsons-staff.com. Website: hutchinsons-staff.com.
In business since 1987.
Placements: professional nannies.
Jobs in: UK (London and country), Europe, Far East and Middle East.
Male positions are sometimes available.
Minimum stay: 1 year.
Wages/pocket money: from £300 net per week.
Qualifications: minimum 2 years live-in experience.
Application procedure: interviews held. All previous references are checked.
Fees: nil.

HYDE PARK INTERNATIONAL LTD
Belmont House, The Dean, Alresford, Near Winchester, Hampshire SO24 9BQ. ☎/fax: 01962 733466. E-mail: info@hyde-park-int.co.uk. Website: www. hyde-park-int.co.uk.
In business since 1982. Member of REC.
Placements: nannies, nanny/housekeepers and maternity nurses.
Jobs in: UK especially London and the Home Counties; also Europe (France, Spain, Italy, Germany, Belgium, Scandinavia), Middle East, Turkey, America, etc.
Nationalities placed: all, provided they are experienced or qualified and have appropriate working visas.
Male positions are rarely available, though agency is prepared to try.
Minimum stay: normally 1 year, though some temporary placements are available.
Wages/pocket money: £250-£450 depending on age and experience.
Qualifications: must have formal qualification or recent relevant experience. Driving licence almost always essential.
Application procedure: interview compulsory. References are checked. Nanny meets prospective family beforehand in all cases.
Fees: nil.
Contact: Samantha Scott (Nanny Division) or Libby Chant (Household Division), Directors.

IAPO UK (INTERNATIONAL AU PAIR ORGANISATION)
Suite 2, 37 Great Russell St, London WC1B 3PP. ☎020-7580 3106. Fax: 0870 762 2149. E-mail: info@iapo.org. Website: www.au-pair.org and www.iapo. org.
In business since 1994. Affiliated to Languages Studies Network Ltd. with partner agencies in a number of Eastern European countries, Germany. USA and Turkey (see next entry for ICEP).
Placements: 600 au pairs.
Jobs in: UK, France, Spain, Italy, USA, Turkey and Germany.
Nationalities placed: EU.
About 2% of applicants placed are male.
Minimum stay: 6 months. Summer au pairs are placed.
Wages/pocket money: £55+ per week.

Qualifications: ages 17-27 and unmarried.
Application procedure: interviews required by local agencies in Europe. Average time to make placements is about 2 weeks.
Other services: au pairs' house in London available for use in emergencies. Social activities and outings arranged for au pairs in London.
Fees: on application.
Contact: Celemet Yener, Placement Co-ordinator.

ICEP - INTERNATIONAL CULTURAL EXCHANGE PROGRAMS
Yuksel Cd. 9/10, Kizilay, Ankara, Turkey. ☎+90 312-418 4460. Fax: +90 312-418 4461. E-mail: ankara@icep.org.tr. Website: www.icep.org.tr.
In business since 1984. IAPA member since 2005. Closely associated with IAPO (above).
Placements: 150 au pairs and nannies.
Jobs in: Turkey; also Turkish au pairs sent to England.
Nationalities placed: EU citizens.
No male applicants can be placed.
Minimum stay: 1-12 months for au pairs in Turkey. Summer placements can be made.
Wages/pocket money: minimum €150 for au pairs, minimum €1000 per month for nannies.
Qualifications: ages 18-28. Good knowledge of English essential.
Application procedure: interviews not required. Average processing time of applications is 2 months. Partner agency in UK is IAPO UK (see address above) though it is concerned mainly with placing Turkish au pairs in the UK.
Other services: part-time jobs are offered, and advice on available classes.
Fees: nil.
Contact in Turkey: Ms. Hande Demirel, Programme Co-ordinator.
Contact in UK: Mr. Celemet Yener, Programme Co-ordinator.

IDEAL NANNIES
4 Stilehall Parade, Chiswick High Road, London W4 3AG. ☎020-8994 5888. Fax: 020-8994 9222. E-mail: info@idealnannies.com. Website: www. idealnannies.com.
In business since 1988.
Placements: nannies, mother's helps and maternity nurses.
Jobs in: UK and overseas.
Nationalities placed: any that are allowed by immigration regulations.
Very few male placements made.
Minimum stay: 1 year.
Wages/pocket money: mother's helps earn £200-£300 per week.
Qualifications: minimum ages 18. Must speak fluent English. Good childcare qualifications or experience essential with references.
Application procedure: all candidates must be interviewed and their references checked.
Other services: full back-up service including introductions to other people.
Fees: nil.
Contact: Karen Murphy, Proprietor.

IMPERIAL NANNIES
17 Radley Mews, Kensington, London W8 6JP. ☎020-7795 6220. Fax: 020-7937 2251. E-mail: nannies@imperialstaff.com. Website: www.imperialnannies.com.
In business since 1996. Member of REC.
Placements: large number of nannies, maternity nurses, mother's helps and all other types of domestic staff.
Jobs in: UK (live-in and daily) and overseas.

Nationalities placed: any that are allowed by immigration regulations.
Minimum stay: temporary and permanent positions.
Qualifications: applicants must have a minimum of two years childcare experience or a relevant nanny qualification plus one year of childcare experience.
Application procedure: personal interviews compulsory. Candidates must provide excellent references, CRB clearance, and verified background.
Contact: Katherine Shields, Manager.

Nannies, Maternity Nurses, Mothers Helps, Au pairs and all Domestic Staff

Providing the very best for your children

We specialise in placing the very best, qualified and experienced childcarers with families in London, the country and overseas. All candidates are personally interviewed, CRB checked, have verified backgrounds with excellent references. Discuss your requirements with our experienced consultants in complete confidence.

Call now on 020 7795 6220

REF: A&NG   View website for our full list of updated vacancies at www.imperialnannies.com

RE C
Recruitment &
Employment
Confederation

☆ Imperial Nannies

17 Radley Mews, Kensington, London W8 6JP
nannies@imperialstaff.com · High St Ken ⊖

INSTITUT EURO'PROVENCE
69 Rue de Rome, 13001 Marseille, France. ☎+33 4-91 33 90 60. Fax: +33 4-91 33 77 36. E-mail: euro.provence@wanadoo.fr. Website: http://perso. wandadoo.fr/euro.provence.
In business since 1989. Non-profit-making association.
Placements: 100 au pairs.
Jobs in: France mainly (Marseille area); send a few au pairs to England, Italy, Spain, Australia and several others.
Nationalities placed: all.
About 5% of applicants placed are male.
Minimum stay: 6-18 months. Only a few summer placements can be made.
Wages/pocket money: minimum €65 per week au pairs (30 hours). Note that families pay a further €150+ a month to the government for social security. Families also provide medical insurance.
Qualifications: ages 18-30. Childcare experience needed.
Application procedure: agency work on average 10-15 hours on each application dossier.
Other services: French classes offered at Institut Euro'Provence. Free social-cultural activities such as museum visits and monthly Provençal meal. Activities organised every day.
Fees: €70 (unless they have paid to register with partner agency in home country).

INTER AU PAIR
Aasstubben 68, 0381 Oslo, Norway. ☎+47 22 52 15 60. Fax: +47 22 50 37 44. E-mail: interaup@online.no. Website: none.
In business since 1992.
Placements: 30-40 au pairs.
Jobs in: Norway (mostly). Outgoing placements in England, Germany, Switzerland, France, Italy, Spain, Austria, etc.
Minimum stay: 6 months; no summer placements available.
Wages/pocket money: NOK 3,000 per month (approx   €375) plus membership of

Norwegian health system *(Trygdekasse)* and less some tax.
Qualifications: must have some experience with children.
Application procedure: average processing time 2-3 weeks.
Other services: agency asks families to help au pair find language course.
Fees: nil, though non-EU au pairs must pay at €100 fee to the Embassy.
Contact: Titti Hartmann, Leader.

INTERCLASS
c/ Bori i Fontestá 14, 6° 4°, 08021 Barcelona, Spain. ☎+34 93-414 29 21. Fax: +34 93-414 29 31. E-mail: info@interclass.es. Website: www.interclass.es.
In business since 1987.
Placements: au pairs, demi pairs and mother's helps. Also work study programmes, hotel and business training, workcamps, etc.
Jobs in: Spain; also England, Ireland, Austria, Belgium, France, Germany, USA, Australia and New Zealand.
Nationalities placed: European.
Male au pairs can be placed in UK and Germany if they have childcare experience on their CV.
Minimum stay: 6 months. Summer stays: 2-3 months.
Wages/pocket money: €60 per week for au pairs; €50 for demi pairs; €84 for mother's helps.
Application procedure: references from teachers and families needed.
Other services: can recommend language schools. Insurance can be arranged.
Fees: €66.
Contact: Pilar, or Fanny Tarré, Programme Director.

INTERLINK
Breton 17, Pral. Izda, 50005 Zaragoza, Spain. ☎+34 976-569358. Fax: +34 976-563745. E-mail: info@interlink-idiomas.com. Website: www.interlink-idiomas.com.
In business since 1994. Member of IAPA.
Placements: 150 au pairs.
Jobs in: Spain; also outgoing programme to Europe and USA.
No male placements.
Minimum stay: 6 months. 2-month summer placements can be made.
Wages/pocket money: €60 per week.
Other services: insurance and flight tickets available though Interlink.
Fees: nil for incoming au pairs. €200 charged to Spaniards on outgoing programme.
Contact: Teresa Santafe.

INTERMEDIATE
Via Bramante 13, 00153 Rome, Italy. ☎+39 06-57 47 444/06-573 00 683. Fax: +39 06-573 00 574. E-mail: aupair@intermediateonline.com. Website: www. intermediateonline.com.
In business since 1990. Member of IAPA.
Placements: 100+ au pairs, au pairs plus, mother's helps and nannies.
Nationalities placed: mainly EU nationals, Americans and Canadians.
Jobs in: Italy, and USA and Europe for Italians (England, France, Germany and Netherlands). Work/study programmes in England.
Agency tries to place male applicants.
Minimum stay: 6 months. Summer stays of minimum 1 month (August) to 3 months are available.
Wages/pocket money: €275 per month for 30 hours of work a week up to €375 for 40

h.p.w. Monthly transport ticket also provided by family.
Qualifications: minimum age 18. Experience of childcare essential.
Other services: Intermediate has its own language school with library in the central Aventino district of Rome (on metro line B). School has programme of visits and excursions. Non-intensive course comprises two 2-hour sessions a week for 8 weeks at a cost of €208. Art history course also offered. Agency organises regular meetings, excursions and social events like a Christmas party and Easter brunch.
Fees: €200.

INTERNATIONAL CATHOLIC SOCIETY FOR GIRLS (ACISJF)
☎020-8777 8371.
In operation since 1929. English branch of the Association Catholique Internationale des Services de la Jeunesse Feminine with counterparts throughout Europe (e.g. In Via in Germany).
Placements: au pairs.
Jobs in: UK.
Nationalities placed: Europeans (in accordance with Home Office regulations).
Minimum stay: 9 months (September-June/July); sometimes 6 months (January-July). Summer stays are available in France.
Wages/pocket money: £55 per week.
Qualifications: minimum age 18 years, though most families prefer older au pairs. Childcare experience required, driving licence an asset. Good basic knowledge of English is essential.
Application procedure: initial enquiries by telephone. Applicants need to submit 2 references (character and childcare experience) plus up-to-date medical certificate and interview if possible. Time to process application is about 2-3 weeks.
Contact: Andrea Watson.

INTERNATIONAL NANNIES
PO Box 33-1291, Takapuna, Auckland, New Zealand. ☎+64 9-489 1026. Mob: 21 826211. Fax: +64 9-235 7940. E-mail: info@nznanny.com or internationalnannies@xtra.co.nz. Website: www.nznanny.com or www. nznanny-aupair.co.nz.
In business since 1990.
Placements: au pairs and nannies.
Jobs in: New Zealand; plus outgoing placement overseas of New Zealand nannies, e.g. to USA, Canada, UK, Europe and Middle East.
Qualifications: must have childcare experience.
Application procedure: e-mail agency for application form. 3 childcare references and a medical certificate required.
Other services: travel insurance available via website.
Fees: nil.
Contact: Louise Munro, Owner.

INTERNATIONAL NANNIES SERVICES
Overseas Division, Box 5030, Alphington, Victoria 3078, Australia. ☎+61 1300 854624. Fax: +61 3-9499 8266. E-mail: nannies@bigfoot.com.au. Website: www.mothersdreamteam.com.au or www.nannyplacements.com.
In business since 1988. Also trading as Placement Solutions (Domestic Division) and Mothers Dream Team Pty Ltd. Member of NICA (National In-home Care Association).
Placements: nannies and mother's helps.
Jobs in: Australia and England.
Male applicants can be placed if they are suitably qualified as nannies.

Minimum stay: 3 months. Summer stays are available. Staff coming to Australia need to be aware of visa restrictions and be prepared to purchase own car for live-out work.
Wages/pocket money: A$15.60-$25 per hour in Australia; rates depend on qualifications.
Qualifications: minimum age 19. Nannies must have 2 years childcare experience. First aid, police clearance certificate and a drivers licence needed.
Application procedure: initial screening by telephone or email; all nannies are given personal interview either in UK or Australia. 6-page application form and 45-minute interview covering hypothetical situations.
Other services: advice given to local candidates travelling to England. Professional development and social activities held four times a year. Newsletter for staff and clients. Accredited national childcare training specially developed for nanny stream.
Fees: A$150-$300 for UK (discounts for nannies already working for agency).
Contact: Louise Dunham, Managing Director.

INTERNATIONAL STUDY VACATION
Via Cartoleria 16/A, 40124 Bologna, Italy. ☎+39 051-272435. Fax: +39 051-296 5364. E-mail: sabrina.masotti@libero.it or info@viaggiaelavora.it. Website: www.viaggiaelavora.it.
In business since 2001. Plans to affiliate to IAPA.
Placements: au pairs and au pairs plus. Also demi pairs in London and Sydney.
Jobs in: England, Ireland, France, Germany, USA and Australia.
No male au pairs are placed.
Minimum stay: short summer placements available e.g. 1 month in France, 2-3 months in England and Ireland.
Wages/pocket money: from £55 a week. More for more hours.
Qualifications: ages 18-27.
Application procedure: average processing time 2-3 weeks.
Fees: from €300.
Contact: Sabrina Masotti, Director.

INTERNATIONAL WORKING HOLIDAYS (IWH)
PO Box 303-220 North Harbour, Auckland 1330. Courier address: Suite 400, 453a Mount Eden Road, Auckland, New Zealand. ☎/fax: +64 9-416 5337. E-mail: nannies@nanniesabroad.co.nz. Website: www.nanniesabroad.co.nz.
In business since 1994.
Placements: nannies; also Camp America.
Jobs in: USA, Canada, UK.
Nationalities placed: New Zealand residents only (since they must be interviewed in person).
About 1% of nannies placed are male.
Minimum stay: 12 months.
Wages/pocket money: up to US$200 a week in USA plus study allowance, subsidised airfares and medical insurance. Up to £250 for nannies placed in the UK depending on experience. All jobs are live-in.
Qualifications: practical childcare experience needed.
Application procedure: processing time depends on speed with which visas are processed (Canada can take 6 months to issue a visa). Personal interviews compulsory.
Fees: none for USA; NZ$50 for Canada and the UK.
Contact: Vicki Kenny, Owner & Recruitment Manager.

INTER-SEJOURS
179 rue de Courcelles, 75017 Paris, France. ☎+33 1-47 63 06 81. E-mail: aideinfo.intersejours@wanadoo.fr. Website: http://asso.intersejours.free.fr.

Metro: Péreire-Maréchal Juin.

Placements: 900 au pairs, demi pairs and au pairs plus per year. Also work placements for European people in hotels/restaurants in England and Spain (Balearics).

Jobs in: au pair in France; plus UK, Ireland, Denmark, Belgium, Netherlands, Sweden, Germany, Austria, Spain, Italy, USA, Canada, Australia and New Zealand.

Nationalities placed: all accepted for France. Outgoing programme for EU nationals.

Minimum stay: 6 months in France, preferably a school year. Summer stays: 2 months minimum. Minimum in other countries of 2 months during summer and 3 months during the rest of the year.

Wages/pocket money: from €300 per month in France.

Qualifications: age limits 18-27 years. Childcare experience helpful but not necessary.

Application procedure: 3 ID photos, medical certificate, 2 references (character, school) and an introductory letter are needed. In the case of au pairs from outside the EU, their birth certificate must be translated into French and certified. The waiting period is usually 1 month, though sometimes families can be found within a fortnight.

Other services: agency can advise on language schools; non-EU au pairs must attend language classes in France. Also organise internships in Ireland, voluntary work in Latin America, etc.

Fees: €130; €170-€180 for outgoing.

Contact: Marie-Helen Pierrot, Director.

IN VIA
Katholische Mädchensozialarbeit, Deutscher Verband e.V., Karlstr. 40, D-79104 Freiburg, Germany. ☎+49 761-200206. Fax: +49 761-200638. E-mail: aupair.invia@caritas.de. Website: www.invia.caritas.de or www.aupair-invia. de. Branches in most German cities.

In operation since 1905. Affiliated to international Catholic organisation ACISJF.

Placements: about 2,500 au pairs.

Au pair placements in: Germany; plus German au pairs sent to French-speaking Belgium, UK, Ireland, France, Italy, Spain, Greece and French-speaking Switzerland.

Nationalities placed: all.

Male positions are available.

Minimum stay: 6 months, 1 year preferred. Summer stays are not possible.

Wages/pocket money: €260 per month.

Qualifications: childcare experience required. Age limits 18-24 years. Basic knowledge of language in question indispensable.

Application procedure: at least 1 reference is required; interviews if possible. Average time to process applications is 3 months.

Other services: agency (which has 40 regional offices in Germany) has au pair clubs in several cities in Germany, for example Munich, Stuttgart and Aachen. Host families assume responsibility for insurance. Agency runs website for au pairs www.au-pair-in-deutschland. de.

Fees: nil.

Contact: Marianne Schmidle, Referee for au pair placements. Foreign branches of IN VIA are: German Catholic Social Centre (see entry) and Foyer Porta, 14 rue Pierre Demours, 75017 Paris, France (+33 1-45 72 18 66).

INWOX (INTERNATIONAL WORK EXPERIENCE)
Zum Oberfeld 17, 55286 Wörrstadt, Germany. ☎+49 6732-937735. Fax: +49 6732-937642. E-mail: info@inwox.com. Website: www.inwox.com.

In business since 2001. Member of IAPA and the German Aupair Society.

Placements: about 100 au pairs as well as interns and volunteers.

Jobs in: Germany. Outgoing exchanges to USA, Europe, Peru and Brazil.

About 2%-4% of applicants placed are male.
Minimum stay: 12 months; no summer placements.
Wages/pocket money: €260 a week.
Qualifications: must have some experience with children and knowledge of target language.
Application procedure: varies according to candidate's application from 1 day to 3 months.
Other services: 24 hour emergency hotline. Emergency accommodation provided if necessary. Replacement families can be arranged.
Fees: nil for applicants for au pair in Europe.
Contact: Sandra Leidemer, Owner.

JANET WHITE AGENCY
67 Jackson Avenue, Leeds LS8 1NS. ☎0113-266 6507. Fax: 0113-268 3077. E-mail: info@janetwhite.com. Website: www.janetwhite.com.
In business since 1978. Member of REC, IAPA and BAPAA.
Placements: several hundred au pairs, nannies and mother's helps.
Jobs in: USA (Northern organiser for Au Pair in America, EduCare and Au Pair Extraordinaire, the qualified nanny programme), Canada (qualified nannies only), Europe and UK (especially Yorkshire and Home Counties). Jobs for nannies in European resorts with UK tour operators.
Nationalities placed: British nannies sent abroad; incoming Europeans (in accordance with Home Office regulations) plus Australians, New Zealanders and Canadians already in Britain and with working holiday visas can be placed in the UK.
Minimum stay: from 6 months for au pairs, 1 year for nannies.
Wages/pocket money: £55 per week for au pairs; £90-£150 for mother's helps; £150-£300 for nannies; $100-$200 for the USA.
Qualifications: minimum age 18 years (Au Pair in America 18-26). Nannies need training and/or previous experience. Mother's helps must be confident and have experience with children and household tasks. Incoming au pairs should be prepared to do housework. Driving licence is a big advantage (essential for USA). Non-smoking almost essential.
Application procedure: appropriate form must be completed and references will be checked. All outbound applicants are interviewed. Placement usually made within weeks (except Canada where it takes a few months).
Other services: advice on visas, travel arrangements, insurance and social introductions wherever possible.
Fees: nil.
Contact: Janet White (BA, MREC), Principal.

JCR AUPAIRS AND NANNIES
2/25 Renown Street, Bentleigh, Victoria 3204, Australia. Postal address: PO Box 497, East Bentleigh, Vic 3165, Australia. ☎+61 3-9557 0300. ☎/fax: +61 3-9557 0400. E-mail: sybil@jcraus.com.au. Website: www.jcraus.com.au.
In business since 1991 in Australia and 2000 in New Zealand. Founder member of UAPA. Part of JCR Intercultural Exchange Programs Pty Ltd. Note that JCR is represented in South Africa: JCR Cultural Exchange Programs (Pty) Ltd, Postnet Fourways Mall #88, Private Bag X033, Rivonia, 2128, South Africa (+27 11-464 2975; fax +27 11-464 2973; renee@aupair.co.za; www.jcr.co.za).
Placements: 250+ au pairs, nannies and mother's helps.
Jobs in: Australia and New Zealand. Outbound programme to 13 countries: UK, USA, Austria, Belgium, Denmark, France, Germany, Greece, Italy, Netherlands, Spain, South Africa and Canada.
Nationalities placed: inbound applicants should have working holiday visa.

About 2% of applicants placed are male, though agency wishes more families were prepared to take on men.

Minimum stay: majority are 12 months but 6 months is acceptable to some Australian families. Summer placements can occasionally be made in certain countries in Europe.

Wages/pocket money: A$150-$195 per week net for au pairs, A$200-$250 per week net for mother's helps. From A$250 for live-in nannies. Au pairs in New Zealand earn NZ$150-200 net per week. Rates in other countries vary.

Qualifications: age limits according to visa stipulations. Nannies must have a qualification and good childcare experience. Mother's helps/au pairs need a minimum of 200 hours childcare experience. For Australia, candidates must have English as first or second language.

Application procedure: first step is to fill up pre-application form on agency website. Agency will then make contact and arrange full application procedures. References needed. Processing of applications for Australia and New Zealand can take 4-8 weeks.

Other services: childcare and orientation booklets and JCR T-shirt given on arrival. Language classes arranged. Agency puts au pairs in touch with others in same area. Full back-up and support and ongoing information given to outbound au pairs regarding prospective family, travel arrangements, insurance and visas. Pre-departure orientation, childcare booklet, T-shirt and flight bag all provided.

Fees: US$200 on placement in Australia and New Zealand if applying directly and not through a JCR office overseas.

Contact: Elise Wald or Sybil Touyz, Directors.

JEUNESSE ET NATIONS AU PAIR
49 rue du Lt Cl de Montbrison, 92500 Rueil-Malmaison, France. ☎/fax: +33 1-41 42 16 19. E-mail: info@jn-aupair.org. Website: www.jn-aupair.org.

In business since 2004. Although not a member of IAPA, agency abides by IAPA code of conduct and co-operates mainly with IAPA agencies.

Placements: au pairs.

Jobs in: France. Outgoing programme to UK, Ireland, Germany, Spain, Austria, Italy and Greece.

Minimum stay: 6 months; summer placements available.

Wages/pocket money: €80 a week.

Qualifications: must have some experience with children and have studied the target language for at least 2 years.

Application procedure: personal interviews conducted if applicant is in Paris area, otherwise by phone.

Other services: advice given on language classes and insurance; in France family pays for health insurance.

Fees: nil for incoming au pairs; €200 for outgoing (€70 registration + €130 placement fee).

Contact: Roselyne Demilly, Manager.

JILL HOLLIDAY
15 Boxgrove Avenue, Guildford, Surrey GU1 1XG. ☎01483 563447. Fax: 01483 570976. E-mail: jill@holliday-aupairs.com. Website: www.holliday-aupairs.com

In business since 1977.

Placements: 200-300 au pairs.

Jobs in: UK.

Nationalities placed: as permitted by Home Office.

Minimum stay: 6 months; September/October to June/July preferred. Summer stays available, minimum 2 months preferred.

Wages/pocket money: minimum £55 per week.
Qualifications: ages 17-27. Regular babysitting shows interest and liking for children.
Application procedure: direct applications encouraged; immediate placements always available.
Other services: contact continued with au pairs through letters, advice, help with courses, etc.
Fees: nil.
Contact: Jill Holliday, Owner.

JOB OPTIONS BUREAU
Tourist House, 40-41 Grand Parade, Cork, Ireland. ☎+353 21-427 5369. Fax: +352 21-427 4829. E-mail: info@joboptionsbureau.ie. Website: www. joboptionsbureau.ie.
In business since 1988. Founder member of IAPA.
Placements: au pairs, nannies and parents' helps, as well as work experience.
Jobs available: all over Ireland. Outgoing au pair programme places candidates throughout Europe, USA and Canada.
Nationalities placed: EU nationals.
Very few male positions are available.
Minimum stay: usually 3-12 months. Summer stays 1-3 months.
Wages/pocket money: €80-€100 per week for au pairs in Ireland.
Qualifications: minimum age 18. Practical childcare experience is essential and must be verified by referees. Candidates must be flexible, mature individuals with a genuine interest in caring for children.
Application procedure: must submit 4 passport photos, at least 2 references (one character and one childcare), photos of family and children for whom candidate has cared, medical certificate, copy of driving licence, passport, police clearance check and a copy of birth certificate. All outbound au pairs are interviewed in various locations around Ireland.
Other services: assistance given in organising travel and arranging English classes. Au pairs are given a contact list of other au pairs working in their area. 24-hour back-up support. Graduates can participate in Internship Programme.
Fees: on request.
Contact: Kathy O'Dwyer (Owner/Manager), Marie O'Driscoll (Childcare Co-ordinator).

JOHNSON'S AU PAIRS
28 Trevor Close, Northolt, Middlesex UB5 6ND. ☎020-8728 1074. Fax: 020-8845 0094. E-mail: johnsonsaupairs@hotmail.com. Website: www. johnsonsaupair.com.
In business since 1994.
Placements: au pairs, demi pairs and mother's helps.
Jobs in: Italy, Germany and England (London area); occasionally Spain and other European countries.
Nationalities placed: all that are approved.
Male applicants can sometimes be placed if requested by family.
Minimum stay: 3 months. Summer stays are available.
Qualifications: ages 17-27. Some childcare experience needed.
Application procedure: personal interview carried out if applicant is in same country as family, otherwise telephone interview. Average processing time is 7-10 days.
Fees: nil.
Contact: Gladys Johnson, Company Manager.

JOLAINE AGENCY
18 Escot Way, Barnet, Herts. EN5 3AN. ☎020-8449 1334. Fax: 020-8449 9183. E-mail: aupair@jolaine.prestel.co.uk. Website: www.jolaineagency.com.

In business since 1975.
Placements: 500-800 au pairs, mother's helps and paying guests (groups and individuals). Also elder care.
Jobs in: UK, France, Italy, Spain, Belgium and Hungary. Paying guest stays arranged in the UK, France, Belgium, Spain, Italy and Turkey.
Nationalities placed: according to Home Office list.
Males can sometimes be placed, though it takes much longer.
Minimum stay: minimum 9-month stays. Summer, Easter and Christmas stays occasionally possible, though not as often as previously.
Wages/pocket money: from £55 per week for au pairs; £75 for au pairs plus; £160 for mother's helps,
Qualifications: minimum age 18. Some knowledge of destination language and childcare experience are needed in most cases.
Fees: £40 for placements abroad.
Contact: Mrs. Irene Rendlick, Principal.

JUNO AU PAIRS BEMIDDELINGSBUREAU
Weide 37, 3121 XV Schiedam, Netherlands. ☎+31 10-471 5431. Fax: +31 10-471 7662. E-mail: juno1990@planet.nl. Website: www.junoaupairs.com.
In business since 1990. Member of IAPA.
Placements: 250-300 au pairs mainly; also domestic help for elderly people, etc.
Jobs in: Netherlands and Belgium.
Very few males can be placed (e.g. 2 a year).
Minimum stay: 1 year. Summer stays can be arranged.
Wages/pocket money: €300-€500 per month (in accordance with IAPA guidelines).
Qualifications: ages 18-30. Good childcare experience and some English needed.
Application procedure: placement normally made within 1 month of receiving application. Interviews may be carried out by partner agency in applicant's home country.
Other services: agency makes sure families provide their au pairs with appropriate medical insurance (which includes up to 10 days' stay in a hotel in an emergency). Agency encourages families to contribute to costs of language course.
Fees: €100.
Contact: Dr. Csaba Tarnay, Director.

JUST AU PAIRS
35 The Grove, Edgware, Middlesex HA8 9QA. ☎020-8905 4400. Fax: 020-8905 3838. Email: hil@aupairs.freeserve.co.uk. Website: www.justaupairs.co.uk.
In business (formerly as Au Pairs & Nannies Direct) since 1996. Member of IAPA.
Placements: 500 au pairs and nannies.
Jobs in: 99% UK, one or two sent to Europe.
Nationalities placed: all that are legal.
5%-10% of applicants placed are male.
Minimum stay: normally 6 months; 1 year preferred. 2-3 month summer placements can be made.
Wages/pocket money: £45-£60 per week au pairs; £200-£350 nannies.
Qualifications: must provide references, police check and medical certificate. Ages 17-27. Good childcare experience and some English needed.
Application procedure: multilingual staff. Place only au pairs who have been vetted by partner agencies abroad.
Other services: phone lines covered 365 days a year in case of emergency.
Fees: nil.
Contact: Mrs. Hilary Perry, Proprietress.

JUST FOR KIDS – SYDNEY'S PREMIER CHILD CARE AGENCY
PO Box 865, Manly, NSW 1655, Australia. Street address: Shop 5, 27 Belgrave St, Manly, Sydney, NSW 2095. ☎+61 1300 765 138 or +61 2-9979 1642. Fax: +61 02-9977 1643. E-mail: info@justforkids.net.au. Website: www.justforkids. net.au.

In business since 2004.

Placements: 150 full-time and 300+ short-term nannies, au pairs and babysitters to work full- and part-time.

Jobs in: Australia. Currently setting up networks with foreign agencies to set up incoming and outgoing programmes for nannies.

About 5% of applicants placed are male.

Minimum stay: family stays are generally 6-9 months as this allows at least 3 months travel. Summer placements can be arranged as well.

Wages/pocket money: au pair's weekly wage A$200-A$250 per week. Nannies earn around A$18-A$22 an hour depending on experience.

Qualifications: minimum age 21 with at least 3 years childcare experience or a childcare qualification. Must have satisfactory references and police check.

Application procedure: personal interview is required and applicants must have an up-to-date CV. Applications are processed in 48 hours following satisfactory reference checks, working with children checks and police checks.

Other services: in cases where the agency pays the staff direct they are fully covered for work cover, professional indemnity and public liability. The agency also pay superannuation which can be reclaimed if the nanny leaves the country.

Fees: nil.

Contact: Leah Kelly, Child Care Consultant.

KENSINGTON NANNIES
3 Hornton Place, London W8 4LZ. ☎020-7937 2333. Fax: 020-7937 1027. E-mail: nannies@easynet.co.uk. Website: www.kensington-nannies.com.

In business since 1967. Member of REC.

Placements: nannies and mother's helps (with minimum 2 years experience).

Jobs in: worldwide (except USA).

Male applicants with training and minimum 2 years experience can be placed.

Minimum stay: 1 year for permanent; temporary posts also available.

Wages/pocket money: varies according to experience.

Qualifications: minimum age 20. Must have knowledge of English. Minimum 2 years nannying experience essential.

Application procedure: personal interviews absolutely essential. Minimum 3 references are taken up. Placement takes 7-21 days if suitable vacancy available in country requested.

Other services: insurance and travel can be arranged if client requests it.

Fees: nil.

Contact: Louise Taylor, Overseas Consultant.

KIDDYKARE AU PAIR AGENCY
Cechova 1104, Dvur Kralove nad Labem, 544 01, Czech Republic. ☎+420 605 722 550. E-mail: info@kiddykare.net. Website: www.kiddykare.net.

Placements: au pairs, au pairs plus, au pair couples.

Jobs in: UK, Germany, France and Spain.

About 3% of applicants placed are male.

Minimum stay: 6 months, usually 1 year. Summer placements available.

Wages/pocket money: from £60 a week in the UK, €200-€280 in other countries.

Qualifications: ages 18-27. Checkable childcare references. Knowledge of the language of host country.

Application procedure: average processing time normally 2 months but can be less. Applicant needs two childcare references, a letter of recommendation, a medical record and a police clearance certificate. Interview is not required.
Fees: nil.
Contact: Renata Prochazkova, Director.

KIDZ AU PAIR AGENCY
Upper Pembroke Rd, Passage West, Cork, Ireland. ☎+353 21-485 9738. Fax: +353 21 484 1905. E-mail: info@kidzaupair.com. Website: www.kidzaupair. com.
In business since 2004. Member of IAPA.
Placements per year: 100 au pairs.
Jobs in: Ireland. Outgoing programme to all EU.
No male placements so far.
Minimum stay: 2-3 months; summer placements available.
Wages/pocket money: from €80 a week.
Qualifications: minimum age 18, with reasonably good English. Must like children and have a pleasant personality.
Application procedure: average processing time 2 weeks. Family interviews the au pair over the phone.
Other services: information given on best language classes for their needs. Meetings held once a fortnight for au pairs to meet up.
Fees: nil.
Contact: Orla Sheehan, Company Director.

KINGSBROOK LANGUAGES & SERVICES
Travessera de Gracia 60, 08006 Barcelona, Spain. ☎+34 93-209 37 63. Fax: +34 93-202 15 98. E-mail: aupair@kingsbrookbcn.com. Web-site: www. kingsbrookbcn.com.
In business since 2001. Member of IAPA, FIYTO, GWEA and ALTO.
Placements: 500 au pairs and babysitters; also internships.
Jobs in: Spain. Also outgoing programme to EU and USA.
UK and France.
About 5% of applicants placed are male.
Minimum stay: 2/3 months in summer; 6/9 months in winter.
Wages/pocket money: €200-€400 per month depending on hours worked.
Qualifications: ages 18-27. Should have a basic knowledge of English or Spanish.
Fees: nil for incoming au pairs.
Contact: Andrea Soares, Au Pair Manager.

KNIGHTSBRIDGE NANNIES
London House, 100 New Kings Road, London SW6 4LX. ☎020-7610 9232. Fax: 020-7610 6409. E-mail: info@knightsbridgenannies.com. Website: www. knightsbridgenannies.com.
In business since 1958.
Placements: nannies, mother's helps and housekeepers.
Jobs available: all over the world.
Nationalities placed: no restrictions, provided work permits can be obtained.
Minimum stay: variable.
Qualifications: one year live-in childcare experience and minimum age 20 required for all overseas and UK posts.
Application procedure: interview with agency essential, with family whenever possible. All references are checked.

Fees: nil.
Contact: Julie Bremner, Director.

KONNEX INTERNATIONAL LTD
12 Newall House, Harper Road, London SE1 6QD. ☎020-7407 5437. Fax: 020-7207 9459. E-mail: information@konnexaupairs.com. Website: www. konnexaupairs.com.
In business since 1997.
Placements: au pairs, au pairs plus, mother's helps and nannies.
Jobs in: UK mainly, also Belgium, France, Germany, Italy, Netherlands and USA (in cooperation with the Au Pair Foundation, California).
About 5% of applicants placed are male.
Minimum stay: normally 6 months. Occasionally 3-4 month summer placements can be made.
Wages/pocket money: minimum £55 per week au pairs.
Application procedure: interviews conducted in London or by partner agency abroad. References are checked.
Fees: none.

THE LINGUAVIVA CENTRE
45 Lower Leeson Street, Dublin 2, Ireland. ☎+353 1-678 9384/661 2106. Fax: +353 1-676 5687. E-mail: enquiries@linguaviva.com.
In business since 1977. Member of MEI-RELSA (Recognised English Language Schools Association) and Dublin Tourism.
Placements: au pairs and demi pairs.
Jobs in: Ireland: Greater Dublin area.
Nationalities placed: all.
Males are difficult to place, but it is sometimes possible.
Minimum stay: 6 months. Summer stays: 3 months (available occasionally for EU nationals only).
Wages/pocket money: about €80 per week. Au pairs from EU countries also get a Dublin public transport pass.
Qualifications: age limits 18-25 years, with some flexibility. Must have intermediate English.
Other services: reduced language classes for au pairs (classes at Linguaviva are compulsory for Linguaviva au pairs) currently €540 for 12 weeks (3 classes twice a week) or €1000 for 24 weeks, Agency organises sports and social activities. Open-door policy for dealing with problems.
Fees: €100 (unless they come via partner agency).

LITTLE LAURA'S
57 Common View, Stedham, Midhurst, West Sussex GU29 0NX. ☎/fax: 01730 814757. E-mail: laura.keates@littlelauras.co.uk. Website: www.littlelauras. co.uk.
In business since 2003.
Placements: 100 mother's helps, live-in/daily nannies, maternity nurses and temporary aid.
Jobs in: UK only.
About 3% of applicants placed are male.
Wages/pocket money: £270-£300 a week; £6-£7 an hour.
Qualifications: childcare qualifications, experience, age and sometimes languages.
Application procedure: all nannies are personally interviewed and references checked. CRB checks carried out if applicants do not already have one.

Fees: nil.
Contact: Laura Keates, Manager.

LLOYD'S
32 Kensington Place, Newport, South Wales NP19 8GP.   ☎01633 216710. Freephone 0800 652 2620. Fax: 01633 841230. E-mail: lloydsservices@aol. com. Website: www.lloydsagency.co.uk. Also office in Swansea for West Wales.
In business since 1989.
Placements: nannies, au pairs, parent's helps and all types of employment in private families. Evening babysitting work available to Lloyd's au pairs.
Jobs in: Wales, UK and international (for example Switzerland, Germany, France and Egypt).
Nationalities placed: Europeans in accordance with Home Office regulations.
Male positions are available; agency is committed to equal opportunities.
Summer stays are available.
Wages/pocket money: £55-£60 per week for au pairs.
Qualifications: childcare experience usually required.
Application procedure: application forms can be competed online. Interviews arranged wherever possible.
Other services: agency helps to arrange social activities, outings and weekly meetings. 24-hour telephone line available. Contracts can be issued. Most families registered with Lloyd's pay some or all of the language course fees for au pairs.
Contact: Gaynor Lloyd, Proprietor.

LOLLIPOP CHILDCARE
50 Testwood Road, Windsor, Berkshire SL4 5RW. ☎01753 832124. E-mail: enquiries@lollipopchildcare.co.uk. Website: www.lollipopchildcare.co.uk.
In business since 2003. Member of REC.
Placements: 100 nannies, mother's helps, night nannies, maternity nurses and crèche staff. Many daily live-out positions available.
Jobs in: UK (Home Counties).
Minimum stay: most positions are permanent.
Qualifications: applicants must have at least 2 years professional childcare experience, at least 2 English-speaking referees, a full working visa and must live in the area (Berkshire, South Buckinghamshire, West Middlesex and North Surrey).
Application procedure: one-hour interview at agency office compulsory. Reference checking takes 3-5 days then interviews set up with families. Applicants must provide police check from their country of nationality.
Contact: Rachel Newson, Owner/Director.

THE LONDON NANNY COMPANY
Vicarage House 58-60 Kensington Church Street, London W8 4DB. ☎020-7368 1603. Fax: 020-7361 0077. E-mail: all@londonnannycompany.co.uk. Website: www.londonnannycompany.co.uk.
In business since 1996. Member of REC.
Placements: nannies, maternity nurses and babysitters.
Jobs available: worldwide.
Nationalities placed: must have full working visa.
Minimum stay: 1 week to 1 year or longer.
Wages/pocket money: live-in nannies earn £250-£350 net per week; daily nannies £350-£450 net; maternity nurses £550-£750 gross.
Qualifications: minimum 3 years nannying experience or 2-year professional childcare

qualification.
Application procedure: interviews required and references are checked. Processing takes a few days.
Other services: agency can help with contracts, with putting nannies in touch with each other and with arranging travel and medical insurance overseas.
Fees: nil.
Contact: Christine Black, Managing Director (chris@londonnannycompany.co.uk).

MARKO AU PAIR AGENCY
38 Usk Way, Didcot, Oxfordshire OX11 7SQ. ☎/fax: 01235 519770. Mobile: 0788 166 4014. E-mail: marketa.clements@yahoo.com. Website: www. markoau-pair.com.
In business since 1999.
Jobs in: England only.
Nationalities placed: mainly Czech but any that are allowed by immigration regulations. About 10% of applicants placed are male.
Minimum stay: 3 months for summer placements.
Wages/pocket money: £55 per week.
Qualifications: ages 17-27. Experience with children and knowledge of English needed.
Application procedure: partner agency in Czech Republic carries out recruitment.
Fees: £70-£200.
Contact: Marketa Clements, Proprietor.

MAR'S AU PAIR AGENCY
16 Spencer Road, Chiswick, London W4 3SN. ☎/fax: 020-8995 6594. E-mail: marsaupairagency@btconnect.com.
In business since 1986. Office hours mainly Monday-Friday 9am-1.30pm.
Placements: 200 au pairs and au pairs plus.
Jobs in: London only (West and Southwest).
Nationalities placed: Europeans in accordance with Home Office regulations. A few positions for male caretakers available each year.
Minimum stay: 6 months from January. Summer stays: June/July to August.
Wages/pocket money: basic wage for au pairs £60 per week; au pairs plus £70.
Qualifications: childcare and household experience required, and a reasonable level of English.
Other services: agent brings au pairs in contact with one another, and can assist with finding a suitable English course. Agency can communicate in Dutch, French and Spanish as well as English.
Fees: nil.
Contact: Marianne Walsh van Elburg, Managing Director.

MARY POPPINS AU PAIR COLLEGE AND PLACEMENT AGENCY
Cape Town Teacher Centre, Molteno Rd, PO Box 44460, Claremont, Cape Town, South Africa ☎+27 21-674 6689. Mobile: +27 834541282. Fax: +27 21-674 4041. E-mail: mpoppins@telkomsa.net. Website: Under construction.
In business since 1998 as a college and 1999 as a recruitment agency. Accredited by the ETDP-SETA (Educational & Training Development Practices) of South Africa.
Placements: on average 7 placements per month of domestic workers, childminding staff, teachers and student nannies/au pairs.
Jobs in: South Africa. Also interview for Au Pair in America and have affiliation with a British agency with occasional placements in Holland, Germany and (rarely) France.
Nationalities placed: all provided they have valid work permit. In practice very few foreigners because of visa difficulties.

Male applicants can rarely be placed (1 in past 2 years).
Minimum stay: 12 months. Could arrange temporary placements over our summer holidays.
Wages/pocket money: R35-R50 per hour and R350-R500 per day.
Qualifications: minimum age 20. English first language, other languages a bonus. Must have childcare experience and/or qualifications, good references and verifiable employment history for past 2-5 years. 95% of positions require a car owner and driver.
Application procedure: interviews compulsory.
Other services: orientation workshop for prospective candidates to prepare them for what South African families will expect of them and what will be acceptable behaviour, etc. Agency ensures contract is in place and is available 24 hours for telephone support.
Fees: €65 per application.
Contact: Ilse Liebenberg, Owner/Director.

MB SCAMBI CULTURALI
Via San Biagio 13, 35121 Padua, Italy. ☎+39 049-875 5297. Fax: +39 049-664186. E-mail: info@mbscambi.com. Website: www.mbscambi.com.
In business since 1989.
Placements: 30-40 au pairs.
Jobs in: UK, Ireland, France, Germany, Spain and USA; no incoming programme in Italy.
Nationalities placed: mainly Italian.
Minimum stay: 3-6 months. Summer placements can be made 3 months minimum.
Application procedure: 2-hour interview required.
Fees: €300 (may vary with country of destination).

MILLENNIUM AU PAIRS & NANNIES
The Coach House, The Crescent, Belmont, Sutton, Surrey SM2 6BP. ☎020-8241 9752. Fax: 020-8643 1268. E-mail: info@millenniumaupairs.co.uk. Website: www.millenniumaupairs.co.uk.
In business since 1998. Founder member of BAPAA. Full member of IAPA.
Placements: 500 au pairs, mother's helps, live-in nannies and housekeepers.
Jobs in: mainly UK; some jobs in Western Europe for British nationals.
Nationalities placed: any permitted by immigration regulations.
Less than 5% of applicants placed are male.
Minimum stay: 6-12 months. Minimum 3 months in summer.
Wages/pocket money: £55-£80 per week for au pairs, £130-£200 for mother's helps and £200-£350 for qualified nannies.
Qualifications: minimum age 18. Childcare and housework experience, and reasonable command of the language of the target country (no beginners) needed.
Application procedure: personal interview held where possible; otherwise by phone. At least 2 good childcare references required.
Fees: free placement in the UK; £50 non-refundable for placements outside the UK.
Contact: Jackie Gallacher, Director.

MIX CULTURE ROMA
Via Nazionale 204, 00184 Rome, Italy. ☎+39 06-474 6914. Fax: +39 06-478 26 164. E-mail: helena@scudit.net. Website: http://web.tiscali.it/mixcultureroma.
In business since 1989. Part of Scuola d'Italiana Roma which offers courses in the Italian language and culture to foreigners.
Placements: 50-100 au pairs.
Jobs in: Italy; also outgoing to EU countries.
Nationalities placed: EU.
About 5% of applicants placed are male.
Minimum stay: September-June or January-June/July. Summer placements are available.

Qualifications: ages 18-27. Good childcare experience and some English needed.
Application procedure: checkable references needed. Usually requests from families exceed number of au pairs.
Other services: 10% discount given at language school. Agency tries to help dissatisfied au pairs find a new family.
Fees: on request.
Contact: Helena Kovàcs.

M KELLY AUPAIR AGENCY
17 Ingram Way, Greenford, Middlesex UB6 8QG. ☎/fax: 020-8575 3336. E-mail: info@mkellyaupair.co.uk. Website: www.mkellyaupair.co.uk.
In business since 2001. Member of IAPA (pending).
Placements: au pairs.
Jobs in: UK only.
About 2% of applicants placed are male.
Minimum stay: 4 weeks in summer.
Wages/pocket money: £55+ a week.
Qualifications: must have some experience with children.
Application procedure: average processing time 2-3 weeks.
Other services: free 24 hour emergency cover if needed.
Fees: nil.
Contact: Marian Kelly, Proprietor.

LE MONDE AU PAIR
7 rue de la Commune Ouest, Bureau 204, Montréal, Québec H2Y 2C5, Canada. ☎+1   514-281-3045. Fax: +1 514-281-1525. Website: www.generation.net/ ~aupair or www.aupairplacement.com.
In business since 1997. Representatives in Paris (c/o Violaine Penzini, 65 blvd Bessières, 75017 Paris, France ; +33 6-73 72 18 18) and in Victoria British Columbia (Suite 112, 1039 Tara Place, View St, Victoria, BC, Canada V8V 4V6 (250-475-1890; toll-free within North America 1-866-475-1890; worldaupair@shaw.ca).
Placements: au pairs and mother's helps.
Jobs in: Canada (Québec, Ontario and British Columbia); outgoing programme to Denmark, France, Germany, Austria, Italy, Netherlands, Norway, Spain, Switzerland, UK, Australia, New Zealand and USA.
Nationalities placed: au pairs in Canada come on tourist visas.
Minimum stay: 4-12 months in Canada. Summer placements begin May or June.
Wages/pocket money: C$100 (€64) per week for 30-35 hours per week plus 2 evenings babysitting.
Qualifications: for Canada, must speak English or French to a pre-intermediate standard. Childcare experience needed. Must be non-smoker.
Application procedure: applications should be made 2-3 months before proposed departure. Last-minute applications may be considered. Application should be submitted in target language, although English is suitable for Canada, Denmark, Norway and the Netherlands. Face-to-face or telephone interviews compulsory for placement in some countries. Telephone contact with host family is arranged.
Other services: specially designed insurance offered by partner broker in Montreal, Claude LePage (450-641-4617).
Fees: C$299/€195 fee plus tax.

MONDIAL/KRYSPOL AUPAIR AGENCIES
van Neijenrodeweg 731, 1082 JE Amsterdam, Netherlands. ☎+31 20-645 8780. Fax: +31 84-213 7435. E-mail: info@aupair-agency.nl. Website: www. aupair-agency.nl.

In business since 1986. IAPA membership pending.
Placements: 100 au pairs and nannies placed by Dutch office; Channel Islands office also offers elder care placements.
Jobs in: Netherlands. UK and France.
Nationalities placed: Polish, Filipino, Slovakian, Baltic and Brazilian.
About 2% of applicants placed are male.
Minimum stay: mostly 3 months; summer placements can be arranged.
Wages/pocket money: €300-€350 per month based on a 30-hour working week. Extra hours will be paid at €3 an hour.
Qualifications: ages 18-25. Basic knowledge of English preferred.
Application procedure: average processing time for EU nationals can be as short as 1 week. Applicants must provide health certificate, copy of ID and have an interview in English.
Other services: Dutch families pay for health and travel insurance and arrange for au pair to attend Dutch or English course.
Fees: €50-€100.
Contact: Tarno Belterman, Managing Director.

MULTIKULTUR INTERNATIONAL EXCHANGE PROGRAMS
Landingstr. 28-30, 63739 Aschaffenburg, Germany. ☎+49 6021-909145. Fax: +49 6021-909146. E-mail: away@aupair-ab.de. Website: www.aupair-ab.de.
In business since 1998. Member of IAPA.
Placements: 400-600 au pairs, nannies, mother's helps, volunteers, working holiday makers and interns.
Jobs in: Germany. Outgoing programmes to Europe, USA and worldwide.
Less than 10% of applicants placed are male.
Minimum stay: 3 months; summer placements available.
Qualifications: must have some experience with children.
Application procedure: average processing time 1-3 months.
Fees: vary.
Contact: Volker Lang, Owner.

MUNICHAUPAIR
Drachenseestr. 13, 81373 Munich, Germany. ☎+49 89-7672 9510. Mobile: +49 160 9936 0319. Fax: +49 89-7672 9511. E-mail: patricia@munichaupair.com. Website: www.munichaupair.com.
In business since 2001. Member of Aupair-Society e.V.
Placements: au pairs.
Jobs in: Germany (Munich and environs); also outgoing to Britain, Ireland, France, Italy, Spain, Greece, Finland and USA.
Nationalities placed: any.
Agency will encourage applications from young men.
Minimum stay: 6 months, as shorter stays are difficult.
Wages/pocket money: €260 per month, though some families pay more.
Qualifications: ages 18-25. Some childcare experience such as babysitting. Basic knowledge of the target language (tests given in case of USA) and basic knowledge of housekeeping needed.
Application procedure: processing of non-EU candidates takes 6-12 weeks while visa is obtained.
Other services: personal contact with foreign au pairs made after arrival. Agency gives information about German culture and Munich in particular, available language courses, guidelines on how to behave in the family, etc. Agency tries to visit the families before registering them. Assistance given with contracts. Families are encouraged to buy

appropriate insurance to cover au pairs. Agency advices au pairs on suitable courses at the Goethe Institute. Monthly au pair get-togethers are organised, for example at a beer garden or as a picnic. Agency co-operates with friendly travel agent which can arrange skiing weekends and other travels.
Fees: nil for incoming au pairs. Outgoing applicants pay €150.
Contact: Patricia Brunner, Owner.

NACEL
BP 829, 12008 Rodez Cedex, France. ☎+33 5-65 76 55 20. Fax: +33 5-65 78 40 61. E-mail: etudiants@nacel.fr. Website: www.nacel.com.
In business since 1954.
Placements: 20 au pairs and 20 work-study per year.
Jobs in: Germany, UK, Spain, Australia and Canada (no placements in France).
Nationalities placed: mainly French.
No male placements.
Minimum stay: 2 months. Summer placements can be made.
Wages/pocket money: minimum £40 per week, depending on number of hours worked.
Qualifications: ages 18-26. Childcare experience and at least intermediate level of English needed.
Application procedure: interviews required. Processing time normally about 3 months.
Other services: insurance and travel assistance given.
Fees: €230.
Contact: Emmanuelle Vaissiere, Head, Head of Individual Student Department.

NANNIES ABROAD
Abbots Worthy House, Abbots Worthy, Winchester, SO21 1DR. ☎01962 882299. Fax: 01962 881888. E-mail: enquiries@nanniesabroad.com. Website: www.nanniesabroad.com.
Placements: 100+ nannies and children's reps with reputable British tour operators.
Jobs in: European resorts including Greece, Spain, Turkey and the French Alps.
Nationalities placed: anyone that has a valid visa to work in Europe (which automatically includes all British and European nationals).
Minimum stay: short-term cover, one full season (normally 17 weeks summer or winter) or permanent (multiple seasons).
Wages/pocket money: £80-£120 a week for no more than 48 hours per week, averaged across a 17-week period. Also free shared accommodation, food allowance, free uniform, free travel to and from place of work at the start and end of the season, use of sports equipment (i.e. free ski hire, ski passes, etc. and in summer, free or discounted water sports as available), plus free medical and travel insurance.
Qualifications: minimum requirement for candidates with no childcare qualifications is at least one year's full time experience in a childcare setting. All recognised childcare qualifications accepted including (but not exclusively): NVQ 2, 3; BTEC; NNEB; CACHE CCE; CACHE DCE; NC; HNC; BA Hons, etc.
Application procedure: recruitment takes place year round. Interviews are essential, normally at head office in Winchester, but sometimes held locally if required.
Other services: agency monitors standard of childcare provided by tour operators.
Fees: nil.
Contact: Ashanti Dickson, Managing Director.

NANNIES OF ST JAMES AND TEMPORARY NANNIES
London House, 100 New Kings Road, London SW6 4LX. ☎+44 (0)20-7348 6100. Fax: +44 (0)1271 817181. E-mail: nanniesstjames@aol.com. Website: www.stjamesandtempnannies.com.

In business since 1991.
Placements: 80-100 nannies and mother's helps.
Jobs in: USA, Europe, i.e. Switzerland, Italy, France, Germany, Austria and the Netherlands; also Hong Kong and a large client base in London and region.
About 5% of applicants placed are male.
Minimum stay: temporary assignments range from 1 week to 6 months; otherwise permanent positions are for a minimum of 1 year. Summer placements are available.
Wages/pocket money: daily nannies in the UK earn £300-£500 net per week; live-in nannies earn £250-£350. Overseas nannies in Europe earn £250-£450 net per week. Overseas nannies in the USA earn £350-£500.
Qualifications: minimum age 18. Must have either a qualification (BTEC, NNEB, NAMCW, GNVQ, NVQ, CACHE) and a year's experience or have at least 2 years experience.
Application procedure: all nannies have to be interviewed personally and appointments are necessary. Applicants must provide copies of their certificates and written references and a CRB enhanced disclosure check. Processing time takes 1-6 weeks.
Other services: travel agent contact can help arrange flights, etc. Advice given on medical insurance policies and contact numbers for other nannies in destination area provided.
Fees: nil.
Contact: John Lincoln (Partner) and Rosemary Newton (Partner).

Specialists in the recruitment of Nannies – Maternity nurses

We provide a professional and personal childcare consultancy for clients throughout the UK, USA and world-wide looking for high calibre staff for the private household. All applicants are personally screened.

NANNIES *of* ST JAMES

Tel: UK +44 (0)207 348 6100 **Fax:** UK +44 (0)1271 817181
Website: www.stjamesandtempnannies.com
E-mail: nanniesstjames@aol.com

NANNY & AU PAIR CONNECTION
435 Chorley New Road, Horwich, Bolton BL6 6EJ. ☎/fax: 01204 694422. E-mail: info@aupairs-nannies.co.uk. Website: www.aupairs-nannies.co.uk.
In business since 1989.
Placements: 400+ nannies, mother's helps, housekeepers, au pairs.
Jobs in: UK, France, Spain, Italy, Germany, Netherlands, etc.
Nationalities placed: any legal UK residents including students who have had childcare experience.
Males are accepted.
Minimum stay: 6, 9 or 12 month placements for au pairs in college terms. 3-month summer stays also available.
Wages/pocket money: £250+ for qualified nannies; £55 per week for au pairs.
Qualifications: au pairs require knowledge of childcare and a basic knowledge of the language. Nannies should have a relevant childcare qualification, first aid and a Police (CRB) check.
Application procedure: applications can be submitted online. For nanny applicants, interviews are required. References are checked. Placements take about 2-3 weeks.
Other services: full back-up service; contracts of employment provided. Contact numbers of other nannies/au pairs in the area are distributed. Help given with travel arrangements

and visas. Welcome pack given on arrival. Christmas party and get-togethers organised for au pairs.
Fees: nil for nannies, mother's helps and incoming au pairs. £40 for British au pairs going to Europe.
Contact: Carole Payne, Proprietor.

NANNY SEARCH LIMITED
7 Broadbent Close, Highgate, London N6 5JW. ☎020-8348 4111. Fax: 0208-347 8383. E-mail: info@nanny-search.co.uk. Website: www.nanny-search.co.uk.
Central branch in Victoria specialises in live-in nannies in London, UK and international. In business since 2000. Agency has been inspected by PANN (Professional Association of Nursery Nurses).
Placements: qualified daily/live-in nannies/mothers helps. Separate babysitting service/maternity/Emergency temps service.
Jobs in: UK and worldwide including USA.
Nationalities placed: any with valid work permit. Must satisfy legal requirements for working in the UK.
About 2% of applicants placed are male. Qualified or experienced male nannies are very welcome.
Minimum stay: from as little as a weekend. Summer placements are available and can often be filled by men. Permanent contracts for a minimum of one year.
Wages/pocket money: Daily nannies earn £300-£450 net per week; live-in nannies £250-£350 + per week; maternity nurses £650-£750 per week
Qualifications: Full CV and excellent references. Driving an advantage as are qualifications, experience and maturity. Sports or a special skill are also good. Minimum age 21. 3 years' minimum experience required.
Application procedure: agency policy is to interview all applicants. Interviews can be arranged in South Africa, Hungary and Croatia as well as the UK. Verbal checks made on references, in translation if necessary. Medical declaration, full CV and CRB check needed.
Other services: consultant visa specialist attorney for placements in the USA; his office can arrange work visas for nannies, usually for expatriate English families. Agency includes Nanny Academy training and support centre with first drop-in centre for nannies and au pairs in the UK. Arrange pediatric First Aid certificate classes for unqualified childcarers at cost, sometimes with Hungarian or Croatian interpreter. The Nanny Academy also runs maternity courses and refresher courses in baby skills for nannies that have been in their jobs long term and need to update their skills. Also runs a course in CV-writing for nannies. Agency hosts social events and produces a contact list and welcome pack. Families are asked by agency to pay return travel costs to the home country. 24-hour emergency telephone number.
Contact: Amanda Cotton, Director.

THE NANNY SERVICE
6 Nottingham St, London W1U 5EJ. ☎020-7935 3515 (Permanent & Temporary Nannies); 020-7935 8247 (Part-time Nannies); 07734 059353 (Maternity Nurses). Fax: 020-7224 0305. E-mail: nannyservice@ukonline.co.uk. Website: www.nannyservice.co.uk.
In business since 1975.
Placements: daily nannies, live-in nannies, part-time nannies, maternity nurses and mother's helps.
Jobs in: London (mostly) and rural England.
Nationalities placed: EU passport holders, South Africans, Australians and New Zealanders and all those eligible for working holiday visas. Students from Europe (outside the EU)

with a student visa are permitted to work up to 20 h.p.w.
Minimum stay: 1 year.
Wages: Live-in nannies earn £300-£350 net per week. Daily nannies earn about £350-£400 net per week in London for working a 10-hour day. Salaries are determined according to age and experience.
Qualifications: minimum age 21 years; relevant childcare experience, references and driving licence essential.
Fees: see website.
Contact: Corrina Slater (Manager), Paul Rendle (Proprietor).

NATIVE SPEAKER
Communicative English Language Training, Business Innovation Centre, IT Sligo Campus, Ballinode, Sligo, Ireland. ☎+353 71-914 7728, Fax: +353 71-914 4500. E-mail: info@nativespeaker.ie. Website: www.nativespeaker.ie.
In business since 2001. Member of ACELS and MEI RELSA.
Placements: handful of au pairs.
Jobs in: Ireland.
Minimum stay: 6-12 months.
Qualifications: ideally candidates should have some experience, but vetting left to partner agencies.
Application procedure: average time taken to process applications is 3 weeks to 4 months. Interviews will be held on request by the family. References required.
Other services: language lessons arranged.
Fees: nil, though au pairs pay for language classes at Native Speaker.
Contact: John Joe Callaghan, Owner/Manager.

NINE MUSES AU PAIR ACTIVITIES
Thrakis 39 and Vas. Sofias 2, 17121 Nea Smyrni, Athens, Greece. ☎+30 210-931 6588. E-mail: ninemuses@ninemuses.gr. Website: www.ninemuses.gr.
In business since 1993.
Placements: au pairs and mother's helps in Greece; Greek au pairs sent abroad. Also place Greek young people in UK hotels for training.
Jobs in: Greece. Outgoing programme to USA, UK, France, Spain, Italy, Belgium, Germany, Denmark, Portugal, Austria, Switzerland, Finland and Luxembourg.
Nationalities placed: EU and American.
Male applicants can rarely be placed.
Minimum stay: 1 month minimum in summer though normal summer stay is from 15th June to beginning of September. Most families prefer someone to stay 9-12 months, though 6-month placements are available.
Wages/pocket money: minimum about €60 per week for au pairs (working 30 hours). Maximum €150 for qualified applicants working full-time.
Qualifications: au pairs must have language skills (usually English, French or German for Greece) and have willing and happy personalities.
Application procedure: references are always necessary. 'Dear family' letter is very important as are photos and medical certificate. Applications processed in 1-3 months (to allow time to visit and interview the host family).
Other services: agency offers Greek language and culture programme (accredited by European Label Award in Brussels). Insurance is normally provided by host family. Agency sends newsletters to au pairs in Greece and organises meetings and excursions. Agency prides itself on its after-care service and in staying in close contact with au pairs. Good back-up in the event of problems. Au pairs can be met at airport.
Fees: nil.
Contact: Kalliope (Popy) Raekou, Owner.

NORTH SOUTH AGENCY
28 Wellington Road, Hastings, East Sussex TN34 3RN. ☎01424 422364/ 0870 751 7304. Fax: 01424 715120. E-mail: Hastings@northsouthagency.co.uk. Website: www.northsouthagency.co.uk.
In business since 1984.
Placements: au pairs, au pairs plus, mother's/father's helps and nannies.
Jobs in: UK only (majority in Greater London and Southeast England) but nationwide.
Nationalities placed: in accordance with Home Office regulations.
About 10% of au pair placements are male due to the efforts the agency makes to promote male au pairs. Male applicants should ideally be in their 20s, able to drive, speak good English, have experience with children and housework and be available to stay for at least 9 months.
Minimum stay: 9-12 months preferred; shorter stays possible depending on demand and starting date. Very limited July/August placements, though openings occur for au pairs available to start summer placements in May or June.
Wages/pocket money: as per Home Office guidelines, currently £55 per week for au pairs (25 h.p.w.), more for longer working week. Live-out nannies are paid in accordance with minimum wage regulations in the UK, qualifications, experience and commitment.
Qualifications: childcare experience necessary for mother's helps and nannies. Qualifications (NNEB or similar) also preferred for nannies. Au pairs should have a genuine liking for children and have some experience, if possible, and also experience with simple household duties including ironing and cooking. Au pairs should be very flexible and not too demanding. Driving licence and experience always an advantage.
Application procedure: information can be obtained from website, by email or phone. Priority given to au pairs who are already in the country, in which case placement can usually be made within a couple of days.
Other services: agency tries to remain in contact with all au pairs and invites them to visit the Hastings office on a day off. Agency can provide reasonably priced accommodation for longer visits to Hastings or for au pairs before or between jobs.
Fees: nil.
Contact: Hanna Matthews.

NORTH WEST CHILDCARE
12 Delahays Road, Hale, Cheshire WA15 8DY. ☎0161-904 0565/ 0161-980 0996. Fax: 0161-903 8040. E-mail: enquiries@childcarerecruitment.co.uk. Website: www.northwestchildcare.co.uk.
Sister companies: The Childcare Recruitment Company and The Housekeeper Company. In business since 1999. Member of REC (Childcare Division).
Placements: 150 nannies, mother's helps, housekeeper/nannies.
Jobs in: UK only.
About 5% of applicants placed are male.
Minimum stay: from as little as 1 week
Wages/pocket money: £55+ a week.
Qualifications: experience and qualifications essential.
Other services: good back-up and support service given.
Fees: nil.
Contact: Julia Harris, Managing Director

NURSE AU PAIR PLACEMENT (N.A.P.P.)
16 Rue le Sueur, 75116 Paris, France. ☎+33 1-45 00 33 88. Fax: +33 1-45 00 33 99. E-mail: nappsarl@aol.com. Website: www.napp.fr; www.nurseaupair. com; www.nappnurseaupair.com.
Métro Agentine, Ligne 1.

In business since 1993 (started by an Australian). Member of IAPA and UFAAP. GoAupair representative since 1993.

Placements: au pairs, nannies, mother's helps, maternity nurses and after school care. 150 incoming, 250 outgoing.

Jobs in: France; also French au pairs sent to USA, Canada (for the Live-in Caregiver Scheme), Australia, South Africa, UK, Ireland, Spain, Italy and Germany.

Nationalities placed: all with either the appropriate visa or an au pair visa.

About 2% of applicants placed as au pairs are male.

Minimum stay: 6 months for EU au pairs and 12 months for non-EU au pairs. Summer placements available, minimum 2 months (i.e. July/August).

Wages/pocket money: at least €70 a week in France plus a *Carte Orange*. Range in other countries from €60 to €85.

Qualifications: incoming au pairs must be 18-29; outgoing age limits 18-26. Must have at least 2 babysitting references. Must have either adequate French or perfect English. Nannies must be at least 20 and either qualified in childcare (NNEB etc) or highly experienced.

Application procedure: Processing can be done very quickly (1 day – 2 weeks) provided references can be verified verbally.

Other services: agency helps with travel and third party insurance arrangements, language courses and any problems between families and au pairs/nurses.

Fees: €185 for Europe and €285 for other countries except USA which is free.

Contact: Sandra Bertrand, Assistant.

OCCASIONAL & PERMANENT NANNIES
2 Cromwell Place, London SW7 2JE. ☎020-7225 1555. Fax: 020-7589 4966. E-mail: all@nannyworld.co.uk. Website: www.nannyworld.co.uk.

In business since 1955. Member of REC.

Placements: nannies, mother's helps, governesses, maternity nurses and all domestic staff.

Jobs in: UK and all over the world (Europe, the Americas, Australia, Africa and the Far East).

Nationalities placed: mainly British, Australian, New Zealand, Irish, Canadian, South African and European, and those who can obtain work permits. Agency has agents in USA, Ireland and Scotland for all positions in private service.

Minimum stay: temporary and permanent positions.

Wages/pocket money: £250-£1,000 per week (depending on age and experience).

Qualifications: ages from 18 upwards. Must be trained and/or experienced (minimum 2 year) with childcare/nursing or teaching experience a strong preference. Good English essential.

Application procedure: initial telephone screening. All applicants are interviewed in person and references checked.

Other services: agency helps with contract details, medical insurance and travel arrangements. Also provides addresses of other nannies in the area.

Fees: nil.

Contact: Angela Hovey, Managing Director.

OLIVER TWIST ASSOCIATION
7 rue Léon Morin, 33600 Pessac, France. ☎+33 5-57 26 93 26. Fax: +33 5-56 36 21 85. E-mail: oliver.twist@wanadoo.fr. Website: www.oliver-twist.fr.

In business since 1991. Member of IAPA.

Placements: 450 au pairs.

Jobs in: France; also outgoing programme to England, Ireland, America and Spain. Occasional placements in Italy, Germany, Austria, Sweden and Netherlands.

About 5% of applicants placed are male (in France, UK and Spain).

Minimum stay: 2 months in summer, 6 months during the year.
Wages/pocket money: €80 per week.
Qualifications: ages 18-27. Good childcare references and some knowledge of French needed for placement in France.
Application procedure: 2-3 childcare references needed. Personal interview held where possible.

O'NEILL SCHOOL OF ENGLISH
Iberluce 20, 48960 Galdakao, Vizcaya, Spain. ☎+34 94-456 49 17. Fax: +34 94-443 2945. E-mail: o.neill@euskalnet.net. Website: http://usuarios.lycos. es/oneillaupair.
In business since 1990.
Placements: about 50 au pairs placed by this language school.
Jobs in: Spain (mostly in the north around Bilbao).
Nationalities placed: all that are legal.
Male applicants can sometimes be placed in families looking for a long-term English-speaking home assistant.
Minimum stay: 2-3 months in summer; very occasionally for just the month of August. Otherwise September/October to end of June.
Wages/pocket money: €90 per week. Extra money paid for extra duties.
Qualifications: native English speakers can always be placed. Minimum age 18 (though families prefer older au pairs). Basic knowledge of Spanish preferred. Driving licence useful.
Application procedure: applications should be sent at least 2 months in advance, though summer placements tend to be made at the last minute.
Other services: advice given on papers necessary to register with Spanish health service and can advise on Spanish courses. Contact arranged with other au pairs.
Fees: one week's pocket money payable once au pair is installed.
Contact: Cristina Tejada, Au-pair Placement Consultant.

ONLY 4 ME AU PAIR AGENCY
Postfach 15 17 01, 80050 Munich, Germany. ☎+49-89-7201 9997. Fax: +49 89-7206 9308. E-mail: info@aupaironly.de. Website: www.aupaironly.de.
In business since 1996.
Placements: au pairs.
Jobs in: Germany (all regions); outgoing to EU.
About 15% of applicants placed are male.
Minimum stay: variable.
Wages/pocket money: €260 per month.
Fees: none.
Contact: Inga Senff.

OPTIMUM CHILDCARE, NANNIES AND SENIORS CAREGIVERS, INC
1-3702 Quebec St, Vancouver, BC V5V 3K4, Canada. ☎+1 604-879-2433. E-mail: opti-mum@shaw.ca. Website: www.opti-mum.com.
In business since 1989. Website databased matching service.
Placements: 100 seniors, caregivers and nannies.
Jobs in: Canada and the USA.
About 5% of applicants placed are male.
Minimum stay: one year.
Qualifications: must have at least one year of relevant experience.
Fees: free to register; $50 fee to access contact information.
Contact: Janet MacDonald, Owner.

PACE LANGUAGE INSTITUTE LTD.
29/30 Dublin Rd, Bray, Co. Wicklow, Ireland. ☎+353 12760922. Fax: +353 12760936. E-mail: liz@paceinstitute.ie. Website: www.paceinstitute.ie.
In business since 1990. Member of IAPA. Member of MEI/RELSA, ACELS, Dept. of Education, Chambers of Commerce for Dublin and Bray.
Placements: 50+ demi pairs (who are given free accommodation and food in exchange for work).
Jobs in: Ireland only.
About 5% of applicants placed are male.
Minimum stay: 12 weeks, winter or summer.
Wages/pocket money: full board and accommodation given in exchange for 15 hours of work a week. Travel pass provided.
Qualifications: minimum age 17. All nationalities provided they can speak intermediate English.
Application procedure: placement within 1 week. No interview needed.
Fees: none, but must take 12-week English course during demi-pair stay. Tuition costs €149 per week.
Contact: Liz Hurley, Director.

PARK AVENUE AU PAIR AGENCY
36 Oakington Avenue, Wembley Park, Middlesex HA9 8HZ. ☎020-8904 0340. E-mail: ruth@aupairlondon.co.uk. Website: www.aupairlondon.co.uk.
In business since 1989.
Placements: au pairs.
Jobs in: UK (mainly London).
Very few males placed.
Minimum stay: 2 months in summer.
Wages/pocket money: minimum £55+ a week.
Application procedure: interview not required. Arrangements can be made quickly by email.
Fees: nil.
Contact: Ruth Rosenthal, Sole Proprietor.

PARK NANNY AGENCY
36 Winchester Ave, London NW6 7TU. ☎020-7604 4000. Fax: 020-7604 4060. E-mail: info@parknannies.co.uk. Website: www.parknannies.co.uk.
In business since April 2001.
Placements: nannies and mother's helps, live-in and live-out, full and part-time.
Jobs in: Europe; also UK especially London.
Agency is happy to place male applicants if they satisfy the requirements.
Wages/pocket money: live-in nannies and mother's helps earn between £175 and £250 net per week. Live-out nannies and mother's helps earn £225-£400.
Qualifications: minimum age 21 with a minimum of 2 years experience in childcare. Applicant must supply references that can be checked verbally. Must be English-speaking.
Application procedure: all nannies are interviewed and their references checked by telephone. Agency pays home visits to families where possible.
Other services: agency keeps in close contact with the family and the nanny throughout the placement procedure. Information on activities in the area is provided and social events are arranged for nannies and their charges.
Fees: nil.
Contact: Hannah Hodgson and Genevieve De Wynter, Partners.

PEEK-A-BOO AU-PAIRS AND NANNIES
10 Ironmonger Lane, London EC2V 8EY, UK. ☎020-7778 0720. Fax: 0870 033 2609. E-mail: info@peekaboochildcare.com. Website: www. peekaboochildcare.com.
In business since 1996.
Placements: about 100 au pairs, nannies, mother's helps, maternity nurses, babysitters.
Jobs in: throughout UK but mainly London. Outgoing programme to USA, France, Germany and many other countries.
About 2% of applicants placed are male.
Minimum stay: 6 months; summer placements available.
Wages/pocket money: £55-£130 a week. Live-in nannies earn £250-£300 per week; live-out nannies earn £350-£400.
Qualifications: ages 18-27. EU nationality plus Romanian, Bulgarian and Turkish for UK jobs. Must have some form of childcare experience. Must speak basic English and have CRB check and all checkable references.
Application procedure: nannies must come in for interview; speed of placement depends on availability and suitability. Au pairs placed in 1 day to 4 weeks.
Other services: trouble-shooting, monthly meetings, VIP club mail list, language classes, au pair courses.
Fees: nil.
Contact: Sara Rahmani, Director.

PEOPLE & PLACES (P & P)
Trewornan, Wadebridge, Cornwall PL27 6EX. ☎01208 812652. Fax: 01208 816121. E-mail: tre.wornan@virgin.net.
In business since 1990.
Placements: 250 au pairs and 20 nannies per year.
Jobs in: au pairs placed in England (mainly) plus a few to France, Germany, Austria, Italy, Netherlands and Spain. Nannies placed in England and Europe.
Minimum stay: 6 weeks in summer.
Wages/pocket money: minimum £45-£50 per week for au pairs; hours in excess of 25 per week should be paid at £1.50 per hour. £200-£350 per week for nannies.
Qualifications: babysitting experience preferred.
Other services: will give phone numbers of other au pairs in the country, on request. Agency tries to contact family after au pair's arrival to make sure all is well.
Fees: nil.
Contact: Lester Tucker (Proprietor), Avril Heard (Au Pair Co-ordinator).

PEOPLE FOR PEOPLE
PO Box W271, Warringah Mall, Brookvale, NSW 2100, Australia. ☎+61 2-9972 0488. E-mail: nanny@peopleforpeople.com.au. Website: www. peopleforpeople.com.au.
In business since 1998.
Placements: live-in nannies and au pairs.
Jobs in: Australia (Sydney only).
Nationalities placed: those eligible for working holiday visas, mainly those from UK, Germany, Canada and Sweden.
Male applicants cannot be placed.
Minimum stay: 3 months. Summer placements can be made (minimum 3 months).
Wages/pocket money: A$180 per week for 30 hours, $240 per week for 40 hours, in addition to free room and board.
Qualifications: ages 18-30. Reasonable spoken English needed.
Application procedure: applicants should complete application form on agency website.

Once arrival date is fixed and references have been sent, agency tries to match family. Applicant is interviewed in person after arrival and then sent to meet 2 or 3 families to give them a choice.
Other services: au pairs put in touch with others in area. New family provided in event of major problems.
Fees: nil.
Contact: Jenell Peel, Manager.

PERFECT PARTNERS
Am Sonnenhügel 2, 97450 Arnstein, Germany. ☎+49 9363-994291. Fax: +49 9363-994292. E-mail: info@perfect-partners.de. Website: www.perfect-partners.de.
In business since 1997.
Placements: 120-150 au pairs and nannies.
Jobs in: mainly Germany; also Europe.
Nationalities placed: any that are allowed by immigration regulations.
5%-10% of applicants placed are male.
Minimum stay: 3-6 months. Summer placements can be made.
Wages/pocket money: according to official German law regarding au pair placements.
Qualifications: childcare experience essential. Basic German language a plus.
Application procedure: processing time approximately 2 months (though strong candidates can be placed within a week).
Other services: if problems arise, agency offers free accommodation.
Fees: nil.
Contact: Sabine Hoppe, Owner.

PERFECT WAY
Hafnerweg 8, 5200 Brugg-AG, Switzerland. ☎+41 56-281 3912. Fax: +41 56-281 3914. E-mail: info@perfectway.ch or perfectway@bluewin.ch. Website: www.perfectway.ch.
In business since 1995.
Placements: 100-200 au pairs mostly, sometimes nannies and secretaries. Also German-speaking nurses, kindergarten teachers and housekeepers.
Jobs in: Switzerland, with Swiss, American and international families.
Nationalities placed: from EU, EFTA, USA and Canada. From 2006, new European countries like Poland and Hungary will be permitted.
Agency very rarely places male applicants.
Minimum stay: 7-18 months for au pairs, 5-10 weeks for nannies. No summer placements.
Wages/pocket money: SFr800 per month for au pairs; SFr3800-8000 per month for nannies plus perks.
Qualifications: ages 18-29. Must be open-minded, flexible, have good manners and some experience in childcare. Nannies must be well educated.
Application procedure: processing takes 4-6 weeks. Applicants must submit CV, letters, 2 references, photos and talk to agency several times on the phone. Some families fly candidates in for interview; otherwise telephone contact.
Other services: representative from agency meets new arrivals at the airport and sees them 3 or 4 times a year. Owner of agency speaks English, German and Swedish.
Fees: nil.
Contact: Karin Schatzmann, Owner.

PERSONAL AU PAIR SERVICE
1 Whites Row, London E1 7NF. ☎020-7377 2744. E-mail: elizabethelder@

thechildcarecompany.co.uk. Website: www.thechildcarecompany.co.uk.
In business since 1985. New management November 2005 by The Childcare Company (see entry).
Placements: about 400 au pairs, au pairs plus and overseas mother's helps.
Jobs in: throughout UK and mainly London.
Nationalities placed: nationalities approved by Home Office.
About 15% of applicants placed are male.
Minimum stay: 3 months (summer months only).
Wages/pocket money: in accordance with Home Office guidelines, a 'reasonable allowance' of £60-£70 per week.
Qualifications: childcare/babysitting experience. Age limits 18-27. It is easier to place applicants with a reasonable level of English, but essential that the level of English is accurately stated on the application form.
Application procedure: complete agency registration form, supply 2 references, passport photo, selection of 4 photographs showing au pair with family, friends and children for whom they have cared. Process takes 2-4 weeks depending on availability of families.
Other services: agency helps with visas and all support during both selection process and stay in the UK. All au pairs receive access to special 'Au Pair Friends' website approved by BAPAA and REC.
Fees: nil to applicants.
Contact: Elizabeth Elder.

PERSONAL TOUCH AUPAIR SERVICE
Siedlungsstrasse 3, 84428 Buchbach, Germany. ☎+49 8086 94 67 16. Fax: +49 8086 94 67 17. E-mail: personal.touch@t-online.de. Website: www. personaltouch.de; www.personaltouch.at.
In business since 1998. Affiliated to International Au Pair Organisation (see entry for IAPO).
Placements: 180-200 au pairs, nannies and household personnel (discounting summer placements).
Jobs in: Germany and Austria mainly. Also outgoing programme to England, Scotland, Ireland, Norway, Denmark, France, Spain, Italy, Switzerland, Canada and USA.
Nationalities placed: all.
About 5% of applicants placed are male.
Minimum stay: 3 months for summer placements, otherwise longer.
Wages/pocket money: from €260 a month to €350 for highly qualified applicants. €60-€80 per week in other European countries.
Qualifications: ages 18-25 in Germany, 18-27 in Austria. Minimum 2 references, 1 childcare (e.g. babysitting), 1 character. Must have basics of the language, enough to communicate with the parents and children; proof of German skills required.
Application procedure: average processing time 4-8 weeks for incoming au pairs; 4 weeks for outgoing except USA which requires an interview and takes 2-3 months.
Other services: information given about insurance, language classes, free-time activities, contacts with other au pairs in the area. 12 months follow-up support given, in case the au pair wants to change family if there are problems.
Fees: nil for incoming. €155 outgoing.
Contact: Andrea Huber, Director.

PHILGLOBE INTERNATIONAL INC.
5165 Queen Mary Ave, Suite 402, Montreal, Quebec H3W 1X7, Canada. ☎+1 514-369-2997. Fax: +1 514-369-0515. E-mail: lsupino@philglobe.com. Website: www.philglobe.com.
In business since 1980. Owner is a member of the Canadian Society of Immigration

Consultants (CSIC).
Placements: nannies (live-in caregivers).
Jobs in: Canada only.
Nationalities placed: all.
Minimum stay: 1 year; many renew for a second year and beyond.
Wages/pocket money: starting salary is C$304 gross (C$256 net) for a 40 hour week with free board and lodging. Working week may be up to 50 hours, but extra hours will be paid extra.
Qualifications: in addition to the requirements of the Live-in Caregiver Program, agency insists on a minimum of 2 years' experience as a nanny or caregiver abroad with references. For foreigners whose mother tongue is neither English nor French, they must submit a certificate of language proficiency (e.g. TOEFEL or IELTS).
Application procedure: once a dossier has been accepted, agency guarantees placement within six months. Visa processing can be very slow so time taken between application and arrival is normally between 8 and 14 months.
Other services: agency offers immigration services and advice on the separate regulations that pertain in Quebec. In Quebec nannies have access to free French classes in their spare time.
Fees: deposit of €150 required with application. Total agency fee is €2000 which covering all services: evaluation and placement with a potential employer, professional legal services for all immigration procedures for obtaining a working permit to work in Canada, legal procedures on arrival in Canada and ongoing support.
Contact: Louisa Supino, Human Resources Local and Overseas Division.

PLAYTIME NANNY AGENCY
55 Queens Road, Knaphill, Woking, Surrey GU21 2ED. ☎/fax: 01483 488511. E-mail: info@playtimenannies.co.uk. Website: www.playtimenannies.co.uk.
In business since 1990.
Placements: nannies.
Jobs in: UK (Surrey only).
Minimum stay: variable. Summer placements available.
Qualifications: experience and/or qualifications needed.
Application procedure: CRB checks carried out which can take up to 8 weeks. All references and certificates checked.
Contact: Lisa Ellesley, Owner.

POPPINS NANNIES & DOMESTIC STAFF
6 Beranburh Field, Wroughton, Swindon SN4 0QL. ☎01793 815313. E-mail: poppins@mac.com or abcpoppins@tiscali.co.uk. Website: www.abcpoppins. com.
In business since 1994. Member of Federation of Small Businesses.
Placements: 100-150 nannies, maternity nurses, mother's helps and occasionally au pairs.
Jobs in: sample destinations in past 12 months include Switzerland, Bermuda, USA, Italy and Norway as well as UK.
About 1% of applicants placed are male.
Minimum stay: summer placements available.
Wages/pocket money: £50-£500 a week, up to £900 a week for maternity nurses.
Qualifications: childcare experience is a pre-requisite.
Application procedure: all candidates are interviewed where possible. CRB and background checks.
Contact: Elizabeth Webster, Proprietor.

PREMIER AUPAIR AGENCY
Bensons Cottage, Woodgreen, Astley, Near Stourport on Severn, Worcs. DY13 0RR. ☎/fax: 01299 828383. E-mail: aupairs@premieraupair.co.uk. Website: www.premieraupair.co.uk.
In business since 1995.
Placements: 500 au pairs and carers.
Jobs in: UK including Scotland and Wales.
Nationalities placed: all that are permitted by Home Office.
About 1% of applicants placed are male.
Minimum stay: 6 months; summer placements available.
Wages/pocket money: £55-£85 a week for au pairs; £4.85 per hour for carers (37.5-40 hours per week).
Qualifications: ages 17-27. Some childcare experience needed. Carers must speak good English.
Application procedure: average processing time 2-3 weeks.
Other services: agency ensures all au pairs are able to attend school. Accommodation can be found before arrival for carers.
Fees: nil.
Contact: Andrea Payne, Co-Director.

PRIORITÉ ENFANTS SÀRL
2 rond-point de Plainpalais, 1205 Geneva, Switzerland. ☎+41 22 321 02 77. Fax: +41 22 329 83 61. E-mail: info@prioriteenfants.ch. Website: www. prioriteenfants.ch.
In business since 1998.
Placements: 40 nannies, mother's helps, babysitters.
Jobs in: Switzerland only.
No male placements.
Minimum stay: 6 months. Full- and part-time positions, permanent and time-limited.
Wages/pocket money: gross salary based on an hourly rate of 20 Swiss francs.
Qualifications: minimum age 20. Minimum 2 years childcare experience. Must be a European citizen, speak English and have references.
Application procedure: candidates undergo an interview process, have their professional references checked, need to provide proof of a clean police record, a medical certificate and character references.
Fees: nil.
Contact: Brigitte Devillers, Director.

PRO FILIA
Nationalsekretariat, Beckenhofstr. 16, Postfach, 8035 Zürich, Switzerland. ☎/fax: +41 1-361 53 31. E-mail: info@profilia.ch. Website: ww.profilia.ch.
Incoming placement office in French-speaking part: 32 Av de Rumine, 1005 Lausanne (+41 21-323 77 66; fax +41 21-323 77 67; vd@profili.ch) and in German-speaking part: Gallusstrasse 34, 9000 St. Gallen; tel/fax +41 71-222 6815; sg@profilia.ch).
In operation since 1896, with 15 branch offices. Swiss member of ACISJF (Association Catholique Internationale de Services pour la Jeunesse Féminine) and related to In Via (see entry).
Placements: 300-350 au pairs in Europe.
Jobs in: Switzerland; plus UK, Ireland, France, Italy, Germany, Spain, Belgium, Holland, Norway and Denmark.
Nationalities placed: Western Europeans, Canadians, Americans, Australians and New Zealanders to Switzerland. Swiss girls abroad.
Minimum stay: 12-18 months in Switzerland.

Wages/pocket money: from SFr600 net per month depending on age, plus board and lodging which is valued at SFr900. Deductions for insurance and contributions amount to about SFr100 per month.

Qualifications: age limits 17-30 years (18 in Geneva). Basic childcare experience and knowledge of household duties needed. Should have some knowledge of the relevant language and be prepared to study it seriously. Au pairs must attend 4-6 hours of language instruction per week.

Application procedure: personal or telephone interviews if possible after written application. Branch office addresses are on website. Opening hours may be limited.

Fees: registration fee SFr40 plus SFr260 placement fee due after placement.

QC HOME SUPPORT SERVICES
21 King St, Suite 112, London, Ontario N6A 5H3, Canada. ☎+1 519-679-2805. Fax: +1 519-645-0698. E-mail: qchs@execulink.com. Website: www. qchomesupport.com.

In business since 1974.

Placements: small number of nannies, nanny/housekeepers and carers for elderly and disabled people. No au pairs.

Jobs in: Canada only.

Nationalities placed: no restrictions.

Male positions rarely available.

Minimum stay: 12 month contracts.

Qualifications: as according to government regulations. Must speak English. Should be non-smokers, able to swim and drivers preferred.

Wages/pocket money: from C$7.45 per hour up to 44 hours per week. Higher salary paid to nannies with NNEB qualification.

Application procedure: contact agency direct for application form. If applicant is already in Canada, a personal interview/screening is arranged.

Fees: nil.

Contact: Viviane E. Logan, Owner/Manager.

QUICK AUPAIR & NANNY AGENCY
Cedar House, 41 Thorpe Road, Norwich NR1 1ES. ☎01603 219191 or 0845 345 5945. Fax: 07092 039873. E-mail: office@quickaupair.co.uk. Website: www.quickaupair.co.uk.

In business since 1998. Member of IAPA, BAPAA and REC.

Placements: 250 au pairs, au pairs plus, mother's helps and nannies.

Jobs in: UK. Outgoing programme to France, Germany, Austria, Italy, Spain, Switzerland, USA and Australia.

Nationalities placed: from any EU country plus Romania, Turkey, Croatia and Macedonia,

About 10% of applicants placed are male.

Minimum stay: 6 months; summer placements available.

Wages/pocket money: £55-£65 a week. £65-£80 for au pairs plus.

Qualifications: must speak 'fair' English, love children and have practical babysitting experience. Must be between 17 and 27, single and in good health. Must be willing to learn about way of life of English-speaking family and be prepared to help with child care and light housework duties.

Application procedure: completed registration form, character references, childcare references, 'Dear Family' letter, medical check, police check, photos (preferably smiling and with children). References are checked but interviews not necessary.

Other services: welcome pack is sent on arrival. Agency introduces new arrivals to other au pairs in the vicinity and keeps in contact. Social functions are organised (through the

auspices of BAPAA). Contact website where au pairs can communicate with others in the UK and make friends with young people of similar backgrounds. Au pairs are given emergency telephone number. Agency mediates in the case of any difficulty and can arrange emergency accommodation if necessary and re-match facility provided the applicant is suitable.
Fees: nil.
Contact: Bryan Levy, Proprietor.

QUICK HELP AGENCY
307A Finchley Road, London NW3 6EH. ☎020-7794 8666. Fax: 020-7433 1993. E-mail: mailbox@quickhelp.freeserve.co.uk. Website: www.quickhelp.co.uk.
In business since 1972. Member of IAPA and BAPAA.
Placements: au pairs, live-in nannies, mother's helps, mini mother's helps, resident housekeepers and elder care. 'Mini mother's helps' fall between au pairs and mother's helps, and work 43 hours a week.
Jobs in: UK only.
Nationalities placed: any that are legal. Many candidates from the new EU countries (Poland, Slovakia, etc.) opt for the mini mother's help option.
Male positions are available.
Minimum stay: 6 months. Summer short stays are available.
Wages/pocket money: £60-£78 per week for au pairs, £150 net for mini mother's helps, £200-£220 net for mother's helps, nannies, housekeepers and 'Living with the Elderly'.
Qualifications: nannies must have training; mother's helps and au pairs must have relevant experience. All applicants should have sufficient language skills to communicate.
Other services: advice given on language schools and ongoing support throughout the applicant's stay. Regular meetings.
Contact: Mrs. Norma Cutner, Owner.

REGENCY NANNIES INTERNATIONAL LTD
50 Hans Crescent, Knightsbridge, London SW1X 0NA. ☎020-7225 1055. E-mail: mail@regencynannies.com. Website: www.regencynannies.com. Additional offices in Hertfordshire (020-8420 4401) and France (14 Avenue de Villars, 75007 Paris).
In business since 1983. Member of REC.
Placements: 100-150 nannies, nurses, mother's helps, governesses and maternity nurses.
Jobs: worldwide, especially London and region, Paris and region, USA, United Arab Emirates and many countries in Europe.
Nationalities placed: any with Home Office permission to work in the UK or abroad.
Minimum stay: 1 year for permanent positions. Maternity nurses are often booked on 1-6 month contracts.
Qualifications: childcare experience and checkable childcare references essential. Driving licence and knowledge of French or German an asset.
Application procedure: interviews with agency essential. Processing application averages 4-7 days.
Fees: nil.

RELACIONES CULTURALES INTERNACIONALES (RCI) - see entry for Club de Relaciones Culturales Internacionales.

RICHMOND & TWICKENHAM AU PAIRS & NANNIES
The Old Rectory, Savey Lane, Yoxall, Staffs. DE13 8PD. ☎01543 473828. Fax: 01543 473838. E-mail: info@aupairsnationwide.co.uk. Website: www. aupairsnationwide.co.uk.

In business since 1992. Member of IAPA.
Placements: 500+ au pairs.
Jobs in: mainly UK (especially Southwest London, Midlands, Merseyside, Jersey, Darlington, Bristol and Cheltenham); also France, Italy and Spain.
Nationalities placed: in accordance with Home Office regulations, especially French, Italian, Spanish, Danish, Turkish, Czech and Slovak.
Minimum stay: minimum 6 months preferred. 6+ weeks in summer. Maximum 2 years.
Qualifications: ages 17-27. Language ability of chosen country. Childcare experience.
Application procedure: application form, 2 references, 'dear family' letter, photos and medical certificate needed.
Other services: contact given between girls.
Contact: Vicki Whitwell, Proprietor (vicki@aupairsnationwide.co.uk).

RIVERSIDE NANNIES & MOTHER'S HELPS
29 Milligan St, London E14 8AT. ☎020-7536 9566. Fax/back-up ansaphone: 020-7374 6363/4. E-mail: riversidechild@btconnect.com.
In business since 1989.
Placements: nannies, mother's helps, maternity nurses and nursery staff.
Jobs in: worldwide (provided work permits can be obtained for nannies).
Nationalities placed: all that are legal including Americans on 6-month BUNAC visas. Agency is prepared to try to place male applicants.
Minimum stay: no minimum though normally 6-12 months.
Qualifications: childcare experience almost always essential.
Application procedure: interviews at agency are compulsory. References meticulously checked including verbal references from past employers overseas.
Other services: training arm Riverside Training Company delivers childcare courses (see 'Introduction: Training').
Fees: nil.
Contact: Gaby Morris or Jill Wheatcroft.

ROMA AU PAIR
Via L. Bellotti Bon 15, 00197 Rome, Italy. ☎+39 06-807 8146. Mobile: +39 339 779 4126. Fax and voicemail: +39 06-2332 8223. Also Bologna office: Via di Frino No. 1, 40136 Bologna, Italy (fax 051-636 0956). E-Mail: info@romaaupair. com. Website: www.romaaupair.it.
In business since 1998.
Placements: 80 au pairs, au pairs plus and mother's helps (summer and long term). Also place Italian applicants as hotel and catering staff in Ireland.
Jobs in: Italy; outgoing programme to UK, France, Germany, Belgium, Spain and Australia.
Nationalities placed: as above plus American, Canadian, Mexican, Australian, South African, etc.
About 2% of applicants sent abroad are male.
Minimum stay: 6/9 months; 1 year preferred. Summer placements can be made.
Wages/pocket money: agency requests family to pay up to €80 weekly pocket money (for au pairs and au pairs plus). Summer placements and mother's helps can earn €100+. Monthly bus card also paid by family.
Qualifications: ages 18-30 and non-smoker. Childcare experience and basic knowledge of the language needed. Driving licence an advantage.
Application procedure: placement normally takes about one month. Complete file includes 2 character and/or job references which will be checked and a medical certificate. Host families are carefully interviewed.
Other services: 24 hour help line. Italian language classes on offer.

Fees: nil for incoming. From €150 for placements abroad.
Contact: Giuseppina Pamphili, Owner & President of Roma Au Pair Cultural Association.

ROWAN NANNIES
The Rowans, Hollybush Close, Potten End, Berkhamsted, Herts. HP4 2SN. ☎01442 876846. Fax: 01442 870865. E-mail: info@rowanagency.com. Website: www.rowanagency.com.
In business since 1991.
Placements: nannies and au pairs.
Jobs in: UK.
Nationalities placed: according to Home Office rules.
About 5% of applicants placed are male.
Minimum stay: 6 months. Summer placements can be made.
Application procedure: personal interview not required. 2-3 weeks taken for processing.
Fees: none.
Contact: Mrs. Lesley Samson, Owner.

SAPA (SLOVAK ACADEMIC & PERSONNEL AGENCY)
Sancová 108, 831 04 Bratislava, Slovakia. ☎+421 2-50 20 66 66. Fax: +421 2-55 41 07 13. E-mail: sapa@sapa.sk. Website: www.au-pair.sk.
In business since 1993. Member of IAPA.
Placements: 1,000 au pairs and cultural exchanges.
Jobs in: worldwide, especially Great Britain and Germany.
Nationalities placed: Slovak and EU.
About 20% of applicants placed are male.
Minimum stay: 3 months for summer placements, otherwise 6 months.
Wages/pocket money: £55 per week or equivalent.
Qualifications: ages 18-27. Childcare experience required. Must have at least intermediate knowledge of English or language of destination.
Application procedure: medical certificates, 4 photos and 2 references required. Interview necessary (though by phone is possible). Processing time 1-3 months.
Other services: SAPA sells insurance, coach and air tickets. SAPA also recruits employees for hotels, factories and care homes.
Fees: US$8 registration fee and US$50 placement fee. Fees vary slightly depending on country (no charge for placement in factories).
Contact: Zuzana Karpinska, Director.

SAPPHIRE PERSONNEL INC
116-92 Caplan Avenue, Barrie, Ontario L4N 0Z7, Canada. ☎+1 705-792-6662. Fax: +1 705-792-1729. E-mail: info@sapphirepersonnel.ca. Website: www. sapphirepersonnel.ca.
In business since 2001.
Placements: 100 nannies, elder care, governesses, housekeepers, mother's helps, home-helps, cottage cleaners, etc.
Jobs in: Canada.
Nationalities placed: from Singapore, India, Africa, England, Caribbean, Philippines, China and Hong Kong.
About 9% of applicants placed are male.
Minimum stay: contracts are usually on a one year basis, but more often run for 2-3 years, depending on the needs of the family. Summer placements are possible.
Wages/pocket money: nannies are paid between C$7.15 and C$18+ an hour depending on experience and number of children to be cared for. Caregivers are paid the same but can go

up to $30 and more for those with a nursing qualification.

Qualifications: must have an equivalency to Canadian grade twelve education and Caregiver or Childcare Diploma plus six months to one year of experience in relevant field. Minimum age 18. Must speak English or French.

Application procedure: 1-2 weeks to finalise contracts if candidate applying from Canada. Overseas applicants must be prepared to wait months for their visa to be processed, varying from 3-12+ months depending on country and how busy the Canadian embassy is.

Other services: overseas applicants receive free Health Care after arriving in Canada.

Fees: nil for local applicants. Overseas applicants are charged US$3000 plus a registration fee of US$200.

Contact: Magdalen Gollop, Managing Director.

S- AU PAIR INTERMEDIATE
Hinthamerstraat 34, 5211 MP 's-Hertogenbosch, Netherlands. ☎+31(0)73 6149483. Fax: +31(0)73 6910889. E-mail: info@saupair.com. Website: www. saupair.com.

In business since 1995. Member of IAPA, NAPO (Netherlands Au Pair Organisation) and exclusive representative of goAUPAIR for the USA Au Pair Programme in the Netherlands and Belgium.

Placements: au pairs only: approximately 400 inbound, 100 outbound.

Jobs in: Netherlands and Belgium. Outgoing programme mainly to USA, Aruba and Dutch Antilles, Spain, France, Italy and UK. Secondary destinations are Ireland, Austria, Switzerland, Denmark and Australia.

Almost no male placements.

Minimum stay: 6 months; summer placements available May-August (applications due before April 1st).

Wages/pocket money: €340 per month in the Netherlands; €450 per month in Belgium. Medical insurance, travel and course fees paid by the family in both countries.

Qualifications: ages 18-25. Must speak basic English and/or French and/or Spanish.

Application procedure: application form can be downloaded from website. Candidates must submit at least 2 childcare references plus preferably a school reference, a medical report, police clearance and official statement of single status. Personal interview conducted at office. After all documents have been submitted, placement normally takes 2-6 weeks.

Other services: non-EU nationals (except Americans, Canadians, Australians and Japanese) require a visa, which will be arranged by agency. One-day orientation course attended by all au pairs within a month of arrival, paid for by family. All au pairs have the opportunity to study any language (not necessarily Dutch) at state-funded schools; course fees are paid by family. In Belgium au pairs must study Dutch, French or German. 24 hour emergency telephone phone in case of problems. Agency guarantees to find a replacement family for an au pair within 15 days of an insoluble problem developing with a host family. Alternative accommodation is made available during that period.

Fees: nil for inbound, €25 subscription fee and €185 placement fee for outgoing.

Contact: Marielys Avila, General Director.

SCANDINAVIAN AU PAIR CENTER (SAPC) DENMARK
Moelledamsvej 2, 9382 Tylstrup, Denmark. ☎+45 98 26 12 42. Fax: on request. E-mail: Scandinavian@aupaircenter.dk. Website: www.aupaircenter.dk.

In business since 2004, though the main office of the Scandinavian Au Pair Service Center in Helsingborg Sweden since 1985.

Placements: 50 au pairs, nannies and housekeepers.

Jobs in: Denmark and the rest of Scandinavia; all of western world but mainly Northern Europe.

Up to 5% of applicants placed are male.

Minimum stay: 6-12 months.
Wages/pocket money: minimum by law is DKK2,500 per month. Host families normally refund travel expenses on completion of contract.
Qualifications: ages 18-30. Must speak German, English, Swedish, Norwegian or Danish.
Application procedure: online questionnaire. Depending on qualifications, placements can be made in as short a time as one week.
Other services: provides web links to assist au pairs meet other au pairs and to join Danish language meet-ups.
Fees: nil.
Contact: Lena Andersen, Manager of Danish department office.

SCANDINAVIAN AUPAIR CENTER NORGE
Torstingbuveien 3, 2322 Hamar, Norway. ☎+47 62 55 22 60. Fax: +47 62 55 22 61. E-mail: info@aupaircenter.no. Website: www.aupaircenter.no.
In business since 2003. Member of IAPA from 2006.
Placements: 150 au pairs.
Jobs in: Norway, Scandinavia, Europe and UK.
Virtually no male applicants are placed.
Nationalities placed: all applicants must comply with terms of Norwegian au pair programme (see www.udi.no).
Minimum stay: 6 months. From 2006/7 summer placements are available.
Wages/pocket money: minimum NOK 3,000 per month.
Application procedure: all registered information must be confirmed by documentation, interviews and information about Au Pair Programme to clarify expectations. Legally binding contracts are drawn up between family and au pair, family and agency, and au pair and agency.
Other services: guaranteed free replacement for both families and au pairs if any challenge occurs during the first three months (provided criminal behaviour is not involved). Every six months, agency organises a one-day meeting for au pairs (free of charge) in different districts for au pairs and families to meet each other, exchange experiences, network, etc.
Fees: nil.
Contact: Anne Marie Platou, Managing Director.

SCOTIA PERSONNEL LTD
6045 Cherry St, Halifax, Nova Scotia B3H 2K4, Canada. ☎+1 902-422-1455. Fax: +1 902-423-6840. E-mail: scotiap@ns.sympatico.ca. Website: www. scotia-personnel-ltd.com.
In business since 1980. Member of IAPA, International Nanny Association, Better Business Bureau and Canadian Nanny Coalition.
Placements: au pairs and nannies, as well as summer camp, hospitality work in England, English teaching/ summer camps in Italy.
Jobs in: Canada and worldwide (USA, England, France, Netherlands, Germany, Australia, Spain, Switzerland, Iceland, Denmark, Ireland, Austria and Italy.).
Nationalities placed: any that are allowed by immigration regulations.
Less than 10% of applicants placed are male.
Minimum stay: 1 month (Spain). 3-4 months over the summer, depending on destination country.
Qualifications: ages 17-27. Good childcare experience and some English needed.
Application procedure: personal interviews required.
Other services: assistance with visa application. Local affiliate agencies assist wherever possible throughout placement.
Fees: varies according to destination.
Contact: Marilyn VanSnick, Director.

SELECT AU-PAIRS
Crosbie House, 1 Moredun Road, Paisley PA2 9LJ, Scotland. ☎0141-884-8361. Fax: 0141-884-1566. E-mail: selectaupairs@aol.com. Website: www. Select-aupairs.com.
Paisley is near Glasgow. In business since 1996. Member of IAPA.
Placements: 100 au pairs and mother's helps.
Jobs in: UK: Scotland and the North of England. A few outgoing placements by special arrangement.
Nationalities placed: according to Home Office guidelines.
About 1% of applicants placed are male.
Minimum stay: 6 weeks to 3 months in summer; 6-8/10 months preferred.
Wages/pocket money: £50-£60 a week.
Qualifications: must have some experience with children.
Application procedure: recruitment arranged with partner agents abroad who personally check references and conduct interviews.
Other services: au pairs are given orientation information from country of origin. Upon arrival a welcome pack and personal visit are the norm. Advice is always available for au pairs in Scotland from the agency.
Fees: variable depending on country of origin.
Contact: Mrs. Nancy Ingram, Director.

SELECT NANNIES
82 Woodlands Avenue, West Byfleet, Surrey KT14 6AP. ☎01932 402146. Fax: 01932 342815. E-mail: selectnannies@hotmail.com. Website: www.select-nannies.co.uk.
In business since 1999.
Placements: nannies.
Jobs in: UK.
Wages/pocket money: £70 net per day.
Qualifications: must have fluent English and driving licence.
Application procedure: all applicants are given lengthy interview.
Contact: Angela Spencer, Owner.

SERVICES DE LA JEUNESSE FEMININE
Rue de Dave 174, 5100 Jambes-Namur, Belgium. ☎+32 81-30 99 80. Fax: +32 81-30 91 35.
In operation since 1954. Affiliated to the international Catholic organisation ACISJF with its headquarters in Switzerland.
Placements: about 100 au pairs.
Jobs in: Belgium (French and Dutch speaking regions); also a few to UK, Germany, Austria, Canada, Spain, Netherlands and Switzerland.
Nationalities placed: EU.
Males cannot be placed.
Minimum stay: 6-12 months.
Qualifications: ages 18-27. Must have experience of childcare. Fluency in French or Dutch required.
Fees: nil.
Contact: Mme. Marie-Jeanne Benoît, Vice President.

SERVIHOGAR
Calle del Pelicano 10, El Puerto de Santa Maria, Cádiz, Spain. ☎/fax: +34 956-85 17 44. E-mail: aupair@servihogar.org. Website: www.servihogar.org.
In business since 2004. Not member of IAPA but follow IAPA guidelines and European Au

Pair agreement.
Placements: 50-70 au pairs, au pairs plus and mother's helps.
Jobs in: Spain. Outgoing programme to UK, Germany and France.
Nationalities placed: EU nationals only.
Very few incoming applicants that are placed are male. Many young Spanish men register for placements abroad.
Minimum stay: 1 year; some summer placements.
Wages/pocket money: €55-€70 per week for 25-30 h.p.w. €75-€100 per week for 30-35 h.p.w.
Qualifications: ages 17-27.
Application procedure: if the candidate applies directly to agency, they must submit 2 references/recommendations which will be checked by telephone. Agency stays in email and telephone contact with applicant throughout the process.
Other services: advice given on what documents are needed to bring in order to apply for insurance and on residence permits. Agency phones au pair soon after arrival to check that all is well. Advice given on where to register for free language classes for foreigners, and contact details of other au pairs. Agency co-operates with other Spanish agencies which makes it easier to find a replacement family if a problem arises. 24-hour emergency contact number.
Fees: nil.
Contact: Laura Martin, Manager.

INTERNATIONAL CHILDCARE RECRUITMENT

Simply angelic

With in excess of 20 years UK recruitment industry experience we feel confident that we can quickly understand your exact requirements, and make the recruitment process as smooth as possible. We place Nannies and Aupairs from overseas with families in the UK, and also British nannies with families overseas.

For full details see **www.simplyangelic.co.uk** where you can also register free online. We will contact you shortly afterwards.

Simply Angelic, 88 Kingsway, London, WC2B 6AA Tel: 0207 6816490   Fax: 0870 7744273   info@simplyangelic.co.uk

SIMPLY ANGELIC LTD
88 Kingsway, Holborn, London WC2B 6AA. ☎020-7681 6490. Fax: 0870 774 4273. Also: Wellington House, East Road, Cambridge CB1 1BH. ☎0870 774 4272. E-mail: info@simplyangelic.co.uk. Website: www.simplyangelic.co.uk.
In business since 2003.
Placements: au pairs and au pair couples (in UK) and nannies (for families in UK and overseas).
Jobs in: UK for nannies and au pairs; qualified nannies also placed with families in Europe, Middle East, USA and the Caribbean.
Nationalities placed: nannies must have English as a first language or speak it fluently. Au pairs must be from a country participating in the UK au pair scheme.
About 1% of applicants placed are male.
Minimum stay: 9 months; some summer placements available for au pairs only.
Wages/pocket money: au pairs earn £55-£120 per week; nannies earn up to £400 net per week.
Qualifications: nannies must be qualified with 1 year's professional full-time sole charge experience or unqualified with 2 years' experience. Maternity nurses must be qualified

with a minimum of 2 years' newborn experience. Mother's helps need to have a level 2 qualification with 1 year's experience or unqualified with 2 years' experience.
Application procedure: nanny applicants must be interviewed in London or Cambridge offices. References and CVs carefully checked and CRB disclosure or clean police check less than 6 months old required.
Other services: advice given on insurance, etc. Ongoing support after placement. Czech and Slovakian spoken at agency.
Fees: nil.
Contact: Glyn Taylor, Director.

SIMPLY DOMESTICS & HOMELINE
65 Colney Hatch Lane, London N10 1LR. ☎020-8444 4304 (5 lines). Fax: 020-8444 4791. E-mail: enquiries@simplydomestics.com. Website: www. simplydomestics.com.
In business since 1989. Member of REC.
Placements: nannies, mother's helps, domestics, housekeepers and au pairs.
Jobs in: UK (North London mainly). Very few placements in Europe.
Nationalities placed: all that are legal.
Male candidates are occasionally placed.
Minimum stay: 3 months especially in summer.
Application procedure: all written and verbal references are checked. Interviews given where possible.
Other services: 24-hour answerphone for problems. Friendship circle organised.
Contact: Judith Ivers, Proprietor.

SNOW AU PAIRS
Kavaljeerintie 6A4, 01520 Vantaa (Helsinki Region), Finland. ☎☎+358 440 434 441 GSM. Fax: +358 440 430 269. E-mail: anne.wright@snowaupairs.com. Website: www.snowaupairs.com.
In business since June 2005.
Placements: 15 au pairs.
Jobs in: Finland.
Nationalities placed: all.
Male applicants can be placed.
Minimum stay: 3 months. Maximum stay 12 months.
Wages/pocket money: at least €252 per month for 30 hours a week. €5 paid for each additional hour worked. Family also pays for au pair's accident insurance (as required by law), language course in Finnish or Swedish and half of travel expenses. Au pairs are given a 2-week paid vacation when working 12 months.
Qualifications: must provide 2 personal references, a background police check and doctor's certificate.
Other services: assistance given with Finnish visa process. Agency organises group meetings and activities with local au pairs to build a sense of community. Assistance provided with contractual and government formalities to ensure the rights of families and au pairs are protected. Agency owner has worked in the area of child welfare and has a degree in Social Welfare.
Fees: €50 application fee. €200 deposit, returnable on successful completion of programme.
Contact: Anne Wright (Programme Director) and Jason Wright (General Manager).

SOAMES PARIS NANNIES
64 rue Anatole France, Levallois-Perret, 92300 France. ☎☎/fax +33 1-47 30 44 04. E-mail: soames.parisnannies@wanadoo.fr. Website: www.soamesparisnannies.com.

In business since 1988. Member of IAPA.
Placements: 150 nannies, au pairs and mother's helps. One department specialises in British nurses and mother's helps.
Jobs in: France (especially Paris and environs); also French nannies sent to England, Ireland, Germany, Italy, Spain, Norway, Netherlands and Belgium.
Nationalities placed: EU and Eastern Europe, Maltese, Australians, Americans. French candidates sent abroad.
Male au pair positions are available.
Minimum stay: 10 months for au pairs, though some 6 month positions available from January. 1 year for nannies and mother's helps. Summer au pair stays of 2-3 months are available.
Wages/pocket money: minimum €75-€80 per week for au pairs; minimum €889 net per month (net) for mother's helps, €1,200 for nannies with diploma; €1,500 for nannies with qualification and experience.
Qualifications: ages 18-29 for Europe. Must have good childcare experience.
Application procedure: interviews necessary for nannies. References are checked.
Other services: private health insurance can be arranged for au pairs. List of language classes given.
Fees: nil for incoming; €160 for outgoing.

SOGGIORNI ALL'ESTERO PER LA GIOVENTU'
Via Tiepolo 28, 20129 Milan, Italy. ☎+39 02-753 00 61 or 02-700 02 568. E-mail: soggiorniallestero@libero.it.
In business since 1957.
Placements: 400 au pairs, demi pairs, work/study, language students and homestays.
Jobs in: UK, Ireland, France, Germany, Austria and Spain. (No placements in Italy.)
Nationalities placed: Italians (mainly).
Minimum stay: 3 months (6 months in Germany).
Qualifications: must have some experience and moderate competence in chosen language.
Fees: €180.
Contact: Nicoletta Casalini.

SOLIHULL AU PAIR & NANNY AGENCY
5 Parklands, Blossomfield Road, Solihull B91 1NG. ☎07973 886 979. Fax: 0121-233 9731. E-mail: aupairs1@btconnect.com.
In business since 1963.
Placements: live-in and live-out nannies plus babysitters for the West Midlands. Au pairs and nannies for Europe and America.
Jobs in: France, Spain, Italy, Germany and America; also UK (West Midlands).
Nationalities placed: Europeans in accordance with Home Office regulations.
Minimum stay: 6 months, preferably 1 year (1 year for USA). Summer stays: 3 months.
Wages/pocket money: £45-£60 per week for au pairs; £250-£300 for nannies, depending on age, experience and duties.
Qualifications: minimum age 18, maximum 26. Driving licence is a help, essential for USA. Childcare experience required for mother's helps and nannies; also for au pairs in the USA.
Application procedure: application form, CV if available, 2 references from teachers and/or previous employers, medical certificate and photos. CRB check. Interview necessary for America plus copy of driving licence and, if possible, life saving qualifications, first aid certificate or any evidence of childcare experience.
Contact: Lorraine Bushell, Proprietor.

SOLUTION AU PAIR
16 rue de l'Abbé Lemire, F-59700 Marcq-en-Baroeul, France. ☎+33 3-20 83 19 50. E-mail: contact@solutionaupair.com. Website: www.solutionaupair. com.

In business since 2002. Member of IAPA and IFAPP. Parent company Coaching Solutions. Located near Lille.

Placements: 90 incoming au pairs and 100 outgoing, including working holiday placements in Australia and New Zealand.

Jobs in: France, especially Pas-de-Calais in northern France. Outgoing programme to UK, USA, Germany, Italy and Spain.

About 20% of applicants placed are male (including working holiday placements in the Antipodes).

Minimum stay: 2 months in summer. Minimum 6 months for a long term placement but preferably 12 months.

Wages/pocket money: about €80 a week plus transport.

Qualifications: childcare experience, language knowledge, ability to survive abroad.

Application procedure: face-to-face interview for both families and outgoing applicants. Processing of files takes from 1 week to 3 months depending on the time of the year and the quality of the file.

Other services: travel insurance provided and close follow-up with language schools. Outgoing au pairs are supported with a strong local network.

Fees: outgoing candidate fee is €195, though differs among countries.

Contact: Annie Labat, Director.

SPANISH TEACHERS S.L.
Ladera de los Almendros 40, 28032 Madrid, Spain. ☎/fax: +34 95-241 7127. E-mail: info@spanishteachers.info. Website: www.spanishteachers.info.

In business since 2005.

Placements: au pairs, babysitters and nannies.

Jobs in: Spain, and outgoing programme to UK, France, Germany and Ireland.

About 1% of applicants placed are male.

Minimum stay: 1-2 months in summer.

Wages/pocket money: standard au pairs in Spain earn €60 a week; au pairs plus earn €85 a week.

Qualifications: ages 17-30. Some childcare experience needed. Must speak Spanish or English.

Application procedure: initial contact by telephone or in person. Clean police record, medical report and references must be submitted. Documents (which should be translated into Spanish) are checked, families are sent au pair profiles and telephone interview is arranged with family.

Other services: agency contacts au pairs and families after arrival to make sure arrangement is successful.

Fees: nil to incoming au pairs; Spanish au pairs on outgoing programme pay €250 for long-term placements, €200 for short-term.

Contact: Ruth Lopez, Manager.

STAR NANNIES
67 Sheldons Court, Winchcombe St, Cheltenham, Glos. GL52 2NR. ☎/fax: 01242 512636. E-mail: tracey@starnannies.co.uk. Website: www.starnannies. co.uk.

In business since 1998.

Placements: 40 nannies.

Jobs in: UK, Europe and Asia but not USA or Canada.

Nationalities placed: must have working visa already arranged.
Male applicants can be placed.
Minimum stay: temporary and permanent positions.
Wages/pocket money: £150-£300 per week net depending on qualifications and experience.
Qualifications: must have childcare qualification or 2 years nannying experience. Must have very good English.
Application procedure: face-to-face interview compulsory.
Contact: Tracey Pountney, Director.

STI TRAVELS
Study Travels International, Via Borgonuovo 6A, 40125 Bologna, Italy. ☎+39 051-233285. Fax: +39 051-291 1707. E-mail: info@stitravels.com. Website: www.stitravels.com.
In business since 1994. Application to IAPA pending.
Placements: au pairs.
Jobs in: Italy; also Ireland, England, France (Nice and Paris areas), Germany (Berlin and Frankfurt), Spain, Monaco, USA, Canada and Australia for Italians.
About 10% of applicants placed are male.
Minimum stay: 6-12 months. Summer stays of 3 months are available in Ireland.
Wages/pocket money: from €77 per week to €165 in USA.
Qualifications: ages 18-27. Childcare experience preferred.
Other services: agency can arrange insurance and travel and give advice on language classes.
Fees: €90 plus varying fees depending on country.
Contact: Bianca Buganè, Director.

STUDENTAFERDIR
Bankastraeti 10, 101 Reykjavik, Iceland. ☎+354 562-2362. Fax: +354 562-9662. E-mail: info@exit.is. Website: www.exit.is.
In business since 1990. Member of IAPA.
Placements: approximately 50 au pairs.
Jobs in: Iceland. Outgoing programme to US, UK, Ireland, Denmark, Norway, Sweden, Holland, Italy, Spain, France, Switzerland, Austria and Germany.
Agency will try to place male applicants.
Minimum stay: usually 9-12 months in Iceland. Some summer placements available.
Wages/pocket money: 10,000 kroner (€138) per week.
Qualifications: ages 18-26, unmarried with no children. Must have experience in childcare and completed secondary school. Must have clean police record, and be in good physical and emotional health. Driving licence essential for US.
Application procedure: processing time may be up to 3 months.
Other services: Families in Iceland pay for au pair's insurance (ISIS insurance). The au pair pays for the language course. The host family pays 4,500 kroner each month to the au pair for the airfare. Agency distributes welcome packs upon arrival and arranges for current au pairs to make contact and welcome new arrivals. Four au pair gatherings held each year.
Fees: nil.
Contact: Hafdis Hardardottir, Project Manager.

STUDENT AGENCY
Basty 2, Brno 602 00, Czech Republic. ☎+420 5-42 42 42 42. Fax: +420 5-42 42 42 40. E-mail: info@studentagency.cz. Website: www.studentagency.cz.
In business since 1993 with 11 offices throughout the Czech and Slovak Republics. Full

member of IAPA, FIYTO, GWEA (Global Work Experience Association) and ALTO (Association of Language Travel Organisations).
Placements: thousands of au pairs, mother's helps, parent's helps, housekeepers, etc. every year.
Jobs in: UK, Ireland, USA, Germany, France, Denmark, Netherlands, Spain, Italy, Belgium, Norway, Sweden and Austria. No incoming programme to Slovak or Czech Republics. About 8% of applicants placed are male.
Nationalities placed: Czech and Slovak.
Minimum stay: varies from country to country. 3-month summer stays are available in England, France, Italy, Ireland, USA and Spain.
Wages/pocket money: £55 per week in Britain, $139 or $200 in USA, €260 in Germany, etc.
Qualifications: vary from country to country. Minimum age 18. Language skills, childcare experience and responsible and flexible attitude needed. Driving licence is essential for USA.
Application procedure: processing time normally 1-2 months for Europe, 2-3 months for USA. Character and childcare references required. Interviews required in some cases.
Other services: agency assists with documentation for obtaining visas and with arranging transport. Emergency back-up given (24-hour helpline) and support throughout stay.
Fees: 1,200 Czech or Slovak crowns for UK; 1,600 crowns for Germany; 1,000 crowns (refundable in some cases) for USA but American partner organisation requires a good faith deposit.
Contact: Ms. Alena Mouckova, Au Pair Programme Manager, and Mr. Radim Jancura, Director.

STUFAM V.Z.W.
Vierwindenlaan 7, 1780 Wemmel, Belgium. ☎+32 2-460 33 95. Fax: +32 2-460 00 71. E-mail: aupair.stufam@scarlet.be. Website: www.aupair-stufam.be.
Office hours: Monday and Friday: 5.30-8pm; Tuesday and Thursday: 3-6pm.
In business since 1985.
Placements: 100-120 au pairs.
Jobs in: Belgium (French, German, Dutch and English speaking families); also Belgian au pairs to UK, Ireland, Netherlands, France, Spain, Italy, Norway, Denmark, Germany, Austria and Switzerland.
Nationalities placed: EU nationals; others must apply for visas.
Minimum stay: 6 months. Summer placements of 2-3 months to au pairs who have a good knowledge of French.
Qualifications: childcare references needed. Must have basic knowledge of the language. Ages 18-28.
Other services: assistance in case of problems. Assist au pairs who need visas. Agency puts au pairs in touch with one another. Families obliged to provide expensive health insurance.
Fees: nil.
Contact: Lieve Deschuymere, Manager.

SUE'S AU-PAIR AGENCY
44 The Reddings, Mill Hill, London NW7 4JR. ☎/fax: 020-8959 2126. E-mail: sueaupair@btinternet.com.
In business since 1985.
Placements: 400 au pairs, mother's helps, nannies, housekeepers.
Jobs in: UK only.
About 1% of applicants placed are male.
Minimum stay: 6-12 months; a very few 3-month summer placements available.

Wages/pocket money: £55 a week for 25 h.p.w. with 2 days off.
Qualifications: must have childcare experience and some English.
Application procedure: au pairs accepted only via agents abroad who have interviewed and vetted au pairs. Candidates are police-checked, and must submit medical report and professional and childcare references.
Other services: agency arranges introductions of au pairs to other au pairs in the area.
Fees: fees may be payable to partner agencies.
Contact: Susan Lee, Proprietor.

SUNFLOWERS CHILDCARE LTD
29 Dover Road, Birkdale, Southport, Lancs. PR8 4TB. ☎01704 564389. Fax: 01704 566662. E-mail: info@sunflowerschildcare.co.uk. Website: www. thenannybureau.co.uk.
Also trades as Nannies International & The Nanny Bureau. In business since 1988.
Placements: 80-100 mother's/father's helps, nannies, nursery nurses, holiday nannies, emergency cover, mobile crèche, nanny/housekeepers and crèche assistants; temporary and permanent.
Jobs available: worldwide but especially UK, France, Belgium, Holland, Germany, Italy, UAE, Canada, Switzerland and Australia.
Minimum stay: varies for each job.
Wages/pocket money: from minimum wage to £650 per week (maternity nurse/ nanny).
Qualifications: must be over 18 and speak English. Some knowledge of other languages an advantage. NNEB, NVQ3 and BTEC where appropriate.
Application procedure: average processing time can be very quick (5-7 days). References are checked. Interview a necessity and follow-up phone calls are made to people who know the applicant well.
Other services: 4-week trial period during which a nanny can keep in touch with the agency. Travel can be organised and general advice on salaries/insurance can be given. Agency also owns and runs Montessori Day Nursery in Southport for children aged 3 months to 8 years.
Fees: none for applicants, vary for families.
Contact: Heather Langridge and Claire Langridge, Directors.

SUNSHINE AU PAIR AGENCY
15 Vy des Crêts, CH-1295 Mies (Geneva), Switzerland. ☎/fax: + 41 22-755 20 81. E-mail: info@au-pair-sunshine.ch. Website: www.au-pair-sunshine.ch.
In business since 1997.
Placements: 20-30 au pairs.
Jobs in: French-speaking Switzerland only (mainly in and around Geneva).
Nationalities placed: EU nationals only.
Very few male au pairs are placed.
Minimum stay: school year (end of August to beginning of July). Some shorter periods possible but minimum 6 months.
Wages/pocket money: SFr760 per month. Au pair must provide valid health insurance.
Qualifications: ages 18-29. Must have childcare references and basic French or English.
Application procedure: medical certificate, 2 references, photos and personal letter to family must be submitted.
Fees: nil.
Contact: Cornelia Odermatt, Owner.

SWANSONS NANNY AGENCY

4 Brackley Road, Chiswick, London W4 2HN. ☎020-8994 5275. Fax: 020-8994 9280. E-mail: anne@swansonsnannies.co.uk. Website: www. swansonsnannies.co.uk.

In business since 1984.

Placements: hundreds of daily and live-in nannies, mother's helps (full-time and shared).

Jobs in: UK.

Nationalities placed: mainly British but also Australians, New Zealanders and Europeans.

About 1% of applicants placed are male.

Minimum stay: temporary and permanent appointments.

Wages/pocket money: from £180 per week up to £450 per week net.

Application procedure: all candidates are interviewed in person and all references and CVs are thoroughly checked.

Other services: nanny contact groups arranged.

Contact: Anne Babb, Owner.

SWAN TRAINING INSTITUTE LTD

9-11 Grafton Street, Dublin 2, Ireland. ☎+353 1-677 5252. Fax: +353 1-677 5254. E-mail: admin@sti.ie. website: www.sti.ie.

In business since 1988. Member of MEI-RELSA.

Placements: au pairs and au pairs plus.

Jobs in: Ireland only.

Nationalities placed: no restrictions.

Minimum stay: 6 months (3 months in summer).

Wages/pocket money: €80-€100 per week for 30-35 hours a week.

Qualifications: ages 18-25. Must be able to speak English at an intermediate level. Some childcare and housework experience needed.

Application procedure: application form should be submitted 3 months before intended departure.

Other services: language classes compulsory for au pairs in Dublin. Swan Training Institute timetables classes for au pairs (3 hours on Tuesday and Thursday evenings) at competitive prices in preparation for Cambridge Examinations.

Fees: placement and tuition cost €524 for 12 weeks.

THE NANNY AGENCY

29 Cranbourne Road, Muswell Hill, London N10 2BT. ☎020-8883 3162. Fax: 020-8245 7641. E-mail: nlondon@thenannyagency.co.uk. Website: www. thenannyagency.co.uk.

In business since 1993.

Placements: up to 50 nannies per year.

Jobs in: UK (North London).

Nationalities placed: mainly British.

Minimum stay: mostly long-term appointments.

Qualifications: checkable references and childcare experience needed. Qualifications useful but not essential.

Contact: Vivienne Kaye, Sole Trader.

TINIES CHILDCARE LTD

Unit 14, 126-128 New Kings Road, London SW6 4LZ. ☎020-7384 0322. Fax: 020-7731 6008. E-mail: info@tinieschildcare.co.uk. Website: www.tinies. com.

In business since 1975. Member of REC. 22 franchised branches across the UK plus

international branches in Australia, New Zealand, South Africa and Poland.
Placements: nannies, maternity nannies, nursery nurses and primary school teachers.
Jobs in: UK, Europe, USA and worldwide especially Australia, New Zealand and South Africa.
Minimum stay: short temporary contracts and permanent posts. Large number of guaranteed jobs also available in nurseries.
Qualifications: nannies must be qualified or experienced. Mother's helps must have at least 2 years full-time childcare experience and references.
Application procedure: interviews arranged if possible. At least 2 childcare references checked verbally plus CRB checks.
Other services: contracts, payroll, childcare training and first aid.
Fees: nil.
Contact: Amanda Coxen.

TOP NOTCH NANNIES
Flat 2, 49 Harrington Gardens, Gloucester Road, London SW7 4JU. ☎020-7259 2626. Fax: 020-7244 9035. E-mail: theteam@topnotchnannies.com. Website: www.topnotchnannies.com.
In business since 1992. Member of REC. Investor in People and accredited by City & Guilds.
Placements: full-time, part-time and temporary nannies, mother's helps, babysitters, maternity nurses and doulas.
Jobs in: worldwide (excluding USA). Good contacts in Australia and New Zealand. Good male nannies can be placed.
Minimum stay: temporary and permanent positions available.
Wages/pocket money: live-in full-time nannies earn £250-£300 net per week; live-out nannies earn £350-£400.
Application procedure: interview essential. Must provide phone numbers for at least 2 and preferably 3 referees.
Fees: nil for UK.
Contact: Jean Birtles, Director.

TOTALNANNIES.COM
37 Leamington Avenue, Morden, London SM4 4DQ. ☎020-8542 3067. Fax: 0870 762 1387. E-mail: info@totalnannies.com. Website: www.totalnannies. com.
Placements: au pairs, mother's helps, nannies, maternity nurses, etc.
Jobs available: worldwide, mainly Italy.
Nationalities placed: most nationalities considered, providing travel and work documents are obtainable.
Minimum stay: 6-12 months. Short-term summer positions of 1-4 months can be made.
Wages/pocket money: maternity nurses earn up to £600 per week, nannies £400, mother's helps £300, au pairs £50. Return airfare to London paid on completion of stay. All positions include holiday pay.
Qualifications: some childcare experience preferred but not essential. Reasonable standard of English essential. Childcare certificate or nanny diploma essential for nanny positions.
Application procedure: 2 passport sized photos, medical certificate (i.e. note from doctor that candidate is in good health) and minimum 2 references preferably related to childcare. Application forms can be sent by post or submitted on-line.
Other services: comprehensive website allows consultation of available positions, members' area with links to other girls placed in families, chat room, round-the-clock support area and free e-mail account. Assigned post-placement co-ordinator assists and supports throughout stay. Free temporary accommodation can sometimes be arranged in

the event of an emergency.
Fees: nil.
Contact: Harry Brasier, Positions Co-ordinator (harry@totalnannies.com).

TRAVEL ACTIVE AU PAIR
PO Box 107, 5800 AC Venray (Maasheseweg 79a, 5804 AB Venray), Netherlands. ☎+31 478-551 900. Fax: +31 478-551 911. E-mail: info@travelactive.nl. Website: www.travelactive.nl.
In business since 1989. Founding member of IAPA and member of FIYTO, GWEA and NAPO. From 1995, incorporating Dutch agency Exis KLIX and from 1999 incorporating Dutch agency Au Pair Discover Holland. Travel Active offers international Work, Study, Au Pair, Volunteer, Language, Internship and Exchange programmes.
Placements: 300 au pairs placed throughout the Netherlands, 150 Dutch young people placed as au pairs abroad. Travel Active places thousands of Dutch participants in a variety of other exchange programmes.
Jobs in: Netherlands. Dutch au pairs placed in the UK, Ireland, France, Spain, Italy, Austria, Iceland and USA.
Nationalities placed: all (inbound) and Dutch (outbound).
Male au pairs with good childcare references are accepted.
Minimum stay: 6-12 months for EU au pairs in Netherlands and 12 months for au pairs who require a visa. For Dutch au pairs: 6-12 months for Europe, 12 or 24 months for USA.
Qualifications: childcare experience necessary of non-relatives and a high school diploma. Maximum age for Holland is 25 years; for rest of Europe maximum is 30.
Other services: for inbound au pairs, insurance is paid by host family and membership is given in Travel Active Au Pair Club which includes welcome package on arrival with an au pair guide, personal counselling, au pair meetings throughout Holland, a weekend trip to Paris, plus flight and/or course reimbursement. Outbound au pairs are personally interviewed and attend pre-departure workshop at the Travel Active office, and are given an au pair guide.
Fees: nil for inbound au pairs (unless a fee is charged by partner agency in another country); €200 for outbound au pairs.
Contact: Esther Terpstra (Programme Manager of the Au Pair department); Elvira Claessen (Travel Active General Manager).

TRUVA INTERNATIONAL AU PAIR AND EDUCATION SERVICE
Osmanaga mh. Sogutlucesme Cd. No.56, Altin Carsi K.4, D.74, Kadikoy, Istanbul, Turkey. ☎+90 216-414 77 50. Fax: +90 216-330 93 30. E-mail: truva@ truva.com.tr. Website: www.truva.com.tr.
In business since 1997. Member of IAPA.
Placements: 250 au pairs.
Jobs in: outgoing programme to England, America and Europe.
About 10% of applicants placed are male.
Nationalities placed: mainly Turkish.
Minimum stay: 6 months – 2 years; some summer placements available.
Qualifications: 18-27. Must have childcare experience.
Application procedure: applicants are interviewed and their references are checked.
Other services: assistance with visas.
Fees: varies.
Contact: Mrs. Fatma Ilhan, General Manager.

UK & OVERSEAS NANNY/AU PAIR AGENCY LTD.

Vigilant House, 120 Wilton Road, London SW1V 1JZ. ☎020-7808 7898. Fax: 020-7808 7899. E-mail: london@nannys.co.uk. Website: www.nannys.co.uk.
In business since 1969.

Placements: 500+ live-in-staff: nannies, au pairs, domestic, housekeepers, etc.

Jobs in: England and worldwide but mostly European countries such as France, Italy, Spain, Switzerland and Germany.

Nationalities placed: any that can work legally. No student visas accepted.
Male au pairs can occasionally be placed if they have childcare experience supported by references and stay for a minimum of 12 months.

Minimum stay: usual stay 12 months plus. Some temp jobs including summer stays available for a minimum of 3 months (no less).

Qualifications: au pairs need good written references only. Mother's helps need to be experienced or/and have good references. Nannies must have NNEB or similar qualification and have good references.

Application procedure: early application encouraged. Interested individuals should send SAE for introduction pack and application form or visit agency (no appointment necessary). Applicants should bring a current CV, references and ID. Processing takes between 1 day and 3 weeks. Agency maintains weekly vacancy lists for the UK.

Other services: advice on insurance, etc.

Contact: Karen Bransgrove, Co-Director.

UK NANNIES AND AU PAIRS

19 The Severals, Newmarket, Cambridgeshire CB8 7YN. ☎01638 560 812. E-mail: help@uknanniesandaupairs.com. Website: www.theukaupairagency.co.uk.
In business since 2000.

Placements: au pairs, au pairs plus, mothers helps, nannies, housekeepers and nanny/ housekeepers.
Jobs in: UK only.
About 25% of applicants placed are male.
Minimum stay: 3 months though many other placements are 6, 12, 18 months or longer.
Wages/pocket money: £60 a week for au pairs, £75 for au pairs plus, £150 for mother's helps, £200+ for nannies.
Qualifications: must have childcare and domestic experience, knowledge of English, police check, medical certificate and references.
Application procedure: average processing time 1-3 weeks.
Fees: nil.
Contact: Ari Hogg, Support Assistant.

UNIVERSAL AUNTS
PO Box 304, London SW4 0NN. ☎020-7738 8937. Fax: 020-7622 4520. E-mail: aunts@universalaunts.co.uk. Website: www.universalaunts.co.uk.
In business since 1921.
Placements: nannies and mother's helps.
Jobs in: UK and Europe.
Agency cannot place male candidates.
Nationalities placed: any, provided they are legal.
Minimum stay: variable. Summer placements possible, but in great demand.
Qualifications: childcare experience needed. Driving licence useful.
Application procedure: after childcare references received and interviews held, placement can usually be made within 10 days. Interviews by appointment only. Family and applicant always put in direct contact.
Fees: no registration fee.

VEREIN FÜR INTERNATIONALE JUGENDARBEIT (VIJ)
Arbeitsgemeinschaft Christlicher Frauen, Bundesverein e. V. Bundesgeschäftsstelle, Goetheallee 10, 53225 Bonn, Germany. ☎+49 228-698952. Fax: +49 228-694166. E-mail: au-pair@vij-bundesgeschaeftsstelle. org. Website: www.vij-deutschland.de or www.au-pair-vij.org.
In operation since 1877. Ten regional offices throughout Germany and many local branches.
Placements: hundreds of au pairs.
Jobs in: Germany. Outgoing programme for German au pairs.
Nationalities placed: all.
Some male applicants are placed.
Qualifications: must have some experience with children and knowledge of the language.
Fees: nil.

WEIGAN NANNIES
1 Whites Row, London E1 7NF. ☎020-7377 2620. E-mail: elizabethelder@ thechildcarecompany.co.uk. Website: www.thechildcarecompany.co.uk.
New management November 2005 by The Childcare Company (see entry).
Placements: nannies and au pairs abroad via tour operator and sponsors.
Jobs in: Greece, Turkey, Spain, Portugal, France and all ski areas with tour operators.
Minimum stay: summer season. Job involves nannying for one or more families, with new arrivals every week. Also work in nurseries and crèches.
Wages/pocket money: wage and package upon request.

Qualifications: minimum age 18. Must have recognised childcare qualification or good experience and EU passport or work permit for UK.
Fees: nil.
Contact: Elizabeth Elder.

WELCOME AGENCY
Corso Moncalieri, 337 bis, 10133 Turin, Italy. ☎/fax: +39 01-661 5647. Mobile: +39 333-439 9015. E-mail: aottone@iol.it. Website: www.welcomeagency.it.
In business since 1998.
Placements: 20 au pairs.
Jobs in: occasionally foreign au pairs are placed in Italian families. Mainly outgoing programme to UK, Ireland and all EU countries.
1 or 2 male applicants placed each year.
Minimum stay: 3 months during the summer.
Wages/pocket money: €70 a week.
Qualifications: must have some experience with children.
Application procedure: written application and all the other documents must be in order (references, dear family letter, doctor certificate, photos). Girls are personally interviewed where possible.
Other services: advice given on insurance, travel and language classes.
Fees: €250.
Contact: Anna Ottone, Director.

WESTMINSTER NANNIES INTERNATIONAL
5 Salisbury Road, Langton Green, Kent TN3 0ES. ☎020-7898 9028. Fax: 020-7898 9101. E-mail: info@westminsternannies.com. Website: www. westminsternannies.com.
In business since 1988.
Placements: nannies, governesses and maternity nurses.
Jobs in: UK and worldwide.
Minimum stay: permanent (1 year) and temporary (variable).
Qualifications: must have training and/or minimum 2 years experience. Minimum age 18.
Application procedure: initial telephone screening followed by a detailed application form. Interviewed personally by appointment.
Contact: Alison Ellershaw, Owner/Manager.

YAKIN BATI EDUCATIONAL COUNSELING SERVICES
Valikonagi Cd. No. 107/E D:11, Nisantasi, Istanbul 80220, Turkey. ☎+90 212-247 58 69. Fax: +90 212-247 91 53. E-mail: info@aupairline.com. Website: www.yakinbati.net/tr.
In business since 1996.
Placements: au pairs.
Jobs in: USA, UK, Denmark, Germany, France and the Netherlands.
Nationalities placed: Turkish mainly.
About 10% of applicants placed are male.
Minimum stay: 6 months though 1 year preferred.
Qualifications: childcare experience and knowledge of English or relevant language needed.
Application procedure: process takes 2 weeks to 2 months provided no documents omitted from application.
Contact: Eren Goker, Educational Advisor.

YORKSHIRE NANNIES
26-27 High Street, Doncaster, South Yorkshire DN1 1DW. ☎01302 349393 (6 lines).
In business since 1970.
Placements: nannies, maternity nurses, mother's helps, housekeepers, carers, couples, butlers, cooks and chauffeurs.
Jobs in: throughout UK and worldwide (excluding USA).
Minimum stay: temporary and permanent positions.
Qualifications: childcare experience and driving licence normally needed.
Application procedure: all applicants are interviewed on premises. Must bring full CV. CRB clearance required. References are checked. High standards expected.
Fees: nil.

YOUTH DISCOVERY PROGRAMMES
PO Box 1813, Cape Town 8001, South Africa. Fax: 21-423 1586. E-mail: aupair@ydp.co.za. Website: www.ydp.co.za.
In business since 1993. Member of IAPA, GWEA and FIYTO.
Placements: 500 au pairs and nannies.
Jobs in: USA mainly; also England.
Nationalities placed: Southern African mainly.
5%-10% of applicants placed are male.
Minimum stay: 12 months for USA, 6 months in Europe.
Qualifications: ages 18-26. 200 hours childcare experience for USA; basic language skills needed for Europe.
Application procedure: detailed interview compulsory. 3 references needed including 2 for childcare. References are checked. Processing time normally 3-6 weeks.
Other services: YDP's partner agencies give 24-hour on-the-ground support to au pairs. International telephone number is given for any medical emergencies.
Fees: R3,995 including flight, insurance and training workshop.
Contact: Kim Leetch, Au Pair Programme Administrator.

Appendix 1: Safety in the Home

Be sure that telephone numbers of the local doctors, hospital and ambulance service are kept in a prominent position by the telephone.

Prevention is better than cure, so let us first examine the potential dangers to children in the home, and how they may be avoided.

Most young children have little or no experience of danger so they are unable to anticipate the consequences of their actions. It is impossible to guard a child all the time, and continually restricting him is bad for developing self-confidence. But making sure the home is a safe place to play can help alleviate the problem. If you are caring for young children and the house has not already been child-proofed, this should be discussed with the employers. Safety catches can be fixed to the doors of cupboards containing dangerous items, and sharp corners on tables and work surfaces may be covered by buffers to help prevent the children hurting their heads. You can also buy slot-in plastic covers for open plug sockets in some countries.

Try to remember that when dealing with a serious first-aid situation, it is imperative that you keep calm. The child will be frightened as well as hurt and will look to you for reassurance. If the wound isn't serious, don't dismiss the child for making a fuss. They will genuinely require your sympathy, but once the initial fear has passed, they should be encouraged to carry on as normal. Absorbing the child in a game or reading a story is a good way of diverting attention from any mild injuries.

SUFFOCATION AND CHOKING

Suffocation of babies can be avoided by removing certain objects from their reach. This includes plastic bibs, pillows, garments with draw-strings or loose buttons and fluffy toys with loose eyes. Don't forget to mend or dispose of any torn blankets. Sharon once looked after a baby who got his head stuck through a hole in his cot-cover in the early hours of the morning. Luckily, she heard him crying and was able to remove it before he strangled himself. If a baby is left outside in a pram, be vigilant of cats in the area. They can sit on a child's face and suffocate him, so use a pram net if this is a problem. Remember, too, that once a baby can sit up by himself, he becomes more active so a safety harness is advisable, especially if the pram is untended at any time.

All objects smaller than a ten pence piece should not be allowed infants and toddlers who are not past the stage of putting everything in their mouths. Peanuts are a common cause of choking in infants and should not be given.

POISONING

Potential poisons should be made inaccessible to children by placing them firmly out of reach or, even better, locking them away. This includes medicines, household cleaners, shampoo and garden chemicals in the shed. Warn the children not to pick berries or fungi which may also be harmful. If in doubt yourself, find out which ones are hazardous.

BURNS

Children are fascinated by fire and, once again, do not appreciate the danger involved. Make sure open fires have guards and beware of clothes that are highly inflammable. Pyjamas are less dangerous for little girls than nightgowns because they fit more closely and there is therefore less danger of the clothing coming into contact with the fire. Keep matches out of sight. Children should never be left alone in the kitchen when the stove is alight. Remember that electric stoves remain hot even after they have been switched off. Handles of pans that are cooking should be turned inwards to avoid accidents. Kettles should point to the wall to prevent the jet of steam pouring towards the child. Never leave buckets of hot water on the floor untended. When running baths, put the cold water in before the hot and then test the temperature with your elbow because it is more sensitive to heat than your hands. Electrical appliances are not safe unless unplugged; just switching items off is not enough.

Table cloths which overhang the edges are dangerous because the child can pull on them, spilling hot food or drinks. Plastic table cloths which can be taped down are best (and are also easier to clean). Place teapots, casserole dishes, etc., in the centre of the table and out of reach, and avoid drinking hot beverages while holding a baby, since their movements are unpredictable.

OTHER DANGERS

It goes without saying that children should never be left in or near a pool unsupervised, no matter how proficient they are at swimming. Garden fish ponds can prove an irresistible attraction to young children who can drown in them in minutes. Ideally they should be covered with strong wire mesh.

The same applies to children in the bath. Even if the water level is low, a child can still drown.

All sharp implements should be kept out of reach, including garden equipment. A gate for the stairs is advisable to prevent falls, and children should not be left alone near open upstairs windows. Either fix the window handle so a child can't open it more than a few inches, or air the room via windows that are well out of reach.

Make sure repairs are kept up on outdoor play equipment such as swings, slides and climbing frames. Do not allow children to play near the road. Quiet streets that are devoid of heavy traffic are just as risky because the children aren't expecting the cars and don't keep alert for them. Teach them road drills as soon as they are old enough to understand. When travelling in cars, children should always be in the back seat, and small children placed in car seats. Keep doors locked.

Above all, keep your eyes and ears open and your wits about you.

FIRST AID

Disasters are unlikely to befall you during your days as an au pair or nanny, but it is unrealistic to assume that the children in your care will never have accidents or health problems. Therefore you should be prepared. Registering in an official first-aid course is a very good idea and the advice below is no substitute. Here is an alphabetical list of the first-aid situations most common to children and instructions on how to cope.

ASTHMA

Asthma is directly caused by the muscles in the air passage going into spasm, which makes breathing difficult. This is distressing for anyone but is particularly frightening for children. Attacks can sometimes be triggered by an allergy or by nervous tension, and they can also occur at night. Whenever the child suffers from an asthma attack you should aim to calm him down. It is vital that you display confidence and reassurance even though such attacks can be alarming to witness. Place the child into a sitting position with his elbows resting on a solid support (a table, for example) and loosen all restricting clothing. This will aid him in his breathing. If possible, provide a source of fresh air. If the attack is prolonged or repeated, or you are in doubt about the child's condition, seek medical aid.

BITES

For superficial animal bites, wash the wound thoroughly with soapy water. Dry it and cover with a sterile, unmedicated dressing and then take the child to a doctor. Severe dog bites should be reported to the police.

If the bite is serious, control any bleeding by applying direct pressure to the wound and elevating the damaged limb. Bandage securely and remove to hospital. Check whether the child is immunised against tetanus.

BURNS AND SCALDS

A burn is caused by dry heat, for example a fire or oven, while a scald is caused by damp heat, for example hot liquid or steam from a kettle.

For serious burns, lay the child down, protecting the burnt area from contact with the ground if possible. Remove any constricting clothing from the injured area before swelling begins, but do not remove anything that is sticking to the burn or apply any lotions or ointments. Cover the burn with a sterile, unmedicated dressing and secure with a bandage. The child will probably be in shock, so you should keep him warm and immobilised. Moisten his lips with water if he complains of thirst. Don't give him anything to drink or eat because it will interfere with the administration of an anaesthetic later on. If breathing and heart-beat stops, begin resuscitation immediately. Remove to hospital.

If the burns are superficial, immerse injury in cold water for as long as the pain persists. If no water is available, improvise with any cold harmless liquid (milk, for example). Remove any jewellery or constricting material and place a sterile dressing on the wound. Once again, do not apply any lotions or use adhesive dressings. In all cases, blisters and loose skin should be left intact.

CHOKING

Hook your fingers inside the child's mouth to dislodge any debris. If dealing with an older child, bend his head over so it is lower than the lungs. Slap him between the shoulder blades four times with the heel of your hand, hard enough to remove the obstruction. Check the mouth again and hook out any visible debris.

For infants, hold them upside down with their body along your forearm and tap them on the back. Small children should be lain over your knee with their head down, while back slaps are applied.

If this method fails, perform *Abdominal Thrust*. This involves standing the child in front of you, or, if small, sitting him on your knee. Place one of your arms around his abdomen, making a clenched fist with your hand. Support his back with your other hand. Press your fist into his abdomen with quick upward and outward strokes, but with less pressure for young children. The thrust must still be hard enough to dislodge the obstruction.

Infants should be placed on a firm surface with their head in the open airway position (see *Emergency Procedures*) below. Apply abdominal thrust but with two fingers only.

CONCUSSION

This can result when a blow is received to the head. A child does not necessarily have to be unconscious to suffer from a concussion and it should be taken seriously in case compression develops. Compression means there is pressure on the brain caused by blood or a depressed fracture, and it may develop up to forty-eight hours later. Therefore, if a child has a bad knock on the head, it would be wise to see a doctor, especially if he or she seems unusually drowsy. Should the casualty be unconscious for any length of time, arrange removal to hospital.

CUTS AND BRUISES

With small wounds, a kiss, a wash and a plaster is all that is necessary. For larger wounds, apply a sterile unmedicated dressing and then bandage it. If your charge has a morbid fear of blood (not uncommon in small children), all you can do is remain calm and reassuring and deal with the wound as gently (but quickly) as possible.

If bleeding is serious, it can be controlled by applying direct pressure to the wound and elevating the injury. For a badly cut arm, for example, apply pressure, bandage and elevate into a sling. Do not bandage so tightly that the circulation is cut-off. Remove to hospital.

For bruises, apply a cold compress to reduce swelling and then dab with witch-hazel.

If you think a cut may be infected you should consult a doctor.

DISLOCATION

If a child has injured a joint so badly that it appears deformed, he may have dislocated it. This is very painful so you should treat the injury particularly gently. Try to immobilise the affected part with bandages or slings and then remove to hospital immediately.

DROWNING

Clear air passages and apply artificial ventilation as soon as possible. When the child is on dry land, check breathing and heart-beat and continue resuscitation if necessary. As soon as the casualty is breathing normally, place in the Recovery Position (see below). Keep him warm and horizontal while removing to hospital.

EMERGENCY PROCEDURES/RESUSCITATION

There may be a time when a child in your care is knocked unconscious and it will be necessary to administer emergency first-aid procedures while you are waiting for medical aid to arrive. Whatever you do, don't forget to call an ambulance before applying the three techniques for resuscitation. If possible, anyone planning to work with children should have some training in First Aid.

To detect whether or not a child is breathing, place your ear above his mouth and look along his chest and abdomen. If you cannot feel or hear any breaths and there is no movement along his torso, apply artificial ventilation. You should first make sure the airway is open by supporting the neck while tilting the head gently backwards. Sweep your fingers around the inside of his mouth to make sure there is nothing obstructing the airway. In children and infants, seal your lips around both the nose and mouth with the head still in the open airway position, and breathe gently into his lungs at a rate of twenty breaths per minute. Check for heart-beat after the first four inflations by feeling for a pulse in the neck. This should be a little off to one side from his Adam's apple.

If there is no pulse you will need to circulate the oxygen around his body via external chest compressions. Lie him on his back on a firm surface and find his breast-bone by tracing the inside edge of his ribs until you find the point where the two sets of ribs join together. Place two of your fingers horizontally side-by-side on this point and then place the heel of your hand just above the mark you have located. For children you should use just one hand, pressing lightly but firmly. After every fifteen compressions, apply two ventilations so you can continue to pump sufficient oxygen around his body. As soon as a pulse returns you should stop the external chest compressions but continue artificial ventilation until natural breathing is restored. The same applies to infants except the chest compressions should be applied with just two fingers. Abdominal thrust and cardiac massage can be dangerous if done by someone untrained.

Once breathing and pulse have returned, place the child in the *Recovery Position*. To do this, you should kneel alongside him and turn his head towards you. Straighten the casualty's arm nearest you, down by his side and tuck his hand under his buttock, palm upwards. Place the other arm over the front of his chest as though supported in a sling. Hold the far leg under the ankle and bring it towards you, crossing it over the nearest leg. Support the head with one hand, while grasping the clothing at the hip furthest away and pull the child towards you. Support the casualty in this position with your knees while adjusting his head (which should be resting on one side on the floor) back into the open airway position, i.e. tilted upwards. Bend the casualty's uppermost arm into a position which will support his upper body. Bend the uppermost leg at the knee to support the lower body. Gently pull the other arm out from underneath the child and leave it lying parallel to his body to prevent him rolling back.

FITS

Sometimes infants between the ages of one and four suffer convulsions (sometimes called fever fits) caused by a high temperature during illness. The eyes may roll up, the breathing stop briefly and the body go stiff and then twitchy. Clear a space around the baby, and ensure a good supply of fresh air. Loosen any clothing around the child's neck and cool him down with a sponge soaked in tepid water. Call a doctor.

If a child in your care suffers from epilepsy, he may experience convulsions from time to time. The most important thing is to prevent the child from hurting himself. You can do this by protecting the head with cushions or clothing and removing anything that is portable and in the way. Do not attempt to open his mouth or restrain him, but once the convulsion has ceased, place him in the recovery position. Advise the child's doctor about this latest attack.

FOREIGN BODIES

If the child has something imbedded in his ear, don't attempt to dislodge it in case you perforate the eardrum. Take the child to hospital.

Should the foreign body be in the child's eye, try to restrain him from rubbing it. Take him into a good light and open the eye wide with your index finger and thumb so you can inspect it. If you can see the cause of the trouble, try to remove it by pouring water into the eye to flush it out. If it is the right eye that is damaged, incline the head also to the right so that the water will not run into the good eye and vice versa. If you cannot remove the foreign body, cover the eye with an eye-pad and remove to hospital.

FRACTURES

If you suspect that the child has a fractured limb, do not move the injured part unless absolutely necessary. Make him as comfortable as possible by padding him around with blankets and cushions, etc. and phone for an ambulance.

HYSTERIA

Sometimes children throw such terrible tantrums that they become hysterical. Do not slap the child since this will only make matters worse, but escort him firmly to a quiet place and keep an eye on him until he recovers. If this sort of reaction happens frequently, you should seek medical advice.

INSECT STINGS

If the sting has been left in the skin, try to remove it with tweezers. Don't attempt to squeeze it out or you will force the rest of the poison into the skin. To help deaden the pain and control swelling, apply a cold compress or a paste of water mixed with baking soda. If the swelling persists or is worse by the next day, consult a doctor.

NOSE BLEEDS

Sit the child down and lean him over a bowl while you persuade him to pinch his nostrils together and breathe through his mouth. Tell him to spit out any blood which accumulates in his mouth. The pressure should be released after ten minutes, but if the bleeding hasn't stopped, repeat the treatment. If it hasn't cleared up in half an hour, seek medical aid.

POISONING

The first thing you should do is try to establish what the child has swallowed. Then call for medical help immediately. If the casualty has swallowed acid, give him something alkaline to drink in the meantime, such as milk of magnesia. If it is something alkaline (ammonia, for instance) give him something acidic to drink, such as vinegar or lemon juice. Should the child have drunk phenol, which is contained in many disinfectants, give him plenty of water to drink. If you are not sure what the substance was, do not give him anything.

Only attempt to make a child vomit if you know he has swallowed a non-corrosive poison such as tablets, insecticides or poisonous plants. The symptoms are nausea and lethargy. Save any remains of the poison or vomit, especially if you are unsure of what he took in the first place. The hospital will need to identify the substance before treatment can be given.

SPLINTERS

Cleanse around the splinter if the area is dirty. Sterilise a pair of tweezers or a sewing needle by passing them through a flame, and gently try to remove the splinter. Don't probe the area or you could make it worse. Seek medical aid.

SPRAINS

Apply a cold compress to help reduce swelling and then bandage. Only seek medical aid if the symptoms persist or you are concerned that it might actually be a fracture.

SUFFOCATION

Remove any obstruction which may be cutting off the air supply, such as a pillow if the baby lies face down. If the child is unconscious but breathing normally, place in the recovery position. If unable to breathe, begin artificial ventilation as soon as an ambulance has been called.

Appendix 2: Childhood Ailments

The moment you become suspicious that a child in your care may be sick, you should inform the parents. If an emergency arises during their absence, always contact them as soon as the crisis is under control, i.e. the doctor has been called and the child has been made as comfortable as possible. If you have to collect a sick child from school, phone the mother immediately after the teacher has alerted you. Should the parents be absent for a period of days and you are worried about the child's health, consult a relative of the family or a close family friend. Ultimately, however, the child is your responsibility so, when in doubt, seek medical advice. One of the most important symptoms to recognise in a child is fever. If the child's temperature is raised for an extended period, always consult a doctor. It might be an indication of a serious illness like pneumonia.

Immunisation programmes against measles, mumps, rubella (i.e. German measles) and whooping cough are now well established in Britain and in most developed countries, so these childhood diseases have been greatly reduced. The only infectious disease against which there is no immunisation to date is chicken pox.

CHICKEN POX

There is no immunisation against chicken pox. With chicken pox, the child may feel generally unwell for a day or two and there will be a slight rise in temperature. He will develop small round spots of a blistery appearance on his body and this will spread to his face, causing itchiness. Scabs will form and these will drop off after a few days, but new crops develop every four or five days, so there are always some spots present. It takes a couple of weeks for all the scabs to clear. The child will feel fine for most of this so there is no reason to keep him at home. However if you go to a park or anywhere where there are other children playing, you should warn the parents (who might even welcome the prospect of their child catching the disease and getting it over with).

Calamine lotion and frequent tepid baths will help relieve itching and nails should be kept short and clean to reduce the risk of infection. It's a good idea to put cotton gloves on the child's hands at night to avoid scratching. If the spots do become infected, they will require special ointment from the doctor.

COLDS

The common cold is caused by a virus, not by cold air or wet clothing (though both of those can increase the likelihood of infection), and it takes about ten days for the body to fight it. Keep the child indoors in a well ventilated, sunny room for a couple of days and encourage plenty of fluids. It has not been scientifically proven that vitamin C fights the virus, but it certainly can't hurt and many people swear by it, so give plenty of fruit juices and citrus fruit.

CONSTIPATION

It is wise to remember that each child is an individual and frequency of bowel movements vary. It is not so much the regularity which is a problem, but whether or not the stools are hard enough to cause the child discomfort. Constipation is also frequently accompanied by headaches, stomach pains, furred tongue and listlessness.

If you have reason to believe your charge is constipated, an increase of roughage in his diet will usually help. Give him plenty of whole-wheat food, vegetables, fruits and fruit juices. Jacket potatoes, popcorn and baked beans are also a good source of roughage and plenty of fluids will encourage softer motions. Make sure the child is getting enough exercise. Remember, too, that most children reach an age where they prefer privacy when opening their bowels and your presence in the bathroom may be inhibiting them.

Never give a child laxatives as a routine means of regulating their bowels. Laxatives are addictive in the sense that the bowel can become lazy and unable to work efficiently without them. Administer them only on a doctor's advice.

COUGHS AND SORE THROATS

If the cough is a loose one (that is to say, one that helps the child to clear mucus from his chest), do not administer cough medicine because this will inhibit its function. If the cough is a dry one and/or the child complains of a sore throat, a mixture of lemon juice and honey in equal parts should help sooth it. Encourage them to gargle with antiseptic mouth-wash if they are old enough to understand not to swallow it.

An older child might like an extra pillow or two to help ease a troublesome night cough, but do not do the same with a baby because of the risk of suffocation. Put the pillows underneath the head of the mattress instead, so it is raised slightly. Turning the child on his front or side at night may also reduce spates of coughing.

If the child becomes breathless at all, has pains in the chest, fever or vomiting, call a doctor straightaway.

CROUP

This is a particularly nasty cough which is more common among two to four year olds than other age groups. The main symptom is a barking cough. If the child is having difficulty in breathing, a doctor should be called immediately. Sit your charge up and stay with him to give reassurance since a serious bout of croup is a frightening experience for a child. Boiling a kettle in the room or leaving a wet sheet over the radiator may offer relief because of the moisture created in the air. Normally croup disappears in a day or two.

DIARRHOEA

This can be serious in small babies because of the risk of dehydration, so call a doctor. Stop milk foods and fruit but encourage all other fluids. In older children it may be due to a digestive upset, so stick to a bland diet for the rest of the day and keep the child warm in a well ventilated room. If the diarrhoea persists, or is accompanied by vomiting or fever, seek medical advice.

EARACHE

Pain from the ear usually warrants a visit to the doctor because it indicates an infection, which may require antibiotics. In the meantime, some relief can be brought by holding a covered hot water bottle or heated pad against the affected ear. One traditional remedy for the pain is to chop up an onion, wrap it in a clean handkerchief and hold it to the ear. Propping up the head-end of the mattress will also help fluid to drain from the ear.

ECZEMA

This condition is usually inherited but can be aggravated by allergy and/or nervous strain. The symptoms are an inflamed, itchy rash most commonly found on the face, inner sides of the arms and behind the knees, and a dry, flaky scalp. It will flare up for a limited time and then fade again, so the condition comes and goes. It is not an infectious ailment.

Prevent your charge from becoming over-heated as much as possible and use cotton fabrics next to the skin to avoid irritation. Keep him out of strong sunlight or winds because this will aggravate the rash, and try to distract the child from scratching. Consult a doctor because he will probably prescribe a special ointment (e.g. hydrocortisone cream), but in the meantime calamine lotion may be helpful.

HEAD-LICE

Head-lice are not the result of dirty hair or unhygienic living conditions, as widely believed. Most children acquire head lice at school since young children often brush heads over their work or at play, allowing lice to jump from one scalp to the next.

The lice lay their eggs in the hair quite close to the scalp and are similar to flakes of dandruff except they are hard. Once the colony is well established, the child will keep scratching the scalp and behind the ears. Any chemist should be able to recommend a medicated shampoo treatment; alternatively schools will probably have an information sheet. Wash the child's hair thoroughly with this, being careful not to get any of it in the eyes. Afterwards, you should go through the hair with a fine comb to remove the nits (lice eggs). This is time consuming and tedious for a child so provide something to amuse him while you are doing it. A new book, or favourite TV programme should encourage him to sit still. It is usually a wise precaution to treat all the members of the family whose heads have been in close contact with the child. Headlice cannot live for very long away from the human scalp, so it is not necessary to wash everything that has come into contact with the child's hair, though of course the comb should be thoroughly rinsed in hot water.

STOMACH PAINS

The main worry with stomach pains is that they might possibly be an indication of appendicitis. If in any doubt call a doctor.

If the condition doesn't appear to be serious, encourage the child to lie down for an hour or so. If the pain persists for longer then two hours, however, or your charge begins vomiting, seek medical advice. In the meantime, it may help the doctor if you manage to obtain a specimen of the child's urine.

TEETHING OR TOOTHACHE

Take the child to a dentist if the problem is toothache. In the meantime you can help deaden the pain by dabbing the affected tooth with oil of cloves. Alternatively, holding a heated pad or covered hot water bottle against the affected side of the face may also help.

If the pain is caused by teething, giving the baby something to chew on will help. Children often find frozen bananas or something hard like a tooth-brush, just as soothing as a teething ring. Various solutions are also available from chemists specially formulated for painful gums.

Don't blame any other symptoms of illness on teething. For example, diarrhoea. This should be dealt with as a separate problem and not left untreated because it is masked by the teething troubles.

VOMITING

A doctor should always be called if vomiting persists or is accompanied by diarrhoea and/ or stomach pain. If the vomiting is just a short bout, stop giving solid food for twenty-four hours and concentrate instead on fluids. A glass of orange juice with one level teaspoon of bicarbonate of soda and a pinch of salt may also help settle the stomach. Avoid fats for forty-eight hours after vomiting has stopped, because these are difficult to digest.

Babies often eject milk after feeds and this is rarely serious. It may be due to swallowing too much air while feeding because they are drinking too quickly. Giving a couple of spoonfuls of water that has been boiled and left to cool prior to feeding times may take the edge off their appetite and encourage them to drink more slowly.

GENERAL CARE DURING SICKNESS

Caring for a sick child will take even more patience than usual, especially once your charge starts to recover and becomes more irritable and demanding. Things can be particularly difficult if there are other children to care for as well, and you still have household chores to attend to. If you have sole charge, try to come to some arrangement with the mother about any additional tasks you usually perform. It is much better for you to concentrate on the sick child rather than the house, and any reasonable family will understand this. Don't try to do too much, but organise yourself and set priorities. Otherwise you, yourself, can become run-down and if you fall ill, the whole family suffers even more.

TAKING TEMPERATURES

In cases of high fever, it is obvious by touch that the child has a high temperature. Kissing the child's forehead is a good way of detecting this because your lips are sensitive to heat. If a precise measure is necessary, you will need to use a thermometer and in general you should take a reading before giving fever-reducing medication.

A normal body temperature is 37°C, and 39°C is dangerously high. A satisfactory thermometer reading can usually be obtained by placing a mercury or digital display thermometer directly against the skin in the child's armpit, and holding it in place with the arm lowered for up to ten minutes. The reading will be half a degree lower than it would be if taken from the mouth. Older children who can be trusted not to bite the thermometer can have the thermometer placed under their tongues for two minutes. If you are taking a temperature orally, remember not to do so immediately after a hot or cold drink or you will have an inaccurate reading. Clean all thermometers after each use by submersion in diluted disinfectant (one teaspoon to five fluid ounces of water) and, with mercury thermometers, shake down the red column to below 37° before the next use.

ADMINISTERING MEDICINES

When giving liquid medicine with an unpleasant taste rub ice over the child's tongue first to inhibit his taste-buds. If the child refuses to take it, gently pinch his nostrils and slip it in when he opens his mouth to breathe. Put your hand over his lips to prevent him from spitting it out and then give him a sweet as a reward for swallowing it. This is one situation in which bribery is well justified! Use a thoroughly cleaned eye-dropper to feed liquid medicines to babies.

In the case of tablets, crush between two spoons and bury the medication in a spoonful of jam, or whatever the child prefers. The same can be done with capsules, by emptying their contents onto a spoon. Note any bad reactions, since some children are allergic to certain kinds of medication. Keep all medicines well out of reach of the children.

DIET

Give sick children plenty of fluids and small, frequent meals if and when they want to eat. Fruit juices provide vitamins and sugar for energy, and soups and milk are very nutritious. Encourage light food such as toast, poached or boiled eggs, poached fish, jellies, milk puddings, fruit purees and sponge cake. Gradually return to a more normal diet as they progress.

AMUSING A SICK CHILD

Try to spend as much time with your charge as possible, and as soon as he is no longer infectious, encourage visitors. If your charge is in bed, reading to him or arranging for him to watch a portable television set in his room should occupy him for a while. Let him draw and colour with crayons, and supply him with jigsaw puzzles on a tray.

If your charge has been seriously ill, assist in a gradual return to normality. Sit him up in bed for longer and longer periods and then gradually increase the time he is permitted to be up. He will require plenty of rest at first, but in the meantime permit him to play with anything which doesn't require too much exertion or excitement.

IMAGINARY ILLNESS

Sometimes children complain of headaches, pains in their stomach or develop bowel problems with no apparent physical cause. These often occur prior to a stressful event such as returning to school after a holiday. If you suspect that a child's illness is an excuse or delaying tactic for something they prefer to avoid, don't dismiss the pain as imaginary. Even children worry, and anxiety can create genuine physical symptoms. Be sympathetic while applying a common sense approach to the problem.

Appendix 3: Cooking for Children

When cooking for children it is important to provide a balanced diet. Even if children will eat only one or two bites of some foods, it is still worth giving them the chance to eat healthy foods. Eating habits developed at a young age will influence the child throughout his or her life. A healthy diet will not only encourage good health by increasing resistance to disease, but also promote growth, regulate the body's processes and provide heat and energy. A balanced diet means one which provides a selection of food which includes protein, carbohydrate, fats, vitamins, minerals and roughage in the right proportions. The chart below gives the sources of the most important nutrients.

NUTRIENT	FUNCTION	SOURCE
PROTEIN	To build	Fish, meat, eggs, milk, cheese, cereals, nuts, beans, lentils, peas
FATS	To provide fuel	Butter, margarine, oils, meat, milk, cheese, fat, ice-cream
CARBOHYDRATES	To provide energy & warmth	Bread, cakes, cereals and biscuits, sugar, potatoes, root vegetables
VITAMIN A	Aids growth & vision	Dairy products, eggs, fruit, carrots
VITAMIN B	Promotes general good health and helps body utilise other nutrients	Wholewheat, oats, yeast, liver, eggs, meat
VITAMIN C	Helps heal wounds & resist infection	Fruit and vegetables
VITAMIN D	For healthy teeth & bones	Oily fish, offal, egg yolk, margarine, butter & sunshine
CALCIUM	For strong bones	Milk, cheese, nuts
IRON	For healthy blood	Eggs, cocoa, meat, offal, green vegetables
HIGH FIBRE	Aids the body's processes & prevents constipation	Bran, beans, brown rice, wholemeal bread, jacket potato

By encouraging your charge to eat a wide selection of food, you reduce the chance of developing food sensitivities which can lead to allergies. Having said that, however, all children go through phases when they are faddish about what they eat. Therefore, the meals that you cook should be interesting and served attractively so as to encourage them to try new and varied foods.

If no suitable cookery books are available and you have run out of ideas, you can always turn to the internet. For example the site www.netmums.com has some food pages with recipes, or the American http://stepbystepcc.com/recipe.html gives some eye-catching snack ideas like 'Ants in a Toilet' made from apples, peanut butter and chocolate chips. 'Ants in a Canoe' sounds more promising: ice cream in scooped-out bananas studded with raisins. Of course these sites all emphasise healthy eating. One claims that you can disguise most vegetables by boiling them and mashing them with potatoes to create 'coloured mash' though this presupposes your charges will eat mashed potatoes in the first place.

The US au pair agency Cultural Care has brought out a charity cookery book for US$15 called *Kids First International Cookbook* which includes 115 recipes suitable for children from 32 countries (www.culturalcare.com/kidsfirst).

BABY'S FIRST SOLIDS

When babies have few teeth, it is important to provide smooth textured food until more teeth develop and they can enjoy chunkier meals. There are many commercial brands of baby-food on the market but these often contain sugar, thickeners and modified starch which provide empty calories and can be damaging to teeth already formed in the gum. They are also highly processed so tend to be less nutritious than fresh food. Reserve their use for travelling and make the baby's food yourself. It really doesn't take much extra time since you can cook it along with your own meals, and just pop it in the blender or mash it by hand.

If there is one particular day when you have less to do than usual, it will save time on your busier days if you prepare food in bulk in advance, and then freeze it in the ice-cube trays, remembering to label all frozen food and date it. Not only do they thaw quickly, it is also easy to select just the right quantity. Most fruit and vegetables puree easily and as the baby develops more teeth, you can add ground pieces of meat or carefully boned fish that has been mashed into flakes. Meat tastes good and moist if pureed with a little natural yoghurt. Do not add salt or sugar to the food you prepare since neither is good for babies and they are quite happy to eat bland food. Any puréed left-overs can be mixed with egg, and baked on cake trays or utilised later as sandwich spreads.

COOKING FOR TODDLERS

Young children prefer food that is not very spicy and it should be served in small portions, cut into little pieces. For this reason, ground beef is usually a success with tiny tots. Try providing finger-food at lunch time such as cheese cubes, strips of cold meat, wholewheat crackers and raw vegetables or fruit. Do not serve food straight from the oven, but let it stand until it is cool enough for a toddler to eat comfortably. Liquid meals such as soups can be cooled quickly by dropping an ice-cube into the dish before serving.

Here are enough suggestions and recipes to get you through one week.

BREAKFAST

Encourage children to eat some protein during breakfast, especially if they are about to go off to school and may not have an opportunity to eat anything else until lunch time. Eggs or cereals with milk provide a good source of protein and the former can be cooked in a variety of ways: boiled, poached, fried or scrambled.

Egg in the Basket (serves one)
1 slice of wholemeal bread, 1 egg, 1 knob of butter.
1. Cut a round hole from the centre of the slice of bread and melt the butter in a frying pan over a moderate-to-high heat.
2. When the butter is bubbling, fry the slice of bread and the round piece in the pan, crack the egg and deposit it into the centre of the hole.
3. When the underneath side is cooked, serve the toasted bread with the egg in the middle, topping it with the round lid that has also been fried.

French Toast (serves one)
1 thick slice of bread with the crusts removed, 1 lge egg, drop of milk and knob of butter.
1. Beat the egg and add a little milk as though making scrambled egg.
2. Soak the bread in the batter on both sides for a few minutes or until it has absorbed most of the liquid without becoming too soggy.
3. Heat the butter in a frying-pan and fry the bread on both sides until golden-brown.

Kids love this served with jam or syrup, but honey would be more nutritious and is just as delicious.

Pancakes (serves two)
2 tbsp oil, 1 lge beaten egg, 2 tbsp sugar, 1 cup flour, 2 tsp baking-powder, ½ tsp salt, approx ½ pint of milk.
1. Beat all the ingredients together in a bowl, adding just enough milk to form a thick batter (about the consistency of a fairly thick milk-shake).
2. Melt the butter in a frying pan and when bubbling, ladle in some of the batter.
3. Turn when underside is cooked to brown and serve while warm.
May be served topped with syrup, honey, lemon juice or brown sugar or with yoghurt and chopped fruit.

Quick Bran Muffins (Makes one dozen)
These store well in the freezer, so they may be baked in advance and stored until required.
25g (1oz) soft marge or butter, 25g (1oz) soft brown sugar, 75g (3oz) wholemeal flour, 50g (2oz) bran, 1 medium egg, 1 level tsp baking powder,½ level tsp bicarbonate of soda, 125ml (5oz) milk and water mixture, pinch of salt.
1. Set the oven to 200°C/400°F/Gas reg 6
2. Cream the fat and sugar, and beat in the egg and milk mixture.
3. Stir in the bran and add the combined dry ingredients.
4. Divide the mixture among 12 well-greased cookie-moulds and bake for approx. 20 mins or until firm to the touch.

LUNCH
These suggestions will also travel easily to school if transported via containers in lunch boxes.

Sandwiches (may be cut into interesting shapes with cookie-cutters and the surplus bread used as bread-crumbs); creamy dip and sliced, raw vegetables; home-made soups (carried to school in flasks); celery sticks stuffed with cottage-cheese or cream cheese (celery keeps longer if stored in the fridge in paper bags instead of plastic, while cottage cheese keeps twice as long stored upside-down.)

Tuna Fish Spread
1 small tin of tuna fish, 1 celery stalk, 1 small onion (if liked), few slices of cucumber, 1 medium hard-boiled egg, mayonnaise, lemon juice and seasoning.
1. Drain the liquid from the tin of tuna and mash up the fish into small flakes.
2. Finely chop the celery, cucumber and onion.
3. Mash the hard-boiled egg.
4. Mix everything together with a few drops of lemon juice and enough mayonnaise to make the mixture moist enough to spread on bread.
5. Season to taste, and use as a sandwich filler or serve with salads.

Chicken Liver Paté (stores well in the freezer)
100g (4oz) chicken livers, 50g (2oz) soft marge/butter, 50g (2oz) cream cheese, 1 tbsp single cream, squeeze of lemon juice, seasoning.
1. Fry the chicken livers gently in a little oil.
2. When cooked, put all the ingredients in a blender and blend to form a paste.
May be used as sandwich filler, or served with hot pieces of toast.

Peanut butter
This can easily be bought in many countries, but it can just as easily be home-made and tastes more delicious than commercial brands. Just melt some butter in a pan and liquidise

with equal weight of peanuts. The longer you liquidise, the smoother it will be. Season to taste with salt and store in an air-tight jar. It can be used for sandwiches, but it is a novelty to serve an ice-cream scoop of it in an ice-cream cone instead.

Creamy Cheese dip for Crudités
100g (4oz) cream cheese, ½ tbsp soured cream, 1 tbsp chopped chives, seasoning and a little milk.
Mix the ingredients together well, adding just enough milk to bring the dip to the required consistency.

Plain Omelette (serves one - may be cut in half to serve two toddlers)
2 eggs, 1tbsp cold water, ½ oz butter, seasoning.
Use a small frying pan, approx. 6in/15cm in diameter.
1. Beat the contents of the two eggs in a bowl, adding the seasoning and water.
2. Melt the butter in the pan, making sure the bottom and sides are coated. When bubbling, pour in the egg mixture.
3. Scrape the mixture slowly, using a wooden spoon, so that all the liquid has a chance to cook.
4. Remove the omelette by folding in half with a palette knife, and slide onto plate.
N.B. Finely chopped vegetables or grated cheese may be added to the mixture. This is also a good way of using up small pieces of meat such as diced ham.

HOMEMADE SOUPS
All the following recipes are enough for two servings, plus a little extra.

Leek and Potato
1 lge leek, 2 lge potatoes, 290ml (½pt) chicken stock, dash of single cream.
1. Chop the leek and peeled potatoes into bite-sized pieces.
2. Simmer in the stock until soft.
3. Pour into blender and blend to form a smooth soup.
4. Re-heat in pan, add seasoning to taste and stir in a dash of cream before serving.

Tomato
1 medium can of peeled tomatoes, 1 small onion, 1 lge carrot, 300ml (½pt) chicken stock, dash of Worcester sauce (optional), knob of butter.
1. Heat the butter in a pan, finely chop the carrot and onion and sauté together until the carrot is soft.
2. Add the tomatoes and juice, stock and Worcester sauce.
3. Simmer for half an hour.
4. Blend in blender and season to taste.

Cream of Mushroom
100g (4oz) mushrooms, 300ml (½pt) chicken stock, 150ml (quarter pt) milk, 50g (20z) butter, 50g (2oz) flour, seasoning.
1. Chop the mushrooms and sauté in the butter.
2. Stir in the flour and cook for three mins.
3. Remove the pan from the heat and gradually add stock and milk.
4. Bring to the boil and cook until soup thickens. Season to taste.

MAIN MEALS
Beef and Spinach Cake
Any mention of 'cake' in the recipe usually inspires children at least to try something. This is also a good way of feeding them spinach since the taste is disguised somewhat by the

other ingredients. The following recipe should be enough for two school-aged children with room for second helpings.

1 pack frozen spinach, 225g (8oz) minced beef, 1 lge egg (lightly beaten), 1 beef stock-cube, ½ dozen button mushrooms, 1 small onion.

1. Heat oven to 200°C/400°F/Gas reg.6
2. Put the frozen spinach in a saucepan and thaw over low heat.
3. Meanwhile, finely chop the onion and mushrooms and sauté in a knob of butter.
4. Turn the heat higher and add the minced beef, stirring all the time so it is evenly browned.
5. Crumble the beef stock cube into the pan and add the thawed spinach, stirring all ingredients together. Add a little boiling water to moisten if ingredients seem too dry and start to stick to pan.
6. Remove pan from heat and stir in the egg.
7. Pour mixture into oven-proof dish and bake uncovered for approx. 20 mins or until firm to the touch. Cut into cake slices and serve.

Homemade Beef Burgers (Recipe will make 2 hamburger patties)
110g (4oz) minced beef, 1 cup of puréed vegetable of your choice, 1 small onion (finely chopped), sprinkling of fine wholewheat breadcrumbs, finely chopped parsley.
1. Mix all the ingredients together.
2. Divide the mixture to form hamburger patties.
3. Grill or fry in a little oil.
These can easily be turned into cheese burgers by topping with a thin slice of cheese and melting it under the grill. Serve in a wholemeal roll with a side dish of cooked vegetables or salad.

Fish Pie (serves 2)
170g (6oz) cooked white fish, deboned; 3 lge potatoes, peeled; 50g (2oz) butter, 570m (1pt) milk, 50g (2oz) flour, chopped parsley, 1 bay leaf and seasoning.
1. Turn the oven to 200°C/400°F/gas reg 6
2. Peel and cut the potatoes into chunks and boil until soft enough to mash.
3. In the meantime, prepare the sauce by melting the butter, adding the bay leaf and flour and stirring while cooking for 1 min.
4. Draw off heat and add milk, stirring all the time.
5. Return to heat and bring slowly to the boil, stirring until you have a thick, creamy sauce, the consistency of custard.
6. Remove the bay leaf and set the sauce aside.
7. Chop the cooked fish into small chunks and place in an oven-proof dish.
8. Pour the sauce on top and spinkle with parsley.
9. Drain potatoes when cooked, and mash.
10. Spread evenly on top of the fish/sauce mixture and run the back of a fork's prongs along it to create a pattern. If you have the time (and the inclination) you can pipe the potato on instead.
11. Bake in the oven for 15 mins, and then slip under the grill for a few minutes to brown it.
Serve with a lemon wedge and some brightly coloured vegetables, such as broccoli or grilled tomatoes. If you really want to catch your charge's interest, you could always put some food colouring in the mashed potato.

Fish cakes (4 servings)
450g (1lb) potatoes, 225g (½lb) cooked, canned fish (drained), 1 lge beaten egg, some dried breadcrumbs, a little milk and some finely chopped parsley.
1. Boil the potatoes, drain and mash.

2. Flake the fish and add to the mash. Sprinkle in the parsley.
3. Season to taste and bind with a little milk.
4. Shape into patties, similar to hamburgers.
5. Dip each patty into the egg and then the breadcrumbs.
6. Store in the fridge for about 1 hr to help the breadcrumbs adhere to the cakes.
7. Heat some oil in a large frying-pan and fry the cakes until crisp and golden.
Serve with chips and peas.

Chicken Baked In Sauce
You can make your own soup for this first but it's much quicker to use a commercial brand, although not as nutritious. The chicken absorbs the flavour but leaves enough liquid to use as a sauce.
Simply put one chicken portion per child in a casserole dish (or substitute chops if you prefer) and pour over a can of soup, for instance onion, mushroom, etc. Cover the dish and bake in the oven at 190°C/375°F/gas reg. 5, for 1½ hrs or until tender. Serve with rice and one or two vegetables.

Risotto (enough for 2 small children)
quarter cup wholegrain rice, 1 cup of water, 1 chicken stock cube, finely chopped vegetables, small pieces of meat such as chicken or pork (optional).
1. Boil the water and add stock cube. When dissolved, and with water still boiling, add rice.
2. Turn to a simmer and cook until soft (approx. 20-30 mins).
3. Lightly fry the vegetables and add the cooked meat, if desired. Mix in the cooked rice.
Serve as a complete meal.

Tomato Sauce (serves 4)
1 small onion and 1 clove of garlic, finely chopped, 1 medium tin tomatoes, 2 rashers streaky bacon and a little oil.
1. Sauté the finely chopped onion and garlic in the oil in a saucepan.
2. Add the bacon, chopped, and cook for 5 mins.
3. Add the tomatoes, but not the juice (may be added later if sauce needs thinning).
4. Simmer, covered, for 20 mins.
5. Blend in blender.
Serve with spaghetti on a slice of wholewheat toast.

DESSERTS
Homemade Vanilla Ice-cream
70g (2½oz) caster sugar, 425ml (3/4pt) double cream, 3 egg yolks, 8 tbsp water, 1 tsp vanilla essence.
1. Dissolve the sugar in the water over a gentle heat.
2. Beat the egg yolks well.
3. Half whip the cream.
4. When the sugar has dissolved, bring the syrup to boiling point. Keep boiling until the mixture is ready. (You can test it by dipping your finger into cold water and then into a little of the syrup. Rub between your finger and thumb and then, when you draw them apart threads should form similar to sticky chewing-gum).
5. Whisk the egg yolks and gradually pour in the sugar-syrup. Whisk until the mixture is thick and mousse-like.
6. Cool, whisking occasionally. Fold in the cream and freeze.
7. When the ice-cream is half frozen, whisk again and return to freezer.
Serve with fresh chopped fruit or chocolate sauce.

Chocolate Sauce
170g (6oz) plain chocolate, 15g (1oz) butter, 2 tbsp water.
1. Melt the chocolate slowly with the water, stirring frequently.
2. Add the butter and heat (don't boil) until the butter is melted and the sauce is blended and shiny.
May be used as a topping for ice-cream, or give the children a dish of it and some chunks of fruit or sponge cake to dip into it.

Strawberry Mousse
This can be made one day ahead, and is enough for 4 servings.
2 egg whites (at room temperature), 1 quarter cup icing sugar, 2 cups strawberries (finely sliced), 2 cups whipping cream, pinch of salt.
1. Whisk egg whites and salt in a small bowl until glossy and stiff.
2. Whip the cream with the sugar in the bowl.
3. Gently fold in the egg whites and fruit, blending well.
4. Spoon the mixture into individual containers and refrigerate at least one hour before serving.

Apple Crumble (serves 4)
450g (1lb) cooking apples, 1½ tbsp brown sugar, pinch of cinnamon, 50g (2oz) butter, straight from the fridge so it is hard, 85g (3oz) plain flour, 30g (1oz) caster sugar and a pinch of salt.
1. Set the oven to 200°C/400°F/gas reg 6.
2. Peel and core the apples. Cut into chunks and place in a saucepan with the brown sugar and cinnamon.
3. Add just enough water to keep the bottom of the pan moist while the apples are stewing.
4. When the apples are soft, allow to cool and then drain any excess juice.
5. Rub the fat into the flour, add salt and when the mixture resembles breadcrumbs, mix in the caster sugar.
6. Pour the stewed apples into an ovenproof dish and sprinkle over the crumble mixture.
7. Bake for 1½ hrs and if the top still isn't brown, place it under the grill until golden.
May be served with cream or custard.

Custard Fruit
Place some chopped fruit in the bottom of a heat-proof container. Make some instant custard and pour over the fruit. Leave to cool and then chill in the fridge so it can be served cold.

Bananas In Caramel Sauce
1 banana per child, 170g (6oz) granulated sugar, 425ml (3/4 pt) water.
1. Melt two-thirds of the sugar slowly in a saucepan.
2. When it is bubbling and brown, pour on the water. (It will fizz dangerously so make sure the children stand well clear if they are watching you make this.)
3. Add the rest of the sugar and reboil, stirring, and then boil until the sauce is of syrupy consistency.
Pour over the banana and leave to cool off a little before serving to your charge.

Other dessert suggestions: fruit salad, jelly or yoghurt.

SNACKS AND BEVERAGES

It is much more nutritious to serve raw vegetables, fruit, nuts, yoghurt or a few small slices of cheese if the children are hungry between meals. However, there will be times when a special treat may be appropriate.

Boiled Cake (very nutritious)
1 cup cold water, 1 cup sultanas, 1 cup raisins, 1 cup currants, 1 cup brown sugar, 2 cups wholewheat flour, peel, cherries and nuts (optional), 1 tsp baking soda, ½ tsp mixed spice, 2 lge beaten eggs, 170g (6oz) marge.
1. Set oven to 190°C/375°F/gas reg 5.
2. Put water, fruit, sugar and margarine in a saucepan and bring to the boil.
3. Boil 5-10 mins.
4. Meanwhile, sieve flour, baking soda and mixed spice into a bowl.
5. Pour in the boiling mixture and beat well.
6. Add beaten eggs and blend well.
7. Pour into prepared 20cm (8in) cake tin and bake for 1-1½ hrs.

Fairy Cakes (makes 18)
100g (4oz) margarine (at room temperature), 100g (4oz) caster sugar, 100g (4oz) self-raising flour, 2 medium eggs.
Icing: 50g (2oz) icing sugar, 75g (3oz) margarine, ½ tsp vanilla essence, 1 tsp milk.
1. Preheat oven to 190°C/375°F/gas reg 5.
2. Place 18 paper cases on a baking sheet.
3. Mix cake ingredients in a bowl and beat until smooth.
4. Deposit a dessert spoonful of the mixture into each paper cup.
5. Bake for ½ an hour or until golden-brown and firm to the touch.
6. Cool on a wire rack while preparing the icing.
7. To make icing, sift icing sugar into a bowl and beat together with the margarine, flavouring and milk until light and fluffy.
8. Deposit a little icing on the top of each cake and decorate with grated pieces of chocolate, chopped nuts or commercial cake decorations.

Chocolate Rice Crispies/Corn Flakes
100g (4oz) plain chocolate, 25g (1oz) butter, 2 tbsp golden syrup, rice crispies/corn flakes.
1. Slowly melt the chocolate and butter in a saucepan.
2. Add the golden syrup.
3. Sprinkle the cereal into the mixture and then form individual chocolate covered heaps on a baking sheet.
4. Chill in the fridge until firm but still gooey.

Chocolate Cake
225g (8oz) margarine or butter, 225g (8oz) self-raising flour.
225g (8oz) caster sugar, 50g (2oz) cocoa, 4 medium eggs.
Filling: 225g (8oz) icing sugar, 30g (1oz) cocoa, 110g (4oz) margarine or butter, 2 tbsp boiling water.
1. Heat oven to 190°C/375°F/gas reg 5.
2. Cream margarine and sugar. Add well beaten eggs and mix.
3. Sieve flour and cocoa and beat into the mixture a little at a time.
4. If mixuture is a little dry, add a small quantity of milk.
5. Place mixture in a 20cm (8in) baking tin.
6. Bake for approx 20 mins. Test to make sure it's cooked by gently pressing the surface with your finger. If the indentation springs back and disappears, it's cooked.
7. While it is baking, prepare the icing by mixing together all the icing ingredients.
8. When the cake has cooled, slice in half horizontally and sandwich together with the icing. Dust the top of the cake with a sprinkling of icing sugar.

Banana Cake (great for using up over-ripe bananas).
2 lge eggs (beaten well), 250g (9oz) self-raising flour, 110g (4oz) margarine, 2 ripe bananas,

170g (6oz) caster sugar.
1. Set oven to 180°C/350°F/gas reg 4.
2. Mash bananas until runny.
3. Beat the marge and the icing sugar together.
4. Add the flour and eggs and bananas.
5. Bake for 1½ hrs or until cooked (using finger test).

Homemade Yoghurt Ice-Lollies (makes 8)
150ml (quarter pt) natural yoghurt, 175ml (6oz) concentrated unsweetened orange juice, 2 drops vanilla essence.
1. Mix all the ingredients together and pour into ice-cube trays.
2. When mixture is half frozen and slushy, insert wooden lolly stick in each individual section.
3. Freeze until firm and serve with a circle of foil around the bottom of the stick to catch any drips.

Homemade Lemonade
Juice and rind of 3 lemons, 2 tbsp clear honey, 1-2 litres (approx. 2 pts) mineral water, ice-cubes.
1. Put lemon juice and rind in a large jug with honey.
2. Pour in water and stir well.
3. Leave to stand for at least 1 hr.
4. Strain out the rind and serve with ice-cubes.

Sparkling Juice
Add two thirds sparkling mineral water to one third orange or pineapple juice to make a fizzy drink. Add a slice of lemon or orange and ice-cubes before serving.

Milk-Shake (serves 1)
1 portion of fruit, 300ml (½pt) milk, 1 scoop of ice-cream. Put all the ingredients into a blender and pour over ice-cubes.

Carrot Cake
225gm (½lb) wholemeal flour, pinch of salt, quarter tsp bicarbonate of soda, 225g (½lb) grated carrots, 1 egg (beaten), 50g (2oz) melted butter, 50g (2oz) runny honey, 50g (2oz) brown sugar, quarter tsp nutmeg, 2 tsp cinnamon.
1. Set oven to 190°C/375°F/gas reg.5. Lightly grease a small loaf tin.
2. Sift flour with salt and bicarbonate of soda. Stir in all remaining ingredients.
3. Spoon mixture into loaf tin and bake for approx. 1 hour. Top should be brown and firm to the touch. Allow to cool before serving.

Appendix 4: Fun and Games

It is essential to appreciate the significance of play in children's lives because it is the main medium through which they learn. Creative play such as drawing or painting will expand their imagination and encourage them to implement ideas. Playing with others will teach them the art of socialising and the importance of co-operation and compromise. By providing stimulating play and encouraging experimentation, the au pair/nanny is making an important contribution to a child's development.

Amusing children doesn't have to be expensive; in fact it is often the simple things that occupy them longest. Odds and ends that are bought can add up, though, so do ask the parents for extra cash if you find it necessary. Dipping into your own wages can prove expensive, especially if you want to plan plenty of outings. Be sensitive to the family budget, however, by keeping expenses in line with what they can afford. Equip yourself with a little notebook so you can record expenses and obtain receipts whenever possible. That way, if any discrepancies arise over finances, you can show the parents exactly how the money has been spent.

Here are some ideas for entertaining children which may provide some inspiration. If the family does not own a book of rainy day activities, then get one out of the library, and before you know it you'll be making creatures out of eggboxes, people out of balloons and necklaces out of pasta. Each child is an individual and some are more advanced than others so select those examples which appear to be most suitable or relevant to your own particular situation. Most are happy with a box of pencils and a pile of scrap paper as long as you interact with them, admiring their drawing and creating some of your own masterpieces to rival theirs.

PLAYING IN THE HOME

At the start of a day when the children need to be kept inside, you will want them to occupy themselves while you get the morning's chores out of the way. Jigsaws, books, cards and board games don't necessarily require your participation but the younger the child, the more likely he is to require your attention. Try to save the more difficult chores which demand a high degree of concentration for when the younger children take a nap, or the older ones are watching television. Chores such as ironing, however, can be done while supervising their play, providing you set them up with everything they need so they don't keep interrupting you except, perhaps, to admire something they have made.

CRAFT WORK

Saving empty packages which have not contained substances harmful to children can come in very handy when it comes to organising craft work. A special box can be set aside to store odds and ends such as empty cotton-reels, egg boxes, bits of silver foil, etc.

Make sure children are supplied with crayons, washable felt tips, paints, brushes, scissors, in fact, anything that is not dangerous and which will help them produce art work. A sticky paste can be made for gluing by simply mixing water and flour together in a small container. If it starts to dry out as the day progresses, just add a little more liquid. A plastic table-cloth to protect the furniture or carpet is a must, as is a plastic apron for the child. Remember to tie back long hair so it doesn't dip into anything.

Children go through reams of paper in no time at all, but a cheap supply can be obtained from office scraps. If one of the parents has access to a computer or telex machine, ask him/her to save the waste print-out material. The reverse side is blank and can be put to good use in the nursery. Alternatively, use the back of an old roll of wallpaper or buy a cheap roll of low-quality paper.

Instead of using paint brushes, you can encourage children to experiment with printing. Put different coloured paints in flat, separate containers (old saucers are ideal) and demonstrate how patterns can be made by dipping different objects in paint and transferring their outlines onto paper. A potato cut in half with a design chipped out of it can create a variety of prints, as can hands and thumbs. Try cotton reels or different types of uncooked pasta.

If you have large sheets of paper, ask your charge to lie down on it and keep still. Draw around the outline of the body and then let him colour himself in. Give him some strands of wool or cotton-wool for the hair, and remnants of material for the clothes.

Modelling clay and plasticine from shops can be expensive but an economic version is homemade play-dough. Combine four cups of flour with one cup of salt and add enough water to form a dough. Too little liquid will make it too crumbly to handle, but too much will make it sticky, so if this happens just add a little more flour/salt. The salt will help prevent it drying out and discourages toddlers from eating it! To provide colour, add powder paint to the flour before mixing, or use food colouring in the water. Provide children with cookie-cutters and a rolling-pin. The play-dough may be stored in the fridge, wrapped in a plastic bag.

Don't forget to praise the art work that is produced and always display it if possible. Blu-tac works well for mounting pictures because it doesn't harm walls, unlike sticky tape or drawing-pins. If sellotape has been used on painted walls, the sticky residue can be removed with methylated spirits. Magnets can be used to pin up pictures on metallic surfaces such as fridge doors. Drawings may be preserved by spraying with hair-lacquer upon completion.

DRESSING UP

All children enjoy the imaginative play involved in dressing up. Get a large cardboard other adult members of the family can be discarded and saved for the children box from the supermarket where old cast-offs from yourself or to use on rainy days. All kinds of interesting clothing and accessories can be obtained from jumble-sales or basement bargains including hats, colourful scarves, jewellery, etc. Little girls should probably be discouraged from wearing high-heeled shoes since they are dangerous to walk in. If they must wear dress-up shoes, buy a cheap pair of ballet slippers or let them wear men's shoes which tend to be flat.

A shoe box filled with cosmetics will keep them occupied for hours, but beware of sensitive skins. The hypo-allergic kind is best. Have plenty of cold-cream in store for removing afterwards.

THE MAGIC BOX

No play-room is complete without a magic box, and the nicest thing about one of these is that it is invisible! Not only does it cost nothing and save on space, it entertains the children for longer and expands their imagination.

It is basically a miming game. You can introduce it by explaining about the invisible box in the corner which is full of magic, and make a great show of opening the heavy (invisible) lid. Roll up the sleeve of one arm and pretend to feel about inside it, drawing out an invisible object. You then have to mime in such a way that the children will guess what you've found. For example, licking an ice-cream cone, pretending to use a bow and arrow or playing a game of catch with an invisible ball. Stick to simple mimes at first until they get the hang of it and make them more complicated as the game progresses, depending on the ability of the child. Encourage your charge to take a turn. You'll be amazed at how resourceful they can be at dreaming up ideas and then communicating them.

INDOOR GAMES

The *Strand Game* can only be played with more than one child because it is competitive. Scatter strands of wool or elastic-bands around the room and then when you are finished the children run around collecting as many of them as they can find. When they have all been gathered, the child who has collected the most wins.

Match-the-Picture requires that the children cut out large pictures from magazines and then cut each picture in half. (Old post-cards will do just as well). Take one half of each picture and distribute them around the room. Divide the other halves evenly among the children and then ask them to search for each of the pieces missing from their individual bundles. The first child to match all the halves together wins.

For *The Memory Game* (also known as Pelmonism or 'Kim's Game' after the novel by Rudyard Kipling), place a variety of objects on a tray (no more than ten) and give the children a chance to study the arrangement. After a few minutes, blind-fold them and remove one of the objects. Then let him study the tray again so he can try to remember which object is missing. If it seems too difficult, try playing it with fewer articles. This game works well as a party game when children have to remember everything that was on the tray after studying it for a minute or so.

A variation on the memory game which needs no actual objects (and is therefore eminently suitable for a long car journey) is the *Saratoga Trunk* game. Someone starts off 'I went on a journey and in my Saratoga trunk I packed X' which can be anything (sunglasses, spectacles, snowball…) and each person adds an object to the list having to remember them all in order from the beginning. The first person to falter loses.

In *Smells and Tastes* you put a variety of objects on a tray - salt, sugar, flour, marmite, jam, etc. - blindfold the children and see if they can identify the substances by taste and smell. Also a good team game and usually gets plenty of laughs.

Are you there, Moriarty? is excellent for older boys and girls. Two contestants are blindfolded and lie face down on the floor supporting head and shoulders on their elbows and holding each other's hands. One has a rolled up newspaper as a weapon and calls 'Are you there Moriarty?' When the other says 'Yes' the attacker tries to hit his head with the rolled up newspaper. Each player gets say five shots and the one to score the most hits is the winner.

Other good party games include the old favourites *Blind Man's Buff, Hunt the Thimble, Musical Chairs, Pass the Parcel* and *Pass the Orange*, where the children divide into teams and have to pass an orange down the line by tucking it under their chins. *Chinese Whispers* is excellent for quite young children. They sit in a circle and the first child whispers something silly like a tongue twister to his next door neighbour who repeats it to his next door neighbour until it gets to the last child who calls it out loud. By this time the original has been turned into complete nonsense which for some reason children find hugely amusing.

Treasure Hunts with rhyming clues can be played indoors or out as can *Sardines* in which you join the hider in the hiding place once you locate him.

PLAYING IN THE GARDEN

On warm days it is nicer to arrange for the children to paint outside in the garden. One of the advantages of this is that you needn't worry so much about mess and spillage because you can hose your charges down if things become serious. Let them collect items such as flowers, leaves and grass to use for making pictures or for floating in a bowl of water to mix their fragrances.

If the weather is especially hot, try to provide something to paddle in. It doesn't have to be a proper pool; any large container will do. Careful supervision is necessary, however, because children can drown even in shallow water. Provide them with plastic cups and a sieve so they can experiment with pouring water, and also a variety of things which will sink and float: a pebble and a cork, for instance. A container of liquid for making bubbles will provide a great deal of entertainment. When the mixture is running low, you can pad it out by adding washing-up liquid and a little water.

Show them how to build a make-shift tent. All you need is a couple of chairs placed back to back with a large space in the middle and a blanket or sheet over the top. Providing a picnic lunch under it can complete the fun.

If you have a garden path, let the children decorate it with coloured chalk. Warn them in advance that they may have to wipe it away at the end of the day, depending on what the parents say. You could appease the children by offering to take a photograph of their handiwork if they still object to it being removed when the time comes.

OUTINGS

Keep in touch with children's activities and forthcoming events in your local area by regularly visiting libraries, community centres, museums or tourist bureaux. As well as play-schools for pre-school children, there may be special gym classes or a regular story-time at the local library where you can safely leave them for half an hour while you browse through the adult section in peace. Children are never too young to learn how to swim, so take your charge to the swimming-baths.

Get together with other au pairs or nannies you know and arrange picnics or visits to the zoo, fun-fairs, adventure playgrounds or the circus. Organise a few unusual outings that would appeal to children such as a visit to a toy factory or the local fire-brigade.

Take advantage of what the particular country you're living in has on offer, whether it be sunshine and beaches, or snow and ice for skating parties and toboggan rides. Remember, the more effort you are prepared to invest in play-time, the more job satisfaction you will reap in return.

AMUSEMENTS WHILE TRAVELLING

Always take some snacks and cans of juice on long journeys with children since it's not always possible to eat meals at the usual time. A damp facecloth, some tissues and a spare carrier bag for containing any rubbish that is accumulated along the way, also come in handy.

Provide them with story books, puzzle books, children's tapes and board games designed for travel such as 'Travel Scrabble' which has a smaller board and magnetic pieces.

Here are some ideas for word games to keep them amused on boring car or train journeys which are educational as well as fun. Take along some paper and pencils for scoring.

(1) Give each child a word to spell backwards. Each correct answer gets a point, and the first to earn ten points, wins. (Young children can spell the words in the usual way.)

(2) When travelling by car, call out a colour and the first child to point to another car of that shade wins a point.

(3) Each child starts out with ten points. During the next ten minutes or so, normal conversation takes place; only none of the children are allowed to say 'yes' or 'no', and if they do, they lose a point. The winner is the one who still has some points left after the others have lost theirs.

(4) Name a category (for example, animal, flower, fruit) and choose a letter from the alphabet. The children have to give the name of something in that category beginning with the appropriate letter.

(5) In the *Silence Game*, no one is supposed to speak and if they do, they lose a point. You can't expect children to play this for long, though, as they'll soon get bored, but it could give you five minutes peace and a chance to think of something else to play.

(6) *Twenty Questions*. Think of someone the children know well and then let them try to guess who it is by asking no more than twenty questions to which you can only answer yes or no. A more difficult variation on this is *Animal, Vegetable, Mineral*, where someone thinks of an object and tells the others whether it is animal, vegetable, mineral or abstract; as above, they have 20 questions to find out what it is.

(7) Give each child a sheet of paper, a pencil and a long word, for example, 'understanding'. They must then write down as many shorter words as they can from those letters. After five minutes the child with the most correct words wins.

(8) *I Spy With My Little Eye*, something beginning with ... Most nannies will remember this from their own childhood but in case you were deprived, here's how you play it. Think of

an object within view of the child, but just give him the first letter. (The North American version uses colour, e.g. 'I spy with my little eye something that is yellow'.) He has to look around him and guess what the object could be.

(9) The *Geography Game* consists of naming any place in the world (continent, river, city, etc.) The children take it in turns to think of another place beginning with the last letter of the one that was named. Usually the one to win is the one who thinks up a place like Essex or Bordeaux.

(10) In the *Alphabet Game* everyone says a letter in turn and the first one to complete a word loses a life. (Three letter words don't count). If you add a letter and, when challenged, you cannot say what word the letters will spell when completed, you lose a life. In the more complicated version, you can add letters at the front as well as at the end.

(11) A fairly rowdy game which everyone in a car enjoys except the driver is *Bus Stop*. It is very simple and you just score one point for spotting a bus stop, two for a letter box and three for a telephone box. Whoever calls out 'bus stop!' etc. gets the points. If you call out the wrong one you lose points to the value of the wrong call. For some reason this game can be relied on to lead to some fearsome arguments.

Appendix 5: Embassies in London & Washington

AUSTRALIA: Australia House, The Strand, London WC2B 4LA (020-7379 4334; www. australia.org.uk) & 1601 Massachusetts Ave NW, Washington DC 20036 (202-797-3000; www.austemb.org)

AUSTRIA: 18 Belgrave Mews West, London SW1X 8HU (020-7235 3731; www.bmaa. gv.at/london) & 3524 International Court NW, Washington DC 20008-3035 (202-895-6700; www.austria.org)

BELGIUM: 103 Eaton Square, London SW1W 9AB (020-7470 3700; www.diplobel.org/uk) & 3330 Garfield St NW, Washington DC 20008 (202-333-6900; www.diplobel.us)

CANADA: 38 Grosvenor Sq, London W1X 4AA (020-7258 6600; www.dfait-maeci.gc.ca/canadaeuropa/united_kingdom) & 501 Pennsylvania Ave NW, Washington, DC 20001 (202-682-1740; www.canadianembassy.org)

DENMARK: 55 Sloane St, London SW1X 9SR (020-7333 0200; www.denmark.org.uk) & 3200 Whitehaven St, Washington, DC 20008 (202-234-4300; www.denmarkemb.org)

FINLAND: 38 Chesham Pl, London SW1X 8HW (020-7838 6200; www.finemb.org.uk) & 3301 Massachusetts Ave NW, Washington DC 20008 (202-298-5800; www.finland.org)

FRANCE: Consular Section, 21 Cromwell Road, London SW7 2EN (020-7073 1200; www.ambafrance-uk.org) & 4101 Reservoir Road NW, Washington DC 20007 (202-944-6000; www.info-france-usa.org)

GERMANY: 23 Belgrave Square, London SW1X 8PZ (020-7824 1300; www.german-embassy.org.uk) & 4645 Reservoir Road NW, Washington DC 20007-1998 (202-298-4000; www.germany-info.org)

GREECE: 1A Holland Park, London W11 3TP (020-7221 6467; www.greekembassy.org.uk) & 2221 Massachusetts Ave NW, Washington DC 20008 (202-939-1300; www.greekembassy.org)

ITALY: 14 Three Kings Yard, Davies St, London W1K 4EH (020-7235 9371; www. embitalia.org.uk) & 3000 Whitehaven St NW, Washington DC 20008 (202-612-4400; www.italyemb.org)

NETHERLANDS: 38 Hyde Park Gate, London SW7 5DP (020-7590 3200; www. netherlands-embassy.org.uk) & 4200 Linnean Ave NW, Washington DC 20008 (202-244-5300; www.netherlands-embassy.org)

NORWAY: 25 Belgrave Sq, London SW1X 8QD (020-7591 5500; www.norway.org.uk) & 2720 34th St NW, Washington, DC 20008 (202-333-6000; www.norway.org)

SPAIN: Consular Section, 20 Draycott Place, London SW3 2RZ (020-7589 8989; http://spain.embassyhomepage.com) & 2375 Pennsylvania Ave NW, Washington, DC 20037 (202-452-0100; www.spainemb.org)

SWEDEN: 11 Montagu Place, London W1H 2AL (020-7917 6411; www.swedish-embassy.org. uk) & 1501 M St NW, Washington, DC 20005 (202-467-2600; www.swedish-embassy.org)

SWITZERLAND: 16/18 Montagu Place, London W1H 2BQ (020-7616 6000; www. swissembassy.org.uk) & 2900 Cathedral Ave NW, Washington DC 20008 (202-745-7900; www.swissemb.org)

TURKEY: Consular Section, Rutland Lodge, Rutland Gardens, London SW7 1BW (020-7591 6900; www.turkishconsulate.org.uk) & 2525 Massachusetts Ave NW, Washington DC 20008 (202-612-6700; www.turkey.org)

UNITED KINGDOM: 3100 Massachusetts Ave NW, Washington, DC 20008 (202-588-6500; www.britainusa.com)

USA: 24 Grosvenor Sq, London W1A 1AE (020-7499 9000; www.usembassy.org.uk)

See the *London Diplomatic List* published frequently by the Foreign & Commonwealth Office available in libraries or check the link to 'UK Embassies Overseas' at www.fco.gov. uk. For all diplomatic representatives in Washington, see www.embassy.org. For all other nations' embassies worldwide, use the search engines www.embassyworld.com.

Vacation Work Publications

Summer Jobs Abroad	£10.99
Summer Jobs in Britain	£10.99
Taking a Gap Year	£12.95
Gap Years for Grown Ups	£11.95
Teaching English Abroad	£12.95
The Directory of Jobs & Careers Abroad	£12.95
The International Directory of Voluntary Work	£11.95
The Au Pair & Nanny's Guide to Working Abroad	£12.95
Work Your Way Around the World	£12.95
Working in Tourism – The UK, Europe & Beyond	£11.95
Working in Aviation	£10.99
Working on Yachts and Superyachts	£10.99
Working on Cruise Ships	£11.95
Working in Ski Resorts – Europe & North America	£11.95
Working with Animals – The UK, Europe & Worldwide	£11.95
Working with the Environment	£11.95
Workabout Australia	£10.99
Live & Work in Australia & New Zealand	£12.95
Live & Work in Belgium, The Netherlands & Luxembourg	£10.99
Live & Work in China	£11.95
Live & Work in France	£11.95
Live & Work in Germany	£10.99
Live & Work in Ireland	£10.99
Live & Work in Italy	£11.95
Live & Work in Japan	£10.99
Live & Work in Portugal	£11.95
Live & Work in Saudi & the Gulf	£10.99
Live & Work in Scandinavia	£10.99
Live & Work in Scotland	£11.95
Live & Work in Spain	£12.95
Live & Work in Spain & Portugal	£10.99
Live & Work in the USA & Canada	£12.95
Buying a House in France	£11.95
Buying a House in Italy	£11.95
Buying a House in Morocco	£12.95
Buying a House in New Zealand	£12.95
Buying a House in Portugal	£11.95
Buying a House in Scotland	£12.95
Buying a House in Spain	£11.95
Buying a House on the Mediterranean	£13.95
Where to Buy Property Abroad – An Investors Guide	£12.95
Retiring to Australia & New Zealand	£10.99
Retiring to Cyprus	£10.99
Retiring to France	£10.99
Retiring to Italy	£10.99
Retiring to Spain	£10.99
Starting a Business in Australia	£12.95
Starting a Business in France	£12.95
Starting a Business in Spain	£12.95
Scottish Islands – Skye & The Western Isles	£12.95
Scottish Islands – Orkney & Shetland	£11.95
Drive USA	£10.99

**Vacation Work Publications, 9 Park End Street, Oxford OX1 1HJ
Tel 01865-241978 Fax 01865-790885**

Visit us online for more information on our unrivalled range of titles for work,
travel and gap years, readers' feedback and regular updates:

www.vacationwork.co.uk

Books are available in the USA from
The Globe Pequot Press, Guilford, Connecticut
www.globepequot.com